THE WORLD
THAT TRADE
CREATED

Kevin Reilly, Series Editor

THE WORLD THAT TRADE CREATED

SOCIETY, CULTURE, AND THE WORLD ECONOMY

1400 TO THE PRESENT

SECOND EDITION

KENNETH POMERANZ AND STEVEN TOPIK

M.E.Sharpe
Armonk, New York
London, England

Library of Congress Cataloging-in-Publication Data

The world that trade created : society, culture, and the world economy, 1400
to present / edited by: Kenneth Pomeranz and Steven Topik.
    p. cm.
Includes bibliographical references and index.
ISBN 0-7656-1708-0 (hardcover : alk. paper) — 0-7656-1709-9 (pbk.: alk. paper)
    1. Commerce—History. 2. Commerce—Social aspects—History. 3.
Culture—History. 4. Industrialization—Social aspects—History. 5.
International economic relations—History. 6. Economic history. I.
Pomeranz, Kenneth. II. Topik, Steven.

HF352.P58W67 2006
382'.09—dc22   2005018044

Printed in the United States of America

The paper used in this publication meets the minimum requirements of
American National Standard for Information Sciences
Permanence of Paper for Printed Library Materials,
ANSI Z 39.48-1984.

∞

BM (c)   10   9   8   7   6   5   4   3   2   1
BM (p)   10   9   8   7   6   5   4   3   2   1

Contents

Foreword

It is a great pleasure for me to introduce this second edition of the most successful volume in my series, "Sources and Studies in World History." The first edition of *The World That Trade Created* engaged more general readers and students in college courses than any other title we have published to date. The secret of that success is simple: the essays are fun to read. The authors write with verve about fascinating topics, often coming to conclusions that surprise us or contradict our expectations. Their style springs from the experience of having written earlier versions of these essays for the *World Trade Magazine*. But Kenneth Pomeranz and Steven Topik are not just literary stylists. They are leading historians who are active in their respective scholarly fields of Chinese and Latin American history and who have developed pioneering approaches to the new field of world history. Consequently, their essays make for delightful reading, even as they introduce us to the latest relevant scholarship, much of it their own.

Readers will be pleasantly surprised to find economic history presented in so lively a manner. In fact, the "dismal science" has produced its share of good writing as well as more than its share of impenetrable prose. But this volume introduces a new economic approach to world history. Instead of abstract markets and theoretical constructs, Pomeranz and Topik show us that economic activity cannot be divorced from social and cultural contexts. This world of trade, they remind us, is made of flesh and blood. Scratch a market, and one finds a myriad of human actors: migrants and merchants, traders and treetappers, pirates and privateers, inventors and industrialists, sailors and slaves, entrepreneurs and engineers, adventurers and advertisers, and gauchos and guano shippers. Even supposedly dead commodities such as gold, silver, silk, cotton, and potatoes live lives determined by time and place.

The remarkable range of topics that these vignettes cover includes histories of particular commodities such as the "drug foods": tea, coffee, sugar, chocolate, tobacco, and opium. Other essays reach unexpected answers to important questions: that fifteenth-century Chinese exploration was too market-driven to surpass the state-sponsored efforts of Spain and Portugal, or that Chinese migration was greater and freer than European migration before 1800. This volume also provides answers to questions we never even thought to ask, such as why railroad tracks span the same 4'8" as ancient

Roman roads, why the can had to wait sixty years for the can opener, and why the keyboard was designed to prevent fast typing.

Today, everyone is acutely aware of how global economic forces have shaped our lives. But one of the lessons of this book is that the world economy is not as new as we imagine. Time and again, Pomeranz and Topik show us that the international economy has a long pedigree. Globalization may be a new word, but we see here that its roots run deep.

For the second edition, the authors have added eighteen pieces on topics as diverse as Shanghai, furs, rubber, Robinson Crusoe, packaging, Coca-Cola, and "American oil." Whether read in sequence or at random, these dozens of essays come together to reflect the mosaic of the world in which we live, reminding us of how closely we are connected by the ordinary objects of our lives.

Kevin Reilly
Series Editor

Introduction

When fifteenth-century China began replacing depreciated paper and copper currency with silver, it set into play forces that would affect remote peoples on five continents. The Chinese traded their silks to the British and the Dutch who bought them with Spanish pesos that had been minted by African slaves in what is today Mexico and Bolivia and mined by indigenous peoples recruited through adapted forms of Incan and Aztec labor tribute. Some of the silver took the more direct route from Mexico to China via the Philippines on Spain's Manila Galleons. European pirates hovered around America's Caribbean and Pacific coasts, in the Mediterranean, and off the east coast of Africa where they struggled with Arab and Indian corsairs who coveted the silver cargos, silk, and spices that they purchased.

The silver found its way east also through Muslim and later Christian purchases of coffee in Yemen's Red Sea port of Mocha, the world's monopoly producer for more than a century. Pilgrims to Mecca spread the taste for coffee from Morocco and Egypt to Persia, India and Java, and the Ottoman Empire. Finally France's King Louis XIV in his soirees introduced his Catholic aristocracy to the Muslim drink, served on Chinese porcelain, sweetened with sugar grown on the slave plantations of the African Atlantic island of São Tomé, and later Brazil, and followed by a smoke of Virginia tobacco. Some noblemen preferred chocolate, a drink of the Aztec nobility so precious that cacao beans served as money, while the English came to favor Chinese tea, also turned into coin in Siberia.

Many lands and cultures were swept into the vortex of the world economy, but that did not mean that they passively accepted its terms. In 1770, a French trader in Senegal was frustrated with local African merchants who, far from readily accepting baubles and beads, refused to trade slaves even for French furniture. They demanded Dutch or British chairs and bureaus, which they found more stylish. At roughly the same time, British merchants in Canada were unable to sell Virginian tobacco to the Iroquois; the Iroquois had already acquired a taste for African cultivated Brazilian tobacco and accepted no substitutes in exchange for the beaver pelts they offered for the elegant garments of northern Europe.

In Naples, earlier in the eighteenth century, enraged consumers threw a shipload of potatoes overboard, convinced that the Peruvian tuber was poison.

At the same time, fashionable men and ladies in London delicately sprinkled grated potato on other foods, believing that the tuber was an aphrodisiac.

Clearly the world economy has connected myriads of far-flung peoples for a long time. Although globalization has today reached unprecedented proportions, there is really nothing new about the New World Order. Nor is diversity a recent invention. The object of this book is to describe, through a series of stories, the long-standing interconnectedness of the world. We attempt to wed the insights of world systems analysis—that the local must be understood in its global context—with the perspective of local studies that see variation and local agency shaping the global environment.

The writings included here began as articles in a column, "Looking Back," which we wrote for the business magazine *World Trade* for more than ten years. The column focused on the history and the creation of the world economy. Steven Topik, and later Kenneth Pomeranz, wrote for the column. Dennis Kortheuer and Julia Topik contributed guest articles. This book is not simply a collection of the articles, however. Rather, it is unified by several central propositions on the nature of the world economy and the forces that shape it. We reject a Eurocentric teleology that sees Europeans as the prime movers and everyone else responding to them; instead the world economy is long-standing and non-Europeans played key roles in its development. To the extent that Europeans had advantages, they often came as much from the use of violence or from luck (as when European-borne diseases devastated New World societies, opening vast territories for conquest). Only in the latter part of our period did Europe clearly have superior productive technology, and it is not clear that it ever had a unique amount of entrepreneurship or social flexibility. Consequently, politics have been as central to shaping international commerce as economics have been. The market structures that are basic to our world were not natural or inevitable, always latent and waiting to be "opened up"; rather, markets are, for better or worse, socially constructed and socially embedded. They required a host of agreements on weights, measures, value, means of payment, and contracts that have not been universal nor permanent, plus still more basic agreements about what things should be for sale, who was entitled to sell them, and which people could haggle about prices (and settle disputes without drawing swords) without compromising their dignity in the eyes of their neighbors. In the process of negotiating these new rules of conduct, the very goods being bought and sold sometimes became the new markers of status and carriers of meaning. Thus "natural" uses and advantages clashed with human-made meanings— as when millions of people resisted the introduction of the potato—and associations so deeply embedded that they probably seemed natural were gradually reversed: over time, chocolate became associated with children, sweetness, and domesticity rather than with warriors, girding for battle, and religious ecstasy. In other words, goods themselves have "social lives" in which their meanings, their usefulness, and value are in flux; "demand" and "supply" are culturally determined by people with loves, hatreds, and addictions, not by reified "market forces."

Moreover, it would be a mistake to assume that pomp and role-playing can be clearly separated from a supposedly more basic level of utilitarian behavior. Thus the Chinese tribute system helped define upper-class style, set rules for various kinds of trade, and conferred enormous value to certain goods that rulers obtained in those exchanges, and so provided them with gifts that helped mark them as important patrons for other aristocrats back home: it was able to play some of the roles we associate today with the World Trade Organization or even the UN (helping to stabilize rulers by recognizing them) precisely because it also played some of the roles now dispersed among fashion designers, elite schools and universities, and international media companies. Success in this complex social, political, and economic arena came to the successful, not necessarily to the most virtuous, hard working, or clever. That is, the world economy has not been a particularly moral arena. Slavery, piracy, and sale of drugs have often been much more profitable than the production of food or other staples. Finally, it is necessary to understand both the local specificity of a transaction or event as well as its international context to appreciate its importance.

We eschew a Eurocentric position while also avoiding simple-minded anti-imperialism. That is, Europeans and North Americans were neither especially gifted, nor especially vile. Rather than focusing on just European trade with the rest of the world or concentrating on one area, we look at numerous areas and their interactions. We are telling the story of the ebbs and flows of the creation of the world economy, done by people with cultures, not by homo economicus or by capital itself. The creation of trade conventions, variations in knowledge and goals, the inter-linking of politics and economics, social organization, and culture all are given attention.

The more things we insist are connected, the more impossible it becomes to describe them comprehensively. Rather than attempt the impossible task of covering the development of the entire world economy over six centuries, we have chosen seven central topics around which to organize chapters; what we take to be the major issues and debates relating to a topic are laid out in an introductory essay. Each chapter then contains a set of brief case studies, which are meant to be illustrative, not exhaustive. Often they are based on the insights of other scholars, though a fair number derive from our own original research or our "take" on lively debates. (We have included a brief bibliography at the end of the book.) Rather than providing the "last word" on any topic, these articles seek to open up discussion, encouraging people to think in different ways about various parts of our world that we often take for granted or assume have always existed and needed only to be "discovered," and to question widely shared (though often implicit) stories of how new ways of making and trading things born in early modern Europe knit together (for better or worse) a world that had previously been composed of separate societies often assumed to have been isolated from each other. Instead we emphasize that complex cross-cultural networks with many centers already existed: the ways in which they were used, reconfigured, and sometimes destroyed is an essential part of understanding the new networks which came to center on Amsterdam, London, New York, or Tokyo.

The chapters are organized by subjects and chronologically. Thus, we begin with the early modern markets and the institutions and conventions necessary for them to function. Then we discuss the role of violence in capital accumulation and market formation. This includes state-directed repression, private initiative, and "outlaws" such as pirates. The third chapter focuses on drugs such as coffee, tobacco, and opium and their contribution to stimulating long-distance trade. Next, we look at the variety of goods that became commodities, from the commonplace potato, and corn, to the coveted gold, silver, and silk, from mundane but useful industrial raw materials such as rubber to the bizarre such as the cochineal bug. Chapter 5 examines the role of transportation improvements in linking up distant markets and intensifying trade. The next section considers features of the modern world economy such as standardization of money, measures, and time, the creation of trade conventions, and corporations. Finally, we discuss episodes of industrialization.

Pomeranz was trained as a historian of China, Topik as a historian of Latin America; each has more recently expanded into writing (for both scholarly and general audiences) and teaching on topics that transcend these regional boundaries. In writing this book, we have allowed each author to present the topics he knows best and to make his own decisions about what to emphasize in the case studies he originally wrote. We have discovered in the chapters themselves a general unity of outlook, which we have tried to systematize in the jointly written chapter introductions, but have not insisted on precise agreement on each point in each article, or on a checklist of particular examples that "must" be included. The result, we hope, is a set of lively vignettes that can be read separately, but which the longer, more synthetic essays reveal to add up to more than just the sum of the book's parts, just as the world economy, while undoubtedly composed of parts worth study in themselves, is more than the sum of those parts. In moving back and forth between the local and the global, the meaning of each is enriched.

We are writing a second edition to *The World That Trade Created* in response to suggestions from readers and instructors who have used it in the classroom. In order to expand its geographic breadth we added four new articles on Africa, four on the Americas, one on the Middle East, three on China, one on South Asia, and two on Europe. We have also brought our story more into the twentieth century with articles on oil, copper, rubber, packaging, marketing—especially Coca-Cola and soap—and the Internet. A number of articles that were redundant have been removed to streamline the book. Maps have been added to locate where our stories occurred. There is also a new epilogue, which discusses some of the changes and controversies over globalization that have occurred in the six years since the first edition was published.

THE WORLD THAT TRADE CREATED

– 1 –

The Making of Market Conventions

Humans might be smart, but there is little evidence that we are by nature "economically rational," that is, that human nature drives people to maximize their independent welfare by accumulating as many material goods as possible. Many of us remember Adam Smith's dictum that it was a basic part of human nature to "truck and barter"—so basic, according to Smith, that this tendency had probably developed along with the ability to speak. Indeed, modern economics has made this a basic principle for analyzing human behavior. But Smith's juxtaposition of trade with speech has an implication that his modern disciples have often forgotten—that trade, like speech, could sometimes serve *expressive* ends. Acquiring a particular good, or sending it to others was (and still is) sometimes a way of making a statement about who a person or group was or wanted to be, or about what social relationships people had or desired with others, as much as it was a way of maximizing strictly material comfort. And because economic activities are social acts, they bring together groups of people who often have very different cultural understandings of production, consumption, and trade.

It is certainly true that people have traded things for thousands of years: evidence of the exchange of shells, arrowheads, and other goods over long distances (and thus of geographically specialized production) goes back well before any written records. But in most cases we can only guess at the motives and mechanisms of trade, and of the way in which the exchange ratios between different goods were determined. We have evidence that even in ancient times there were some markets in which multiple buyers and sellers competed and prices were set by supply and demand; but we also have a great many cases in which exchange reached a fairly large scale while governed by very different principles. Where supply and demand did set prices— as appears to have been the case, for instance, for many goods in ancient Greece, and at roughly the same time in China—the exchange value of goods—what they could fetch in other goods—became more important than their inherent usefulness (use value) or their status. But even price-determining competitive markets were affected by the fact that they were understood to be just one of various ways of exchanging. In the second century B.C.E., the Chinese emperor held a debate at court about whether the state (and the people, though he cared less about them) were best served by competing merchants or government monopolies over crucial goods such as salt and iron; and though the ruler's decision for monopoly could never be fully implemented even for these goods, the debate reverberated through the centuries, shaping notions of what was and was not acceptable behavior both for unregulated merchants and their would-be regulators.

Everywhere it took a very long time for the concept of prices settled by supply and demand to overcome more traditional notions of reciprocity (equal exchange of goods and favors), status bargaining, which was more ritualistic trading between acknowledged unequals, or Aristotle's notion of a just price, set not by barter in the market but rather by ethical notions of a moral economy, of just exchanges.

Some people resembled the fleet Ouetaca of Brazil. As we see in reading 1.7, they were what we today unkindly call Indian givers. The chase after the exchange was as important as the actual exchange itself. Both parties mistrusted the other, and there was only a very dim sense of property values.

Others were like the Brazilian Tupinamba, who thought the French traders "great madmen" for crossing an ocean and working hard in order to accumulate wealth for future generations. Once the Tupinamba had enough goods, they instead spent their time, according to a Jesuit priest, "drinking wines in their villages, starting wars, and doing much mischief." And among the Kwakiutl of the Pacific Northwest, giving large amounts of goods away could be either a way of procuring witnesses to one's accession to a new rank (and of outcompeting for that rank people who could not assemble enough goods to give away fast enough), or a way of deliberately embarrassing a rival; but whether the purpose was to proclaim solidarity or hostility, the giver was the winner, and goods were accumulated in order to get rid of them on the right occasion as ritual gifts or Christmas presents.

Even large, sophisticated civilizations were often not based on market principles. The storied Inca of Peru knit together millions of people over thousands of miles in a prosperous, strong state that seems to have had no markets, no money, and no capital. Instead, trade was based upon the familial unit known as the *ayllu* and overseen by the state. Reciprocity and redistribution were more guiding concepts than profit and accumulation. The Aztecs and Maya of Mexico also had great empires that engaged in long-distance trade. The Aztecs (reading 1.6) enjoyed an enormous marketplace in their capital city of Tenochtitlan (today Mexico City), which hosted as many as ten thousand shoppers and sellers at a time. The Maya, on the other hand, apparently had no local markets in their considerable cities. Both empires traded goods in an area that stretched from New Mexico to Nicaragua, the equivalent distance in Europe from its northernmost to farthest southern point. Yet long-distance trade was completely separate from the local markets of

Aztec cities. Long-distance traders dealt in luxury goods as emissaries of their imperial aristocracies. They were essentially state bureaucrats. These sophisticated long-distance traders would completely disappear once their states collapsed and European merchants arrived.

Asia, linked by busy sea networks rather than the difficult overland routes of Peru and Mexico, had much more active private trading. As reading 1.4 demonstrates, diasporas of trading peoples such as the overseas Chinese, Muslims, and Hindus joined together an enormous and complex network of commerce; we will return to these trade diasporas shortly. Moreover, the Chinese "tribute system" (see reading 1.2) helped provide a framework for trade across vast areas of East and Southeast Asia. Though its primary purposes were political and cultural rather than economic, it helped provide an "international" monetary system, promoted shared luxury tastes across a huge area (making the market big enough for specialized producers to target), created quality standards for many goods, and promoted at least some common expectations of what constituted decent behavior. The leaders of ethnic trading communities (reading 1.1) provided other elements of a shared framework for trade; so did the accumulated practices in certain long-established entrepôts (usually city-states that were convenient meeting places for East and South Asians because of the patterns of the monsoon winds—see reading 2.1). These trading networks were linked to states, but they had also gained a life of their own. Thus, when Europeans finally entered the waters of the Indian Ocean in the sixteenth century and tried to wrest away the trade, they found their Asian competitors resilient. We see in reading 1.4 that for a long while, Europeans were treated as simply one more competitor who had to be tolerated, but not obeyed. Unlike New World traders, Asians were less dependent upon their states and hence could persist, even thrive, in the face of European cannon.

But saying that Asian trade was more independent of the state than that of the Incas or Aztecs does not mean that it operated in a purely economic realm outside politics and culture. On the contrary, even "merchants" often derived more profit from state concessions and monopolies than from clever entrepreneurship. Muhammed Sayyid Ardestani (reading 1.11) amassed a huge fortune as a tax farmer and a contractor for government purchases. The importance of good relations with government officials was obvious even to the representatives of the English East India Company (reading 1.12). In order to impress the Indian princes with whom they dealt, agents of the company spent lavishly to maintain themselves in the lifestyle of local princes and made frequent shows of military power. Being a successful trader required spending as much as accumulating: minimizing costs was not a consistent high priority.

Success for many Europeans in Asia also demanded intermarrying with the local population. Agents of the Dutch East India Company took Malay, Javanese, Filipina, and especially Balinese wives (reading 1.9) to implicate themselves in the local market and society. Even though the British and Dutch agents represented some of the first modern capitalist enterprises organized as joint stock companies, they relied on the traditional means of business alliances: marriage. But while a high-level European marriage generally linked two "houses" in which males controlled the capital and managed the business by exchanging a woman—almost as if she were a trade item herself—in Southeast Asia it was often the bride herself who had the liquid funds and the business acumen (her aristocratic male relatives considered themselves above such haggling). Some European men were delighted to get a domestic partner and a business partner in the same person; many more seem to have found the independent spirit of these women irksome. But for a long time they had little choice but to adapt if they wished to prosper. In fact, the European sojourners often indirectly reinforced the importance of these women even while they (and the missionaries who accompanied them) complained about it. Not being used to the tropics, these men tended to die well before their "local" wives; with inheritances in hand, these women then had even more bargaining chips for their next venture or next marriage.

Europeans had to "go native" in the first centuries of contact because of their own weakness and because of the variety of local laws and traditions that governed commerce. A diversity of states, religions, and trade diasporas and no agreed-upon commercial law left room for violent disputes. As we see in reading 1.10, the intensification of trade in the sixteenth and seventeenth centuries led to greater contact and increasing agreements on trade conventions. The spread of Islam also provided an ethical basis for conflict resolutions. But a convergence of practices was not inevitable. In fact, a depression in the late seventeenth and early eighteenth centuries led to a reversal of the trend, at least in what is now Indonesia; commercial customs again became more local and disparate.

Moreover, "native" was a relative term. The typical Asian port housed Gujaratis, Fujianese, Persians, Armenians, Jews, and Arabs, just as European trading centers housed separate groups of Genoese, Florentine, Dutch, English, and Hanseatic merchants. Only the most nearsighted European could fail to see that these groups differed. (The greatly increased power of Europeans in the nineteenth century encouraged such myopia and allowed more Europeans to get away with it; but earlier traders, lacking the aid of a colonial state, could not survive if they were that obtuse.) The individuals who made up these "trade diasporas" may have expected to leave someday, but the accumulated knowledge, contacts, and ways of operating that each group created was much more enduring—sometimes more important and lasting than the laws of the supposedly rooted "local" authority.

Under the circumstances, it is not surprising that trade diasporas remained the most efficient way of organizing commerce across much of Afro-Eurasia and the Americas until the nineteenth century, as they had been for centuries. Trade diasporas made sense from many points of view. In an era when contracts could be hard to enforce, especially across political boundaries, it helped to deal with people who came from the same place you did. You were likely to understand them better than you did strangers: not only did you speak the same language but you shared an understanding of what was good merchandise, of when a deal could (and could not) be called off, and of what to do in embarrassing but inevitable situations such as bankruptcy or accident. If you traded with somebody with whom you did not share these understandings you ran a higher risk of trouble, including having to deal with the culturally alien, sometimes arbitrary, principles of the local ruler's courts. And in case a trading partner was tempted to cheat you, it helped that their relatives and yours lived near each other. If worse came to absolute worst, there were people to take your anger out on, but more often a shared home base enforced honesty in a less physical way. Somebody who eventually hoped to return home, to inherit his parents' business, or to marry his children to members of other elite families back in his home territory would think twice before hurting the reputation of his family back home. The same principles not only kept traders abroad—two Gujaratis doing a deal in Melaka, for instance—honest with each other; it worked even better to keep either one from enriching himself at the expense of his partners or employers back at their native place. One practice used by Fujianese in early modern times drew particularly heavily on social rank at home to enforce honest dealings abroad. Great merchant families often sent their indentured servants off to manage their most far-flung business interests, especially in Southeast Asia. (Among other things, they may have wished to keep their actual sons at home—for company, safety, to maximize the chance of grandchildren, or to protect the family's other interests by managing their land or training to become a government official.) The servants understood that if—and only if—they returned home having done well would they be given their freedom, adopted into the family as a son, and furnished with an elite bride selected by their new parents. Until they succeeded, there was not much point in coming home.

The rulers of port cities also found it convenient to have trade handled this way. Concentration of wealth in the hands of aliens was less threatening than concentrations of wealth in the hands of, say, local aristocrats who might have the right blood and connections to make a bid for the throne; and if many of the aliens came from the same place, they could be assigned to keep each other orderly. Even Stamford Raffles (see reading 2.6), who saw himself as a child of the English Enlightenment and professed a belief in the rule of law, not men, found it convenient to organize Singapore (which he founded in 1819) as series of separate ethnic quarters, with a few leading merchants in each quarter responsible for governing according to the customs they were used to. And twenty-five years after that, the founders of the International Settlement in Shanghai initially imagined an all-white settlement where they would rule only themselves; it took a civil war, which brought wealthy Chinese refugees who sent rents soaring, to trump the desire for racial separation and create a mostly Chinese community under Western rule.

In the best of all possible worlds, a ruler might even convince a key figure in a trade diaspora to pay a handsome sum to be named "captain" over his ethnic fellows: if the ruler chose the right person, he got revenue, a grateful (and wealthy) follower, and good government in the merchant quarter at no cost to himself. With so many advantages, trade diasporas remained an indispensable way of organizing trade until full-fledged colonial rule (and with it Western commercial law) was established across much of the globe in the nineteenth century. And even then—and in fact today—such networks remain an important part of global trade. Condemned by much of Western social theory as nepotistic, irrational, "traditional" (and thus hostile to innovation), groups of Fujianese, Lebanese, Jews, and Armenians continue to organize trade through ethnicity, and to compete successfully with allegedly more rational ways of doing business. When the "past" thrives in the present, it's a sure sign that reality is more complex than the blackboard diagrams of either economists or sociologists.

Even when distant areas conformed to European standards of law and values, many other impediments stood in the way. Reading 1.8 reveals how difficult business conditions were for an English merchant in Brazil in the years right after its 1822 independence. By this time, European military power was far greater, allowing Europeans to force some reluctant people (and their land and goods) into the kind of market they wanted. Moreover, Europe had made a quantum leap in methods of producing some goods (such as cloth) at low prices, allowing them to trade on very favorable terms with anyone who wanted those goods. And meanwhile, conventions of trade (and ways of thinking about trade), which fit well with our notions of profit maximization, had come to the fore in Europe, so that Europeans had a much clearer idea of what market conventions they wished to impose in Brazil and elsewhere. But even so, the creation of a world economy was far from finished. Just how far will become clear in Chapter 6, on the institutions of *modern* world trade.

1.1 The Fujian Trade Diaspora

Any trader knows that personal contacts matter. But before the age of tele-communications, enforceable commercial codes, and standardized measures, it was even more important to have some nonbusiness tie with your partners, agents, and opposite numbers in other ports. So all over the world, trade was organized through networks of people who shared the same native place—and thus a dialect, a deity (or several) to swear on, and other trust-inducing connections. Genoese, Gujaratis, Armenians, Jews (though for the latter the shared "native place" had long been lost), and others fanned out across the world and linked its cities to each other.

The Fujianese diaspora, based on China's Southeast Coast, has been among the largest and most durable of these. (In 1984, Fujian's Pujiang county had 1,026,000 residents—and over 1,100,000 known descendants abroad.) It also has an unusual feature. While most of the other trading diasporas were purely urban, Fujian also sent millions of its children to clear land and grow crops elsewhere: from the Chinese interior to Southeast Asia, the Caribbean, and California. Yet oddly enough, the two diasporas had little to do with each other until the late nineteenth century, and then largely under the aegis of Western colonialists.

Fujian has long been crowded and rocky, so that, as one Chinese official put it, "men have made fields from the sea"; it has been a center of boat-building, fishing, and trade for over 1,000 years. Even after deforestation forced boat-building to move to places like Thailand, Fujianese remained the principal shippers and traders of Southeast Asia: many also became tax collectors, harbor masters, and financial advisers in the region's kingdoms, and later in Europe's colonies there. As transportation improved in the nineteenth century, the networks extended further—most of the Chinese who came to gold-rush California, for instance, came *not* from the counties hardest hit by poverty and violence, but from counties in Fujian and neighboring Guangdong whose commercial networks gave their sons access to superior information and start-up capital for venturing abroad. The firms that managed these overseas activities were usually organized on family lines, and used those connections strategically. The opportunity to return home to a carefully selected bride was often used as an incentive to make a sojourning family member produce and remit a certain level of profit; some young men without families were entrusted with difficult ventures and told that their adoption would be formalized when they returned successful. Lineages often specialized in particular lines of trade and passed on valuable techniques to their members; and affection and loyalty made the sometimes vague boundary between personal and firm assets much less important than it might otherwise have been.

Meanwhile, Fujian also produced agricultural migrants who fanned out across both China and Southeast Asia. Here, too, the home base's resources could help in getting started, and important skills could be transferred to new locations. Fujian has grown sugar for hundreds of years, and Fujianese brought the crop (and/or new ways of growing it) to many new places: Jiangxi and Sichuan in the Chinese interior, Taiwan, Java, and parts of the Philippines. Indeed, Fujianese were so known for their skill in growing sugar that Europeans deliberately sought them out as sugar-growers for their plantations, from Sri Lanka to Cuba to Hawaii.

Where Fujianese farmworkers went, a few Fujianese merchants usually followed—providing retail goods (including the right kinds of rice and condiments, and sometimes opium), credit, and help in sending money back home. But given how strong Chinese merchant groups were in Southeast Asia, the vast undeveloped tracts of potential farmland, and the crowded conditions back home, what is striking is that the two diasporas weren't more tightly linked—in particular that Chinese merchants very rarely tried (except on Taiwan) to develop overseas farms with labor from home. As early as 1600, Chinese Manila was as big as New York or Philadelphia would be in the 1770s, and there was plenty of unused farmland nearby—but no significant rural Chinese settlement. Why?

One simple but important factor was that the Chinese state would not support such ventures. It appreciated that commerce helped keep South China prosperous, but distrusted those who would leave the center of civilization for long. The compromise was a ban on people staying abroad over a year—a mere inconvenience for merchants (who sometimes had to pay bribes to return after two trading seasons), but a very strong deterrent for farmers, who would have to stay abroad much longer before their travels paid off and they could return home rich (as sojourners generally hoped to).

Just as importantly, the Chinese state's indifference to colonization meant that its subjects overseas had little security. Anti-Chinese violence was not infrequent, and though the Qing occasionally made gestures in support of their "good" subjects who were abroad temporarily, they would not even do that for "bad" subjects who had been gone longer. The best security for Chinese overseas was the ability to run and/or make payoffs—both much easier for a relatively liquid merchant than for even a very successful farmer.

Not only was the Chinese state unwilling to flex its muscles to provide law and order for its subjects abroad, it would not help merchants do so themselves. European countries, of course, licensed private companies (the East and West India Companies, for instance) to themselves use force, conquer overseas areas, provide government, and move in settlers; and as the Zheng family (see reading 4.10, "Saved from Sugar Shock") showed, Chinese merchants had the skills to do that, too. What they didn't have, though, was any incentive. European companies that bore the high start-up costs of creating a colony could recoup those costs because they had a guaranteed market back home for whatever exports they could generate: tobacco, sugar, and so on. Even when high taxes and profit margins were tacked on, the goods faced very little competition in Europe: revenue-hungry governments gladly kept out other countries' colonial exports, and climate and geography decreed that there would be no home production of sugar or tea. But the Chinese state was under less pressure to increase its revenues—it had no neighbors of comparable might, and it ran big budget surpluses through most of the 1700s. Even if it had wished to work with overseas merchants to create a stream of heavily taxed colonial imports, it would have found this difficult: China had tropics within its borders and grew plenty of sugar and other overseas goods. Faced with domestic competition, people exporting back to China could not charge spectacular markups—and so had no reason to risk lots of money starting overseas settlements that would eventually increase their supplies.

Things changed after 1850, when European colonial rule became more secure and demand back in industrializing Europe soared. Then a new generation of overwhelmingly white investors took the steps to match sparsely populated tracts of the tropics—from the newly drained Mekong Delta to Hawaii—with vast numbers of Chinese (and Indians) whose good farming skills were available cheap since they had so little land back home to farm. Fujianese traders were involved again—as labor recruiters, grocers, pawnbrokers, writers of letters home—but not as the prime movers, and not as the people who profited most from the sweat of their countrymen. Having lost the chance to create new "homelands" for themselves, these two Chinese diasporas would both spend the next century as essential but underpaid helpers of those who were aggressive enough to do so—for a while.

1.2 The Chinese Tribute System

When nineteenth-century Europeans came banging on the gates of China, one of their most vociferous demands was the abolition of the "tribute system," in which foreign trade was licensed as part of an elaborate set of diplomatic exchanges in Beijing. While part of their hostility was due to the way in which tributary diplomacy was symbolically different from diplomatic exchange among equals—John Quincy Adams even claimed that the demand that foreign diplomats kneel was "the true cause" of the Opium War—they also ridiculed the tribute system for forcing the practical matters of trade into a straitjacket of ritual. To a nineteenth-century Western European, convinced that humans naturally sought economic gain above all, no further proof could be needed that China stifled normal human impulses and would be better off if it was "opened up" to laissez faire—even by violence.

But were pomp and pragmatism really at odds in the tribute system? A closer look shows that they complemented each other—but only once we recognize that economics is always embedded in cultural and social practices.

For the Chinese court, "foreign" and "domestic" trade were not distinguished in the same way as today. Their world was not one of sharply separated sovereign nations, each with its own laws, customs, and relatively stable boundaries. Instead, they saw one true civilization—their own—which was based on principles appropriate to all people, wherever they came from, and one ruler—the Chinese emperor, or "son of heaven," who represented all humanity before the heavens. Those who were ruled directly by the emperor and by officials he hired and fired comprised an inner circle of humanity; they paid compulsory taxes, though they might also offer (theoretically) voluntary "tribute." Those who lived under partially assimilated native chiefs or kings (even if they occupied the hill country in China itself, with Chinese settlements and military garrisons in the valley all around them) and followed at least some customs and laws of their own comprised a second circle: their representatives brought tribute frequently, and private trade in virtually any articles was encouraged as well. A further circle of less assimilated rulers brought tribute less frequently, received fewer gifts in return, and had more restrictions on their private traders. An outermost group of "barbarians" who did not pay even lip service to Sinocentrism was excluded from the tribute rituals entirely; they were either allowed very limited trading rights at one or two specific border spots (the British at Canton in the eighteenth century, the Russians at Kiakhta) or traded indirectly by having their goods included in the tribute offered by somebody else. (Portuguese goods, for instance, might be purchased by a Siamese ruler and included in his tribute offerings.)

By exchanging gifts with these emissaries, the emperor confirmed his approval of them as rulers, but he also made clear who was the superior and who was the inferior in this relationship. The foreign emissaries, even if they were kings themselves, bowed to him, but not vice versa. Moreover, the nature of the goods exchanged was heavy with symbolic importance. The goods foreigners presented were supposed to be exotic, and valued more for what owning them said about the emperor than for any use value: by including exotic animals in their zoo, for instance, Ming rulers reinforced their claims to universal overlordship. The goods given by the emperor in return were symbols of refinement and civilization: books (especially the Confucian classics), musical instruments, silk, porcelain, paper money (a uniquely Chinese product for several centuries after its creation in the 1100s), and so on. Many were most useful to the rulers of tributary states as gifts that they could give to their followers, creating clients and reinforcing their right to rule by reminding other aristocrats back home that they were the ones with a special pipeline to the court that defined elegance for much of the world.

Clearly, then, the design and basic dynamics of the system came from concerns about culture, politics, and status, not about profit maximization. But at the same time, it defined the ground rules for a vigorous trade. When the Qing rewarded Siam's "civilized behavior" in shipping rice to Canton (rather than a frivolous good such as sugar, much less opium) by expanding tribute trade (which was more profitable for the Siamese than the rice shipments) they were rewarding political loyalty—but they were also keeping South China food prices down.

And when we look closely at the tribute missions themselves, moral order and economic profit prove to be linked in many ways. Not only did merchants accompany the tribute mission, bringing trade goods that they could sell privately while in Beijing; even gifts from the emperor were often quickly recycled. (Indeed, Chinese traders joined some foreigners in complaining that the court did not give the foreigners enough gifts; they knew well that it was a portion of these gifts, quickly off-loaded for cash, that gave foreigners the wherewithal to buy other Chinese goods.) And the tribute exchanges established value for many Chinese goods, making them valued luxuries abroad *because* they were the sorts of things that emperors gave.

This not only applied to things like ivory chopsticks (even in countries where people ate with their hands) but to money itself. When Chinese governments printed too much paper currency (as they often did), the tribute-bearers who were given some had little to gain by swapping it for goods within China; but back home it still had cachet, and so value (even if that value was unrelated to what denomination was printed on it). So, was somebody who brought his paper currency home chasing a useless status symbol, or was he, like any good trader, simply not disposing of it where there was already a glut? And was the man who carried silk home that different? True, printed Chinese silks could be worn, unlike paper money, but they were also—like paper money—an acknowledged store of value that was almost as hard to counterfeit then as a greenback is today; and they were also a status symbol, even if one never wore them. So silks became both the fabric of the elite and a form of money: in many areas one could (or even had to) pay part of one's taxes in silk. (Until roughly 1600, this was true in China itself—and Ming rulers often used a substantial portion of this silk to buy peace with the Mongols and other potential invaders.) So the tribute system—which so clearly subordinated economic gain to other priorities—at the same time helped define a vast common market, giving it its currencies, defining tastes that helped create markets worth producing for, and creating the standards (both of fashion and of behavior) by which its elites recognized in each other the people they could deal with without either lowering themselves or running too much risk of default. Today, we may have dispersed those functions among many seemingly unrelated players—from the IMF to Yves Saint-Laurent—but we have not dispensed with any of them. When they were centralized in Beijing, the tribute trade was no less commerce for being ritualized—and no less ritualized for being commerce.

1.3 Funny Money, Real Growth

Endless books have been written about the dangers of governments printing too much money. But for centuries the opposite problem was just as common: governments often couldn't mint enough coins (or the right coins) to meet their subjects' needs. When currency famine struck one of the most dynamic premodern economies—that of Tang (645–907) and Song (960–1127) China—it spawned innovations that ranged from coins made of lead and pottery on the one hand, to the world's first paper money on the other. And, surprisingly, the awkward coins survived longer than the modern-sounding paper money. Therein lurks a surprising lesson: a single convenient currency isn't always what a complex economy needs.

The basic problem was simple: "medieval" China's economy was growing and commercializing too fast for both its political institutions and its metal supply. The Chinese had used copper, bronze, and (more rarely) gold coins for centuries, but the dizzying speed of economic change meant that too many exchanges were happening for the supply of coins. The eleventh century alone saw a twentyfold increase in the annual output of government mints, plus lots of private coinage—and it still wasn't enough. Lead and iron coins were used locally where those metals were plentiful, despite their inconvenience; and silk, tea, and other luxury commodities were regularly used as "money" for large transactions. Then, to avoid the costs and hazards of transporting commodity "money," both tax collectors and long-distance traders began printing commodity-based notes: thus somebody delivering, say, salt to Hangzhou could receive not silk or copper to take home, but a piece of paper that could be exchanged for silk or copper once he got home. Then the government—concerned about the confusion, fraud, and high transaction costs created by the wide variety of moneys—began issuing more notes of its own, making them exchangeable for *any* commodity, and insisting that merchants use those notes instead of printing others. By 1024—centuries before anything comparable in the West—we find Chinese governments printing recognizable paper money.

Just one more step—issuing standard notes in small denominations to replace most of the varied mass of coins—would have created the kind of currency system we're used to. So why didn't this happen? The problem was that "money" had at least three distinct functions in this period, which often clashed. It was the way of settling accounts for large, long-distance transactions: forwarding taxes from the provinces to the capital, provisioning armies, and buying rare luxuries. It was the essential lubricant for the millions of small daily transactions in a society far more market-driven than the Europe of its day. And, as something that the Chinese made more skillfully than others in East and Southeast Asia (who trailed in both printing and minting technology), it was an export good in high demand.

Paper money was ideal for large-scale domestic trade and made considerable headway against coins of all sorts. High-quality copper (and some gold) coins were good to export, since foreigners could test their reliability more easily than paper, and remint them if they chose. As a result, paper, gold, and copper shared a tendency to disappear from *local* circulation—especially in areas that imported necessities (such as salt) from elsewhere in China, or had trouble meeting their tax bills. Those areas suffered frequent liquidity crises and adjusted by minting whatever was at hand. In fact, for such areas, very awkward currencies—lead, iron, pottery—were actually ideal; since it would not be very profitable to carry such bulky currencies away, it was better for merchants who sold in these markets to take home commodities. Thus "junk money" not only ensured that there would be some money around to fuel local circuits of exchange in poor areas; it also provided a hidden subsidy to the "exports" those areas needed to balance their "imports." (In areas that exported necessities like salt, "bad" money was not needed and seems to have been much less common.) So while one reformer after another sought to curb these local moneys, it was no accident that none ever succeeded—and it would have been disastrous if they had. Instead, sophisticated markets developed in which local currencies could be exchanged for more standard moneys, but only in limited quantities—a solution that balanced the needs of a huge interdependent economy with the "protectionist" needs of poorer localities.

And in the long run, paper money proved more vulnerable than clumsy coins. Since paper was supposed to be trustworthy enough to circulate over huge distances, periodic printing press inflation compromised its usefulness much more than overminting damaged local currencies. And as the currency designed for large, long-distance transactions, paper money became far less useful when political disruptions—particularly the wars that accompanied the collapse of Mongol rule in the mid-1300s—obstructed long-distance trade. Long-distance trade recovered and then reached new heights in the 1500s, but by then a new medium of exchange was available: silver, which came first from Japan, Vietnam, and Burma, and then, in unprecedented amounts, from the New World. For the next 300 years, close to half the world's silver production found its way into China's money supply, joining but not replacing other local coins, while becoming the standard for long-distance trade. Meanwhile the rest of the world enjoyed silks, porcelain, and other goodies they could not have purchased had China's experiment with paper money not proved abortive.

Only after the nineteenth-century opium trade reversed this silver inflow did the Chinese government return to printing paper money. And as poorer areas once again found silver and copper scarce, bronze, iron, and other local coins again proliferated, much to the dismay of foreigners. But what Westerners thought was monetary chaos permitted by a government that had never cared enough about trade to create a reliable currency was really something very different: the return of mechanisms that mediated the many levels of a complex economy in a way that no one currency could do.

1.4 When Asia Was the World Economy

Every schoolchild knows that Columbus was looking for India when he stumbled upon the Americas. But the Portuguese actually reached India by sea in the 1490s. And while they did not overwhelm the societies they encountered as the Spanish did in the New World, they did help to undermine a vast commercial system centered on the Indian Ocean.

This Asia-centered world economy had been taking shape since the rise of Islam in the seventh century. As the first Arab converts conquered much of the Byzantine world (especially Egypt and Syria) to their west and the Sassanid lands (Iran and Iraq) to their east, they laid down few economic rules; both the converted and unconverted (mostly Jewish or Christian) traders of Cairo, Damascus, Baghdad, and Tashkent continued business as usual. The conquest meant that a single power, the Islamic caliphate, could guarantee safe passage between two worlds—the Mediterranean and the Indian Ocean—separated since the decline of Rome.

As later generations extended the Islamic conquests from Spain to Somalia, West Africa, and Java, the networks of Hindu and other traders were welded to those of the West and Near East. Commerce boomed. At the edges of the empire, merchants dealt with a still larger world. Traders bought Chinese porcelain and silk in Canton and Malaysia. Europeans shipped Indonesian spices via the Red and Mediterranean Seas. And from Eastern Europe, Turkey, and sub-Saharan Africa came other crucial imports: gold (principally for coining money), iron, timber, and slaves both white and black.

The limited unity that the caliphate created—particularly in currency—

was essential to this burgeoning trade. So was the urban elite's insatiable demand for exotica. But the looseness of Islamic rule was even more important: as long as tribute was paid, local rulers were allowed to do much as they pleased. Most rulers allowed traders of all faiths to move freely from port to port. Wars were frequent, but usually limited to land, while the seas remained open. Merchants who encountered problems in one port simply moved to another. Piracy was common, but manageable. Merchant groups, often organized on ethnic or religious lines, maintained insurance funds to ransom any members captured at sea. Kidnapping became so pervasive a business pursuit that, in the 1200s, a standard ransom rate prevailed throughout the Mediterranean.

Within this cosmopolitan world, businesses spanned vast areas. The letters of one group of Jewish merchants, found centuries later in a Cairo synagogue, reveal a family firm with branches in India, Iran, Tunisia, and Egypt. Moreover, a complex international division of labor developed: the soldiers who resisted the Crusades wore chain mail from the Caucasus and carried steel swords smelted in India from iron mined in present-day Tanzania. Not only luxury goods, but such bulky necessities as flour and firewood, were exchanged across huge distances. The density of exchange also favored the worldwide diffusion of knowledge and products. Rice-growing, which had spread slowly from Eastern Asia to India and parts of Mesopotamia, was now adopted in Egypt, Morocco, and Southern Spain; sorghum spread from Africa to the Mediterranean. Cotton was introduced from India to Iraq as early as the 600s; from there it followed the trade routes to Syria, Cyprus, Sicily, Tunisia, Morocco, Spain, and eventually to the Nile Valley. Islamic trade routes brought papermaking from China to Europe, and Greek medicine back into a Europe that had lost it.

By the time the Portuguese arrived, this system was already in trouble. Revolts by slaves, overtaxed peasants, and the urban poor; invasions; and ecological problems had led to economic contraction and fragmentation. Yet the volume of trade was still enormous, and the basic rules by which it was conducted still held. The Portuguese government was the first to attack the principle—common throughout the region—that the sea belonged to no one, and the first to use force to redirect trade. Within twenty years of sailing into Asian waters, they created forts at two of the three places where major westbound trade routes could be blocked: Malacca, in the straits that connect the Indian and Pacific Oceans, and Hormuz, at the entrance to the Persian Gulf. (They failed to take Aden, at the mouth of the Red Sea, but succeeded in blockading it during the annual sailing season.) They also built numerous coastal forts, mostly in India. They claimed a monopoly in the pepper trade and the right to board or sink any ship in the hemisphere to which they had not issued a pass, or *cartaz*. The *cartaz* was cheap, but the buyer also had to agree not to trade in certain commodities and to boycott certain ports.

Portuguese pretensions far exceeded their power. Their settlements were always vulnerable because they were not self-sufficient. Indeed, most survived only because they were obviously too weak to threaten major land powers; thus nearby kingdoms felt free to feed the Portuguese in return for *cartazes* and safety at sea. And though Portuguese ships dealt harshly with those whom they caught violating their monopoly—sinking ships, bombarding ports, and burning crops—they could not truly rule the ocean.

By the middle 1500s, the counterattack began. The sultan of Acheh led an offensive on land and sea, reopening the Red Sea trade routes in the 1540s with the help of Indian merchants, and besieging Malacca (with Turkish help) over and over in the late 1500s. Before long, more powerful Europeans appeared: the Dutch and English. By the early 1600s, the Portuguese Empire in Asia was in irreversible decline. But the age of mercantilism, trade wars, and a Europe-centered world economy was just beginning.

1.5 Treating Good News as No News

Imports from Asia to Europe date back to Greek times, if not earlier. The writings of Roman moralists contain diatribes against patricians "wasting" valuable gold and silver to clothe themselves in Chinese silk. And most people today associate East–West trade before 1500 with one name above all: Marco Polo (1254–1324), the Venetian trader who spent twenty-five years in China and other parts of Asia. But to his contemporaries, Polo seemed more a crank than a trailblazer. Undoubtedly Polo, his father, and his uncle had done something right while in Asia, since they returned with enormous profits; but too many of Polo's stories clashed with European preconceptions for him to be believed.

Polo's *Travels* are today the most famous account of international trade ever written. They have gone through hundreds of printings and have been the basis of movies; a recent list of scholarly studies runs 354 pages. Most of what Polo told his readers about China, Persia, Sumatra, and elsewhere has since been substantiated. (He was less reliable about Japan, Java, and other places, for which he relied on hearsay.) But for a long time his accounts were treated less as a medieval Fodor's than as fantasies.

Polo told his stories to his cellmates after he was captured by Genoa in one phase of its centuries-long war with Venice for commercial and maritime dominance; and it was one of these fellow prisoners, a professional writer of romances, who wrote out and published the *Travels*. For a good 200 years thereafter, Polo's *Travels* were usually classified as romances as well.

Beginning shortly after Polo's death, carnivals in Venice featured a clown named "Marco of the Millions" (a nickname for Polo himself) who amused the crowd by telling increasingly outrageous stories; "a Marco Polo" became a proverbial English expression for lies. Meanwhile the "travel diaries" of John Mandeville, a fourteenth-century scholar who never left Europe, went through far more editions and were far more widely believed, even well beyond the days of Columbus and Magellan. Though Mandeville carefully borrowed accurate accounts from numerous other travelers (including Polo), he also borrowed much well-worn nonsense: eighty-foot-tall cannibals, giant ants that mined gold for their human master, and so forth.

Why the credibility problem? The question is even more puzzling because earlier Europeans had known much of what Polo's contemporaries would not believe. Though Europe had traded with East Asia for centuries, it had always been done through intermediaries, and political changes had made the European role increasingly marginal. After the collapse of the Eastern Roman Empire and the rise of Arab and Persian power, the amount of silks and spices moving by land across Central Asia had declined; instead, these goods moved by land and sea to Alexandria. From the tenth century on, Venice had obtained a virtual monopoly on the transshipment of spices from Alexandria to Europe and thus had no interest in seeing other Europeans develop alternatives to Alexandria. (This intimacy with Arab traders made the Venetians something of an exception in the age of the Crusades; when they went so far as to begin their contracts with the Egyptians with "In the name of God and Mohammed," the Pope drew the line. Few Venetians stopped making such contracts, but many "made up for it" on their deathbed by willing their profits to the Church.) It was only with the consolidation of Mongol power in Central Asia that the northern trade routes reopened, bringing Polo and other Europeans back into Central Asia for the first time, and into direct contact with China for the first time ever.

Thus, many of the physical wonders Polo described—such as the Baku oil fields in present-day Armenia—had been used by the Romans; however, the use of oil for heating had lapsed with the empire, and did not return to the Mediterranean until the 1700s. (Petroleum-based bombs had also been used in war, but had been banned as inhumane in 1139; the ban was largely obeyed until napalm made its appearance in the twentieth century.) But few people knew this in Polo's day, and his accounts of wonders like the black stones that could be burned for heat (coal) struck many as implausible. But the greatest doubts were reserved for his stories of life in China, which had become the heart of the Mongol Empire.

Europeans certainly knew of Mongol military power, since the armies of Genghis Khan had conquered as far as Poland and Hungary before turning back in 1222 (due to a succession crisis at home). European traders and missionaries had encountered dependents of the Great Khan ruling many parts of India, Persia, and Central Asia; and after the slaughter that accompanied the early Mongol conquests, most of Asia lived relatively peacefully under their rule, allowing the Polos and others to revive land-based commerce. But to most Europeans, the fabled Eastern land of wealth and wonders was India; they were simply unprepared for the wealth and sophistication that Polo reported in China. Tales of cities of perhaps 2 million people (Quinsay, or present-day Hangzhou); a canal over 1,000 miles long; and an economy that ran on paper money were simply too much for Polo's fellow Venetians (who had just built their first mint in his absence).

Most confusing of all, though, were probably Polo's claims that public safety and commercial honesty were far better maintained in China than in Europe, without Christianity as a basis for morals. Europeans had long believed that a fabulously rich, quasi utopia existed in the Far East, founded by an itinerant Christian named Prester John; but a non-Christian kingdom as excellent as Polo's version of China was something else again. (The Prester John story died hard, even after Polo and other European travelers debunked it; before long, common belief had simply moved this utopia to uncharted parts of Africa.)

Some merchants and missionaries did follow Polo to China, drawn to a field where (unlike in India) they faced little Moslem competition. But the opportunities Polo described did not last long. Within a generation of Polo's death, the Mongol Empire was breaking apart into separate warring states, the trade routes across Central Asia became treacherous again, and several of the great cities Polo had seen on his way across Eurasia all but disappeared. In China itself, the Ming dynasty reestablished order, but on a far less cosmopolitan basis. As outsiders themselves, the Mongols had been perfectly happy to deal with other non-Chinese; Polo himself had served Kublai Khan during his stay in Asia. The Ming dynasty saw no need for foreign officials and before long was taking steps to restrict all kinds of foreign contact.

Between European blindness and Asian tumult, Polo's *Travels* seemed destined to remain more a curiosity than a business guide. His fellow Venetians even ignored his notes from a stop he made in Sumatra on the way home; this, he noted, was where the spices that Europeans coveted actually came from, and where they could be bought for a fraction of the prices Venetians paid in Alexandria.

It was left for Venice's rivals to take the hint. The first map to use Polo's information was made in Catalonia; Prince Henry ("The Navigator") of Portugal read the *Travels* avidly; and a copy of the book is preserved today in Seville, with notes made in the margins by a Genoese—Christopher Columbus.

1.6 Aztec Traders

When Europeans finally arrived in the Indian Ocean and the South China Sea, they discovered thriving Arab, Indian, and Chinese trade networks. It would take centuries for the Europeans to break the dominance of these traders in Asia, the Middle East, and Africa. But in the Americas, the Spanish and the Portuguese immediately controlled long-distance commerce. Why did the indigenous peoples of the Americas so quickly and easily cede trade?

The Europeans had theories that explained Indians' failure in commerce. Indians were racially inferior, lazy, and, most of all, uninterested in profit. With a strong sense of communal property and a desire to self-sufficiency, Indians were uninterested in European goods and the broader world. While soothing to European consciences, these explanations had little truth in the historical record.

In fact, pre-Colombian Indians traded extensively. It was no fluke that Columbus early in his first voyage discovered an Indian canoe from an island he had just visited already paddling to a neighboring people with the Spanish goods they had just acquired for trade. Caribbean islanders had frequent commercial intercourse.

But that was very small-scale compared with the commerce of Mesoamerica: turquoise and silver from New Mexico was traded down to Tenochtitlan (present-day Mexico City) in exchange for either bowls, knives, combs, blankets, and featherwork manufactured there or the wide array of trade goods the Aztecs and their neighbors accumulated: rubber from Veracruz, chocolate from Chiapas, jaguar pelts and honey from the Yucatán, gold from Nicaragua, cacao and obsidian from Honduras or El Salvador, and gold from Costa Rica. A tremendous area, equal to the distance from southern Spain to Finland, separated Mesoamerican traders.

The urge to barter and truck was strong enough to push goods over two thousand miles. This was a feat rarely matched in the world because Mesoamerica had few rivers to tie together its far-flung populations. Most people lived in the high valleys of the center of the continent distant from the coast. Although the island of Cozumel seems to have been a major trading center for the Yucatán, no other coastal entrepôts have been discovered. Trade centers were inland. They were separated by rugged and precipitous ravines and ten- to twelve-thousand-foot-high mountains. To further disrupt travel, unlike everywhere else in the world that was densely populated, Mesoamerica had no large beasts of burden to carry the turquoise, cotton blankets, and cacao. Nor were wheeled vehicles used. Thousands of humans carried the loads on their backs and heads up and down the mountainsides on narrow, treacherous paths (see reading 2.10, "A Brief Trip Across the Centuries").

Yet trade was vigorous enough that the Aztecs, and perhaps the Maya, had their own caste that specialized in commerce. The *pochteca* lived on the island of Tlateloco, next to the aristocratic Tenochtitlan. They had special exemptions, were well respected, and lived well. They supplied a market in Tenochtitlan that stunned the Spanish Conquistadors when they first saw it. Hernán Cortés reported: "The city has many squares where markets are held, and trading is carried on. There is one square, twice as large as that of Salamanca, all surrounded by arcades, where daily more than sixty thousand souls buy and sell, and where are found all the kinds of merchandise produced in these countries." A fellow soldier, Bernal Diáz, enthused: "We were astounded at the great number of people and the quantities of merchandise, and at the orderliness and good arrangements that prevailed, for we had never seen such a thing before."

With such a dazzling array of precious and manufactured goods, intricate and intensive trade routes, and a special merchant caste well acquainted with the trade and able to converse across many language barriers, why did the Aztec commercial class come to a crashing halt with the arrival of the Spanish? Why did they not continue to prosper as in Asia, the Middle East, and Africa?

The answer is twofold. First, although extensive and well developed, Aztec and Mayan commerce was not really commodity commerce. Money and private property were still in the beginning stages of use. Commerce was an extension of statecraft, and merchants were essentially government officials. Trade was largely in tribute goods exacted through force or the threat of force; it was not private property created with the intention of profit. Thus this was a commercial system greatly dependent upon the political empire it served. Without Aztec or Mayan force there would be no tribute goods; and with no tribute there would be no trade.

The astounding destruction brought by the Spanish conquest ended not only Aztec and Mayan political power, it also destroyed the large cities (Tenochtitlan may have had as many as 500,000 inhabitants, ten times the size of the largest city in Spain) and even much of the rural indigenous population. The remaining population was either drafted into working for the Spanish or attempted to close itself off from the Spanish world in tightly guarded local economies. Most of their luxury goods such as featherwork and skins did not interest the Spanish. Those goods that did, such as cacao and gold, were soon produced under the control of Spaniards, who also oversaw their trade.

Within a few short years, a vast thriving commercial emporium had disappeared. Indians were condemned as nonenterprising and marginalized from the economy. Global trade not only created commercial networks, it also destroyed them.

1.7 Primitive Accumulation: Brazilwood

There are few countries in the world so much created by the world economy as Brazil. It is one of the very few countries to receive its name from a trade good. Greece and Turkey, for example, never exported lard or fowl. Yes, some countries and areas gave their names to goods, China comes immediately to mind. But in Brazil it was the trade good—the Brazilwood used for dye—that christened the area. The *pau Brasil* first attracted European interest in the distant subcontinent, but its boom was brief and its harvest difficult.

The problem was that to harvest dyewood from the sweltering tropical forests, the large trees had to be cut and transported to the coast. This, of course, required labor. Europeans had not come to the tropics to do such arduous work. But they found it difficult to induce the local population to work for them. Although there may have been as many as 6 million people living in Brazil in 1500 and they were concentrated close to the coast and rivers, the men had no tradition of hard work and the women could not cut and haul the logs.

The seminomadic Tupi people whom the Portuguese encountered gained most of their sustenance through hunting, fishing, and gathering. Women conducted their rudimentary agriculture; labor was little specialized nor had capital been accumulated. These people were so "backward" that they did not pay taxes or work for others. The Tupi classless subsistence societies also engaged in little trade and produced for themselves only simple artifacts.

For some of them, trade was more a contest than a profession. Jean Lery, a French huguenot who visited Brazil in the 1550s, wrote of the most peculiar exchanges of the fierce Ouetaca. When another people, say the Tupinamba, wanted to trade with the Ouetaca, they would show their trade good from afar, as would the Ouetaca. If both agreed to exchange, the Tupinamba placed his item, for example green stones, on a rock two hundred steps away and returned to his original place. The Ouetaca would then walk to the rock, take the stones, place down his featherwork, and retreat. The Tupinamba would then return to get the featherwork. Then the exchange became interesting: "As soon as each one has returned with his object of exchange, and gone past the boundaries of the place where he had first come to present himself, the truce is broken, and it is then a question of which one can catch the other and take back from him what he was carrying away." Since the Ouetaca ran like greyhounds, they usually won the contest. Lery advised his European readers: "Therefore, unless the lame, gouty, or otherwise slow-footed folk from over here want to lose their merchandise, I do not recommend that they negotiate or barter with the Ouetaca."

The Ouetaca were exceptional, to be sure. Most Tupis willingly traded some goods and were not "Indian givers." However, their needs were limited. They had no sense of private property, commodities, or acquisitiveness. Lery became aware of this in a conversation with an older native who was curious why the Portuguese came from such a distance in search of Brazilwood: "Do you not have wood in your country?" he wondered. When Lery explained that the wood was for dye, not firewood, his interlocutor asked why they needed so much of it. The Frenchman replied that in his "country there are traders who own more cloth, knives, scissors, mirrors and other goods than you can imagine." The Tupi considered this a while then mused: "this rich man you are telling me about, does he not die?" Assured that Frenchmen too died, the old man wondered what became of the traders' goods after death. Lery patiently explained that they were bequeathed to heirs. The Tupi had heard enough: "I now see that you Frenchmen are great Madmen. You cross the sea and suffer great inconvenience . . . and work so hard to accumulate riches for your children or for those who survive you. Is the land that nourished you not sufficient to feed them too? We have fathers, mothers and children whom we love. But we are certain that after our death the land that nourished us will also feed them. We therefore rest without further cares." The budding mercantile capitalists of Portugal ran up against this culture that they considered backward. They could not see that the native Brazilians already had the advanced values of a leisure-oriented ecologically sensitive society.

To convince the Tupi to sweat and toil carrying heavy logs that they no doubt believed were better left to stand erect as trees, the Portuguese and French exploited traditional local values and attempted to create demand. First, some of the Europeans went native. Unlike Robinson Crusoe (see reading 5.5, "The Luxurious Life of Robinson Crusoe"), who attempted to remake in the image of Europe the desert island on which he was shipwrecked, some Portuguese and French adopted native (un)dress, learned their languages, and married into their communities. They then played upon traditions of reciprocal labor to begin to send the forest to Europe. The European traders also offered steel swords and axes, which the warlike Tupi found useful in combat. By allying with selected villages and providing them with weapons, the Portuguese attempted to create demand for arms by raising the level of violence. The French would then use the threat of Portuguese-armed villages to strike up alliances with their enemies. Here in the remote tropical forests of the southern hemisphere, the quest for dyewood was replicating the wars of Europe.

But the Europeans could not inculcate in the Brazilians the virtues of accumulation and property. John Hemming recounts the complaints of a Jesuit priest, one of the vanguards of the culture of capitalism, who objected that the Tupi had "their houses full of metal tools. . . . Indians who formerly were nobodies and always dying of hunger through not having axes to clear fields now have as many tools and fields as they want, and eat and drink continually. They are always drinking wines in their villages, starting wars and doing much mischief." The introduction of steel axes had permitted entire villages of Brazilians to act as if they were European aristocrats. With their needs met, the Tupi were hard to exploit.

It became clear to the Portuguese that if they wanted more than simply enough, more than a healthy sustenance, in short, if they wanted capital, they had to turn to another form of labor. The rules of the Tupi labor market were set too much in favor of the aborigines. Since the small Portuguese population was not anxious to cross the Atlantic to break their backs in tropical agriculture, the Portuguese in Brazil took to enslaving their Brazilian hosts. But this was not ideal either. Many male Tupi, disdainful of agriculture, which they considered woman's work, preferred to die rather than dig. Others used their knowledge of the areas to escape. So traders turned to a people well equipped for the tropics and accustomed to agriculture: African slaves. But to purchase them required more money than dyewood could provide. Hence the Portuguese turned to sugar plantations. The "golden age" of Brazil began as the age of dyewood ended. Dyewood became an unimportant trade good, and the native peoples were driven ever farther into the remote interior. Today, the only trace left of the age of dyewood is the country's name: Brazil.

1.8 A British Merchant in the Tropics

You are a young Liverpool merchant of modest means, and you want to make your way in the world. The year is 1824, and you are going to help lead the British commercial assault on South America. You know that Brazil, that legendary treasure chest of sugar and gold, has just recently opened her ports to foreign traders and three years ago became independent. You have heard fellow merchants talking of setting out to take advantage of this new opportunity. No longer would you have to trade through Portuguese middlemen.

In fact, as an Englishman, you would enjoy special privileges the Portuguese did not share. In 1810, Portugal's king signed a treaty expressing his gratitude toward the English for helping him and his court flee Napoleon's army and cross the Atlantic. Now you, as an Englishman, would have access to special English-run courts and have the advantage of specially low tariff rates. You are also allowed to practice Protestant religions, as long as you are not too public about it. As a Liverpool native, you are acquainted with many merchants and representatives of British manufacturers. Sharing a language and customs with them, they trust you. You will be able to serve as a consignment and shipping agent and have privileged access to British credit for exports.

While this newfound opportunity seems promising, you are aware of the many dangers that surround you. The newly independent country is wracked with discord. Moreover, the economy has been depressed for almost a decade as international prices for sugar crashed and Minas Gerais's fabled gold fields dried up.

There is a new, promising product that might rescue Brazil—and you. Europeans have been drinking coffee now for over a century in ever greater gulps. Haiti, the world's largest producer for much of last century, suffered a bloody social revolution that ended her coffee supremacy. Cuba and Jamaica have made some headway in replacing Haiti, but neither has the vast fertile forests and large army of slaves that Brazil does. Introduced almost a century ago, coffee is now spreading among Rio de Janeiro's hills. Yes, you think, Brazil is a good country for an Englishman on the make.

But what problems do you face doing business in this exotic land? Fortunately, in many ways Brazil is Europeanized. Having been a Portuguese colony for over three centuries, it has Portuguese laws and customs. As an export colony, Brazil's economy has long been oriented to foreign markets. But it is also the world's largest slave society, with over a million slaves. You don't worry about the moral implications of trading in a slave country, of course. But what problems will slave culture present you in turning a profit?

Brazil has no banks. Except for the state-run Banco do Brasil, which mostly lends to the government, lending is on a personal basis. Loans are generally short term at high interest rates and based on slaves' collateral or trust in the planters' honor. Although coffee growers own vast lands, rural real estate cannot serve as collateral because it is poorly demarcated, titles are usually faulty, and planters have so crafted the legal system that foreclosure is almost impossible. Under these circumstances, you are not likely to lend to the grower unless you are personally acquainted with him. Since transportation is so horrible in the interior that it can take weeks to go a few hundred miles, you rarely see planters.

A group of intermediaries springs up to transfer credit and bring coffee to port: they are the *comissários*, or factors. Mostly Portuguese, these men borrow from you and other exporters and in turn open up accounts for their planter clients. They sell the coffee that arrives in Rio to sackers who blend and sack it and sell it to you. You must inspect the bags carefully, however, because there is no government oversight or coffee exchange that inspects quality. Indeed, pickers and growers are notorious for stuffing sticks and stones into their coffee shipments. Moreover, there are no standards of quality, no accepted size of lots. Information is also scarce. With a government that rarely intrudes into the interior and planters who rarely keep close accounts, information on the size of the crop is poor. Since coffee crops can vary by more than 50 percent from year to year this is a serious shortcoming. With no warehouses of any size, a glut can smash prices and scarcity can drive them way up.

You have some customers in England who issue you ninety-day notes in exchange, which you use to pay your bills and lend to comissários. Because of Brazil's long history as a colony and the great expense of importing some 3 million African slaves, little capital is available locally; you must borrow abroad.

This, of course, is in your favor because it is in the international link that your advantage lies. But there are serious problems in selling abroad. Just as supply and price in Rio are unpredictable, so are international prices. There are no coffee exchanges yet in Europe or the United States. Prices are made on the spot in the street. It can take months for news of the latest prices to reach Rio by clipper. And you cannot be certain when ships will put into port to carry your exports because there are no lines that regularly stop in Rio. Fortunately, the industrial revolution is creating a vast market for coffee that your competitors in Cuba, Jamaica, and Java cannot satisfy as well as you can.

Less certain is the import trade, in which you also dabble. Because slaves constitute maybe a third of the inhabitants and most of the country's largely rural population is outside the money economy, the market is small. Supply is uncertain not only because of the vagaries of shipping, but also because poor docks and lighters mean goods are often spoiled in transit. And the customs house is a disaster! Even with the judicious application of bribes, goods can take weeks to be released. Moreover, with slow transport and little money in the economy, Brazilian and Portuguese retail merchants demand as much as six months to pay for goods. And if you guessed wrong about demand for certain products in this new market, you may not be repaid at all. The legal system makes foreclosure difficult.

Under these circumstances, it is not surprising that you and your fellow Englishmen will be able to control the trade for the whole of the nineteenth century; but it is surprising that you took the many initial risks to create the coffee market in the first place.

1.9 How the Other Half Traded

Even today, companies often find that keeping up the morale of employees sent overseas is difficult. But consider an earlier multinational: the Dutch East India Company (VOC) of the seventeenth and eighteenth centuries. Its outposts in India, Southeast Asia, Japan, and Taiwan were places where few

Dutchwomen were willing to live; and while most men working for the company were quite willing to seek mates among indigenous women, this brought complications of its own. Given the cultural gulf separating these couples, it may be no great surprise that the private letters of these men are full of references to how hard it was to "tame" these women into the kinds of wives they expected. What may be more surprising is how hard the VOC, the Dutch Reformed Church, and other Europeans in Southeast Asia found it to break the *commercial* power of these women, many of whom were substantial traders in their own right.

Long before Europeans arrived, maritime Southeast Asia (including present-day Malaysia, Indonesia, and the Philippines) carried on a substantial long-distance trade. Many of the merchants were women—in some cases because commerce was thought too base an occupation for upper-class men, but too lucrative for elite families to abstain from completely. (Some elites carried this snobbery a step further, and held that noble women were also too lofty to barter in the marketplace or to visit the Chinese settlements where much long-distance trading was arranged; they were not, however, too noble to supervise a team of servants who carried out these businesses.) Malay proverbs of the 1500s spoke of the importance of teaching daughters how to calculate and make a profit.

More generally, these societies typically allowed women to control their own property, gave them considerable voice in the choice of husbands, and were often quite tolerant of other liaisons. The long journeys away from home that some of these women took even made it necessary to allow them, within the crude limits of available technology, to control their own fertility. (Herbal medicines, jumping from rocks to induce miscarriages, and even occasional infanticides were among the methods used.) Both the Islamic missionaries, who swept through the area in the 1400s, and the Christians, who followed a hundred years later, were appalled and hoped to bring such women to heel.

But despite these qualms, the Portuguese, the first Europeans to establish themselves in this world, had found intermarrying with such women to be an indispensable part of creating profitable and defensible colonies. When the VOC gave up on importing Dutch women—having sometimes found "willing" candidates only in the orphanages or even brothels of Holland, and facing discontent among the intended husbands of these women—it turned to the daughters of these earlier Portuguese-Asian unions: they at least spoke a Western language and were at least nominally Christian. Many had also learned from their mothers how useful a European husband could be for protecting their business interests in an increasingly multinational and often violent trading world. Councillors of the Dutch court in Batavia (present-day Jakarta), who were rarely rich themselves, but were very well placed to prevent the VOC's rules and monopoly claims from interfering with their wives' trade, were often particularly good matches for the richest of these women. Thus, arranging elite interracial marriages proved relatively easy: but making the resulting families conform to visions hatched in Amsterdam proved harder.

The VOC's principal goal, of course, was profit, and profit was best secured by monopolizing the export of all sorts of Asian goods—from pepper to porcelain—back to Europe. In theory, the Company also claimed—at least intermittently—the right to license and tax (or sink) all the ships participating in the much larger intra-Asian trade, including those of Southeast Asia's women traders. But the realities of huge oceans and numerous rivals made enforcing such a system impossible, and the VOC also faced powerful enemies within. Most Company servants soon discovered that while smuggling goods back to Holland was risky and difficult, they could earn sums by trading illegally (or semi-legally) within Asia that dwarfed their official salaries. Here their wives were a perfect vehicle for making a fortune: they were well connected in and knowledgeable about local markets, often possessed of considerable capital, and able to manage the family business continuously without being susceptible to sudden transfer by the Company.

And for some particularly unscrupulous Dutchmen there was the possibility of a kind of lucrative cultural arbitrage: after profiting from the relatively high status of Southeast Asian women, one might take advantage of their low status in Dutch law to gain sole control of the family fortune, and then perhaps even return to the Netherlands to settle down with a "proper" wife. (Though even with the law on the man's side, such a process could be very complex if the woman used her informal influence cleverly and hid her assets—in one such case the man eventually won control of most of his wife's profits, but the legal proceedings took nineteen years.)

But if men had powerful allies in the Dutch law and church, women had the climate on their side. Foreigners tended to die young in India and Southeast Asia, leaving behind wealthy widows. Such women were often eagerly sought after by the next wave of incoming European adventurers, enabling them to strike marriage bargains that safeguarded at least some of their independence; many wed and survived three or four husbands. The rare Dutchman who did live a long life in Batavia was likely to rise quite high in the VOC, become very wealthy, and marry more than once himself; but since such men (not needing a particularly well-connected or rich spouse once they'd risen this high) often chose a last wife much younger than themselves, they tended to leave behind a small circle of *very* wealthy widows, whose behavior often scandalized those Dutchmen who took their Calvinism seriously.

From the founding of Batavia in 1619 until the late 1800s, Dutch moralists and monopolists waged an endless battle to "tame" these women, and at least partially succeeded; later generations, for instance, seem to have conformed much more than earlier ones to European sexual mores. And as the scale of capital and international contacts needed to succeed in long-distance trade grew larger, European companies and their Chinese or Indian merchant allies—all of them male—did increasingly shrink the sphere in which these women operated.

Eventually, when late nineteenth-century innovations—the Suez Canal, telegraphs, refrigerated shipping, vaccinations, and so on—made it more and more possible to live a truly European lifestyle in Southeast Asia, a new generation of Dutch officials chose to bring wives with them, or to assume they would quickly return to Holland and marry there. Even so, trade managed by Eurasian women remained a crucial part of local and regional economies: many, for instance, managed commercial real estate and money-lending operations through which they funneled profits from their husbands' activities into local development around the fringes of Southeast Asian trading cities. (Ironically, this niche may have been kept for them in part through the racism of many of their husbands, who preferred to deal with the locals as little as possible.)

As late as the turn of the twentieth century, this sphere and those who managed it refused to disappear—the Indonesian novelist Pramoedaya Toer has painted a powerful portrait of one such woman, who waged a running battle to hold on to the businesses (and children) she had handled for years against her half-mad Dutch consort and his "legal" family back in Holland. Along with most of her real-life counterparts, this fictional woman was ultimately defeated; but for three centuries, women like her had built and sustained much of the world their husbands claimed was theirs.

1.10 Deals and Ordeals: World Trade and Early Modern Legal Culture

People can't trade without sharing some rules of the game. But societies have different ideas about who should pay what if merchandise is spoiled, prices change suddenly, and so on. Today, elaborate contracts, commercial treaties, and international law cover most eventualities, but in sixteenth-century Southeast Asian ports, such things barely existed. As trade boomed throughout the region—thanks to soaring demand for Southeast Asian spices in India, Europe, and above all China, and the increased availability of silver (mostly from Japan and Peru) to pay for it—commercial law evolved rapidly, but not always in the ways you'd expect.

In most Southeast Asian ports, traders were organized into ethnic communities, each of which had a headman who was supposed to keep order. So if, say, a Gujarati and a Dutch merchant fell out, their respective headmen would first meet to settle the dispute. This had its own perils for the merchants—they often lost the chance to speak for themselves, and might find their own case sacrificed to the broader interests of their communities, or the political ambitions of their headman. But the alternative—a lawsuit in the king's court—could be far more perilous. Witnesses on both sides might be tortured, and conflicting claims were often resolved by ordeal, in the belief that heavenly strength would enable the truthful party to endure longer. In Acheh, for instance, a common practice was to make the parties put one of their hands in molten lead, searching for a piece of pottery with sacred writing on it.

Such methods were not necessarily any more "backward" than those in use back in Europe—this was, after all, the era of witch-burnings, and the use of torture to extract truthful testimony was common to many places. In fact, a Portuguese sailor arrested for smuggling in China (and eventually freed on appeal) could not get over how much fairer Chinese justice seemed than his own. He was particularly struck by the practices of cross-examining witnesses in public (which he thought inhibited bribery) and by how everyone could swear oaths on their own sacred books (a practice that would have been unthinkable back home).

Nonetheless, polyglot trading centers, in which religious differences had to be tolerated, put the problems of relying on oaths, ordeals, and supernatural truth-finding in particularly sharp relief. And since Southeast Asia had many independent and competing ports, each hungry for the revenue that came when traders chose them as an entrepôt, the sixteenth- and seventeenth-century trade boom created powerful incentives to adopt a different kind of legal system.

Since the great trade boom also sparked a wave of conversions to Islam in Southeast Asia, the new legal codes often were based on the Koran. While that particular inspiration may have displeased Chinese and especially European traders, they could hardly deny that what resulted was a better system of dispute resolution. Increasingly, judgments were based on written laws or precedents that could be checked in advance; open interrogation of witnesses increased, and—probably most comforting of all—the use of ordeal declined in major ports. This new kind of law was seeping into cases that involved no foreigners, too, and there are even some signs that it was spreading to rural areas.

But by the eighteenth century this story of legal progress had gone into sharp reverse: ordeal was becoming more common again in various cities, and complaints about lawlessness and interethnic violence became more common. What had happened?

Once again, trade patterns were central. The mid-seventeenth century saw major depressions in both China and Europe: demand for Southeast Asian products slumped, customs revenues fell, and many kingdoms turned increasingly toward a rural, less cosmopolitan orientation. Worse yet, the increased power of armed, monopoly-seeking, European traders (especially the Dutch East India Company) forced more and more of the remaining trade onto their boats and into their fortified cities. Other Southeast Asian ports shrank, either through direct destruction by European guns or loss of revenue; and as these cities became less important to their rulers so did the relatively secular and tolerant way of life that they had exemplified. Ironically, the situation was often worst of all where European trading companies became the powers behind the throne. There, the desire to keep administrative costs to a minimum often led them to try to rule based on "local custom," which they thought would be the easiest kind of law to enforce: that preference often involved reviving whatever practices seemed most "ancient," and minimizing the importance of more recent, and sophisticated, urban practices that they attributed to "foreigners." (These European rulers were also all too willing to believe that the most "savage" practices they could find were the most "authentic"; and if letting custom reign in some places drove more and more business into a handful of European strongholds, this was all right with them, too.) As colonialism flourished, foreign trade ceased to be an opening wedge for legal reform throughout the region; instead it became a force that widened the gulf between "advanced" and "backward" legal systems.

1.11 Traveling Salesmen, Traveling Taxmen

We usually think of our own era as particularly cosmopolitan, especially in economics; the globalization of finance, production, and consumer tastes and the shrinking importance of national boundaries are clichés of our time. But for certain entrepreneurs, an earlier time and place—the Middle East, South Asia, and Southeast Asia, from about 1500 to 1750—offered a much closer approximation of a borderless world than anything being contemplated today. And for many of these itinerant traders, it was their intense involvement in the politics of their host countries—not the creation of markets that ignored nations—that yielded the greatest rewards.

These entrepreneurs—mostly Persian and Chinese—fanned out across the Indian Ocean world, establishing bases from present-day Mozambique to Indonesia, and most places in between. They traded in virtually every commodity available, from textiles and grain to gold and diamonds. But what gave them their entry into kingdom after kingdom was their skill at providing a different kind of service, which today is usually reserved for a country's own nationals: collecting public revenue. They were tax farmers who, in return for a free hand for themselves and their employees, would contract with rulers to provide a set amount of revenue by taxing an agreed-upon set of commodities over a given space.

From 1500 on, virtually every state bordering the Indian Ocean auctioned off the right to collect at least some of its taxes; Chinese entrepreneurs won many of the auctions in Southeast Asia, while Persians won a few contracts there and most of the auctions elsewhere. Once established as tax farmers, and granted important rights that went with those posts—the right, for instance, to inspect every cargo that went in and out of a port where they collected the customs—they gained a valuable advantage for their efforts as more conventional shippers, wholesalers, financiers, and arbitragers. And once they were locked into commitments to deliver large amounts of revenue, or had already advanced money to cash-hungry rulers, they often found themselves assuming other roles that modern states rarely give to foreigners—as generals and admirals, for instance, raising armies to protect "their" country's claims on a particular territory or trade. When Europeans arrived on the Indian Ocean scene, they, too, usually found these political merchants to be indispensable intermediaries and trading partners.

Consider, for instance, Muhammed Sayyid Ardestani. Born in Persia in 1591, he turned up in the Indian sultanate of Golconda in the 1620s, making a fortune as a horse trader. To modern ears, "horse trading" may suggest small-scale peddling in wide open markets, but it was something very different in seventeenth-century South Asia. From the 1400s on, the scale of warfare on the Indian subcontinent increased dramatically as the Mughal Empire (itself of Persian origin) sought to conquer as much as possible of present-day India, Pakistan, Bangladesh, and Afghanistan, while other states (and leagues of states) sought control over areas big enough to be viable bases for resistance. Horses were one of the two crucial sinews of power that no Indian state could produce for itself—adequate war mounts had to come from Arabia, Persia, or Central Asia, at enormous cost. (The other major military import was a new type of cannon, available after 1500 from European traders.) In fact, horses were probably the single biggest import into India (unless we count silver, much of which was reexported to get more horses)—and since India was probably the world's largest exporter from 1500 to 1700, the horse trade was a crucial link in world trade. Because horses had such strategic importance, virtually every state intervened heavily in the horse trade, often making it a state monopoly. Thus a would-be large-scale horse trader was likely to have two choices: accept appointment as an official of one of the importing states and play the game of court politics, or find another line of work.

Having established himself at court (where Golconda's Muslim rulers preferred Persian Muslims to indigenous Hindu traders), Ardestani soon wangled another enormously lucrative concession: running one of Golconda's fabled diamond mines. Thus enriched, he was prepared to help the sultan procure the most basic military necessity: money.

With armies growing larger and their equipment fancier, the cost of war was soaring. Thus, rulers needed to extract more revenue from both trade and agriculture. While some kings tried trading on their own account, most found it more efficient to license existing traders and sell to one of them the position of collector of license fees and customs; such a person was in the best position to figure what the traffic would bear. Once appointed, he could easily benefit his own interests: by monopolizing information, detaining competing cargoes while he sold his, or even by accusing a competitor of "smuggling."

Sometime in the 1630s Ardestani became governor and tax farmer for the province that included Masulipatnam, then the biggest port on India's Eastern coast. Here both Asians and Europeans came to buy the textiles that unlocked the other riches of the globe: they were exchanged for spices in Southeast Asia, gold in East Africa, slaves in West Africa, tobacco and sugar in the New World, and silver in Europe. As the port's principal tax collector, Ardestani soon developed ties to the British, Dutch, and Portuguese, despite their often violent quarrels with each other. The Dutch East India Company, eager to retain Ardestani's favor, gave his ships safe conduct passes for the seas they patrolled, even while denying them to most others. With this help, Ardestani's personal trading empire soon extended east to Burma and Indonesia. This one-man conglomerate gained still greater synergy through the interaction of these international interests with his state-licensed involvement in Golconda's village economy.

Foreign traders at Indian Ocean ports had a problem. Though monsoon shifts determined when they could arrive and when they had to leave, orders had to be placed several months in advance for the intricate woven goods they so prized. The companies were hard-pressed to finance these substantial advances and would have been devastated if weavers or middlemen had absconded with them. Here a local partner like Ardestani had an enormous edge: not only was he cash-rich, but he had successfully bid for the right to collect the land and other taxes from a number of weaving villages, too. Golconda got more revenue by letting Ardestani collect than it could have by relying on elites within the village (who had closer ties to fellow villagers, and fewer to the court); and Ardestani, even if he promised the court enough revenue so that he couldn't squeeze out much extra for himself, gained a vital hold over the peasants, weavers, and local brokers whose tax obligations he effectively bought from the court. He could thus lock up much of the best cloth for himself and his preferred clients; both the British and Dutch learned to their cost how hard it was to bypass such middlemen and deal directly with producers.

For years, Ardestani went from triumph to triumph. In the 1640s he served as a general in one of Golconda's many campaigns to capture more of coastal India; he bought up more and more tax farms; and he amassed a personal bodyguard of over 5,000, complete with European-made artillery.

Eventually, he fell in what was probably the only way he could have fallen. After losing a factional quarrel at court, Ardestani was arrested by a new sultan who feared he had become too powerful. But even that defeat was temporary; using some of his immense wealth to buy his release, Ardestani soon defected to the Mughal court, where he was given an aristocratic title and resumed his old activities on new terrain. Such a switch was not unusual. Many tax-farming merchants served several courts during their careers: arresting one and then letting him buy his release was often just a way of squeezing one last bit of cash from a laid-off political appointee. And it would not do to treat such people too harshly, even when dismissing them. Most of these successful itinerants had relatives who performed the same functions elsewhere, and nobody needed to make enemies who were powerful at the courts of other states; besides, many of the records that the new tax farmer would need were in the old farmer's private hands. (In fact, the transfer of accounting methods from business to the tax rolls was one of the most important long-term legacies of merchant tax-farming to statecraft all around the Indian Ocean littoral.) Indeed, foreign tax farmers were such an essential part of South Asian commerce and politics that it was a long time before anyone tried to do without them. Thus, when the English East India Company conquered Bengal in 1757, it did not try to install a new sovereign; instead the Company forced the existing ruler to appoint it—a new, corporate type of merchant—to the time-honored post of chief tax farmer.

1.12 Going Nonnative: Expense Accounts and the End of the Age of Merchant Courtiers

Corporations have always wanted to keep their employees' expense accounts under control, right? Well, it hasn't always been that simple. In fact, the British East India Company of the seventeenth and eighteenth centuries—one of the first recognizable antecedents of today's multinational corporations—found that it wasn't at all easy to get this point across. When the company's accountants started to balk at items like the bill for feeding a tiger on the estate of their chief representative in Madras, they weren't enforcing norms that everyone understood. They were, in fact, establishing a modern way of doing business that was rather shocking at the time, and which was only sold to their employees as part of a much broader set of ideas about race, purity, and the honor of a good English businessman.

Part of what was new was that the East India Company was a corporation. Earlier firms that had far-flung networks were partnerships of various sorts, so that a firm's agent in a distant city had an equity interest in the business's profit. If he wasn't yet a partner, he still usually had some interest in the firm's long-term health, or at least in his reputation back home. (Chinese merchant families, for instance, often sent young nephews or servants to manage the business overseas for a while; only when they returned with adequate accounts were they permitted to buy into the firm, and only then was a marriage arranged for them.) But EIC employees rarely held much stock in the firm—people who had enough capital for that were not usually the ones willing to go to India to try to make their fortunes. So the Company's new organizational form intensified its potential conflicts with its agents.

But what was more important yet was that the EIC (and its Dutch, French, Danish, and other European cousins) was not just any corporation: it had a legal monopoly on imports from Asia back to the mother country and a license to seek monopolies or monopsonies in other markets, using force if necessary. Indeed, as a firm that had what for the time were enormous upfront costs to cover—costs for building forts, providing armed escorts to protect its ships from other European powers, and so on, as well as more routine business costs—the firm more or less had to seek monopolies elsewhere, too, using its fighting forces offensively in order to help pay for them. But that pushed the company in two contradictory directions at once, with fateful consequences for both our modern idea of doing business and the development of colonialism.

On the one hand, trying to maintain monopolies required giving the company's local agents enormous latitude to use company funds for politics: to butter up princes who might grant lucrative local concessions, to socialize with local merchants and nobles (often the same people) who controlled stocks of desired goods, and to use force and make alliances with local power-holders who might offer a better deal than the incumbent rulers of some area. Thus a successful merchant had to be a general and a courtier as well. When the Madras agent sent in the bill for his tiger's upkeep, he no doubt felt that he was quite justified in charging the firm for the cost of looking grand enough to gain access to the necessary court circles. And when Christian merchants took local Hindu wives (even if they also had a wife back in Europe), patronized religiously oriented local cultural events, and so on, they were not only enjoying themselves, they were fitting in as they needed to. For the first century or so of the EIC's operations, London apparently agreed; becoming deeply enmeshed in local society was understood to be an essential part of doing business.

But on the other hand, running a far-flung business—especially one that sought monopoly—required keeping a very tight reign on these same employees. Very few of them expected to get rich on their salaries alone: instead they also carried on extensive trading on their own account. Inevitably, some of these activities conflicted with profit maximizing for the EIC. London became more and more concerned about whose interests were actually served when agents were living it up in the company of local elites.

As accounting methods became more sophisticated, headquarters tried very hard to impose more precise rules about allowable expenses, but it was never all that hard to evade them if you wanted to. One just had to learn that one's tiger, banquet staff, and so forth needed to be called something else on one's account books.

So morality would have to be called on to plug the gaps in long-distance supervision. Increasingly, these dry financial rules were accompanied by more general moral instructions, trying to convince the company's agents that they could not remain true Englishmen (or Scots, or whatever) if they mixed too much with "the natives." (These changes went along with, and fed into, a general hardening of European racial attitudes and increased belief in Europeans' own superiority in the 1700s, and an increased sense that the sober businessman should be different from the libertine aristocrat.) By the end of the 1700s, local "wives" had been redefined as "concubines" or even "whores"; both they and the men who lived with them were even excluded from the fortified European settlements during certain wars and panics near the end of the century. Entertaining local elites never ceased, but it was increasingly seen as a regrettable necessity and a threat to the soul (and national identity) of any European who overindulged: a powerful supplement to the much drier observation that it was a threat to the firm's dividends. The era of great merchants as cosmopolitan princes, joining in whatever the local version of the noble life was, was ending; the era of the Western trader or colonial bureaucrat in a separate house on the hill, living by the customs of his home country and trying to keep as neatly separated from local customs as the two sides of a ledger, was dawning.

1.13 Empire on a Shoestring: British Adventurers and Indian Financiers in Calcutta, 1750–1850

It's as basic as Econ 101: give investors in a capital rich country the chance, and they will jump at the higher returns available in a country where capital is scarce. The notion still drives hopes and fears wherever rich and poor economies are being linked, from the Rio Grande to the Elbe. (Though in fact, capital often still flows the other way, as it did out of Latin America in the 1980s.) This expectation of how money should flow was just as strong 200 years ago, when the British East India Company established new colonies at Madras, Bombay, and Fort William (Calcutta)—beachheads, through which investment was expected to follow an already lively trade. The highest hopes were generally held out for Calcutta, which offered access to the huge and relatively rich Bengal region.

So at the end of Britain's first century in Calcutta, who was financing Anglo-Bengali trade, India's first steam-powered industries, and the British administration itself—Ram Gopal Ghosh, Motilal Seal, Dwarkanath Tagore, Ashutosh Day—Bengali merchants all. In fact, it was not until the 1860s that significant British investment flowed to India. By that time a financial panic begun in London had bankrupted the great Bengali merchants—and the interracial import—export agencies and banks they had founded—leaving a clear field for the British. The children of Bengal's trading elite had turned to other pursuits. Before long some Europeans could be heard explaining that Indians simply weren't cut out for entrepreneurship.

The rise and fall of these financier-merchants began before the British with the tribute system of the Mughal dynasty. As conquerors from India's relatively poor far North, the Mughals exacted tribute from farther South, where an ecology suited to paddy rice, combined with easy access to coastal shipping, had created a much richer, more commercialized society. Much of the tribute money then went back south to purchase luxury goods for the elites of Delhi and Agra. Merchants who already did a booming export trade in Indian textiles and other goods (mostly to the Middle East and Southeast Asia) arranged this trade, too. Before long, those rich enough to take more risks moved into finance, helping both the government and the noble family anticipate their revenues.

When the Mughals crumbled in the 1700s, this trade shifted but did not dry up, and these merchants continued to handle public finance for their various successor states. Indeed, the increased bargaining power of merchants dealing with a plurality of states and the revenue needs of warring principalities made the commercialization of political power one of the growth industries of eighteenth-century India. At first the British coastal colonies were just three more states formed by cash-short militarists, little different in their needs from Oudh, Rohilkhand, or other pieces of the collapsing empire. They paid their bills (at 8 to 12 percent interest) no more or less reliably than others; and the complexities of remitting their savings to home meant big business for Calcutta bill-changers who could add a London bank to their already far-flung network of correspondents.

But these remittances were part of why the English *were* different. Most of them aspired to make fortunes and send them home, not to be the princely patrons of an Indian court. As a result, they were not inclined to spend the tribute they exacted on Indian cloth or jewelry; they wanted to export currency. And that was a big problem: India, poor in precious metals, had imported bullion for centuries. Now, a sudden net drain of coin (5–6 million pounds a year from India as a whole) created chronic liquidity problems, even as growing trade and the tantalizing possibilities of new technology begged for investment funds.

Bengali merchants in Calcutta tried to fill the region's diverse financial needs by founding interracial "agency houses" in partnership with British sojourners. The Bengalis provided capital, local knowledge, and contacts in the vast hinterland along the Ganges. Some of the British were mechanics, who provided knowledge of new wonders like the steam engine and mechanized cotton spinning; others offered little besides presumed access to their powerful countrymen. Very few were significant merchants in their own right. Meanwhile, the uncertainties and rumors of corruption surrounding the East India Company—which sometimes supported and sometimes obstructed new developments in its dominions—discouraged long-term commitments of money from London.

Along with financing government and trade, the agency houses pioneered many promising new ventures: coal mines with steam-driven pumps, new salt-making methods, tugboats, iron bridges, tea plantations, sugar-refining, and even railways (though in this last case, only on paper). They even bid on projects beyond India, such as a proposed steamer mail service from Calcutta to Suez. But their efforts were perpetually undercapitalized: there was simply too little money around for simultaneous expansion in so many areas, and what money the merchants could amass from Calcutta's Europeans was always subject to sudden withdrawal. Moreover, the relatively small number of these houses created numerous conflicts of interest. It was common, for instance, for a house that managed a firm it did not own to make suspicious deals between itself and a firm in which the house (or one of its partners as an individual) had a big stake.

Worst of all, none of these houses could escape heavy dependence on the tail that sometimes wagged the East Indian dog: Britishers' attempts to send money home. Unable to take out as much currency as they wanted, the English looked for other easily negotiable export commodities: opium, indigo, cotton, and (a bit later) tea. But since the supply of these exports was often driven more by the need to find *some* vehicle with which to take home wealth than by changes in demand (largely a function of harvests elsewhere), all were subject to periodic booms and busts.

When a gigantic bust hit indigo in the 1840s, it became clear that the diversity of the houses' investments was more apparent than real. Firms that foreclosed on indigo plantations kept them running despite low prices, needing to realize some cash to stay in the rapid-turnover remittance business; with supply and low prices thus sustained, other plantations then followed into bankruptcy. Coal mines found that their biggest customers—the same plantations, who used coal for the extensive boiling that indigo needed—were defaulting; tax arrears shook the governments the houses lent to. Since indigo and opium were essentially functioning as a substitute for money, the collapse of indigo prices left everyone illiquid. Desperate directors—both Indian and British—resorted to creative accounting, lent themselves large quantities of their firms' money, and waited for prices to rise again; but since nobody could afford to withhold their indigo from the market, the spiral continued. When a London correspondent refused to honor drafts on the Union Bank, Calcutta's largest, the house of cards tumbled down; censorious British newspapers focused on the scandals of the panic's last stage and "the lack of business ethics in Bengal," rather than on deeper causes closer to home.

The ruined Bengali merchants did not return to commerce. Many sought the relative safety of landholding, or of the civil service (soon to expand greatly as all of India was absorbed into the British Empire in 1858); others chose education, medicine, or the arts. (Dwarkanath Tagore's grandson Rabindranath won a Nobel Prize for his poetry.) A new corporation law encouraged the creation of all-British banks—which then rarely lent to non-Europeans. And in the 1860s, railway construction—requiring patient capital on a scale only industrialized nations could provide—finally began to elicit the English investment that had been absent before. Alone at the top of the new Indian economy, the British now began to "introduce" entrepreneurship.

– 2 –

The Tactics of Transport

To trade, goods have to be moved from seller to buyer—the more cheaply, the more trade there is and the greater the profit. People have struggled for centuries to bring down transport costs, often in ways that are barely perceptible: a careful study of the pottery containers in which olive oil was shipped in Roman times shows a slow but steady trend toward thinner walls, so that less weight was added per volume of oil shipped. But until the age of steam power, there were some fundamental limits to what could be done. Even since then, the story of transportation is not a simple one of technology conquering distance, much less one of the conquest of distance always bringing people closer together or increasing trade.

Natural Limits

Until the invention of the railroad, water transport was much more energy efficient than land transport. A bag of grain in late imperial China rose almost 3 percent in price for every mile it had to be carried overland; a lump of coal, 4 percent. So where goods were heavy, the cost advantages of water transport could be immense: as late as 1828, some Atlantic seacoast towns in the United States found it cheaper to use English coal for heating than to lug wood from the enormous forests that started just a few miles inland.

Nonetheless, far more ton-miles of goods went by land than by water. Much of this was simple geography: since the vast majority of production and consumption didn't take place right next to waterways, almost everything that moved went at least part way by land. Moreover, energy efficiency and economic efficiency were not the same thing. True, an animal carrying a load had to eat, but if there was plenty of grass by the side of the road, this might not cost the shipper anything. And if the animal was going to be on the move in search of grass anyway—as was the case with the huge Indian bullock trains described in reading 2.3—even long-distance land transport could be astonishingly inexpensive. Often one didn't even need to build much of a road—if the land was flat and enough of it uncultivated, the beasts would simply make their own paths as they went. Only where the population was too dense (and land too expensive) for foraging along meandering paths was preindustrial land transport bound to be painfully expensive—and these were often places where waterways were good. (Both the Netherlands and China's Yangzi Delta, for instance, despite plenty of money, trade, and engineering skills, had dismal road systems: there was simply no way to bring the costs of land transport down to where they could compete with water anyway.) But traveling through sparsely populated areas raised its own issues: the highest costs of the Great Silk Road caravans, for instance were usually for security. (See chapter 5 on the economics of violence.)

In Mesoamerica, the absence of waterways and large beasts of burden did not prevent the Maya and Aztecs from moving goods over enormous and astoundingly difficult terrains. Trade traveled thousands of miles on the backs of men. Packtrains of hundred of *tamames* (carriers) linked the aristocracy of distant areas. But here it was coerced labor and tributary goods, not commodities produced for profit, that filled the roads (see reading 1.6). This continued after the end of colonialism through private coercion of human beasts of burden (see reading 2.10, "A Brief Trip Across the Centuries"). Status and power, not economic calculation of gain and loss, motivated trade.

Whether on land or on water, natural constraints mattered. Except where geography was unusually favorable, it was mostly products with high price-to-bulk ratios that were worth shipping long distances: silks, gold and silver, sugar, coffee and medicinal herbs, not wheat, limestone, or wood. Thus transport powerfully shaped the geographic division of labor and the nature of demand, even where it was good enough to allow a long-distance division of labor to emerge. Sending bulky rice down the Yangzi River and expensive textiles back up against the current was economically viable; reversing those directions would not have been. Shipping fine swords and linens from Spain through Argentina to Potosí was profitable, but exporting wheat, mules, or wine from northern Argentina to Spain was inconceivable (see reading 5.2).

Transport costs limited the size of cities as well, because bulky goods like food and fuel could only come so far before they became too expensive (see reading 2.3)—unless, as in the exceptional case of Potosí, the lonely city sat atop a mountain of silver, enabling the residents to pay sky-high prices without flinching.

Before the nineteenth century, maintaining a competitive edge in trade was difficult. Centers of overland commerce such as the cities along the famous Silk Road depended upon political peace to ward off the depredations of armies and bandits. Overland trade routes varied with the fortunes of war. Maritime trade advantages were also at risk because the key to cheap shipping was ships. And ships, in turn, needed masts made from large, difficult to transport timbers. From Venice to Xiamen to the Americas, great shipping and trading powers found that they either had to secure increasingly remote waterside sources of big trees or allow others to take over shipbuilding. By the eighteenth century, South China had many of its big junks built in Southeast Asia; on the eve of the American Revolution, one-third of the British merchant fleet was built in the New World, while the Royal Navy struggled to monopolize potential masts from places as remote as Quebec and Madras (see reading 2.1). Many of the Portuguese ships that plied the triangular trade between Europe, Africa, and America were built in Bahia, Brazil, and the Spanish built them in Guayaquil, Ecuador.

Nature also shaped the rhythms of trade and the places where it was conducted by constraining transportation. All across maritime Asia—from Canton to Mocca—trading schedules were dictated by the monsoon winds. Since strong winds blew consistently in one direction for several months and then stopped, and then blew consistently the other way for months, it made no sense to fight those winds. A trader went as far as he (or occasionally she) could in one direction and then stayed around until the wind reversed; his goods were then picked up by another merchant who had arrived earlier and knew precisely how long into the next season he could safely stay and still have enough days of favorable wind to get home (see reading 2.1). Thus, instead of Chinese traders spending two or more monsoon seasons (and years) sailing all the way to, say, Persia with silks, it made more sense to sail out one monsoon season and exchange with intermediaries based in between and thereby return home with frankincense and rugs. A series of emporia developed at sites such as Melaka, Surat, and the Muscat that had more to do with how far one could travel from there in one sailing season than with what goods could be produced locally. The result was a remarkably lively and cosmopolitan chain of port cities along the Asian littoral, but in many cases these cities had only weak relationships with their immediate hinterlands. (See also reading 1.10.)

And despite its remarkable efficiency, the system had certain natural limits that no advances in either seafaring or commercial institutions could exceed in the days before steam. Since no merchant could turn back to home before the wind shifted, there was no way to cut the amount of time away from home (and thus the cost of sustaining the crew away from home, as well as the turnover time for capital) below a certain level. In the Atlantic, by contrast, the wind patterns imposed less severe constraints. Major ports arose either because Spanish mercantilism designated them as monopoly entrepôts such as Havana, Cuba, Veracruz, Mexico, and Cartegena, Colombia, or because relatively free, mostly British traders found them convenient. In the former case, government fiat rather than winds set the departure time. In the British case, a shipper who could cut his turnaround time in port could turn his capital over faster, and cut his expenditures on wages for his crew as well.

This is precisely what happened in the eighteenth century, as Scottish traders built warehouses, appointed agents to collect goods in advance, and found other ways to cut their time in New World ports by several weeks on each trip. The results were dramatic. As transatlantic shipping costs fell, colonists could move further inland (thus incurring higher local shipping costs) and still get their tobacco, rice, and other goods back to Europe at competitive prices. Only when one could successfully export from farther inland did Europeans begin populating areas farther from the coast—with all that implied for them and the people they displaced. (See reading 2.4.)

Limits of Nature

But even if geography and meteorology shaped preindustrial transport—and thus economies—their rule was not absolute. Atlantic winds may have been necessary for the breakthrough in shipping costs discussed above, but they were not in themselves sufficient to cause innovation. One not only needed the cost-conscious Scottish traders themselves, but a more or less monocultural pattern of trade. Delegating responsibility for acquiring goods in Baltimore to a local agent was relatively easy if the agent knew that the only thing to purchase in the Chesapeake was tobacco, and that the market back home for tobacco had become so huge that no one ship's cargo could glut it. (It would become even easier in later centuries as standardized grading for commodities developed—see chapter 6, "Making Modern Markets.") Delegating to an agent was much more difficult when he had to prepurchase your cargo for a trip home from, say, Melaka, where a typical ship carried a little silk, a little tea, a little porcelain, some incense, some sugar, and so on—whatever was available at a good price (none of it produced locally) in quantities small enough that they would not glut the market back home.

Sometimes it wasn't even clear whether a particular innovation was more a matter of improved control of nature or improved control over people. Shortly before 1600, the Dutch began using a new kind of ship called the *fluitschip,* on their voyages to and from the Baltic. Though clunky and slow-moving, the fluitschip could be sailed with a much smaller crew than most then in use, cutting costs enormously. But the Dutch did not use these cheaper ships in their push into Mediterranean shipping, much less on Atlantic, Pacific, or Indian Ocean routes. The reason? The Baltic routes had been cleared of pirates (and rival governments, often pretty much the same thing) but these other routes had not. The much smaller crew of a fluitschip, on a slow-moving vessel with minimal gunports, would have been a sitting duck.

Natural port advantages did not guarantee continued success. The port of Mocca, a major entrepôt between Europe and Egypt on one hand and Persia and India on the other, became land-bound as its harbor silted up (see reading 3.3). Other times, rather than nature dooming a port, humans who inherited, bought, or stole a site with favorable geography could try to exploit it too much, and so lose their advantage. In other cases, just the *possibility* that people might try to monopolize a locational advantage could spur preemptive action. Thus fears that the Dutch might squeeze traffic through the straits connecting the Indian Ocean and South China Sea once they were restored to power there were enough to convince Stamford Raffles to set up an alternate port, committed to free trade, at this choke-point of world trade: the city of Singapore. (For this, Raffles was punished by his more cautious, diplomacy-minded superiors; see reading 2.6.)

Power-Driven Transport: New Time, New Space, Old Conflicts

Steam and the railroad would scramble the world's trade geography in the nineteenth century. With the rise of steam power human control increased enormously—but not infinitely. Steamships could go upstream almost as easily as downstream and could sail the ocean at any time of year. But in at least some stormy seas, they did so at their peril. Steam shovels could dig canals, dredge harbors, and so on, much faster and more effectively than ever before. Peacetime freight rates went into free fall, or so it seemed: about 80 percent per pound for most commodities crossing the Atlantic between 1815 and 1850, and then another 70 percent from 1870 to 1900, for a cumulative fall of almost 95 percent.

The changes on land were even bigger. Railroads could, for the first time, move heavy loads cheaply over long overland stretches, but not where there was too steep a grade. (Since trains are far too heavy to rely on inflatable tires, they use smooth wheels. Thus, there is very little friction between railroad wheels and track, and going up steep grades is almost impossible—even today, it is impossible to build railroads on grades as steep as those that cars and trucks, with road-gripping tires, can handle.) Moreover, the enormous expense of railroad building through underdeveloped areas meant that even a large amount of transport cost savings could go with disappointing earnings (see reading 2.9, "Guaranteed Profits and Half-Fulfilled Hopes").

Railroads also created their own peculiar needs. It was, for instance, very expensive to keep a steam locomotive waiting at a station to be loaded, and extremely slow to start one up again if you turned it off. Thus, loading stops had to be brief, and grain (for instance) came to be loaded from elevators that released a flood of wheat into the car when opened, rather than loaded in separate bags. But using grain elevators meant giving up on keeping farmer Jones's wheat separate from Farmer Smith's—with far-reaching consequences that we explore in reading 6.4 on commodities in the modern world economy.

By vastly increasing the speed and volume of the carrying trade while dramatically slashing prices, railroads and steamships set into motion a conceptual revolution in time, space, and commodification. With steam, the Atlantic and Pacific shrank to ponds and continents to small principalities. Distant neighbors became proximate, indeed closer to others in ports or on the same rail lines than they were to people nearer in terms of miles but removed from the transportation networks. With the transportation bottlenecks gone, time was money. Greater volume meant greater profit rather than gluts. As time and distance evaporated, the middleman between buyer and seller often lost importance. Manufacturers and financiers often gained ascendancy over merchants; advertisers—who tried to bridge cultural distances, which closed more slowly than physical ones—also grew in importance. The global supermarket began taking shape in the nineteenth century. Luxuries no longer dominated the long-distance trade. Beef and mutton from Argentina, Uruguay, and the United States and wheat from Australia, the United States, and India fed hungry European populations; Japanese mills mixed U.S., Indian, and Chinese cotton. As goods from numerous countries competed in the world's markets, the need for standardization and commodity markets arose. (See reading 6.4.) Thus transportation not only determined profit, loss, and volume of trade. It created neighbors, shaped the sense of time, redrew the maps, and unleashed the conceptual revolutions known today as commodification and globalization. But as much as the transport revolution changed, it still has not, as some people predicted (and continue to predict), made geography irrelevant.

For one thing, people need to seize opportunities, and even societies very attuned to profit do not pursue every chance. The late nineteenth-century United States, for instance, busily developing a conquered continent, largely turned its back on the sea, letting a once-powerful merchant marine evaporate and abandoning even routes (such as those to Brazil) where it seemed to have a natural advantage. In other cases, people did seize opportunities to bridge physical distances, but inadvertently increased cultural distances. In the Dutch East Indies (now Indonesia), for instance, a barrage of late nineteenth-century changes seemed destined to strengthen relations between colony and motherland. Improvements in ocean shipping were compounded by the building of the Suez Canal, which helped cut sailing times by almost two-thirds in just a decade; transoceanic cables meant that the news could now, for the first time, move almost instantaneously—at a fraction of the cost of goods. But in the context of colonialism and late-nineteenth-century racism, divisions actually increased: Dutch felt closer to the Netherlands,

Chinese to China, and Muslims to more accessible centers of Islamic learning in the Middle East. (See reading 2.8.) So here, at least, advances in transport and communications did more to create separations (both within the colony and between it and the metropole) than to bring people together. Technology can change the ease with which people move themselves and their goods elsewhere; but only humans determine what they think of themselves, each other, and their goods.

2.1 Woods, Winds, Shipbuilding, and Shipping: Why China Didn't Rule the Waves

Quick—what were the largest ships in the preindustrial world? Not the Spanish galleons that brought New World silver across the Atlantic; and not the British men-o'-war that finally drove those galleons from the sea. Both were outclassed by the "treasure ships" made for the Chinese navy.

First put afloat centuries before those European vessels, the treasure ships ranged far and wide in the 1300s and early 1400s, touching the East African coastline and, some believe, rounding the Cape of Good Hope—unmatched distances for that era. At 7,800 tons, the biggest of these were three times the size of anything the British navy put afloat before the 1800s.

With such a big lead in naval affairs, it seems a wonder that the Chinese never became a sea power on par with latter-day England, Spain, Holland, or Portugal. No wonder, though, if you examine history closely.

China's stint as a sea power all but ended when the Ming dynasty withdrew support for treasure ship journeys after 1433. From then on, Chinese ships stayed to the east of present-day Singapore. Within a few decades, the initiative in long-distance exploration—and later in trade, too—passed to the Europeans.

The government's policy shift began when a new faction gained influence in China's Ming court. Its members advocated a greater focus on domestic and continental matters, emphasizing agricultural production, internal stability, a military buildup and colonization at the edges of the Central Asian steppe, and refurbishment of the Great Wall, designed to repel invaders.

That explains the end of government-sponsored navigation. But, though many think all of China turned inward along with the government, the real story is very different. The curtailing of private sector ocean trips involved more complex factors. Private traders became more active than ever on the Southeast Asian shipping routes, but never went as far as the treasure ships had. Unlike the Ming court, private traders based their decision on market forces.

Timber for big boats was expensive, especially in busy trade centers, since large populations meant heavy use of firewood and building wood. China wasn't alone in the wood shortage. Until coal became widely available as a suitable cooking and heating fuel, Europeans struggled with shortages. All over Europe, as well as in Japan and parts of India, governments went to great lengths to control the price and supply of wood. Venice's shipyards fell silent for lack of lumber, while the British took extraordinary measures to save theirs, even passing laws that reserved all trees of a certain height and strength in the forests of New England for the Royal Navy. (Enforcing the laws proved to be another matter, though.)

The Chinese government simply let the timber market work. Once the Ming stopped building massive and expensive treasure ships, they paid little attention to timber prices. Their successors in the Qing dynasty, which held sway from 1644 to 1912, engaged in a short-lived attempt to fix prices during an early palace-building spree, but quickly left it to the market.

The market responded by developing a huge private trade in timber, which grew up wherever there was water transport. Logs were floated hundreds of miles from interior forests down all of China's major rivers and canals to meet the needs of the densely populated regions near present-day Shanghai, Canton, and Beijing. Regional centers sent back cloth, iron goods, and other manufactures. Wood also moved on the seas, from Manchuria, Fujian, and even from present-day Vietnam and Thailand.

But these methods were only good for tapping resources already close to water routes, and coastal and riverside forests were quickly used up. Moving logs from the deep forests used too much labor, so by the eighteenth century the cost of building a boat on the central China coast had risen about three times as fast as the price of rice, China's staple food, and our most reliable indicator of the general cost of living.

Chinese shippers took the logical, market-driven way out: contracting for construction of boats at various Southeast Asian locations, often in shipyards run by their relatives or other Chinese emigrants. China wasn't closed, and the market didn't halt because of artificial factors. There just wasn't a market for the outsized "treasure ships" anymore.

Instead of financing big ships for long hauls to India and the Middle East, Chinese traders commissioned smaller vessels, capable of carrying porcelain and silk to midway points, where traders would buy Indian cotton and indigo for the return trip.

The shorter routes also fit better with weather patterns, keeping Chinese merchants out of far-flung ports where shifting monsoon winds could strand a ship for months. Maximizing profit meant relying on the entrepôts that developed where the winds made it convenient to meet; a series of these meeting places created an efficient marketing network that allowed the exchange of products all the way from the Mediterranean to Japan, China, and Korea, without anyone being gone for more than one season.

Deference to the weather proved good business, but was a detriment to the development of shipbuilding and open ocean navigation. To make big ships and long voyages worth the investment required ulterior motives, such as missionary work, military competition, or the desire to monopolize the seas and bypass the competitive markets in all these port cities. The Chinese left such ambitious projects to the Europeans, who proved willing to defy market principles, thereby launching a new era and pattern for world trade.

2.2 Better to Be Lucky than Smart

Christopher Columbus has been presented to us since our first days in school as the exemplary visionary. Single-handedly he seems to have torn Europe from the Middle Ages and shoved it into the modern era. He forced provincial Europe to become a world power and to dominate the world economy because of his splendid grasp of the real world and its possibilities. Was Christopher Columbus truly the Great Man in History, the keen European entrepreneur who overcame ignorance and superstition to reshape the world?

Cristoforo Colombo (he came to prefer the Spanish "Colón" but never used "Columbus" in his life) was very much a man of the Mediterranean mercantile world. The son of a Genoese wool weaver and merchant, he went to sea by the age of fourteen, visiting much of the Mediterranean. Genoa was not only a thriving center of trade in general in the newly emerging capitalist world economy, it was also a center of the African slave and gold trades. It was not an accident that Columbus would become the New World's first slave trader. From an early age he became enamored of the hunt for wealth and was not too scrupulous about how he obtained it. He served for at least a time with a corsair crew plundering ships. When he was shipwrecked off the coast of Portugal in 1476, he had been raiding Venetian compatriots. For the rest of his life, Columbus would demonstrate a facile ability to shift allegiances to suit his own interests.

Providence had thrown Columbus onto the shores of the world's greatest seafaring nation, where great strides in mapmaking, shipbuilding, and navigation were well under way. Since early in the fifteenth century, the Portuguese had developed the quick, maneuverable lateen-rigged caravel ships, charted the seas and skies, and developed navigational instruments such as the quadrant to determine latitude. These advances were driven not by an abstract love of knowledge, but a desire to enrich themselves in the fabulous markets of Africa and the Orient. By the time Columbus was carried by chance to Portugal, the Portuguese, by design, had discovered and peopled the Atlantic islands of Madeira, the Azores, and the Canaries, and had sailed more than halfway down the coast of West Africa.

Columbus became inspired to sail west by the fever of discovery and navigational derring-do that was in the Portuguese air. He studied maps. Most importantly, he married the daughter of the governor of one of the islands of Madeira, Europe's farthest western point. The odd birds and branches that washed ashore and local legends inspired the Genoese.

Yet no one would finance his daring expedition to the west. The king of Portugal turned him down because of the failure of an earlier expedition west that the sovereign had authorized. Experience, not superstition, worked against Columbus. Queen Isabel of Castile, engaged in the last act of the eight hundred-year-long reconquest of Iberia from the Moors, turned him down despite Columbus's conviction and charm. Christopher and his brother sought out the kings of France and England, also to no avail.

Queen Isabel had second thoughts and decided to call together a group of experts to study Columbus's project. Partly because of his secrecy and fear of "industrial espionage," he revealed little of his plan. The experts, after four years of deliberation (no rush to judgment) turned him down, but not because the queen had surrounded herself with ignorant, superstitious sycophants who feared falling off the edge of the flat earth.

Rather, her learned councilors, well aware of the world's spherical shape, as were virtually all European intellectuals at the time, concluded that Columbus had miscalculated the circumference of the earth. As Columbus would later write to the queen, he based his plans not on maps and astronomy, but on the Bible. Columbus was less a modern man than the advisers who denied his plan. He was a deeply religious medieval thinker who based his unshakable conviction of the path west on biblical prophecy. Taking cues from scripture and converting with the smaller Italian mile, rather than the more appropriate Arab unit, he calculated a world one-third smaller than it actually was. He had assumed that 2,400 miles to the west lay the Indies. We know today that this is actually closer to Indiana. Isabel's advisers realized that the great distance to the Indies precluded an ocean expedition because of the difficulty of provisioning such a long trip.

The king of Portugal recalled Columbus for a second discussion of his plans. This again failed because as the Genoese arrived at court, Bartholomeu Dias arrived in Lisbon announcing he had reached Africa's Cape of Good Hope. The path to the Indies was open—to the east. There was no need for Columbus's adventure.

Finally, Columbus's faith was confirmed when Queen Isabel again asked him to return to court. Enthused by her just completed victory over Muslim

Granada and swayed by her husband, King Ferdinand, who argued that the amount Columbus required was relatively small, Isabel consented to financing most of the expedition despite her doubts of its success.

As we know, Columbus guided his three small ships across the Atlantic. Thirty-three days after leaving the Canary Islands, he reached the Bahamas. Not only did he really not know where he was going because of his confused idea of the size of the earth, but he did not recognize where he was when he got there. So anxious was he to enrich himself with the trade of the Indies, that he remained convinced that Cuba was Cipango (Japan). All of the inhabitants of these "new lands" suffered from his mistakes as they came to be called "Indians." In a little over a decade he would lead four expeditions to the Indies, would sail off the coast of Venezuela and Honduras, spend a long time on Jamaica, Hispaniola, and Cuba, and yet he persisted to the end in believing that he had indeed found the East Indies. This man who had redrawn the maps of the world still had a medieval belief that the world was pear-shaped and that the turbulent waters of the Orinoco River were one of the four rivers at the top, near the earthly paradise. This man whose exploits would revolutionize the world economy was driven by a desire for gold to finance the reconquest of Jerusalem. Christopher Columbus bumped into the modern world by accident and didn't recognize it when he found it. Sometimes it is better to be lucky than smart.

2.3 Seats of Government and Their Stomachs: An Eighteenth-Century Tour

People today who complain about "big government" don't care where its employees live: an IRS agent in Topeka is still part of "Washington." But in pre-railroad days, what often set people off was the size of the capital cities themselves. Why did the growth of London or Paris cause so many riots, and the growth of Beijing and Delhi so many fewer?

The size of most cities was limited by the need for food and timber. Few farm regions had over 20 percent of their crop to sell once the farmers themselves had eaten. And it was hard to draw on a very large hinterland because land transport quite literally ate into that surplus: a team of horses that traveled over twenty miles would eat enough of the grain they hauled to make the trip (usually) unprofitable. So if a city got too big, food prices soared, wages followed, its products became uncompetitive, and growth stopped.

But capitals were different. There was no real competitor for the services they provided, and they included residents who could raise their incomes by edict to keep up with higher prices. As European empires, armies, and bureaucracies grew between 1500 and 1800, so did capitals, causing horrible problems for their neighbors. London, surrounded by unusually productive and market-oriented farms, and with excellent water transport, was not that big a problem: but even there, various new laws were needed to direct enough grain to the city.

Paris, less favored by circumstance, was a disaster. Nearby farmers typically consumed over 80 percent of what they grew themselves, marketing only what was left over. So if the harvest fell short by, say, 10 percent—a common event—it hit the grain market the way a 50 percent shortfall might today. Traders would scour ever-larger areas buying grain for the capital, where people could afford high prices. Rural grain buyers—village artisans, wage laborers, and farmers of grapes, flax, and other non-grains—went hungry. Thanks to the extra waves Paris made, they could drown in what were actually pretty calm seas; their only defense was to riot, trying to stop the grain wagons from leaving. And even Paris was not Europe's worst case: that was Madrid, swollen with American silver, but located in a very dry region that mostly raised sheep.

The cost of suppressing these rural grain riots—and of keeping prices down for the poor in the capital—was a brake on the growth of European capitals. But if few European cities could exceed 200,000 people, and none could exceed 500,000, how did other societies feed cities of over a million?

A few of these capitals were perfectly positioned near bountiful harvests, excellent water transport, or both. Thus Cairo lived off the Nile Delta, and off seaborne imports when needed; Istanbul sat next to major shipping routes as well as a fertile plain. And Edo (now Tokyo)—probably the eighteenth century's biggest city—not only ruled a country where almost everyone lived within striking distance of coastal shipping: it was also lucky that its subjects grew rice, which yields far larger surpluses per acre than wheat, and stores and ships better. But even so, feeding Edo took massive road-building, a huge merchant network, and—at times—plenty of force to collect rice tribute from unhappy farmers.

Perhaps the greatest wonders were the Qing and Mughal capitals: Beijing and Delhi. Though both empires ruled plenty of rice-growing areas, their capitals were hundreds of miles away, on dry plains that yielded little surplus at all. And both were among the largest cities of the preindustrial world. So why weren't they five times as catastrophic as Madrid? The solution in each case was an ingenious and unique transport system, enabling the capitals to tap remote rice surpluses.

In Beijing's case, rice was carried north by the world's most extensive system of canals, including the Grand Canal, a 1,400–mile-long engineering marvel that borrowed water from, and linked Beijing to, several of China's major rivers. It had been built bit by bit beginning back in the

600s, and was finished in 1420; by the 1700s, it carried enough rice to feed at least 1 million people a year. Moreover, the Qing oversaw a huge national network of both state-run and private charitable granaries: they stockpiled grain in good years and sold at a below-market price in bad ones. The system was expensive, but it worked: Chinese grain prices even in the worst eighteenth-century harvest failures almost never rose more than 100 percent, while French food prices would sometimes soar 300 or 400 percent.

The Mughals neither dug canals nor built many granaries—though they did encourage temples and rich families near the capital to invest heavily in well-digging, making the plain a little less dry and a little more productive. But the real solution was land transport, provided by the *banjara* caste.

The banjara were hereditary, migratory livestock herders; for centuries they had gone from village to village, trading some of their newborn oxen to farmers needing plow animals, and some of the oldest animals for hides. Not surprisingly, they soon got involved in transport, too. And since their caravans often had over 10,000 bullocks (they had perhaps 9 million in all), each able to cart about 275 pounds, they were a natural for big bulky loads. By Mughal times, they were regularly employed to haul grain to the capital, with more lucrative opportunities to carry salt, cloth, and even diamonds acting as a sweetener.

Moreover, banjara shipping was cheap, because it took advantage of what you found on a semiarid plain: plenty of unfarmed and unfenced grassland. Unlike European teamsters, who usually had to pay to feed their wagon teams, the banjara herds ate for free along the roadside. This made the caravans slow, and—to European visitors—strange-looking; but the system worked. And had those visitors been blacksmiths from outside Paris or Madrid, they might have seen the beauty of it all.

2.4 Pioneers of Dusty Rooms: Warehouses, Transatlantic Trade, and the Opening of the North American Frontier

The story of Westward expansion is probably America's most popular epic, and the figures involved are, for good or bad, the culture's most enduring icons: Native Americans, fur traders, loggers, farmers, soldiers . . . and warehouse managers. Warehouse managers? Yup. During at least the first two centuries of European settlement the pace of Westward expansion was in large part dependent on the settlers' ability to market cash crops back in

Europe; and the ability to remain competitive in European markets while shipping goods from farther and farther inland depended on being able to cut the shipping costs incurred down the line, after one's crop reached the Atlantic Coast. Between 1700 and the outbreak of the American Revolution, those costs fell by half, without any technological change in shipping; and a big part of the explanation lay in warehouses along the East Coast.

We often imagine the farmers who cleared the western parts of, say, Pennsylvania or the Carolinas as self-sufficient folk who mostly grew food for their own use; but two simple facts made most of them dependent on sales to Europe. First, most of them started out in debt, either for their passage to the New World or their land. Second, complete self-sufficiency was simply too inefficient, and the colonial market was too small and spread out to support much in the way of industry; so nails, cloth, and other necessities—not to mention status symbols like mirrors, clocks, or tea—were generally imported. In return, Pennsylvanians and New Yorkers sent grain; Carolinians rice, naval stores, and later cotton; and Virginians and Marylanders mostly tobacco. The markets for most of these goods were volatile and competitive, so trying to produce them in more remote locations was a chancy business, unless costs could be cut elsewhere.

Basically, two sets of changes brought down shipping costs, even before the advent of either steam or improved sailing ships, and so made this expansion possible. The first came from the British side—the largely successful suppression of piracy in the eighteenth century. This not only cut insurance costs, but made it possible to send freight across the Atlantic in unarmed (or only lightly armed) ships. Such ships were cheaper to build and much cheaper to operate, because they could function with a smaller crew. But this was only part of the story, and one that benefited the Caribbean colonies and Brazil—in some cases competitors of the mainland colonies—at least as much as the North Americans.

The other part of the fall in costs came from reducing ships' time in port. Sailors had to be paid for shore time in any port other than their home (they could hardly have survived otherwise); this made time spent acquiring a cargo expensive. Traditionally, that time could be quite long, because buyers had to visit each plantation, examine its crop, and dicker over the price. In 1700, an average ship going between England and the Chesapeake tobacco country spent over 100 days per voyage going around the mouth of the river collecting cargo; port times elsewhere were similar, and similarly expensive. (In the Indian Ocean and South China Sea, where the impossibility of returning home until the monsoon winds shifted made port times even longer, a radically different solution was found. Instead of hiring sailors for wages, ship owners recruited merchants as crew members, exchanging on-board services for a right to use a certain amount of cargo space; these merchant-sailors supported themselves by trading on their own account while in port, relieving the ship owner of any need to support them.)

The solution, in retrospect, seems remarkably simple: contract with agents on the spot, who have bought up the desired crop in advance, and have it warehoused and ready to load when the ships from Europe arrive. Yet at the time this was quite an innovative solution: merchants were not used to providing the scale of credit that such arrangements often required, or delegating that much responsibility for choosing what goods to acquire. Part of what made this possible in the New World, however, was precisely the narrow range of goods sought in any particular American location. A ship arriving in, say, Alexandria, Calcutta, or Canton faced complicated choices among commodities—was pepper a better buy this season than silk, or tea a better buy than either? Or given the need to stop off in Surat on the way back, might it be better to buy cotton and figure on swapping it there for something to take back to Europe? But shippers arriving in Baltimore were buying tobacco and little else; in Charleston, rice, cotton, or maybe naval stores; in Kingston almost certainly sugar. Moreover, they were taking these goods straight back to Europe: unlike in Old World commerce, on the transatlantic route there were no stopovers where you might exchange part of this cargo for a different one. So decisions were simpler and easier to delegate, and those who saw that could greatly cut their port time.

Interestingly, it took the well-established English trading companies quite a while to figure this out: independent Scottish traders were the first to see the potential of financing Americans who would build and manage warehouses. But it gradually became clear how much time and money could be saved—by 1770, port time in the Chesapeake was down to fifty days, much of which was needed for repairs anyway—and other shippers followed suit. As transatlantic shipping costs fell, the volume of American goods demanded in Europe rose. But English ships exporting to America were partly empty, since manufactured exports, many of them luxury goods, took up much less space than bulky New World farm and forest products. Thus, they always had room for a new batch of European immigrants, immigrants who could now more easily move into the less crowded interior of the colonies, in part thanks to the quiet pioneering on the wharves and in the warehouses of the coast.

2.5 People Patterns: Was the Real America Sichuan?

After Columbus came other Europeans. Since so many Europeans, were, like people everywhere, short on land, resources, and opportunities, the opening of two empty continents was an enormous draw. By 1800—when the United States had broken away from England and much of Latin America was about to break away from Spain—an unparalleled number of people had joined the adventure, creating new societies while greatly relieving population pressure in the Old World.

Oops! Scratch all that; it may be in your high school textbook, but it's mostly wrong. In fact, the flow of Europeans to the New World before 1800 did not stand out, at least numerically. Somewhere between 1 million and 2 million Europeans came to the New World between 1500 and 1800; by contrast, over 8 million Africans came via the slave trade. (The predominantly European population of North America resulted from very high birthrates—what Ben Franklin called "the American multiplication table"— while wretched conditions and an absence of females kept the African population down.) Indeed, slaves were needed in some parts of the New World precisely because not enough Europeans were willing to come for the sort of jobs that were being offered once the privileged and powerful had grabbed much of the best land and turned it into plantations. Much better examples of people moving vast distances to seek free land—and by far the largest voluntary migrations of the pre-steamship era—were occurring among the Chinese, who are often portrayed as people too tied to the soil of their ancestors to move.

Consider the numbers, or what we know of them. About 4 million Chinese moved to the Southwest frontier alone between 1500 and 1800, clearing previously uncultivated lands and pushing out the indigenous tribal peoples. Over 1 million people relocated (some voluntarily, some not) to Manchuria just in the mid-1600s; and though further migration to the area was banned in the 1700s, the amount of land found to be cultivated by Chinese in a 1779 survey suggests an influx of at least 1 million more. Other people crossed the straits to Taiwan, or headed for other frontier spots. One of the few things we know about migration to Sichuan—not a new frontier, but an area that again had open land after war and plague ravaged it in the mid-1600s—is that for about 200 years it was the most popular destination of all.

Why so many? It wasn't that Chinese were any poorer or more desperate than their European contemporaries; on average they may even have been a little more fortunate than preindustrial Westerners. And the lands they sought out were certainly no richer; nor were the hardships necessarily less than for those crossing the Atlantic.

In some cases, government policy provides an answer. Some of the migrants—perhaps 1 million of those going to the Southwest, for instance— were soldiers and their families, sent by the state to help shore up China's hold on contested regions. Elsewhere, the frontier was one of *re*settlement after depopulation, and the state often aided voluntary migrants: it provided free seed and breeding stock (for draft animals), helped with irrigation and flood control projects. Most basically, it guaranteed title to abandoned or newly cleared land, and frequently didn't put such land on the tax rolls.

But on truly new frontiers, the state was often less accommodating, and even discouraging. Migration to Taiwan and Manchuria were banned for long periods, as the government sought to protect the indigenous peoples of these areas—or at least avoid the costs of putting down rebellions. In Manchuria, the Qing dynasty (1644–1912) was protecting its own ances-tral homeland, a place that nurtured the horsemanship and martial values that had made the Qing conquest of China. Moreover, the forests were the source of ginseng root—a lucrative royal trade monopoly. The soybeans and wheat the settlers would grow instead might have filled stomachs, but not the imperial treasury. (In the New World, by contrast, it was usually the colonists' crops—sugar, tobacco, coffee, and so forth—that entered for-eign trade on a large scale, generating government revenues far beyond what furs and skins could yield.)

Taiwan also had forest exports—the indigenous people sold deerskins and other forest products to the Dutch traders who arrived after 1600—and the Qing feared that too many farmers clearing the forests would create an ex-plosive anti-Chinese alliance. So even once it became clear that the govern-ment couldn't stop Chinese from settling Taiwan, the state worked hard to make sure the natives didn't lose everything. They insisted, for instance, that Chinese farmers could not own the land they cleared; while they might gain permanent surface rights, and be allowed to sell, rent, or pass on those rights, those who had been there before still owned the subsoil, and thus could col-lect rent that might partly offset losses from the shrinking forest. And when convinced that settlers were pushing too hard and causing instability, the government was willing to arm and ally with native peoples to restore the status quo—hardly a likely scenario in the New World.

So why did so many more Chinese than Europeans pull up stakes? In part, no doubt, because migration offered them farms of their own almost imme-diately. In many European colonies, on the other hand, elites were allowed to gobble up all the land, so ordinary folk could only hope to gain land after surviving a period of indentured servitude. And in part because, contrary to most stereotypes, they started out less encumbered than most Europeans. Until the French Revolution, many Europeans were legally bound to a piece of land and/or a feudal master. Even those who had the right to leave often could not have sold their interest in the land to finance their passage. By contrast, the overwhelming majority of Chinese peasants were independent smallholders, or tenants whose relations with their landlords were based on contract, not legal subordination. In the economic sphere, they were simply freer than their European contemporaries—and that meant, among other things, freer to move. It was only once European peasants and artisans "caught up" in this regard—and once many of them lost their livelihood in the tumult of the nineteenth century—that they became equally footloose and sought out new lands on a scale that justified the immigrant legend that we have now read back into the first three centuries of New World colonization.

2.6 Winning Raffles

In the fifteen years he served the British East India Company in Asia, Stamford Raffles conquered Java, wrote three books, gathered much of the original collection of the London Zoo, and above all, founded Singapore. The Company denied him a pension and dunned his widow for expenses he had claimed while creating Southeast Asia's greatest trading center.

Few people did more to promote British commerce in Asia than Stamford Raffles; and perhaps nobody did more to define the values of the empire in its nineteenth-century "liberal" phase. Born in 1781—just three months before the British defeat at Yorktown that sealed the thirteen colonies' independence and signaled the limits of an empire of white settler colonies—Raffles started work at age fourteen for the flag-bearer of a different kind of British Empire, the East India Company, which traded with and sometimes ruled over long-established societies in South Asia. (Raffles began work so young because his father died suddenly and in debt. This side of his story also made him a fitting emblem of the nineteenth-century British Empire; though such rags-to-riches stories were actually rare, the idea that any enterprising young man could make his way by helping British commerce expand to reach new fields overseas was a myth dear to English hearts.)

For ten years, Raffles labored anonymously in the firm's London offices; when given a chance to go to Penang, on the Malay Peninsula, in 1805, he grabbed it. Always extremely ambitious (in several of his letters, he compares himself to Napoleon), Raffles made himself nearly indispensable by teaching himself Malay on the voyage to Penang; almost nobody else in the company's employ spoke the language. Though he was fascinated by every aspect of the area (on a leave back to London, he took with him over thirty tons of sketches, plants, animals, and local artifacts), Raffles had his eye from the beginning on bigger things, and on points farther east. The Napoleonic Wars gave him his chance, for with Holland, the colonial master of present-day Indonesia, under Bonaparte's rule, its loosely held possessions were up for grabs. And in fact, Raffles thought even bigger than that: his very first memo about Southeast Asian affairs stressed the value that a new British settlement in the Netherlands Indies would have as a base for expanding British trade with China. In 1811, he sailed as the number two civilian (and chief strategist) of a force of 9,500 that took Java from the Dutch; he then served as its governor for the next four and a half years.

Raffles was also fired by a vision of a simultaneously liberal and authoritarian empire, with free trade as its cornerstone; he was convinced this would be good for the natives, as well as the British. At least on paper, he abolished the Dutch system in which villages were forced to do a quota of unpaid labor cultivating export crops in order to keep access to the land on which they grew rice for themselves. Auctioning the land to the highest bidder and assessing taxes on it, he reasoned, would be enough to ensure a steady stream of sugar, coffee, and other exports, while giving peasants a chance to participate in the market. Slavery was to be abolished; tax money was to be used to build roads and make other improvements favorable to trade. But quite aside from the chaos that resulted from trying to introduce capitalism overnight, Raffles had another problem in Java: neither his employers nor the British foreign ministry favored this application of English principles. Whitehall Street was eager to have Holland as an ally in post-Napoleonic Europe, and so planned to return their empire to them, and for the East India Company that made Raffles's road-building and other reforms an expensive investment from which they would never see much profit. Within a year of the war's end, Raffles was sent to the backwater post of Bencoolen (also in Malaya) and given a decidedly mixed personnel review; probably only the high-ranking friends (including the crown prince) that he had made on a furlough back in London—where he was celebrated as a war hero, explorer, naturalist, and anthropologist—guaranteed him even that much.

As frustrating to Raffles as the detour in his own career was the opportunity he was sure Britain was missing. Not only had they restored the East Indies to the Dutch, they tolerated Holland's reimposition of its monopoly on almost all trade with this vast archipelago. (As London saw it, such tolerance was necessary, since spoils from Indonesia were essential to rebuilding and stabilizing a Holland ravaged during the war.) To enforce that monopoly, the Dutch continually harassed foreign ships in their waters and often refused to serve those that entered their ports. And since Indonesia stood along the only possible sea routes linking the Indian Ocean with the Pacific, this placed the Dutch firmly in the way of non-Dutch merchants dreaming of great profits to be made in China and Japan. For Raffles's bosses at the East India Company, this was only an irritation, but for smaller "country" traders, it was a disaster. Their smaller ships were more often in need of taking on supplies in between India and China; and they had a special financial need as well. Being less well capitalized than the EIC, they found it a great hardship to wait the several months of an ocean voyage to China before seeing any return on the working capital they had invested in cargo, crew, and stores; they needed to turn over their stock sooner and above all had to avoid failing to return before the monsoon shifted, becalming ships and forcing several months' more wait before a trip's profits returned home. For centuries before the Europeans came, this problem had been solved by having ships coming from China meet those coming from India and the Middle East somewhere in the straits of Malacca; a variety of towns there had had their decades (or centuries) of glory before greedy pirates or monarchs killed them off by charging too much for protection. Now it was the Dutch who monopolized this perfect spot for an entrepôt: Raffles, who may have known the area's commercial history better than any European, was determined to plant an outpost for free trade there.

By swamping his supervisor—the governor-general of India, based in Calcutta—with memos about how the Dutch were tightening a noose around the Calcutta-Canton trade, one of the EIC's biggest moneymakers (largely thanks to opium sales), Raffles eventually obtained vaguely worded instructions, which could conceivably be said to include permission for armed intervention. That was all he wanted: taking advantage of a succession dispute between two brothers of a deceased sultan, Raffles arrived at the future site of Singapore on January 29, 1819, recognized the brother who had lost out, persuaded him (and his uncle, the real power in the family) to lease Singapore for 8,000 silver dollars per year, and sent in a token force of British soldiers to deter any Dutch action against the new town. The whole process took a week.

The controversy lasted longer. The Dutch protested vehemently, but ultimately did nothing; meanwhile, the EIC and the British foreign ministry, afraid of new commitments and of giving offense, delayed recognizing the settlement. But as Raffles had guessed, time was on his side. Independent merchants in both Calcutta and London saw things as he did and wrote volumes of letters, editorials, and leaflets demanding support for the new colony. Perhaps more important, these merchants voted with feet, their boats, and their capital. Within two and a half years, the little fishing village had over 10,000 inhabitants (mostly Chinese merchants); 2,839 vessels (all but 383 of them Asian owned) had cleared port. And the next year's figures exceeded those for the first two and a half combined. From Singapore, Britain could join in and piggyback on an intra-Asian trade much larger than the direct England-Asia commerce for which the EIC had a licensed monopoly; they could also bend that trade to their own purposes, pushing old and new exports from India to the Far East (spices, indigo, opium) in place of those from Indonesia. In March 1824, both Britain and Holland ratified the inevitable, recognizing the bustling free trade port of Singapore as a British possession.

The new city's success heralded major changes not only for Southeast Asia, but for Britain—and that, perhaps, helps explain why Raffles's superiors were so grudging about giving him credit. When the EIC had been created 200 years earlier, part of the thinking had been that a licensed monopoly, with strong ties to the government, would make for a stronger British presence in Asia; equally important, such an entity would be easier to control, so that it would not pursue policies that conflicted with London's. Even after the company became deeply involved in military actions on the Indian mainland (becoming de facto rulers of Bengal after 1755), this logic persisted; Parliament's response had been to tighten oversight of the Company, not to abandon it or take away its monopoly on bringing Indian goods to England.

Moreover, the way in which the EIC ruled its new possessions, at least at first, was somewhat like the way in Dutch Java that had so infuriated Raffles. Essentially, the Company acted as the stern leader of a coalition of princes, big merchants, and landlords (which was how it had come to power). Plenty of consultation with local elites took place, and many early EIC governors styled themselves as merchant princes (see reading 1.2, "The Chinese Tribute System"). At the same time, the Company—like many indigenous elites—obtained many of its trade goods through direct use of force against local, nonelite populations, rather than free contracting (see reading 7.4, "Killing the Golden Goose," for one example).

Raffles operated differently. There was little in the way of an indigenous elite to consult with in Singapore, and even if there had been, he would not have been interested. Convinced that he and other Europeans knew best, he created a government system with almost all real power in the hands of the colonial governor, and no need to consult anyone. On the other hand, since Singapore was an entrepôt rather than a place where many goods were produced, there was no need for the kind of coercive labor control measures widely used in both Java and India. That formula of free markets and undemocratic government has proved a lasting legacy.

In pushing in this direction, though, Raffles represented more than just himself. Increasingly, it was becoming clear that the real profits for Europeans in Asia would come from pursuing intra-Asian trade; and the Europeans seizing these opportunities were more often private parties than the chartered companies, who remained oriented toward the home markets in which they had legally protected monopolies. These "country traders"—some English, many more Indian or Chinese—provided indispensable economic dynamism for Britain's new empire, but were not so easy to control. Their power to upset London's Eurocentric calculations was vividly demonstrated in their pressure on the government to keep Singapore no matter what the Dutch said or did; the demands of many that Britain force open the ports of China and Japan—where Whitehall and the EIC preferred to move more slowly—was an omen for the future. (Another omen for the future was that the government of Singapore, having committed itself to a no-tariff policy and having little land to tax, found itself almost entirely dependent for revenue on one exception to its free trade ethos: an opium monopoly.)

This new "free trade" empire brought unprecedented profits, but also unprecedented change. As the man who unleashed the whirlwind, Raffles caused discomfort among the supposed leaders of this transformation, many of whom actually preferred the supposedly safer profits of a world that moved slowly enough for London to call the shots.

2.7 Trade, Disorder, and Progress: Creating Shanghai, 1840–1930

Commerce built Shanghai. It is probably the largest city that has never been even a provincial capital, and it was the world's sixth largest city in the 1920s, when it still had very little mechanized industry. But beyond that, very little about its growth is what you'd expect—or what its builders expected.

Foreigners often claimed that Shanghai was just a "fishing village" when they made it a treaty port after the Opium War. What became the British concession, and later the heart of downtown, probably had only 500 residents when foreigners set up shop there. But just across the river was a Chinese city of perhaps 250,000, which was the hub of a booming *domestic* trade. Here the Yangzi River valley (home to more than one-third of China's population) met the sea, and the handicrafts produced by the bustling Yangzi Delta's 30 million-plus inhabitants—especially silk and cotton cloth—went upriver and along the coast to be exchanged for rice, timber, sugar, wheat, soybeans, and many other goods in which such a crowded place could not be self-sufficient. Even in the 1830s, some foreigners estimated that Shanghai's annual volume of trade matched London's. After all, the delta around it had more people than Britain, and like Britain, it was "the workshop" of its particular "world."

Foreigners, of course, were in the process of delivering a rude shock to that world, yet Shanghai seemed to gain even from national calamities. As the opium trade boomed in the 1820s and 1830s, Shanghai became one of its main centers; after the Opium War, it became the dominant one. Millions suffered as use of the drug spread, but many Shanghai merchants, shippers, and bankers grew rich. And an even greater disaster—the civil war that shook China in the 1850s—gave Shanghai a huge boost.

The Taiping Rebellion (1851–1864) may be the most destructive civil war ever, claiming more than 20 million lives. But Shanghai benefited. First, the war ended a centuries-old practice of sending huge amounts of rice from South China up the Grand Canal to help feed Beijing and the northern armies. The grain now went by sea instead, departing from Shanghai. This gave a lucrative guaranteed cargo to shippers who had once sailed north more than half empty (since the cloth and other manufactures Shanghai exported took far less space than the timber, soybeans, wheat, and other bulk goods coming from the south). The profits paid for substantial modernization of wharves, ships, and so on. And as the government began to recognize that foreigners were an even greater threat than the steppe peoples used to worry about—but also a potential source of cash and new technologies—Shanghai and other ports became the targets of new "development" efforts.

Above all, the civil war changed plans for the treaty port itself and its relationship to the Chinese city. The Qing government had originally seen the treaty ports as a way of keeping foreigners out of the Chinese city; the foreigners planned on a settlement "free" from Chinese residents. But as fighting drew near, Chinese sought safety in the concessions for themselves and their money. Population soared from 500 to 20,000, and when British officials planned to throw the migrants out, their merchant compatriots protested. The Chinese influx had sent rents soaring, and landlords were not about to give these gains up. Greed trumped racism, and British authorities agreed to let Chinese settle in their concession.

From then on, there was no turning back. Chinese came in wave after wave, both to the foreign concessions and to the Chinese city; before long they had become one metropolis. While the welter of conflicting jurisdictions made Shanghai a heaven for smugglers and racketeers, it also made it a remarkably open place: a haven for all kinds of business, for political radicals (both the Chinese and the foreign authorities despised such people, but they could often cross from one zone to another before a warrant was filled out), for refugees from around the world (50,000 White Russians after 1917, and more than 20,000 European Jews during the Nazi era) and for both the good and bad of modern culture. Shanghai was the home to China's first newspapers, department stores, and movies, and it spawned inventive combinations of Western and Chinese-style civic associations. Western innovations in steam power, telegraphy, insurance, and many other areas spurred the city's commercial growth.

But openness was far from being entirely good. Shanghai's various governments largely lived off lawlessness rather than combating it. In the 1920s,

Shanghai had the highest number of slot machines in the world, probably the most prostitutes per capita, and an enormous drug trade; vice was central to the city's fiscal base, and inequalities were so large that at least one hotel had servants iron the guests' morning newspapers. To millions, both in China and abroad, Shanghai was the paramount symbol of both the possibilities and the horrors of a new world where everything was for sale and nothing happened as planned.

2.8 E Unum Pluribus

When the Suez Canal opened in 1869, it fulfilled a centuries-old dream: a short-cut between Europe and Asia. In just three months, shipping costs between London and Bombay fell 30 percent; over the course of a decade the canal, plus improved steamships, cut the trip from Marseilles to Shanghai from 110 to 37 days. Goods, people, and ideas moved on an unprecedented scale.

Nowhere were the changes more revolutionary than in the Dutch East Indies—the "Spice Islands" of Columbus's day, and the Indonesia of ours. Many Europeans confidently predicted that as the colony became more closely tied to Europe, Western ways would triumph, too. And as a common culture spread through the increasingly interdependent archipelago, their fractious mix of Malays, Indians, Chinese, and others would forge a common identity and society—under European leadership, of course. But instead, the canal had the opposite effect. By the early twentieth century Indonesia was physically united, but bitterly divided along class, ethnic, and religious lines, loosening Dutch control, while creating inter-Asian hostilities that still linger today.

The map changed swiftly. The telegraph reached Batavia (today's Jakarta) a year after Suez opened. Two years later (1872) the Dutch opened their colony to investments from other Europeans: tobacco, coffee, cocoa, and rubber plantations boomed in the previously sparsely populated outer islands. (They would soon be followed by tin mines and oil wells.) To secure the most valuable outer island—Sumatra—the Dutch launched the Acheh War in 1873, a bloody thirty-year campaign that finally filled out the borders Indonesia would have at independence. And within those borders a new type of enterprise took shape, more like modern agribusiness than the older colonial system.

Before 1870, most of the Indies' exports came from Java and were produced by peasants. Wishing to rule Java cheaply, the Dutch had supported much of the old way of life. Peasants were kept in their villages, growing their own food, and ruled by their traditional princes and village heads; the sugar and other exports they produced were cultivated by additional forced labor, allocated through a tribute system in which each prince was assigned a quota for "his" lands and peasants. But the growth of international trade now created new possibilities. The French and British drained the Mekong and Irrawaddy Deltas; soon rice from Southern Vietnam and Lower Burma was being eaten from Coventry to Canton. Once Indies laborers could eat imported rice, Europeans turned the outer islands into gigantic plantations worked by wage laborers and producing only export crops. To keep labor cheap, huge numbers of "coolies" were imported from crowded China, India, and Java. Better-off Chinese moved in to handle rice retailing, pawnbroking, and opium-dealing; and atop this society of immigrants sat European planters. The native princes and headmen so carefully propped up in Java were cast aside here in favor of more "modern" administrators: foremen, debt collectors, courts, police, and private guards. And even in Java itself, rising rice imports permitted specialization in exports, and brought more peasants directly into the cash economy.

But what the canal pulled together, it also tore apart, partly by changing the way Europeans lived and ruled. As it became easier to get goods (even ice!) and news from home, a different kind of European came to the Indies. Called *trekkers* (sojourners), as distinct from the older *blijvers* (stayers), they saw the Indies as just one stop on a career path that would end up back in Europe. While there, they intended to live as they did at home. Since it was now possible to do just that, the new wave of Europeans brought European wives with them; the blijvers had married local women, who brought them into local elite society. The new Europeans avoided direct contact with the local population; most declined to learn Malay, which for centuries (starting well before the European arrival) had been the near universal second language and language of trade from Sumatra all the way to Luzon. Many unmarried trekkers were so scornful of "natives" that they preferred importing Japanese concubines (considered a "better class of Asians" in that frankly racist and Social Darwinist era). The "Eurasian" children of earlier mixed marriages, previously treated more or less as equals, now became a distinct caste, inferior to "pure" Europeans; many responded by trying to shed their "Indisch" ways and disavow their Asian roots.

Others also partook of the growing racial exclusiveness. The new wave of Chinese migrants also found that it was much easier to keep in touch with their homeland than it used to be; following the Europeans, they too created segregated neighborhoods, schools that stressed the culture of the home country, and racially exclusive trade and civic groups. Mindful of the scorn of the Europeans above them and the hostility of the Malay peoples below (not surprising given Chinese dominance of moneylending, tax-farming, and the

drug trade), Chinese set up the first "nationalist" organizations in the Indies—
but the nation they were concerned with was China. Early activities included
fund-raising for political causes back home (including the 1911 revolution)
and demanding that the colonial administration grant the Chinese "European" status, as they had the Japanese.

Soon the Indies' majority got into the act, too. But for Javanese, Achenese,
Minangkabauans, and so many other groups to promote their shared interests against Europeans and Chinese, they needed a sense of shared identity,
which they had not had before. And here, too, the canal lent a hand: since the
main shipping routes between Europe and Asia now went through the Middle
East rather than around South Africa, the colony's Moslem majority was also
brought closer to a far-away cultural "heartland." Pilgrimages to Mecca, once
exceedingly rare, now became common for the more religious, town-dwell-
ing *santri* Moslems. This happened just as the "modernist Islam" movement
was sweeping the Middle East. Modernists argued that the true Islam of the
Koran was not incompatible with life in the modern world. The false impres-
sion that Islam clashed with the modern stemmed from mixing Islam with
various local customs; these had to be purged in the interest of both religious
truth and survival in a competitive world. Duly inspired, Indies santri set up
schools that combined Koran study with Western sciences and social sciences; formed cooperatives of Moslem merchants to fight Chinese inroads
into cigarette making and batik making; and campaigned for Moslem political rights. Having indeed opened the Indies to greater outside influence with
their steamships and cables, the Europeans discovered that foreign ideas did
not have to mean European ones. Sarekat Islam, founded by modernist Moslem merchants in 1911, became the training ground for most of the major
agitators against European rule.

But a stronger "Islamic" identity was not the same as an Indonesian one.
Not only were the Chinese left out and blamed for the Indies' ills (as they
often still are), modernism intensified divisions between the more prosperous, religious, and educated santri and a larger, poorer group of rural *abangan*
Moslems. The latter had mixed their Islam with any number of indigenous
practices that the santri sought to eliminate—from a system of female family
heads (once widespread but by this time limited to parts of Sumatra), to lax
sexual practices, to mystical cults, "wasteful" feasts, and "superstitious" rites
not sanctioned by the Koran. Since the santri were far more organized and
educated than the abangan, it was their views that the Europeans usually
recorded as being the "customary law"; but victory on paper produced neither real conformity nor Islamic unity. The abangan naturally resented santri
meddling, and denied that having been to Mecca conferred any credit on
santri; instead they often said (and say) that these trips were financed by an

immoral and alien miserliness toward abangan tenants, debtors, and custom-ers. As more worldly Indonesians formed mutually hostile groups tied to foreign places and ideas, the unorganized rural majority was left to face a strange and harsh world alone. More or less by default, many abangan later flocked to the radical wing of Sukarno's nationalism, and to one more im-ported idea—communism. When those large but poorly organized move-ments collided with the better organized santri, the army, and their foreign allies in 1965, perhaps 500,000 died—bloody testimony to a lasting disunity built in part by better communications.

2.9 Guaranteed Profits and Half-Fulfilled Hopes: Railroad Building in British India

The preeminent symbol of global transformation in the nineteenth century was the railroad. It cut land freight costs by as much as 95 percent and mul-tiplied trade accordingly. It gave us standardized time, as it became neces-sary for people long distances apart to coordinate their movements to the minute. It standardized commodities: loading separate bags of wheat from Jones's farm and Smith's farm while a train waited under full steam was too slow and expensive, so we got the grain elevator. People understood that it required a certain mind-set to live in the railroad's world: one that empha-sized reasoned calculation and overthrew old and "inexact" habits. In fact, late-nineteenth-century Social Darwinists often used the perceived ability (or lack thereof) of various people to build, run, and take advantage of rail-ways as standard gauge of the supposedly genetic "fitness" of various peoples for modern life.

So when India—which by 1910 had the fourth largest rail network in the world, with 85 percent of Asia's total track—did not promptly become a modern society, and the railroads themselves earned only modest profits, the search for what was wrong with the "natives" was on. But if Europeans had looked a bit more closely at how the railroads were built, and what they did, these mysteries might have vanished.

First, the huge extent of the rail network should not have raised expecta-tions but lowered them. Many of the lines (including some very long ones out to the frontiers) were built to move troops, not goods; others, explicitly referred to as "famine lines," went to India's poorest areas, which frequently suffered harvest failure and also had poor transit—areas so poor that they were unlikely to provide much rail traffic except when others brought in food to save lives (and social stability). Moreover, Britain arranged private

financing for these financially questionable lines by making the colonial regime give investors a guarantee: if any approved line failed to earn a 5 percent return on capital in any year, the Indian taxpayers would make up the
difference. (Similar guarantees were made on Ottoman and some other railroads.) The result was a boon to London financiers—and to other British
firms, who provided virtually all the track, rolling stock, skilled laborers,
and even much of the coal. This led to even more building of lines with
limited commercial potential—and a lot of gold-plated construction, as banker
and boilermaker both benefited from raising the amount of capital on which
a return was guaranteed. (Another result was that, unlike elsewhere, Indian
railroad-building did not stimulate indigenous steel-making, engineering, or
even coal-mining; nor did it train a group of skilled people who could then
transfer knowledge to other industries.)

The giant rail net did, of course, make rates for overland freight fall sharply,
but in some places (especially along the Ganges) traditional transport was
still competitive. And while the volume of commerce did boom, neither its
growth nor the displacement of traditional transport was as rapid as people
expected. In 1882 (after thirty years of building) India's rails carried about 4
billion ton-km of freight; but in 1800, bullock caravans in North India alone
had probably carried over 3 billion, and population had doubled in between.
Moreover, even these falling shipping rates were still high relative to the
population's spending power. In 1890, it still cost 22 percent of average per
capita income to move 200 kilograms 1,500 kilometers; in the United States,
the same transport cost 1 percent of the average person's income. And the
rate structure made it much cheaper to ship on trunk lines leading to ports
than on branch lines: good for India's booming exports, but bad for the development of domestic markets.

The part of these disappointing results most apparent to the English themselves was that most of the lines made little money. In 1900, 70 percent of
India's track belonged to lines that needed subsidies from Indian taxpayers
to reach their 5 percent return; most earned under 3.5 percent. In 1881, two
lines accounted for 56 percent of all Indian railway earnings. The subsidies,
though quite small relative to the transport costs saved by railroads, were
bitterly resented in India. Meanwhile, Englishmen who had prophesied that
"Railways are opening the eyes of the people . . . they teach them that time is
worth money . . . introduce them to men of other ideas . . . above all they
induce in them habits of self-dependence" and that "30 miles an hour is fatal
to paganism and superstition," now sneered that "all civilization disappeared
beyond 100 yards on either side of the track."

But the railroads were making a difference—just not as fast as the English
had assumed, not in every case, and not always quite the difference that had

been expected. By the 1920s, shipping rates had declined 80 percent relative to income (the same rate at which they fell in the United States over those years), and the volume of traffic soared 1,000 percent between 1882 and 1947. More frontier areas developed cash crops, generating civilian uses for lines once built for largely military purposes. Rice- and wheat-growing areas each began to eat more of the other grain, so the effects of a blight striking either crop were reduced. Perhaps most important, the so-called famine lines proved their worth repeatedly as suppliers of relief, making harvest failures in marginal areas far less catastrophic than they had been. And so, while being covered with a rail net did not transform India's economy, much less its culture, as some foreigners had expected it to do, it did give India a stronger safety net, giving railroads a powerful impact even where their own earnings suggested that they were not much in demand. Thus, in colonial India, railroads built to suit English generals, investors, and steel-makers may actually have done more to make certain parts of the old society *more* viable than they did to usher in a new one.

2.10 A Brief Trip Across the Centuries

We tend to think of transportation as a means of conveying things from here to there, often from producers to consumers. Transportation relates to changes in geography. But in fact means of transport often straddle not only different physical areas, but also different social areas and even almost different historical epochs. A good example is the passage of coffee from the plantations of Chiapas, Mexico, to the roasters in the United States.

Coffee was grown in Soconusco, a remote sparsely populated area in the south of the Mexican state of Chiapas starting in the 1870s. It had considerable disadvantages: it had a sparse population, steep, difficult terrain, few rivers, and until late, few roads and no railroads. But the land was ideal for coffee and equally important, it was cheap and available.

But it was only going to be profitable if the coffee grown there could be exported. The connection to the modern world of coffee drinkers was done with a most archaic, Stone Age form of labor. Some of the areas were so isolated that even horses had great difficulty reaching them. Anthropologist Jan Rus has calculated that 5,000 Mayan Indians were coerced through a debt peonage form know as habilitacion to each carry 110-pound loads of coffee on their backs. Maya carried the coffee down steep, slippery paths and across dozens of rope bridges to river ports, from which they were loaded for the coast. The trip was at least three or four days each way. The form of transport was dictated not by simple technical issues—capital, terrain, power available—but by the labor system based on brute force. Even at the end of the nineteenth century, coerced labor was the rule. Many observers called it slavery. Wealthy landlords in the Chiapas highlands were able to demand labor from the Mayan Indians. The Mayan communities enforced the labor tax in return for a modicum of self-government. The Indians were paid a pittance so that it was cheaper to use an Indian carrier than a mule. And better yet, the Indian could be trapped by debt, which was passed on to his family. Large convoys of Indians snaked through the tropical valleys balancing Arabica bags on their backs.

This archaic labor form persisted into the twentieth century. The Pan American Railroad was begun in 1901 and completed in 1908 connecting up with the Gulf Coast. The train encouraged coffee planting so that production doubled between 1900 and 1910. But this modern form of transport actually *increased* the demand for Mayan *cargadores* to bring the coffee from the fincas to it. As late as 1925 there were only seven trucks in the entire state of Chiapas!

The bags of coffee were loaded on board ship on the backs of stevedores. But once they reached New York, they entered a different world! Often they would steam over to the New York Dock Company in Brooklyn, which was two and one-half miles long with thirty-four piers and a storage capacity of more than 65 million cubic feet. Twenty steamship lines regularly berthed there. Slings unloaded ten to fifteen 132-pound bags at a time. Then four-wheeled trucks carried twenty-five bags to an electric hoist that lifted them to one of three floors. Next the coffee was sampled, sold, and loaded onto trains, because the major trunk lines all had tracks running to the dock company.

Green coffee was shipped by train to roasting factories. The Woolson Spice Company's plant in Toledo, Ohio, was in 1910 one of the most modern and largest in the world. Conveyor belts brought the green coffee from the private rail sidings to the Burns roaster feed hoppers where it was roasted. After roasting, it was discharged through chutes into coolers and from there into storage hoppers where there were screens and chaffers to clean the coffee. Then it was moved to automatic weighing and packaging machines. Automation allowed the 500 workers in the five-story factory to roast one million pounds of coffee a week! From there it was sold in some 200,000 stores in forty-one states. By 1910 a vast fleet of trucks carried the roasted coffee from the trains to the retailers.

That coffee, which had been picked by the hands of indebted Indians and carried on their backs in the tropics of Mexico, finished its voyage motored by steam, coal, electric conveyor belts, and gasoline engines. It had moved not only from one continent to another, from one country to another, but from one historical epoch to another. Yet as dissimilar as the factories and docks of New York where from the jungles of Chiapas, the two were intimately tied together by world trade.

– 3 –
The Economic Culture of Drugs

Today the word "drugs" refers to outlaw commodities, socially harmful and criminal goods that dwell in the underworld of the black market. They are not considered part of the gross national product. Indeed, they are thought to subtract from the total of goods and services produced, because drug use prevents consumers from contributing through hard work or by the consumption of legal, wholesome products. Drugs are viewed as an embarrassment to capitalism, a throwback to primitive times before bourgeois ethics and consumption patterns took hold. Drug company CEOs are called "barons" or "lords" as if they were medieval princes and their organizations "clans" or "cartels." Free trade, which is said to bring great advantages to everyone involved by increasing profits to the most efficient producers and costs to consumers, does not apply to the world of drugs. This is the rare area in which government surveillance and control is demanded to *reduce* commerce and profits. Drug control is done not through market mechanisms, but through "wars" waged by drug "czars." But are drugs really such exceptions? Are they economic outcasts with different rules?

The fact is that historically, goods considered drugs, that is, products ingested, smoked, sniffed, or drunk to produce an altered state of being, have been central to exchange and consumption. What has changed is not the commercial and social value of these goods, but the definition of "drug." New foods introduced from what seem to be exotic lands have historically passed through different phases in their social lives. They often started as drugs that caused pleasant pharmacological effects. As drugs they were seen as both medicines and sacraments of religious rites. That is, they were thought to have both spiritual and physiological effects. They either transported consumers into spiritual states of bodylessness, or, conversely, heightened sensuality by serving as aphrodisiacs. They either heightened or dulled senses; but in either case they transported users away from the drudgery of the work-a-day world. (A surprising array of foods were thought to arouse sexual ardor, from the plain potato to the succulent tomato—called the "love apple.") Although the introduction of new foods no doubt had these social uses for millennia, only the transportation revolution of the sixteenth century caused these foods to occupy an important place in international trade. As the world economy made them valuable, they were transformed from spiritual or sensual balms into the foundations of vast, secular fortunes.

In the seventeenth century affluent people all over the world began to drink, smoke, and eat exotic plants that came from long distances. Coffee, tea, cocoa, tobacco, and sugar all became popular at roughly the same time. Both European and Asian consumers became addicted to these American, Asian, and African products. For three centuries they constituted the most valuable agricultural goods in world trade. Although today advocates of free trade exempt drugs from the free circulation of goods, in fact the plants that gave birth to the modern world economy were considered drugs. Sometimes, as with coffee and tobacco, they were initially outlawed in consuming countries. But their appeal became so strong that government after government decided that it was better to tax consumers of these delicacies and accept their use, even cultivate it, than to spend large amounts to prevent drug addiction.

However, producers attempted to maintain their natural monopolies since most drug foods were indigenous to a specific place: Arabica coffee to Ethiopia then domesticated in Yemen, cacao to Mexico, coca to the Andes, tea to China, tobacco to the Americas. Non-European originators of these exports such as the Chinese, Ottoman, Aztecs, and Incas attempted to control the trade and to prevent the export of seed or seedlings. They failed when Europeans used the persuasion of trade and the force of warfare to open ports. Before long, most of the drug foods were being produced in new, distant parts of the world that Europeans had colonized. Botanical gardens that nurtured exotic seedlings became the advance guard of empire. Colonial empires were built on the foundation of drug trades. So were many domestic bureaucracies and armies. Tariffs on tea, sugar, and tobacco accounted for a significant part of the revenue of numerous seventeenth- and eighteenth-century states. In fact, reliance on taxes on drugs is still one of the main sources of public revenues today. Known as sin taxes, charges on tobacco products and alcohol fund our schools and public health programs.

The popularization of drug foods by Europeans often transformed their meanings, uses, and location of production. Tea and coffee gained initial favor in China and the Middle East because their caffeine contributed to the wakefulness necessary for religious rites. Muslim Sufi holy men and Buddhist priests popularized the drinks, which long were closely associated with religious observances (readings 3.2, 3.3). Cacao drinking was restricted to the Aztec theocracy and aristocracy in Mexico (reading 3.1). In Europe, all three beverages became tied to secular uses. Over time their class appeal changed: they began as aristocratic privilege, diffused to bourgeois pleasures, and eventually became mass delights and finally common necessities (reading 3.4). The drugs that began as nourishment for spiritual contemplation became the sustenance of industrial workers. Along that path, the way they were consumed also changed. From hot drinks with no sweeteners (the Aztecs added chile to cacao, the Arabs sometimes nutmeg or cardamom to coffee), so many additives were included that the original beverage was hardly discernible.

Once they gained acceptance and began creating fortunes for merchants and state treasuries, most of the drugs became respectable. In areas marginal to world trade, they sometimes served as money. Cacao beans in Central America, tobacco in West Africa, opium in Southwest China, and tea bricks in Siberian Russia were currency. But usually the goal was to transmute them into gold or silver. At first they were foundations of mercantilist empires. The Spanish doted on chocolate because of their dominion over most of Latin America, which had a natural monopoly on cacao until traders later moved it to Africa. The British, who were the first Europeans to become coffee crazed, found tea more to the advantage of their trade plans in China and India (reading 3.7). The French and Americans, oriented to Latin America, became coffee addicts.

These exotic drugs emerged from the outlaw underground to become central parts of the nascent bourgeois lifestyle in Europe. They went from the stuff of community, such as the tobacco smoked by Native Americans in council meetings or by West Africans in religious ceremonies, to the fuel of individualism. Coffeehouses (which served other drinks as well) served as centers for trade and politicking in Europe. The first newspapers, men's clubs, and political parties were organized, and revolutions plotted, around tables serving coffee and tea (reading 3.4). Smoking brought together men who created civil society amid the acrid clouds of tobacco. (Indeed, the coffeehouse was the world economy in miniature; it was an international emporium, joining coffee from Java, Yemen, or the Americas, tea from China, sugar and rum from Africa's Atlantic islands or the Caribbean, and tobacco from North America or Brazil.

The nineteenth century would popularize these goods so much that they lost their revolutionary appeal and their sense of social distinction. Tobacco descended from elegant snuff and fine cigars to vulgar chewing tobacco. Dandy Parisian aristocrats at Versailles who delicately took snuff would not have recognized that this was the same substance that U.S. baseball players later called chaw and spit out on the sidelines or teenagers smoked furtively in school restrooms. Sugar was debased from extravagant culinary dessert masterpieces to a huge source of working-class calories in beverages to an industrial additive in something so prosaic as, say, ketchup; coffee and tea descended from the elegant salons to become popularized with instant coffee and iced tea in military rations and in cafeterias.

As the drug foods became more popular and respectable, they lost their original histories. Instead of distinguishing the land of their origin, they became central to the cultures of the consuming countries. As agents of the consuming nations transplanted the drug crops around the world, the native countries lost their birthright. When coffee could come from any one of a hundred countries around the globe, what did it have to do with Yemen, where it was first domesticated? Indeed, Yemen's principal port, Mocca, became associated with *chocolate* rather than coffee.

In the consuming countries of the north, drugs created *culture*, social practices. Who could imagine the British without their spot of tea, the French without their café au lait, the Italians without their espresso, or the Americans without their coffee break? The drugs not only helped create national identities in the consuming nations, they also distinguished different sectors of them. Chocolate was considered the drink of women and children, while coffee and tobacco were associated with men. Snuff and later cigars were for the elite, chewing tobacco for the commoner. The rich drank their tea poured from Mexican silver teapots into Chinese porcelain cups in an elegant salon; the commoner sipped from a dirty, crude mug lent by a street vendor.

At the same time, in the producing countries the drugs born with so many religious and communitarian meanings became mere commodities. Rather than symbolizing identities, they became a means to make money in order to buy something else or to create capital. As the first international drugs became mass products, new drugs entered the world market. First gaining international demand in the nineteenth century, coca (transformed into cocaine) and opium were initially acceptable mass products. In fact, coca had been chewed for hundreds if not thousands of years in the Andes to dampen hunger and cold and to give energy to workers, much as American workers drank coffee or British laborers, tea. The Inca had overseen the coca trade. It was also used in religious rituals. When cocaine was developed in the nineteenth century, it was first a pain killer and later an additive in the popular drink Coca-Cola (reading 3.8). Opium, on the other hand, was forbidden by the Chinese emperors after 1729 in an attempt to protect their subjects. It became wildly popular only after British gunboats forced open China's ports so that the British would have something to sell in China in exchange for all of the Chinese tea the English addiction demanded. Opium was an engine of growth for the world economy in the nineteenth century, as it allowed the British to capitalize Western Europe with Chinese and Indian bullion, much of which had originated in the Americas (reading 3.7).

Only in the twentieth century, with the rising tide of prohibition of alcohol consumption, did opium and cocaine revert to the outlaw category. The inebriation they created was considered to be more harmful than the virtue of sales. A morality campaign defeated the possibility of profit. But this might be another brief interlude—as we have seen in the past—before the lure of profit outweighs concerns about the social consequences of drug consumption. After all, we are witnessing today struggles between those who would legalize marijuana, as in the Netherlands, restrict it for medical purposes, as a California law did, and those who want to continue criminalization. In the opposite vein, efforts are being made to include tobacco as a drug under Federal Drug Administration authority, rather than an unregulated food as it is today.

In the past, moral scruples were ignored when fortunes were at stake. Catholics were willing to drink a heretic beverage such as Muslim coffee (though they quickly began producing it in supposedly Christian European colonies). French revolutionaries saw no contradiction in drafting the high-minded Rights of Man while consuming sweetened coffee and smoking pipes of tobacco produced by New World slaves. British traders in China sold opium off one side of their ships to feed addictions and gave out Bibles off the other to deliver salvation, confirming both Marx's dictum that religion was the opium of the masses and the twentieth-century wit who countered that opium had become the religion of the masses.

European and North American consumers were not bothered by the fact that these food drugs that contributed so much to leisure and pleasure in northern consuming countries caused exploitation, landlessness, and impoverishment of the producing class in the South and East. In every case they were produced in poor countries for use in rich lands and enriched the rich disproportionately. Drug foods had very different effects in the countries where they were produced than in those where they were consumed. While stimulating fortunes, monetarization, and wage labor in Europe and North America, they spread slavery in the producing countries (readings 3.6, 5.1, and 5.5). Coerced labor often was needed to cultivate these drugs. States usually oversaw the coercion as, for example, the African slave trade, and organized the production of drugs. In other cases, such as in Southwest China in the nineteenth century and Burma and Colombia today, production of criminal contraband led to increased violence and criminal influence in the producing areas. Drugs have been both the foundations and the bane of states. Thus, foods that were first consumed for the earthly pleasures they bestowed, the "taste of paradise," became commodities that many producers found satanic. But they must be recognized as a foundation of the world economy, not an aberration.

3.1 Chocolate: From Coin to Commodity

When Christopher Columbus encountered a large Maya trading canoe in 1502 he knew he had stumbled upon something of value. Some of the Maya traders dropped almond-like objects and began to furiously scramble to pick them up "as if their eyes had fallen out of their heads." These curious beans were known in Mayan as *ka-ka-wa*, which the Aztecs changed to *cacao* and the Spanish eventually corrupted into *chocolate.*

The cacao bean had been prized in Mesoamerica for more than two thousand years. The Olmecs, the Americas' first civilization, used cacao and in turn passed on the custom to the Maya. Grown only in the tropical lowlands, cacao was traded to the highland civilizations of Teotihuacán and later the Aztecs. It was as much coveted for its pharmacological effects and rarity as for its taste.

Cacao was considered to be a stimulant, intoxicant, hallucinogen, and aphrodisiac. Warriors would count on cacao's theobromine to steel them in battle. Others would drink fermented chocolate and feel intoxicated by the beans, especially if they were still green (and when consumed in conjunction with the psilocybin mushroom, as in some religious festivities). And men such as the Emperor Moctezuma would imbibe the potion before going to make love with their many wives. The drink also served as a cure for anxiety, fever, and coughs.

Taste was also important. They added many spices, some of which we today might not appreciate. Usually made into a beverage by adding water, chocolate was commonly drunk with chile peppers, flowers that resembled black pepper, the seeds of the pizle—which gave a bitter almond taste—or lime water. Maize was used to thicken it. Only when the Maya or Aztecs added honey and vanilla does the drink sound familiar.

Chocolate occupied a unique position in the Aztec marketplace. It was greatly desired, but rare. Natural stands of cacao trees grew in the tropical lowlands, but the Maya peoples who lived in these areas were largely self-sufficient peasants. Although we now know there were large Mayan cities, no evidence of marketplaces in them has yet been unearthed. Tribute served to bring surplus to the aristocrats. There was some long-distance trade of precious goods, but there is no evidence of an important merchant class among the Maya. Hence, despite substantial demand for cacao in the Mexican highlands, production was small.

Indeed, cacao beans were so precious and rare that they were used as money. Since the Aztec economy was mostly on the basis of face-to-face barter, cacao represented an important opening to monetarization. That cacao really was thought of as a form of money was demonstrated by the fact that cacao beans were sometimes counterfeited! Empty cacao shells were filled with clay, which, according to the first Spanish viceroy, looked "exactly the same, some grains better some worse."

It might seem absurd to have money growing on trees. But in fact the Spanish continued this tradition in central Mexico for decades and in parts of

Central America for centuries. In Costa Rica, the governor was still making his purchases with cacao beans in the eighteenth century. Some Catholic friars, who played a large part in introducing cacao to Europe, suggested that the beans be used as money in Spain as well. No doubt the idea of money rotting away appealed to these critics of capitalism and usury.

Ascetic priests were the first to popularize chocolate in Spain and neighboring countries. Chocolate was considered a Catholic drink just as coffee was first a Muslim drink and then a Protestant beverage. The Jesuits in particular were so taken by chocolate that they became involved in cacao production. Indeed, they were denounced by some secular competitors for trying to monopolize the trade. (The same impulse convinced Jesuits in Paraguay to commercialize mate tea.)

Although introduced into Spain as a spiritual drink of abstinence, it soon became, as in Mexico, the aristocracy's drink of leisure, luxury, and distinction. In early sixteenth-century Spain, chocolate was mixed with water, sugar, cinnamon, and vanilla. Two centuries later, hot chocolate was finally made with milk. The first stimulant to gain favor in Europe, cacao became Spanish America's primary export agricultural good.

European imperialists, unlike pre-Columbian imperialists such as the Aztecs, were able to control production as well as distribution. Driven by the capitalist world economy, production now moved away from Mexico's wild stands to plantation agriculture. Cacao trees were cultivated in Venezuela and Central America and then transplanted to the Philippines and Indonesia, Brazil, and finally Africa. The cacao bean became a commodity rather than a coin. A colonial crop until the eighteenth century, its production only became really large once the colonial aristocracy ceased being the principal customers. Chocolate became domesticated as women and children drank cocoa (invented in 1828 by the Dutchman Van Houten) and ate the many sweets that were made after milk chocolate was developed in the second half of the nineteenth century.

Chocolate today is a sweet treat, a small indulgence. But let us not forget its heroic days when it was the beverage of princes and warriors, the days when money grew on trees.

3.2 Brewing up a Storm

In the 300 years between Columbus's voyages and the industrial revolution, three kinds of transcontinental trade boomed. One was the slave trade from Africa to the New World. Another was the export of huge amounts of gold and silver from the American mines to both Europe and Asia. The third—and the only kind to last well into the industrial age—was a boom in what have been called the drug foods: coffee, tea, sugar, chocolate, tobacco, and later opium.

Most of these mildly addictive little luxuries went to Europe; and most became cheap enough for the masses because (regardless of where they originated) they began to be grown on vast New World plantations, combining plentiful cheap land and cheap slave labor.

Only tea production never shifted to the New World, remaining an Asian peasant crop that eluded direct Western control for 400 years. Yet tea also became the national drink of England, an industrial and colonial superpower that spared no effort to control production of its other necessary raw materials. What made tea so important, and so different from its "drug food" cousins?

Tea was known in China at least as far back as A.D. 600 and spread to Japan and Korea not long afterward. The earliest exporters of the new beverage were Buddhist monks, who went to Chinese temples seeking enlightenment—and brought back stimulation, too. (The two may not have been unconnected: legend has it that monks became big consumers of tea when they realized it would keep them awake as they struggled to prepare for ordination exams.) The drink was not cheap and never won universal acceptance, even in China; poor people in the North generally drank boiled water instead. Yet enough people wanted it that it soon covered many South China hillsides (the only places it would grow), and helped fuel medieval China's commercial revolution. The drink also became widely associated with Chinese civilization, hospitality, and discussions among the cultured elite, and so acquired a prestige that made it a valuable export to the rest of East, Southeast, and Central Asia. (In a backhanded tribute to the symbolic association of tea and sociability, poor North Chinese often drank their boiled water with the same rituals that accompanied tea drinking in the South, and sometimes even called their beverage tea.)

In fact, tea found such a welcome abroad that it soon became a strategic good in which the Chinese state took an interest. The nomadic and seminomadic peoples of Central Asia—Mongols, Eleuths, Turks, and others—so coveted tea that it soon became the principal item sold them in exchange for the warhorses they raised—the world's best. As a result, the Chinese government tried at times to organize a state monopoly to produce and transport tea, making sure that enough was available for this trade at a price they could afford. (After a hard-pressed government set tea-procurement prices too low and wrecked some centers of production in the 1100s, later regimes turned to a more successful policy of regulating the trade rather than running it.)

And from Central Asia, the tea habit reached other new markets: Russia, India, and the Middle East, where sweetened tea (something not found in East Asia) provided a welcome substitute for wine, which was forbidden in the Islamic world and impossible to grow in Russia.

But in part because of tea's strategic function, its cultivation spread far more slowly than its use. It was a crime to take tea plants out of China, and until the mid-nineteenth century that country remained the source for most of the world's production. (Japan was more or less self-sufficient, but not a source of exports.) And while most of Asia was content to rely on China for much of its tea supply, the Europeans—who began to import the beverage in the 1600s—were, in the long run, less willing to accept this monopoly arrangement.

The Portuguese found Chinese tea for sale when they ventured into Southeast Asia in the 1500s. But it was mostly the lower-quality variety, which survived the long trip from China better than the best tea. And while tea is noted in England, France, and Holland in the 1600s, it did not find a wide market. Indeed, Western Europeans seemed primarily interested in using tea as a medicine rather than as an everyday drink. In 1693, even the English probably imported less than one-tenth of an ounce of tea per person.

The story changed completely in the eighteenth century. By 1793, the English imported over a pound of tea per person; the country's total imports of tea had risen perhaps 40,000 percent. Although the reasons for this sudden shift in taste are not clear, the sudden availability of a cheap sweetener was certainly a factor. It was in the late seventeenth and eighteenth centuries that slave plantations in the New World first made sugar affordable for the European masses. And changes in social life no doubt mattered, too. More and more artisans came to labor in workshops (or in some cases, early factories) separate from their homes; work hours became more regimented, and going home at midday for a long lunch less likely. In such a setting, short breaks that provided a shot of caffeine and sugar became an important part of work routines. And even if these early stirrings of industrialization did not quite cause the taste for tea, they certainly benefited from it. Tea, after all, replaced gin and beer as the national drinks in England—early factories were dangerous enough as it was without stupefied workers fumbling about their duties. Had tea and sugar not replaced alcohol as the country's principal cheap drink (and source of supplementary calories), the situation could have been far grimmer yet.

Dependence on tea, of course, had its price—one that the British did not wish to continue paying. As its import bills (all settled in silver) soared, the English sought in vain for a good they could sell to China in equal amounts. The answer they eventually found was opium grown in their Indian colonies, leading to war, dislocation, and a massive addiction problem in China.

Only after that "solution" was in place did Europeans begin to get their hands on the plants they needed to grow tea in their own colonies (growing it in Europe itself was impossible). Tea plants finally made it to

Dutch-occupied Java in 1827, and to British-ruled Ceylon in 1877. Even then, production from these islands alone was insufficient to meet European demand.

Ultimately, a still larger area was needed: Assam, a very sparsely inhabited region of Northeast India filled the bill nicely. The Assam Tea Company was formed in 1839, just as the Opium War was beginning; but production did not really take off until the 1880s. The Assam Tea Clearance Act of 1854 gave any European planter who promised to cultivate tea for export up to 3,000 acres in the region. But the indigenous population had other ideas: clearing the forests for tea plantations (or any other form of private property) would mean the end of their seminomadic way of life.

It took no small amount of force—from outright warfare to tax collection that forced people into debt to laws against "trespassing" and "poaching" on the forest lands suddenly granted to foreigners—to displace these people. And it took plenty more effort to create the transport net, including heavily subsidized railroads, to ship large amounts of tea out of this remote and mountainous region.

In the long run, it worked: between about 1870 and 1900, Assam's exports jumped twentyfold, and other regions in the Himalayan foothills also saw tea-growing take off. (One of the most famous, Darjeeling, is within sight of Mt. Everest.) At last, the West had a tea supply equal to its thirst, and as safely controlled by the consuming countries as were its supplies of coffee, sugar, and other little "pick-me-ups." But the tea plant's road from China to India had been even harder—and more surprising—than a trek over the dizzying peaks between them.

3.3 Mocca Is Not Chocolate

When Jean de la Roque and three French East Indian Company ships arrived in Yemen's port of Mocca in 1708, they were the first Frenchmen ever to round Africa and sail into the Red Sea. They had undertaken this dangerous yearlong voyage with one purpose in mind: to purchase coffee directly.

Although coffee has long been associated with Latin America, for some three hundred years—half of coffee's lifetime as a commodity—*coffea arabica* was an Arabian monopoly. Not only was all of the world's commercial coffee produced in the mountains of Yemen, but the great majority of it was consumed in the Middle East and Southwest Asia. Most galling to the Gauls, the commercial middlemen were also mostly Arabian, Egyptian, and Indians. But this would soon change. De la Roque was an integral part of a tide that would sweep away that monopoly, leaving behind only a faint and distorted memory.

Although coffea arabica appeared as a native plant in Ethiopia, the coffee beverage was probably developed around 1400 in the Yemeni city of Mocca. By 1500 the beverage became ubiquitous on the Arabian peninsula. Muslims adopted it in their worship and spread the beverage throughout the Islamic world as far as India and Indonesia, as religious pilgrims brought beans back from their pilgrimages to Mecca. Coffee also became intimately related to the growth of secular society. The café was born in the Middle East. Restaurants were almost unknown, and taverns were forbidden to Muslims. Hence, coffeehouses became one of the few approved secular public places in Muslim lands short on public space.

Europeans were slow to adopt the coffee habit for several reasons. First, as a Muslim drink, it was viewed as heretical. Second, the Turkish fashion of a very thick, hot, black unsweetened drink did not please European palates. Finally, the rather rare caffeine spice or drug was quite expensive. In fact, Europeans rarely consumed the drink before the last quarter of the eighteenth century.

Coffee's role in sociability and prestige in Europe was enhanced by the arrival of emissaries of the Ottoman Sultan in France and Austria in 1665–1666, who poured the exotic liquor for their aristocratic European guests during extravagant soirees. The Turks also propagated European coffee drinking unintentionally. When their siege of Vienna in 1683 failed to break the Austrians' spirit, the Turks departed, leaving behind bags of coffee. The owner of the first Viennese coffeehouse then thought to remove the sediment from Turkish coffee and add honey and milk, which made it much more attractive to Europeans. But the arabica remained a rather exceptional specialty product.

The problem was coffee's high price. Yemen's artisanal production, layers of commercial intermediaries, and expensive transport made coffee something of a luxury. Until the 1690s it was grown only in Yemen on small, steep, irrigated mountain gardens by hundreds of peasants in three coffee districts.

The town of Betelfaguy, a two-day trip inland from Mocca, was one of the major markets. Farmers brought their beans down from their nearby plots throughout the year. De la Roque noted that the harvest was "not fixed and regular so that the Arabians know no crop." Growers brought their coffee in small increments six days a week; when the price was low they held back. In the marketplace Indian merchants and Arabs controlled the trade. Even though the Dutch and British East Indian Companies had representatives in Mocca beginning in the early seventeenth century, they—as did de la Roque—used Indian intermediaries who were said to drive the hardest bargain. The Europeans' commercial position was weak because they had no political influence and the only European good the Yemeni wanted was Mexican silver piasters—on the spot.

Although coffee was one of world trade's most precious goods, de la Roque discovered that this was still very much petty, face-to-face commerce embedded in a tributary state. He had to sign a treaty with the governor of Mocca to be permitted to trade in the first place. Then he had to wait patiently for coffee to come to the market. He ultimately purchased some 600 tons of coffee, but it took six months to acquire that amount. When de la Roque attempted to solve this bottleneck by advancing a large sum to an Indian merchant who claimed special access to coffee, he was swindled.

Not only did assembling the cargo require a lengthy stay, the sudden burst of demand that the Frenchmen represented caused prices to escalate. Prices had already swollen tenfold in twenty-five years because of Europeans' growing taste for the arabica. Now de la Roque caused another spurt, so irritating the Turks that the sultan's ambassador complained to Yemen's king about the European's direct purchases. In addition to suffering rising prices, the sultan was losing customs duties.

The Ottoman had good reason to be concerned. Theirs was already an expensive and cumbersome route from Yemen's mountains to their own cafés. They transported their purchases from Betelfaguy to a small port ten leagues away on camelback. Then they shipped the cargo sixty leagues to the major Ottoman port on the Red Sea, Jeddah, where it was transferred to Turkish ships and sailed to Suez. At Suez, the coffee returned to camelback for the trip to Cairo or Alexandria. From Alexandria the cargo was again shipped, this time to Constantinople. Until de la Roque's voyage, almost all French coffee was also bought in Alexandria and shipped to Marseilles. This was such an expensive route that de la Roque found his direct venture all the way around the Cape of Africa to Mocca profitable—even though it took two and a half years to complete!

Pleased by the success of the voyage, de la Roque returned to Mocca two years later when he made a visit to the king of Yemen, whom he found planting a large garden of coffee trees. The Frenchman criticized the monarch, explaining that European kings planted only decorative plants in their botanical gardens, adding "if there was any fruit, they generally left it to their courtiers." The king was unimpressed by this argument.

What made this discussion so poignant was de la Roque's discovery upon returning to Paris that he was wrong about Louis XIV's botanical garden. The merchant ended his account of his adventure: "We cannot end this treatise more properly, nor agreeably than by speaking of . . . the coffee tree which is at length arrived from Holland."

Planted in the Sun King's garden, this plant was a progenitor of European colonialism in the Americas. It would be the ancestor of many of the coffee trees that would be planted in the Americas as its seedlings were taken across the Atlantic. The French had found a way to break the Arab coffee monopoly. Within fifty years, coffee grown in Martinique was displacing Mocca coffee in the Cairo market! Yemen could not compete with colonial production. By 1900 Yemen produced less than 1 percent of the world's coffee, and the formerly thriving port city of Mocca had fallen to four hundred stragglers living amidst its landlocked ruins. Today, the only memory of proud Mocca's three hundred-year hold on the world coffee market is a drink distinctive for adulterating coffee grown in the Americas with chocolate!

3.4 The Brew of Business: Coffee's Life Story

Coffee starts our morning, organizes our work breaks, and complements our meals. The world's second most traded commodity is such an integral part of modern life that the world before coffee is unthinkable. Yet it took a five hundred-year voyage to reach your breakfast table. Along the way it passed through four continents and wore many masks.

The fictional Ethiopian shepherd who hopped around after tasting the bitter berries that left his flock animated and in disarray, discovered the secret that eventually led to coffee's domestication in Yemen. The Arabs who transported the berries across the Red Sea may well have been slave hunters, linking from the beginning the beverage and human chattel, a horrible marriage that would last four hundred years. At first welcomed by the mystical Sufi in Arabia who wished to stay awake to contemplate the infinite in the mid-fifteenth century, coffee soon was denounced by conservative mullahs who feared that its addictive properties would divert men's minds from exploring the sublime; already in 1511 they burned bags of coffee in the streets of Mecca. Later, the Turkish grand vizier decreed that the punishment for operating a coffeehouse was cudgeling; for a second offense the perpetrator was sewn into a leather bag and thrown into the Bosporous.

These rulers were right to fear the sociability of coffee. Coffeehouses in Cairo, Istanbul, Damascus, and Algiers became centers of political intrigue and fleshly vice. From stimulating, to addictive, to subversive, coffee's trajectory would be repeated in other centuries and on other continents.

In Europe, coffee's favor rose in the seventeenth century along with the emergence of commercial capitalism. The medieval Mideastern bean evolved into a Western capitalist commodity. Fittingly, it was first brought to Europe by Venetian traders. Thank God! Otherwise we might not have espresso and cappuccino. But the first purveyors of coffee regarded it as a medicinal drug that could cure sore eyes, dropsy, gout, and scurvy. London merchants soon were imbibing the potion in coffeehouses that doubled as centers of commerce. Jonathan's and Garraway's also served for three-quarters of a century as England's main stock exchanges; the Virginia and the Baltic doubled as mercantile shipping exchanges; and Lloyd's café became the world's largest insurance company. The coffeehouses served as office buildings, "penny universities" that disseminated the latest news, and the first men's clubs. Coffee helped stimulate business but outraged wives who, resenting their husbands' addictions to the dark, noisy coffeehouses, issued broadsides against the "base, black, thick nasty bitter stinking nauseous Puddle water" alleging that coffee caused impotence. King Charles II, concerned more with café patrons' political discussions than their familial responsibilities, tried unsuccessfully to close them down. It would take the rise of the East Indian Company and Indian colonies to make Britain a tea-totaling country.

On the continent, cafés came to symbolize and serve the beneficiaries of capitalist prosperity who constituted the new leisure class that would become known as café society. But not without a fight. Debates raged about coffee's medicinal value. In the best scientific tradition, Sweden's King Gustav III commuted the death sentences of twin brothers convicted of murder on the condition that one be given just tea to drink and the other coffee. The tea drinker died first—at age eighty-three—and Sweden became the world's largest per capita coffee consumer. Frederick the Great was less open-minded and less concerned with his subjects' health than with their political proclivities and the balance of trade. He sought to prevent commoners from drinking the brew by making it a royal monopoly. He failed, though the high import duties restricted consumption to the relatively affluent in major cities. The same was true in France and Austria.

But in the capitals cafés prospered. Their great popularity in Paris, according to Thomas Brennan, attested "to the elite's determination to gather separately from its social inferiors." Yet this was an elite of achievement, a bourgeois elite. Coffee's great virtue, in contradistinction to alcohol, was that it stimulated the body while clearing the mind. Some coffeehouses such as Paris's Procope served as centers of intellectual and artistic life where men like Voltaire skewered aristocratic foibles. The Café Heinrichhof in Vienna inspired Brahms and other great composers as well as merchants who preferred the sound of money. Other coffeehouses, such as my grandmother's Café Mozart in Vienna, hosted cards and billiards and other such less inspired diversions. The leisure of the coffeehouse was serious business. Coffee "speakeasies" were intimately involved in the birth of civil society, public space, and the democratization of a semifeudal aristocracy. Appropriately, then, it was at Paris's Café Foy that Camille Desmoulins sat on

July 13, 1789, planning the assault on the Bastille that some argue ushered in the modern world. Coffeehouses continued to serve as bastions of intrigue and agitation during the French Revolution.

As clanging factories gave birth to the industrial age, coffee came to represent not only leisure, but also labor. In the United States coffee became democratic as a drug to prop up the drooping eyelids and awaken the flagging consciousness of an army of laborers. No longer primarily the beverage of spiritual contemplation, commerce, or leisure, coffee became the alarm clock that marked industrial time. By the late nineteenth century the café yielded to the cafeteria and café society to the coffee break. North Americans' coffee imports swelled almost ninetyfold in the nineteenth century. Now instead of seeking divine inspiration as did those early Moslem patrons, profit as did London's businessmen, or the artistic inspiration of continental drinkers, the straggling customers at the factory cafeteria sought survival. In some coffeehouses they plotted to subvert bourgeois society. And, in an ironic twist, temperance societies promoted coffee and coffeehouses as the antidote to the alcoholism of the saloon. The mullahs would have been dumbfounded to see coffee, derived from the arabic *qahwah*, meaning wine, lauded as a remedy for one of the principal social ills of the industrial world: wine addiction.

Coffee consumption has continued to expand in the twentieth century, though it is now attacked for causing heart attacks and ulcers rather than praised for its invigorating qualities. Rather than a moment for spiritual contemplation or socializing, coffee drinking is often a hurried gulp while sitting at the wheel of the car or on the run. Coffee not only fuels the agitated pace of modern industrial life, it has become itself an industrial commodity. Some of the modern processed concoctions that shamelessly masquerade as coffee are more the invention of chemists than farmers. Coffee has become domesticated, commodified, and adulterated; although some religions still denounce it, coffee has lost its subversive edge. From Ethiopia to Yemen to Europe and then the fields of Latin America, coffee has accompanied the development of the modern world. From divine elixir to bourgeois beverage to industrial commodity, coffee has become the brew of business.

3.5 America and the Coffee Bean

Americans love coffee. For a long time now, we have been the world's largest coffee drinker. Indeed, our love of coffee rather than tea is often seen as a mark of national identity that distinguishes us from the British. Historians even see coffee-drinking as noble and patriotic. Most agree that the coffee habit was an intimate part of the creation of the nation: Colonists took up the beverage as an act of rebellion against the British.

Every schoolchild has heard of the Boston Tea Party, in which American patriots, dressed as Indians, threw cases of Chinese tea into Massachusetts Bay. This is an inspiring story that infuses a consumption habit with glory. Unfortunately, as with too many glorious stories, it is not true. Quite simply, avarice and profit, not glory and patriotism, animated America's turn from tea to coffee.

Tradition has it that the American colonists, as British subjects, loved tea rather than coffee. The truth is that Jamestown's John Smith—who earlier spent more than a year pressed into the service of the Turkish vizier—is said to have brought the Turkish coffee habit to America as early as 1607. It is true, however, that colonial Americans drank more tea than coffee.

Colonial imports of tea ballooned from a meager 2.5 million pounds in the 1790s to almost 90 million pounds one hundred years later. But, at the same time, coffee consumption grew seven times as fast. By 1909, Americans downed an average of 1.25 pounds of tea and 11.5 pounds of coffee per person per year. That was 40 percent of all the coffee consumed in the world. By the 1950s, Americans drank a fifth more coffee annually that all of the rest of the world combined.

How did this coffee mania come about?

Not because of American patriotism or Anglophobia. Rather, the cause was, in a word, slavery. American shippers carried off the products of Haiti's huge slave labor force (the world's largest at the time) and supplied many of their basic necessities. Haiti's slaves produced huge amounts of sugar on large plantations. However, Haiti's yeoman and freedman population lacked the capital to carve out sugar plantations. Instead, the rural middle class opened up smaller and cheaper coffee farms to sell to the island's elite who were anxious to imbibe Paris fashion. Coffee became sufficiently profitable that production soon exceeded local demand.

Yankee merchants came to the rescue. New England and Chesapeake traders had long been involved in a triangular trade with the sugar island that saw Americans deliver foodstuffs to feed Haitian slaves, as well as lumber and British manufactures in exchange for sugar and rum, which in part would be sold in Britain to obtain other manufactured goods. These shippers sometimes found themselves with carrying space to bring back consignment goods seeking new markets. Coffee, which withstood sea travel and was slow to spoil, was ideal freight.

The price of coffee plummeted. The drop in price from 18 shillings per pound in 1683 for Arabian coffee to 9 shillings in 1774 for Haitian coffee under British mercantilism and even further to 1 shilling in the independent United States made the beverage available to a far wider public. By 1790, coffee imports were a third greater than tea imports, and a decade later coffee shipments outstripped those of tea tenfold.

When Haiti's slaves, inspired by the American and French Revolutions, revolted in the 1790s—abolishing slavery and declaring independence in the process—coffee production slumped severely, prices shot up, and exports to the United States were cut in half. This might have spelled the end of America's love affair with the coffee bean, if another country, also based on slavery, had not taken advantage of the situation and turned its land into coffee groves. The first Brazilian coffee reached New York in 1809. By mid-century Brazil was supplying two-thirds of the coffee consumed in the United States.

Previously, Lisbon's tight control of Brazil's commerce had shut out Yankee traders from doing business with the vast Portuguese colony. But again the French Revolution intervened. Napoleon, bent on seizing Lisbon—one of the finest ports in Western Europe—convinced Portugal's King João VI to decamp to Rio de Janeiro and throw open Brazil's ports to the world. U.S. flag ships now could enter Rio easily to load coffee, but what could they sell? Brazil—a continent-sized colony—was self-sufficient in provisions, unlike its Caribbean competitors. But it needed more slaves.

As world demand for coffee swelled in the 1830s, Brazilian planters sought more African chattel to work the coffee groves. Antislave sentiment—and eventually an act of Parliament—virtually ended the traditional British participation in the "peculiar institution." By the early 1840s, American ships carried one-fifth of Brazil's record slave imports across the Atlantic. By the last year of the slave trade—1850—one-half of the bound unfortunates came to Brazil in ships flying the Stars and Stripes.

Brazilian slaves toiled to grow the coffee to which America's teeming urban and industrial masses became addicted. Coffee became an integral part of the American way of life, not so much because Americans rejected the "Britishness" of tea but simply because slavery made coffee cheap—and profitable.

3.6 Sweet Revolutions

Tens of thousands of Haitian refugees have landed on U.S. shores to flee the misery of their island. Haiti, with its staggering child mortality rates (about one-tenth die in their first year), life expectancy of about fifty years, per capita income of less than $400 a year, and 25 percent literacy rate is the American disaster area.

Two centuries ago, however, the island was coveted as one of the richest in the world—the pearl of the Antilles. But while sugar made her delicious to outsiders, it rotted the fabric of Haitian society.

Sweetness was a taste little known to mankind before the early modern period. Honey was the only natural sweetener (which is why paradise was a land of milk and honey), and it was not in great or widespread supply. People had to rely on bland diets of gruel, or rice, or tortillas. Only seasonal fruits relieved the tedium.

Sugar began its march to global acceptance in the Far East or perhaps the South Pacific. A tall grass, it was first domesticated in India by 300 B.C., but spread slowly. A thousand years later it had reached China, Japan, and the Middle East. The Arabs were the first great sugar cultivators; Egyptian sugar was regarded as the world's finest. The bitter Arabian conquest of the Iberian peninsula brought with it the planting of the sweet spice. Other Europeans became familiar with this new plant as they battled their way to Jerusalem during the Crusades. Sugar and violence became intertwined.

The merchants of Venice used their large commercial fleet and navy, combined with their forts and trading posts that dotted the Mediterranean, to dominate the European sugar trade of the Middle Ages. They prospered though the spice was still a luxury good with a small market.

Sugar continued its westward march with the rise of the Ottoman Turks who, by the fifteenth century, had deprived the Venetians of their Moslem sources. The Italians turned first to the recently reconquered areas of Sicily and Iberia. Then they joined with the Portuguese in a momentous departure that would reshape the world economy.

Sailing their seaworthy and maneuverable *naus* and *caravelas*, the Portuguese discovered Atlantic islands such as Madeira and, off the African coast, São Tomé. In São Tomé, sugar production was revolutionized. But it was a terrible revolution. Africans were enslaved and brought to work on sugar plantations. The small, previously desert island became a bonanza for its Portuguese lords and Italian merchants—and a hell for its tens of thousands of slaves. Europe's dramatic prosperity during the sixteenth century created a considerably larger group of people who could afford to indulge their sweet tooth.

To meet this new demand, the Portuguese decided to expand production further by bringing sugar to Brazil. America became the fourth continent to be pulled into the world sugar market. It was a truly international crop, combining an Asian plant, European capital, African labor, and American soil.

Although Columbus was the first to bring the spice to the Americas since his father-in-law owned a sugar plantation on Madeira, it was in Brazil that sugar first flourished on a large scale. For a hundred years the Portuguese dominated world sugar production. In 1513, to demonstrate his newfound majesty and wealth, the king of Portugal offered to the pope a life-size effigy of the pontiff surrounded by twelve cardinals and three hundred four-foot-high candles—all made of sugar!

Then came the Caribbean's turn and particularly Haiti's moment of glory. The lush tropical French island became a vast sugar plantation and slave prison. Some 30,000 free whites shared the island with a like number of free mulattos and 480,000 slaves. Sugar brought the ancient labor form of slavery and the modern forms of industrial capitalism into a gruesome marriage. The sugar plantation was perhaps the first modern factory. It had a large, disciplined labor force and specialization and integration of tasks almost in assembly line fashion. It required sophisticated refining techniques and expensive equipment. The planters were often prominent absentee members of the French bourgeoisie such as merchants and bankers.

But they relied on an archaic and brutal form of labor. Slavery had died out in Europe and was on the wane in Africa when sugar combined with the Age of Discovery (read: imperialism) to give it new life. Between 1500 and 1880 some 10 million Africans were shipped across the Atlantic under the most indescribably horrible conditions. Most of these people were destined for sugar plantations, a large share for Haiti (which imported twice as many Africans as the United States). No wonder that the historian and former prime minister of Trinidad-Tobago, Eric Williams, after noting: "no sugar, no Negro," rued: "Strange that an article like sugar, so sweet and necessary to human existence, should have occasioned such crimes and bloodshed." Williams went on to claim a second paradox: he made the controversial argument that it was the profits accumulated from the sugar-inspired slave trade that financed the industrial revolution in Europe.

In Haiti the contradictions between industrialism and slavery, between the bourgeois and the archaic could no longer be contained once the French had their revolution. The island exploded when the bourgeois Rights of Man clashed with French colonial intentions. Although the revolutionaries in Paris were willing to extend suffrage to free white Haitians and eventually to free brown ones, they had no intentions of undermining one of France's main sources of revenue by abolishing slavery. So Haiti's black Jacobins freed themselves. One of the world's first modern wars of national liberation was also arguably its first race war. Fighting almost continuously from 1791 to 1804, the ex-slaves seized the island, killing or exiling the free population.

After more than a century of the bitterly harsh slave regime, the freedmen were ready for a vacation. Once they returned to work, they refused to work for plantations; instead they undertook their own land reform, breaking up the large estates into small parcels. The black Jacobins became black peasants. They also refused to grow sugar. Although the individual black peasants no doubt were far better off than they had been while the sugar economy was booming, Haiti no longer played a role of importance in the international economy. Today the island ranks 112 out of 125 countries in per capita exports. The island found itself with little infrastructure, little capital (for sugar's wealth had always been mostly invested in France), and an uneducated peasantry with no political experience. A small mulatto aristocracy arose who exploited the population for their own benefit but brought little development. When their rule wavered, the United States lent a hand (as during the U.S. occupation between 1915 and 1934) to maintain "stability" and keep the peasants quiescent. After 1804 Haiti found nothing to replace sugar as the island's population swelled. Certainly an economy based on exporting baseballs and blood was not likely to be dynamic. Europe's sweet tooth turned a tropical paradise into a miserable, impoverished backwater. The world economy does not only bring progress.

3.7 How Opium Made the World Go "Round"

It's a vaguely familiar story, though not a pretty one. One hundred fifty years ago, British seapower forced China to accept the Treaty of Nanjing, ending the three-year Opium War. China was forced to tolerate massive imports of a powerful addictive drug and various other injuries; but the treaty's clauses and defenders spoke more generally of promoting free trade and "opening" China.

Not only British generals, but supposed liberals and radicals throughout the West, assured their audiences that opium was a side issue. Former U.S. president John Quincy Adams, no lover of European colonialism, explained that "Britain has the righteous cause . . . but to prove it, I have been obliged to show that the opium question is not the cause of the war. The cause of the war is . . . the arrogant and insupportable pretension of China that she will hold commercial intercourse with the rest of mankind . . . upon the insulting and degrading forms of lord and vassal." Even Karl Marx argued that the *real* significance of the Opium War was that the global bourgeoisie's insistence on "battering down the Great Wall" would bring a "stagnant" China not only into the world market, but into world history.

Nobody today would defend dope-peddling at gunpoint; but the received wisdom remains that drugs per se were not the big story. John King Fairbank, dean of U.S. sinologists, explained the war in words Adams could have endorsed: "the Chinese position on foreign relations . . . was out of date and insupportable. . . . Britain represented all the Western states in demanding diplomatic equality and commercial opportunity . . . it was an accident of history that the dynamic British commercial interest in the China trade was centered not only on tea, but on opium." One of his students wrote that had war not broken out over opium, it could as easily have happened over cotton or molasses.

But in fact, opium was not incidental. A closer look shows that it was central to promoting world trade and accelerated economic growth—not for China, of course, but for Europe and the Americas.

The international opium trade began in the 1700s as an answer to a crisis in Europe's (especially Britain's) international trade. For centuries, Europe had consumed spices, silk, and other Asian products, but exported very little to Asia. Spain's conquests in the New World provided a temporary solution. New World gold and silver were shipped in huge quantities to Asia—perhaps 50 percent of these metals found their way to China alone—in return for things that Europeans could actually consume. But by the mid-1700s, Europe's Asian imports were reaching new levels (particularly in England, where tea became the national drink). Meanwhile, the New World mines were yielding less ore, and new cargoes from the Americas (mostly sugar and tobacco) were also draining Europe's cash hoard.

So how to pay for all these new tastes? Force was one answer: conquer producing areas in Asia directly and make them export to meet new taxes. The Dutch (in Indonesia) and the British (in India) each had some success, but not enough; and the Chinese state was still far too strong to contemplate such measures there. Meanwhile, attempts to sell European products—including British woolens in semitropical Canton—remained frustrating.

Eventually the British East India Company turned to opium, which could be produced in its Indian colony. The drug (previously used in China as a medicine, but rarely as a narcotic) was initially a luxury: bored government clerks, soldiers garrisoned at long-pacified sites, and wealthy women confined to home were among the early users. This traffic grew more than twentyfold between 1729 and 1800, which helped stanch the flow of bullion from Britain to China. But the flow was not decisively reversed. For China these imports—enough to supply perhaps one hundred thousand addicts in a nation of 300 million—were serious but not catastrophic.

The consequences became more grave when in 1818 somebody developed a cheaper, more potent blend of opium. The results were as spectacular as those that the Medellín drug cartel would later achieve by turning expensive cocaine into cheap crack. The Indian opium entering China in 1839 was enough to supply 10 million addicts. Enough silver now flowed out of China to buy opium to offset much of Britain's world-leading import bill—and cause monetary havoc in parts of China.

The number of addicts became sufficiently alarming that China took a stand in 1839, with dreadful results. The Chinese not only lost their battle to exclude dope and their war with the British navy: they lost their tariff autonomy, a large indemnity, the right to subject foreign residents to Chinese law, and the land that would soon be Hong Kong. The worst was yet to come:

its military weakness exposed, China entered a calamitous century of foreign aggression, domestic disorder, and civil war. Skyrocketing opium use—to perhaps 40 million addicts by 1900—played no small role in this.

One might think that the opium trade—and all the suffering it caused—would have become unnecessary to Britain just about the time that they went to war over it. After all, by the 1840s Britain was the world's industrial leader, and would remain so until the eve of World War I. It seems a good guess that "the workshop of the world" would not need to sell drugs to pay its import bills. Had China granted the British the free trade they demanded, couldn't the civilized Europeans have done without selling this one commodity? No. The British still needed opium, even in the early 1900s. Industrial superiority did not guarantee adequate foreign exchange in an era when most of the world still used few mass-produced goods and Britain's appetite for foreign foods (and raw materials) grew as fast as its industrial might. When Britain had turned to free trade in the 1830s and 1840s, the problem got worse: a flood of New World grain and meat was now added to tea, sugar, tobacco, and cotton. Meanwhile, most of Europe and North America stuck to protectionism, limiting British sales in the world's richest markets for manufactured goods—and nurturing new industrial competitors. By 1910 Britain's deficit with the Atlantic world was so large that even doubling British exports to the United States and industrial Europe would not quite have balanced the books.

Invisibles—returns on foreign investment, shipping, insurance fees, and the like—helped a bit, but not nearly enough. Moreover, Britain was a large and vital supplier of capital to the very countries with which it ran huge deficits.

This imbalanced trade, which subsidized living standards in England and rapid growth elsewhere in the West, was sustained for decades by Britain's trade with India and China, in which opium played a key part. As late as 1910, Britain's 120 million-pound deficit in the Atlantic world was largely balanced by its trade with Asia. The empire (not counting India) had a 13 million-pound surplus with China; and aside from cotton thread, manufactures contributed less to this surplus than did farm products, including non-Indian opium.

Most important of all was Britain's annual 60 million-pound surplus with India—about half of its deficit in the Atlantic world. British manufactures of all sorts—from cloth to kerosene to railroad cars—completely dominated the Indian market, aided by protection against other industrial countries and (in the case of textiles) laws that hobbled India's own producers. The foreign exchange that enabled India to keep buying all these British goods came in large part from China, especially from drugs.

Britain itself was India's biggest customer (taking 54 percent of exports in 1870), but obviously not the source of India's cash hoard. India earned large surpluses on its trade primarily in Asia—and especially China. From 1870 to 1914, India ran an annual surplus of about 20 million pounds with China; by 1910, its surplus with the rest of Asia as a whole was about 45 million pounds.

And how did India earn those surpluses? With rice, cotton, and indigo, but above all with opium. In 1870, opium accounted for at least 13 million pounds, or two-thirds of India's surplus with China. It remained the most important item in Sino-Indian trade until the early twentieth century, and also figured prominently in exports to Southeast Asia. In other words, dope not only helped create Britain's direct surplus with China, it made possible the even larger British surplus with India. Without those surpluses, Britain could not have remained the West's chief consumer and financier; and the Atlantic economy as a whole would have grown much more slowly. Though a century of British-led industrialization transformed much of the West, it was only near the end of that century that the West outgrew its reliance on piracy in Asia.

This equation still leaves a mystery: China had no countries with which it ran huge surpluses. So how did it pay for its century of unbalanced trade with Britain and India, which was so important to the growth of the world economy? Records are not good enough to offer a definitive answer. But the best bet is that remittances from Chinese workers and merchants overseas plugged the gap.

The already substantial Chinese communities in Southeast Asia grew much more rapidly as late-nineteenth-century colonialism opened up new areas for export-oriented production. The California gold rush created openings in the New World; plantations from Cuba to Hawaii sought cheap and skilled sugar-growers; and new channels of information made it easier to know what opportunities existed in the first place. Since millions of these workers came without wives and children (often at the insistence of their "host" societies), those laborers who resisted gambling and brothels could send a fair amount home even out of tiny paychecks; and telegraphs and new financial institutions made the transfers easier. No hard numbers are available, but the totals must have been quite large. Thus the Chinese laborer laying track for the Union Pacific may not only have provided muscle to build the railroads: his earnings, routed through China to India to England to the United States may have helped provide the capital, too.

Thus opium not only bound together China, India, England, and the United States in a quadrilateral of trade, but also played a central role in sustaining Britain's industrialization drive and the revolutionary nineteenth-century expansion of the world economy.

3.8 Chewing Is Good, Snorting Isn't: How Chemistry Turned a Good Thing Bad (Coca)

We tend to associate technology with modernity and modernity with improvement. Thus the transformation of coca leaves from a ritualistic, almost magical potion to the more complex medicinal extract, cocaine, would appear to be progress. From a simple, natural leaf, sophisticated chemistry made coca into an industrial medicine. From a natural substance that was used in reciprocal exchanges and state tribute payments and was used locally for spiritual ceremonies, it became a valuable commodity that was traded internationally. The world economy helped change the meanings and consequences of coca, unfortunately for the worse. It became much more valuable, but also more dangerous and socially corrosive.

The coca tree is indigenous to the lower lying tropical valleys that cut into the high altiplano of Bolivia and Peru. Although the Inca asserted that coca was one of their great contributions to Andean culture, in fact humans have probably consumed its leaves for thousands of years. Certainly the people of Tiawanaku, which preceded the Inca by 600 years, already knew and took advantage of the leaf's effects. By chewing the leaf into a cud and adding a bit of lime paste, the user released alkaloids that had an effect similar to caffeine: they alleviated hunger, thirst, and fatigue. Coca is not hallucinogenic and probably not addictive.

Prior to the Spanish, it seems that coca consumption was not widespread. Although cultivation and harvest techniques were simple, the trees grew only in a restricted ecological niche. Coca was not a commodity; the Andean societies did not use money. Instead, they exchanged through barter, often within kin groups. Coca's importance was its use, not its exchange value. It created social networks and ceremonies, not markets.

The Incan "divine plant" was mostly used in religious rites and medical applications. It was burned by wise men to initiate religious ceremonies, offered as a ritual sacrifice, and also taken to maintain wakefulness for nocturnal spiritual rituals. Its leaves were used like tea leaves to foretell the future or to diagnose the cause of a disease. It was also seen as a medicine to treat digestive problems or to cleanse wounds. Little bags of coca were exchanged as hospitality gifts and were used to pay tribute to local and imperial leaders. The Inca redistributed to local political leaders some of the coca they acquired in order to win allegiance. Coca was thus central to the spiritual and social rituals that held together Andean societies and allowed the creation of large empires such as Tiawanaku and the Inca.

tary offensives, sometimes through attempts to transplant the crops, and from the late nineteenth century on, through attempts to synthesize substitutes—but with mixed success.

Where the obstacles to stable, cheap supplies were largely sociopolitical, transplanting was quite effective. Thus, for three centuries, Europeans failed to break the monopoly of Arabs and Indians over the supply of coffee; but once coffee trees flourished in several European colonies, power in this market shifted to the processors and to the consuming countries. British attempts to find alternatives to U.S. cotton supplies as civil war loomed were less completely successful, and often led to bitter disappointment for producers when U.S. production recovered and glutted the market. But considering the scale of the potential problem—the United States produced two-thirds of global exports in 1860—Manchester weathered the storm fairly well (see reading 7.3).

Sugar was first brought to the New World by Christopher Columbus to be grown in the Caribbean. Europe's sweet tooth led to massive slavery, turning a tropical paradise into a concentration camp. After the slaves of Haiti revolted and abolished the inhumane institution, sugar moved elsewhere. Hawaii (reading 4.9) began to produce for the U.S. market. While this brought prosperity for some, it cost the Hawaiian monarchy its kingdom, as U.S. marines conspired with the American sugar plutocrats to make it American. Sometimes, though, sugar was not so ruthless. The Chinese state was more interested in encouraging rice production than sugar production—even though East China developed a sweet tooth to match Europe's in the seventeenth and eighteenth centuries—and was interested most of all in ensuring stability on its frontiers. Thus, although Fujian, Guangdong, and Taiwan (reading 4.10) were among the world's largest sugar producers between 1650 and 1800, none of them were ever allowed to become a monoculture dominated by sugar.

Rubber (reading 4.2) became valuable in the nineteenth century. When world demand for rubber boomed (thanks to the bicycle craze and pneumatic tires), Brazil, the world's major producer, did not hold up the world for ransom: indeed, it expanded production as best it could, often by enslaving people to work as rubber-tappers. But neither did the tapping of Amazonian trees conform to "rational" capitalist standards. Trees grew at great distances from each other, interspersed with other jungle vegetation, so tappers "wasted" much time wandering from one to another and were hard to supervise, and workers in Brazil were in short supply. Thus, when the Englishman Henry Wickham smuggled some rubber tree seeds from Brazil to London, the plan was clear. Rubber trees were planted on newly cleared plantations in British Malaya and other tropical colonies—and planted in nice neat rows at the minimum possible distance apart. Then more bountiful Indian and Chinese laborers were imported and placed in barracks, adding an engineered immigrant labor force to the engineered "immigrant" landscape. The result was rubber cultivation too efficient for Brazil to compete. But control wasn't perfect here either—for instance the all-male workforce eventually won the right to bring women and start families and received higher wages to support this improvement in lifestyle. (They extracted this partly by being so unruly that plantation owners decided the stability of family life might be worth its costs.)

And the ups and downs of rubber were just beginning. In the twentieth century, cars, trucks, tanks, and airplanes—and thus everyone from joyriders to generals—came to depend on rubber tires with ever-changing specifications. But most of the world's greatest consumers—the United States, Germany, Japan, and Russia—lacked suitable colonies in which to grow adequate and reliable supplies of rubber. The resulting scramble of labs, plantations, merchants, and officials created huge fortunes, tragic errors (e.g., Japan's attempt to conquer Southeast Asia), environmental disasters (Henry Ford's failed Brazilian plantations), bizarre alliances (Germany's I.G. Farben and the U.S. Dupont Standard Oil and General Motors sharing strategic patents for synthetic rubber and airplane fuel even as World War II loomed), and, by turns, both prosperous and impoverished rubber growers: in fact, just about everything except long-term stability for any given place.

Where serious natural limits on transplanting coincided with strong resistance to control by the producing society, the struggle could be protracted and nasty. As early as the 1600s, Europeans showed an interest in cultivating Chinese tea plants elsewhere and made many attempts. But the fragility of the plants, the long sailing times of the pre-steamship age, and a Chinese ban on exporting seeds meant that transplanting that was even partly successful had to wait until the 1820s. Since British tea demand multiplied about 400 times over the course of the eighteenth century and would rise still further in the nineteenth—partly, as with cocoa, because it was combined with ever-cheaper sugar from slave plantations—the Chinese monopoly became quite expensive. British strategies ranged from selling opium to China at gunpoint to bloody and expensive campaigns to conquer Assam (northeast India), move out the nomadic peoples, and plant tea on the hillsides, but it was only in the 1880s that they finally got a significant crop—and then they had to spend more money on a long railway line through a rugged region that otherwise had little need for it. The cost of these measures to Chinese and Indians was incalculable, but it is worth noting that they were not cheap for Europeans either. But, tea was apparently worth it to them: initially a status symbol associated with the prosperity and refinement of Chinese civilization, it eventually became a taken-for-granted part of everyday life (see reading 3.2).

So changes in what certain commodities were used for and struggles over their control go way back: but both were probably greatest from the late eighteenth to the early twentieth centuries. In this era, population, industrial production, and per capita demand soared. But in other respects the world was a Malthusian one. Land was finite, and in a pre-synthetic era, food, clothing fiber, and building materials all had to be harvested from it annually; there was not yet a chemical industry that could revolutionize per-acre yields through petrochemicals. Supply bottlenecks for burgeoning industries could suddenly bring massive global demand to bear on surprisingly obscure places and commodities, creating bizarre social changes.

Economic historian William Parker has pointed out that bottlenecks created by technological innovation can be solved in one of two ways: either by a new technological innovation or by applying vastly more resources to old production processes. Thus, for instance, when cotton spinning was mechanized, it created two bottlenecks: a shortage of weavers to use all the yarn and a lack of cotton to be turned into yarn. The first bottleneck led to a further technological change—mechanized weaving. The second led to a massive expansion of cotton planting, which for various reasons could not be done in Europe. Instead it was done with slaves in the American South, and when that supply proved inadequate (or was threatened by politics), by spreading the particular cotton varieties that mills needed to India, Egypt, and China—where peasants who preferred older varieties (and had tailored social customs such as the scheduling of harvests, gleaning, and festivals to the rhythms of that particular plant) were attacked by special, armed patrols—which still couldn't stamp out the old customs everywhere (see reading 4.13).

Slave-planted cotton in the United States is probably the outstanding example of technological progress in one place leading to the extension of drudgery and misery elsewhere, but there are others. When the McCormick reaper conquered the American Midwest—making freehold family farming possible and profitable on a staggering scale—the demand for twine boomed, too, and much of it came from the Yucatán where conditions of near-slavery were introduced in order to grow cheap henequen (reading 4.12). In other cases, the social results were just as dramatic, but harder to evaluate. When the late-nineteenth-century silk boom made rural Japanese women work longer hours—but made their incomes more equal to those of their menfolk—the shifts in power, lifestyle, and attitudes were subtle but far-reaching.

But whatever their local social results, global trade, specialization, and the (re)making of commodities rolled on. Cotton, for instance, went from being just one fiber plant among many to being the global standard. Here the physical realities of the plant mattered. Flax, for instance, was very labor-

and fertilizer-intensive to grow, and it took longer to figure out how to spin flax fibers mechanically. Thus, despite a long-established linen industry, flax couldn't compete with cotton for most uses in an age of factories and plantations, as Ireland, Silesia, and other linen-producing regions learned to their cost (see reading 7.2).

With other products, the bottleneck-induced boom was as intense as with cotton, but didn't last as long: chemistry intervened, and land- and labor-intensive solutions gave way to technological ones. We have already discussed rubber and guano, but there are many other examples. The peanut (reading 4.8), a marginal food grown mostly for subsistence, suddenly became a hot commodity when its oil proved to be a useful industrial lubricant—and violent feuds erupted over sandy strips of North China that would grow nothing else and so had never been worth claiming legally. But just as quickly as the boom started, it died—undercut first by cheaper Indian and African peanuts and then by new chemical processes. In other places, the boom-bust cycle was even more painful. When the Amazon rubber boom subsided (readings 4.2 and 4.15), the people who had been moved there to work tapping trees tried clearing and farming the land instead. Since the soil underneath was thin, stripping the heavy canopy of foliage that used to replenish the land when its leaves fell quickly created an ecological nightmare.

Coffee's longer-lived success was even more devastating for Brazil's huge Atlantic Forest (reading 4.1). Felling trees to make way first to grow manioc and then to plant coffee caused serious problems of erosion. But the culprit was not ignorance. The less technologically sophisticated the farmer, the less harm he did. The real tragedy came with modern coffee farmers and their railroads, which made even distant forests accessible and turned the land into a commodity.

Development may have been particularly rapacious in Brazil, where the land at first seemed infinite and the investors were often foreigners who had little direct stake in the rainforest and little understanding of how indigenous people lived with it, but more carefully managed enterprises still present conundrums. Indeed, modern notions of economic development exist in a basic tension with ecological stability.

One of the prime motors of economic progress is increased division of labor and specialization. But specialization in a particular crop works against biodiversity, which (among other things) makes ecosystems able to survive external shocks. The standardization of crops, in which a few out of hundreds of varieties of wheat or rice are selected, is also part of modern development, since only interchangeable products can be traded sight unseen (see reading 6.4), and it, too, reduces biodiversity.

Even more fundamentally, neoclassical economic theory, ever since its birth, has held to some version of a "labor theory of value"—that is, a notion that the price of a thing depends on the amount of labor-time required to bring it to market, and the amount of production (or other benefits, such as leisure) foregone by using that labor-time to produce the good. This notion is visible, in fact, even before economists such as David Ricardo formalized it, in the ideas about "the state of nature" and the *origins* of property in such English classics as John Locke's philosophy and Daniel Defoe's *Robinson Crusoe*. (Marxism, which was for a century the main alternative to these economic theories, was in this area no alternative at all, holding to a particularly rigid version of the labor theory of value and justifying tragic undervaluations of the "free gifts of nature.") But this often clashes with what we take to be "value" in nature: few people think that the value of a redwood is adequately measured by the work it takes to cut one down. At the same time, the value we may attribute to "nature" is often also more a matter of our own tastes than of scientific laws. Whatever the merits of redwoods, from a strictly biological point of view, it is hard to explain why one very old, magnificent tree is better than two newer ones: in fact the younger, faster-growing trees provide more of certain "forest services," such as oxygenating the air. While the consequences of replacing a local social and cultural code for valuing some object with a global one may be huge, as several examples in this chapter show, we at least know how to map and compare the "before" and "after" points in ecological terms or in economic ones; when we compare the values of commodities on the market to their "value" in nature, however, we are doing something important, but considerably murkier.

Solving problems through long-distance trade also often had consequences nobody could have guessed at for the outsiders (usually Europeans) who represented the globalizing, commoditizing side of the story. After all, they, too, came from "local" cultures and societies, which were inevitably affected by the arrival of foreign alternatives to local resources and local ways of doing things. While the mountains of guano Europeans and North Americans imported proved finite—leaving the places they came from as poor once the boom was over as when it began—the idea of mining nutrients and hauling them to the farm had quite a future. It led eventually to synthetic fertilizer (which essentially turns coal or petroleum into plant growth)—a soil-conserving strategy that has now completely overwhelmed the older one, based on careful tailoring of endlessly varied seeds to localities. Generations of carefully accumulated local knowledge—the main "human capital" of millions of peasants—became obsolete, rendering peasants "ignorant" in the eyes of those promoting a new farming of uniform seeds (which themselves became a major internationally traded commodity) and chemical inputs. (Much of that knowledge has only recently been rediscovered due to interest in organic farming.) This is a process that seems about to be repeated today, as we move toward bioengineered plants whose patented seeds are already impregnated with the qualities that help them respond optimally to particular, patented fertilizers, insecticides, and so on.

Yet in this context of biological standardization, societies still create unsuspected "needs," touching off mini-gold rushes for items previously considered worthless. The new prosperity of South China, for instance has created sudden demand for geoducks, a species of large clams living off the Pacific Coast of the United States, making struggling fishermen rich, and quite possibly making the clams themselves extinct. And in an irony that millions of peasants would have appreciated, water shortages and high labor costs in the United States have touched off a search for slower-growing, hardier, and less thirsty grass varieties to be bred for the next generation of American lawns. This has sent the heirs of the folks who promoted standardized cotton, transplanted rubber trees, and so on scrambling to see if, somewhere in the cracks of some pavement or under a railway trestle, they might find an overlooked bit of biodiversity with which to meet new needs.

4.1 Unnatural Resources

> *Children, you live in a desert; let us tell you*
> *how you have been disinherited.*
> —Warren Dean

When the first Portuguese arrived on the coast of Brazil almost five hundred years ago, they encountered the vast Atlantic Forest that spread along the country's southeastern coast and far inland. While a few stood in awe at its grandeur, admiring it as landscape, most Europeans viewed it as an area of frightening animals, a barrier to movement, or as a resource to cut down. In a real sense they did not see the forest for the trees and would not see it until it was almost all felled. As a result, economic calculations were always shortsighted. For centuries, Brazilians lived off of the inheritance of their children.

Man cannot truly live *in* the dense Atlantic Forest, for he must cut clearings, but he can live with the trees. For four hundred generations indigenous peoples had been living with the forest. Largely hunters and gatherers, they also developed a sophisticated slash/burn agriculture. While destroying forest and undergrowth with fire, this method required movement to new forested land every several years, allowing the cleared spaces to grow over. Since the indigenous population reached no more than 3 million people over an enormous area, their sparse settlements did little harm to most of the forest. And since they sustained themselves in good part with the fish and game of the forest, they would quickly notice if an area was overhunted and move, allowing the fauna to recover.

Then came the modern enlightened Portuguese. For much of the first century after contact, the Portuguese relied on native techniques and native labor to extract resources from the forest. This was not so much production as plunder. Some Portuguese colonizers, especially the clergy, hoped to create a devout settler society in the New World. They named the colony Holy Cross, but the rest of the world recognized the truth of the colony and knew it by the trade good that was being cut from its forests—brazilwood, used to make a red dye. In its first century, six thousand square kilometers of the Atlantic Forest were affected by this trade. Still, the forest was vast, so not much damage was done.

Indeed, in a perverse way, the Portuguese may actually have helped restore the forest in the sixteenth and seventeenth centuries. Disease and slave raids exterminated most of the native Tupi people. Survivors often hid in remote forests, afraid to engage in agriculture for their fields would reveal them to the slave-hunting Portuguese. Indigenous agriculture virtually ceased and the forests returned.

The small Portuguese population of 300,000 in 1700 hugged the coast. Instead of using native knowledge to cultivate native crops, they transferred the slave-based sugar economy from their Atlantic island colonies. Land was given out to the politically favored in enormous grants. Salvador da Sa received 1,300 square kilometers! But the state in actuality had little control over land. Ownership depended upon who could conquer and hold territory. The result was a predatory, hierarchical society in which a few controlled the land and the majority worked in some capacity for them. Agriculturalists were increasingly African slaves. Although at home the Portuguese had worked the same land for many generations and the Africans were skilled agriculturalists, the New World slave society disdained reverence for land. The Europeans brought a new religion and language; they introduced an exotic crop and foreign laborers; and they imposed the concept of commodity production for a foreign market. But underneath the facade of colonizing, Christianizing modernity lay the same slash-and-burn techniques it learned from Brazil's original inhabitants. Land was worked and then quickly abandoned. But now, with a population five or six times more dense, and a greater need for firewood, some of the forest close to the coast had little time to recover. Equally seriously, rather than living from the hunt, the neo-Europeans brought livestock. For the pigs, cattle, goats, oxen, horses, and mules the forest was not a shelter but an enemy. Domesticated animals sped the assault on the Atlantic Forest. Still, when Brazil secured independence in 1822 the great majority of the Atlantic Forest remained. After all, the entire country's population was only at most 5 million people, less than one-third the current population of the city of São Paulo.

Another exotic crop, coffee, led the attack on the interior. Introduced at the end of the eighteenth century, by 1900 Brazil's coffee production surpassed that of the rest of the world combined. Although coffee has been widely heralded as a "modernizing" crop and Brazilian coffee planters as enlightened entrepreneurs, in fact this was hardly agriculture at all. It was not simply coincidence that the same word for miner (*lavrador*) was also applied to agriculture workers. Trees were wantonly cut and burned; then coffee seedlings were planted around their stumps. No shade, no fertilizers, and no tools beyond the hoe were used. After twenty or thirty years, coffee trees had consumed the nutrition of the virgin forest, so they were abandoned to pasture, which in turn often became denuded wastelands. Planters recognized that this was less cultivation than devastation. In the coffee-growing state of Minas Gerais in the early twentieth century, uncleared forest land was worth 70 percent *more* than coffee lands because forest soil was more fertile. Brazil was able to capture the world's market for low-priced coffee precisely because land was cheap and fertile. No one calculated depreciation or replacement cost of the living "capital stock." In this sense, coffee planters were feasting and leaving the bill for future generations.

It was an expensive bill because the Atlantic Forest was not a renewable resource. Deforestation had enormous consequences. Once the mangroves around Rio de Janeiro's bay were cut down, shellfish and fish numbers declined, as did the game that had fed on them. The rivers that ran into the bay silted over, halting much maritime traffic and increasing the threat of malaria, because of now stagnant waters and the mosquitoes they attracted. Elsewhere the destruction of trees caused periodic droughts and greater extremes in temperatures. Many species disappeared.

Depredations were not caused primarily by ignorant Indians or colonizing Europeans. Even the primitive techniques of coffee planters were not the main culprit. Rather, modern technology accelerated the destruction of the Atlantic Forest. The railroad made distant forests accessible, encouraging planters to leave their existing groves more quickly to assault more distant virgin forests. The iron horse made great demands for cross ties and wood for fuel. It also enabled other industries, especially iron smelters, to grow by expanding the area in which they sought charcoal.

The state had not been willing or able to protect the forest on its own lands in good part because it was poor, weak, and dominated by the landed elite. This changed in the 1930s with the establishment of a populist state, and the sense of the forest as an inexhaustible resource began to change by the 1970s. Some efforts to create nature preserves and safeguard public lands followed.

But the pace of the assault on forests has slackened little. The response to Brazil's tremendous social inequalities has been to stress economic development rather than redistribution of wealth. Under this mind-set forests are not a patrimony, a treasure, but rather are "unexploited resources." All animals and plants exist for the plunder and profit of humans. Populists and even leftists share conservatives' disdain for other species. They argue that conservation is a luxury for the rich. The poor countries must cut down ever more to feed their burgeoning populations. Never mind that the land itself is being exhausted.

This is not a new story of course. Areas of longer dense human settlement cut down their forests long ago. As historian Warren Dean bitterly noted: "South America is the forest historian's freshest battleground, where all the fallen still lie sprawled and unburied and where the victors still wander about, looting and burning the train." Today, at most 8 percent of the original Atlantic Forest remains. Will its value be recognized before the only remnants of the forest available to our children are stuffed into ill-tended botanical gardens?

4.2 Bouncing Around

In the early hours of March 28, 1876, in Santarém, Brazil, Henry Wickham loaded a cargo of seeds onto the London-bound British freighter *Amazonas*. Wickham—a colorful world trader given to self-promotion and not, perhaps, the most reliable source—would later tell eager audiences that he secreted the contraband seeds on board in sight of a menacing Brazilian gunboat and then later slipped them by Brazilian customs agents in the capital city of Belém. Once in London, botanists quickly planted the seeds in the Kew Gardens. Nature handled much of the rest: the seeds sprouted, giving birth to rubber trees, heretofore confined to South and Central America. Some were transplanted in Malaya and, later, in other European colonies in the East Indies. By the outbreak of World War I, these colonies had seized control of the world rubber market from its former leader, Brazil.

The story Wickham told earned him a British knighthood and the eternal enmity of Brazilian nationalists. Whether or not the British adventurer's exploits were as swashbuckling as he painted them, the transfer of rubber across the world certainly had dramatic consequences, only one of which was the decline and fall of the Brazilian rubber empire.

But until the Scotsman Charles Macintosh found a solvent for rubber in 1820 and the American Charles Goodyear discovered the vulcanization process in 1839, no one much cared where rubber grew. The ancient Maya and Aztecs had kicked rubber balls in their ceremonial games, and Europeans had long noted rubber's peculiar characteristics. But before Macintosh and

Goodyear, rubber was too weather-sensitive. It melted in the heat. It became brittle in the cold. After Macintosh's process and vulcanization, rubber's impermeability made it ideal for raincoats (known as "mackintoshes"), boots ("rubbers"), and more personal waterproof wear. But it took the bicycle craze and John Dunlop's pneumatic tire at the turn of the century, and later the automobile, to create the enormous demand that would revolutionize production and bring far-flung populations into its orbit.

Initially, rubber production could not increase rapidly enough to meet worldwide demand. That provoked a dizzying rise in prices. Nor, at first, was there much rubber merchants could do to increase supply, because the rubber tapping process itself was unwieldy. Rubber trees did not grow naturally in convenient, concentrated stands, but in isolation across the immense Amazon rain forest. Tappers, known as *seringueiros,* wandered trails several miles long to gather the rubbermilk. As a result, the tapping process was slow and inefficient.

One way to expand production was to hire more tappers. Rubber merchants did so, contracting with more and more of the independent seringueiros, and reaching into ever more distant tributaries of the Amazon. But finding tappers was difficult. Because of the climate, disease, and the previous lack of valuable natural resources, few people lived in the Amazon area. Many who did were indigenous peoples uninterested in money or working for someone else. Rubber did not care. The native populations became victims of the Amazon's integration into the world economy. This last bastion of pre-Columbian culture fell to the disease or weapons carried into the jungle by the Europeanized seringueiros. Luckier natives sometimes suffered enslavement as coerced tappers. Survivors settled in ever more distant, isolated corners of the Amazon.

But Indian labor was the exception. More often rubber employed seringueiros from the arid, overpopulated, and desperate northeast of Brazil. A devastating drought between 1878 and 1881, followed by another in 1889, starved hundreds of thousands of people and uprooted additional hundreds of thousands. Their misery drove them into the rubber forests of the Amazon. Even malaria and other tropical diseases that hid in the jungle did not frighten men, women, and children driven by hunger.

Although the rubber boom caused much suffering, it also brought unprecedented wealth to the main cities of the Amazon. Great, colorful mansions that captured the world's imagination popped up in remote Manaus, 900 miles upriver from the coast. More fantastic yet was the ornate Manaus Opera House where Enrico Caruso sang opening night. So extravagant were the nouveau riche merchant princes of Manaus, that they reportedly sent their laundry out. To France.

The wealth created by the rubber boom changed international boundary lines. As the virtually uninhabited, uncharted expanses of the tropical forest now became valuable, neighboring countries laid claim to them. The most notable area of dispute was the rubber-rich Bolivian province of Acre. Ignored by the highland populations of Bolivia, the Bolivian government attempted to profit from its territory by leasing the area to a U.S. company, all but issuing them sovereign rights in return for rent. The neighboring Brazilians protested loudly. Since the area was settled de facto by Brazilian citizens, the Bolivian government had little choice but to renounce the agreement. This did not satisfy Brazilian squatters, who seized the area and proclaimed its independence. After brief skirmishes and diplomatic wranglings, the area became incorporated into Brazil.

The frenzy and euphoria of the "black gold" rush were doomed, by Wickham's theft, to be short-lived. East Indian plantations financed by European capital, supervised by European botanists, and amply staffed by the abundant populations of Southeast Asia soon overshadowed South American production. Brazil's labor-intensive cultivation of wild trees was no match for industrial plantation production. World Wars I and II gave great impetus to the creation of synthetic rubber, which today provides most of the world's rubber needs. By 1960 Brazil produced only 2 percent of the world's rubber and indeed imported or synthesized from petroleum most of its own rubber needs.

The story is not an unrelieved tragedy for Brazil. If world trade eventually stripped the country of its rubber industry, it has also provided Brazilians with markets for coffee, sugar, and soybeans—the exotic crops that blazed the trails rubber followed later.

4.3 Golden Misfortune: John Sutter in the Wilds of California

John Sutter, born in 1803 close to the Swiss border seemed destined to be a provincial. Clerking in a draper's shop, Sutter married, had four children and settled down to a modest bourgeois life. But his imagination, charm, ambition, and lack of business sense would lead him across an ocean and then across a continent.

Running from creditors, Sutter abandoned his family and headed for the Wild West, which in 1834 was Missouri. He traded on his European heritage, his ability to speak four languages, and his Old World charm. Hoping to take advantage of the thriving Western fur trade, he borrowed money and set out with trade goods for Santa Fe, at the time still part of Old Mexico. There he set a pattern that would follow him his whole life. A business partner cheated

Sutter out of his goods. But rather than giving up his Western adventure, he left behind creditors and headed for a land he had heard of called California.

His trip to California demonstrated how remote and backward the Mexican province was and what a multinational world it occupied. He went overland to Vancouver to the British Hudson Bay Company west coast headquarters. But California was still far. He waited weeks before boarding a ship to the kingdom of Hawaii, which was an active part of this Pacific Rim. At every stop along the way he made friends and collected letters of reference, which he presented at the next port. After four months in Hawaii, Sutter returned to Sitka, Alaska, a Russian province. Finally, twenty-one months after leaving Missouri, he reached Monterrey, California, where, although indebted, he presented his letters of introduction, his tales of past feats, and his plans for the future to Mexican authorities.

This province was rather pristine with some 300,000 Indians and 15,000 Mexicans living in an almost natural economy. No mail, no banks, and cattle hides for money. But Sutter had big plans. Not gold mining or trading. Instead, he proposed to transform California's small pastoral economy from cattle herding to agriculture and industry.

The Mexican governor, afraid of the covetous eyes of neighboring British, Russian, and U.S. adventurers, warmly embraced Sutter's settlement plan, giving him some 50,000 acres in the wild interior of the province on the Sacramento River. Although an American citizen before adopting Mexican citizenship, Sutter's plan to bring European immigrants to the colony he named New Helvetia after his homeland eased Mexican fears. Sutter set about building a large fort to protect against Indian raids and turned the fertile land to wheat, pea, corn, bean, and grape fields.

He also brought the trappings of "civilization" to his settlement, introducing irrigation and shipping on the Sacramento River. Many of the tools he brought in from Fort Ross, which the Russians sold to him. Sutter became a branch of the Mexican government. He granted passports, married couples, and handed out land deeds. He was the principal Indian agent and the head of the militia, becoming a captain. The 225 troops he commanded in English, Spanish, German, and pidgin Moquelumnan and dressed in cast-off Russian uniforms were the law in the interior. One of the cannons he placed in his impregnable stockade (walls eighteen feet high and ten feet thick) had come from Moscow where Napoleon's army left it after their attempted siege. Though often called a soldier of fortune, Sutter sought peace and order. He wanted to sell his land to colonists and then sell them goods once their farms flourished. He was looking for sturdy development, not an overnight bonanza.

His goals put him in a contradictory position. His land and position came from his high standing with the Mexican officials. But there were not enough Mexicans to work the land. So he sought European and Hawaiian immigrants, who were coming in great numbers to the United States at the time. There was also an increasing number of American trappers who, like Sutter, happened onto the West Coast but who were interested in quick wealth, not development. This was a volatile mixture with which to build a new settlement.

But Sutter went on. He built gristmills for his large fields of wheat to sell to the Russians. He planted grapes for wine and aguardiente. And he built a lumber mill on the American River to provide the raw material for the new settlements he was planning.

It was at that lumber mill that James Marshall found glittering stones. When he brought them to Sutter, the captain was not sure what they were. So little had he thought of gold that Sutter had to go to his *Encyclopedia Americana* and look up "gold."

But Sutter was not overjoyed. He recognized "the curse of the thing" and saw that the gold would "greatly interfere with my plans." In time he came to recognize this discovery as his downfall. But even before finding gold, Sutter's settlement was collapsing because the United States seized Alta California in 1848, something that Sutter had anticipated. Sutter's political power, however, was gravely reduced and his land titles were mostly not recognized by the new government. Then, despite Sutter's efforts to keep the discovery of gold a secret, swarming forty-niners changed the face of California. They squatted on his land, mined his gold, slaughtered his cattle, and mistreated his Indian workers. They overran Sutter's fort to the extent that he abandoned it. The sturdy fortress was dismantled for lumber.

Sutter was at the right place and at the right time and had a prescient vision, but he was the wrong man. He was capable of settling the frontier but ill-adept at taking advantage of the new business climate. As a merchant he should have been able to mine the miners. But business partners constantly got the better of him. Cheated out of his land, his planned city, to be called Sutterville, was developed by others and named Sacramento. Nearly bankrupt and heartbroken, Sutter left California going east to Pennsylvania where he squeaked by on a modest pension. He would not be the last person to have his California dreams broken.

4.4 California Gold and the World

The first time James Marshall mentioned to his crew that he thought he had found gold in the stream where they were building a sawmill for John Sutter, they shrugged their shoulders unimpressed and went back to work. The second time, the whole world listened; and soon came rushing to the distant outpost known as California—which would pass from Mexico to the United States nine days after Marshall's discovery.

The story of how California, with only some 15,000 nonindigenous residents in the beginning of 1848, became a beehive of human activity with over 100,000 residents in two years and 250,000 in four is well known. So is the tale of San Francisco, slumbering on the forgotten Pacific with 850 inhabitants; it soon became a boisterous painted madame and then an elegant lady with over 30,000 newcomers crammed onto its hills and along its coast. California prospered much more than did John Sutter. Less well known is the impact of Marshall's gold specks on the world economy. Long before Hollywood captured the world's imagination, before Disneyland, before surfers, hippies, and yuppies, a "California Dream" enthralled the world.

In fact, foreigners arrived first. Word of the strike at Sutter's Mill reached foreigners well before the East Coast of the United States became infected with gold fever. Great distances and poor transportation made California much closer to other Pacific nations than to the Atlantic seaboard. Even as intrepid a traveler as the famous scout Kit Carson took three months to rush the news of gold from the fields to Washington, DC. Most travelers in the early days, whether they sailed around the horn or drove a covered wagon across the plains, took twice as long. Thus, gold fever did not break out in New York until ten months after Marshall's discovery. By then, some five thousand Mexicans had already marched across the desert from Sonora. Thousands more Chileans and Peruvians heard word from ships coasting down around the horn and joined in the rush. Hawaii and Tahiti, too, sent hundreds of prospectors. As a Honolulu editor wrote of California: "If it isn't the land that flows with milk and honey, it abounds with wine and money, which some folks like better."

More distant areas got the news later; but even they quickly joined East Coast Americans in the race to the gold fields. Within the year thirty-six ships delivered more than two thousand Frenchmen. (Louis Napoleon hoped to dump his unemployed and threatening proletarians in the California gold fields; he established a national lottery to raise funds to that end and succeeded ultimately in ridding himself of almost four thousand of his countrymen.) Several dozen British convicts sentenced to labor in Australia also found their way from down under to the San Francisco Bay, where they formed a much feared band of thugs. The Chinese comprised the single largest nationality, besides Americans. China may have been across an ocean, but the ocean served as a highway, not a barrier. Clippers crossed it in as little as thirty days. Within five years some forty thousand Cantonese arrived on the credit-ticket system (a form of indentured servitude). By the 1860s they were the predominant nationality in the mines. All in all, foreigners from twenty-five different countries constituted one-quarter of the California population.

Working together, these forty-niners dug up more gold between 1848 and 1860 than the world had uncovered in the previous 150 years. The gold was quick to find its way abroad; in the early years Californians imported almost everything they needed and paid up to ten times East Coast prices. All of that gold flowing out of California reversed the global deflation of the previous three decades. The minting of coins increased six- or sevenfold. This sparked the greatest boom in international commerce the world had ever seen, as world trade almost tripled between 1850 and 1870. California ore also helped pave the yellow brick road that allowed gold to replace silver as the standard metal for world currencies.

The fact that a formerly ignored area like California now had tremendous purchasing power also created a revolution in transportation. For the United States, of course, the lure of the West Coast greatly accelerated the building of the transcontinental railroad, which connected in Logan, Utah, in 1869. But the implications of California's wealth were even more important for shipping. The Pacific Coast of the Americas had been largely cut off from world commerce since Peruvian silver declined in the eighteenth century. Only a few ships a year worked their way up and down the coast of South and Central America. Now, all of a sudden, seven steamship lines connected Panama (which in 1855 received a railroad that cut the isthmian crossing to less than five hours) with New York, California, South America, the West Indies, and Europe. Nicaragua, Mexico, and Cape Horn, the other trans-American routes, also enjoyed much greater maritime traffic. Chile and Peru now had a market in California for their wheat; so did sleepy El Salvador. More reliable and cheaper shipping also allowed West Coast coffee producers in El Salvador, Costa Rica, and Guatemala to begin exporting to Europe and the East Coast of the United States. Hills Brothers and Folgers began roasting coffee in San Francisco.

But the South American export boom was not an unmixed blessing. The ports on the eastern coast of Central America fell into abandonment. More seriously, in all of these countries the export booms led to increased land value and greater demand for labor, which in turn encouraged land concentration and repressive labor relations and despoiling of indigenous peoples.

The discovery at Sutter's Mill also sucked the United States into the Pacific Rim. Hawaii came more tightly into the U.S. commercial orbit now that Yankee skippers ventured more frequently into the Pacific. Within a half century the island kingdom would become U.S. territory. China also slowly increased its trade with Americans, though the much coveted "China Market" never lived up to expectations. And even Japan, long suspicious of foreigners and reluctant to trade, was forced by Admiral Perry in 1854 to open her ports to U.S. goods.

The Gold Rush also signaled the beginning of a new international position for the United States. While the thirteen colonies were huddled on the Atlantic seaboard, the United States had been preoccupied with Europe. Now that the country had become bicoastal, its economic and strategic concerns grew. Suddenly South America was in the United States' "backyard" because it stood between the two coasts. Now a Central American canal became important to U.S. national integration. A failed California gold miner, William Walker, briefly became president of one of the favored Istmus transit points, Nicaragua, in 1857, and fewer than fifty years later, the Panama Canal Zone became a U.S. territory for almost a century. The Caribbean, the sentinel of a canal, also became strategically important. The Pacific—Hawaii, Guam, Japan—had suddenly moved closer to American shores, and its affairs became of consequence to the United States.

James Marshall might have wished he had kept his mouth shut. His mill never came into use, and Sutter's agricultural empire was overrun by gold-crazed arrivals. Marshall died broke, and Sutter ended his years in Pennsylvania. The local Californios fled to the southern part of the state, and the indigenous population was decimated. Instead of building a sawmill, Marshall changed the face of California and helped build a new world economy.

4.5 Beautiful Bugs

When wealthy Dutch burghers sat down to sumptuous feasts, they took great pride in the sophisticated and lavish decorations that appointed their dining rooms. They were particularly fond of the exquisite Flemish tapestries that covered their walls. Crafted from wool or silk, bordered by silver, and dyed with brilliant scarlets and crimsons, these wall hangings declared not only their owners' wealth, but their worldliness: they were a creation of world trade. But for two centuries few Europeans knew how these lovely creations were bathed in color. Yes, they knew that the mysterious cochineal dye had been sent back to Spain by Hernán Cortés after the conquest of Mexico. But they were not exactly sure what it was made from. They assumed that it was a seed like many other vegetable dyes. Not until the end of the seventeenth century did Italian chemists discover that the cochineal seeds were not seeds at all; they were the dried bodies of insects. The stately, elegant tapestries were smeared with dead bugs!

Of course Indians in southern Mexico and Central America had long known this. The Aztecs had already demanded cochineal as a tribute good from the southern regions of Chiapas and Oaxaca. But Enlightenment Europeans could not imagine asking Indians about a matter of natural science. So they remained ignorant for a couple of hundred years. The superior knowledge of the Mixtec and Mayan Indian producers meant that they would continue to dominate production for centuries.

Most Mixtecs knew that cochineal was made from the female cochineal insect (*Dactylopius coccus*), which fed on a particular nopal cactus that inhabited a limited range. In the wild, Indians would pluck them off the cactus and plunge them into hot water or into an oven. This was a precise, laborious business, since it took some 70,000 dead bugs to make one pound of cochineal. Only the female insect would do, but since she outnumbered the males by 150–200 to 1 (talk about a man-hungry world!) this was not a great problem. However, mature virgin bugs, which were more prevalent early in the season, gave off stronger colors. So timing was important. Wandering the countryside hunting for female bugs was a time-consuming business for Indians who had children and other crops to tend to. Thus a more intense form of "cultivation" was developed. "Seed" pregnant cochineals were placed in bags made of maize leaves and pinned to cactus leaves. Shortly, the insects began to breed, and the young crawled out onto the cactus. After roughly three months—depending on the weather—they were ready for harvesting. In good climates three crops a year were possible. After about five years new nopals had to be found or planted, since by that time the guests had eaten the host. This practice was termed agriculture with "seed" and "harvests." But it really was livestock raising. (Instead of a flea circus, one had a herd of bugs.)

The tiny scale of the livestock, however, meant that the social implications were quite different from cattle raising. Whereas grazing bovines usually caused land to be concentrated in the hands of Europeans who expelled Indians and left the pastures sparsely inhabited, a herd of cochineals, as one would imagine, required very little space. Consequently, they did not much affect other activities or living arrangements. Indeed, the nopals were usually interspersed among subsistence crops such as maize and beans. Often they occupied the house plots. In Guatemala's former capital of Antigua, destroyed by a volcano, cochineals were raised in the ruins of what used to be elegant houses and stables.

Indian communities were not harmed and, indeed, were sometimes strengthened by cochineal. There were no economies of scale. Small plots tended to produce better quality dye than larger ones, where labor and supervision were lacking. Moreover, this was a very risky trade that required considerable expertise. Only the proper cactus and climate yielded cochineal. Even then, unseasonably heavy rains or locusts could slaughter the little bugs. The unglamorous, backbreaking, neck-craning work of "cultivation" meant that few Spaniards ever attempted to ferret out the Indian trade secrets. Instead, they allowed the Indians to maintain their domination of this pre-Columbian crop.

For most of the boom period of cochineal, the colonial Spanish state was responsible for collecting the insects as tribute. In the late colonial period, to expand production, the *reparto de mercancías* was sometimes employed. This was the forced sale of goods by government officials and sometimes churchmen to Indians who were required to purchase the often unwanted goods with cochineal. In effect, the bugs could not only be sold for money, they served as money themselves.

When state coercion officially ended after independence, in few places did Indians lose control of the "industry." Indians usually rented communal land to grow the cactus, so much of the income went to village coffers for collective celebrations and public buildings. Only in a few places did Europeanized ladinos appropriate the land and dominate production.

In virtually every other case in Latin America the increased export of indigenous crops such as cacao, rubber, and henequen led to subjugation and impoverishment of Indians. They were only able to keep their grip on cochineal bugs because of the precarious and labor-intensive nature of the enterprise and special-expertise harvesting required.

The result was that many of the finest drapes, silks, and tapestries of Europe depended upon the Indians of Mexico, Guatemala, and later Peru for their eye-catching crimsons and scarlets. The jackets that the famed British "redcoats" wore on their backs were colored with the bug dye, as were the scarlet letters real-life Hester Prynnes wore on their breasts.

For four centuries the world economy could not crack the Indian monopoly on cochineal. After the 1850s German and British chemists substituted for it by inventing aniline dyes. Although initially not as brilliant and color-fast as natural dyes, they were cheaper and could be produced in the great amounts that the cotton textile revolution was demanding. Sterile factories replaced the gathering of insects. The heroic cochineal bug, which sacrificed her brilliant body to palpably introduce the cactus-strewn countryside of the New World into the wealthy dining halls of Amsterdam and other major European cities, disappeared from the world economy. The new industrial dyes became just as colorful as cochineal, but alas, their stories were not.

4.6 How to Turn Nothing into Something: Guano's Ephemeral Fortunes

This is the story of how hungry yet prosperous people in Europe turned mountains of excrement on remote, barren islands halfway around the world into piles of gold—and how that sudden wealth led to disaster.

The Chincha islands off of the coast of Peru are barren dots in the Pacific. Uninhabitable to humans because of their lack of rain, they became paradise to cormorants, pelicans, and other birds. The birds thrived on one of the world's richest fishing waters, refreshed by the cold Humboldt current. Feasting on anchovies and facing no natural predators, the cormorants stretched their land legs on the Chinchas where they created a virtual aviary carpet. As many as 5.6 million birds per square mile crowded onto the specks of land, making not only a tremendous racket, but mountains of excrements hundreds of feet deep. The lack of rain allowed the manure to pile higher and higher, generation after generation.

Although no humans lived on the islands, humans did know about the bird manure. Indeed, the Incas had a name for it: *huanu,* which meant dung. It was later corrupted into "guano," one of the few Quechua words still current in the English language.

The Incas, marvelous agriculturalists, used guano to fertilize fields in the coastal valleys to feed their dense populations. But its use fell into abeyance after the Spanish conquest. The dramatic fall of the Indian population because of disease, and the marginalization of survivors to the Andes mountains, where transporting guano was infeasible, virtually ended demand. The small Spanish population that commanded the best lands had no need for fertilizers beyond the cow manure they introduced along with cattle. But the cormorants kept working their magic and the islands' treasure grew.

Three centuries after the Spanish conquest, in the late 1830s, the world once again woke up to guano's wonders. Europe's burgeoning population put a strain on its agriculture. Urbanization, the end of the frontier and the spread to marginal lands, and increasing prosperity meant there was greater demand for food than ever, yet fewer natural resources to meet that demand.

Science, as well as hunger, led Europeans to look to guano. Only at the end of the eighteenth century did European scientists begin to understand plant nutrition; the first field experiments were undertaken in 1834 by Jean Baptiste Boussingault, and only in 1840 did Justus von Liebig disprove the theory that plants derived nutrition from humus. Agriculturalists began experimenting with soil supplements besides the age-old use of manure and lime.

Of course demand and knowledge needed their handmaiden: feasibility. To bring fertilizer economically from halfway around the world required a revolution in transportation. Great advances in sailing ships' size and speed, the steamship that began to be important in the 1840s, and more efficient port facilities combined with the new railroad to transport the landed guano all radically lowered carrying costs.

All of a sudden, Peru, driven by internecine fighting in the two decades since independence and reeling from the loss of most of its silver mines, found itself rich. The guano boom was literally like finding a pot of gold, for it required almost no investment.

Imagine the perfect employee: he does not need to be fed because he hunts his own food, needs no shelter because he gladly lives outdoors, is productive even while seeking food or at leisure. He never goes on vacation. The worker needs no tools or machines. Indeed, this employee is actually the factory himself. He finds the raw material, which he obtains for free, transports it, processes it, and delivers it, then steps aside while it is taken at no charge. Aside from the tens of millions of cormorant worker/factories, the guano trade needed only some 1,000 to 1,600 humans. Chinese and Polynesian indentured servants as well as Peruvian convicts shoveled the sweltering manure into the holds of awaiting ships. It was transferred, virtually untouched, to the fields of Europe.

Initially, Peruvians had little to do with the trade. The British house of Gibbs won the monopoly contract, contracted British ships, and marketed guano primarily in France, England, and the southern United States where it nurtured crops such as turnips, grains, and tobacco.

Surprisingly, in this age of empire the weak Peruvian state was able to maintain a monopoly over the guano trade and indeed, for a while, award the concession to a Peruvian company. Historian Shane Hunt has estimated that 65 to 70 percent of the final sales price reverted to the Peruvian government; that was more than 100 percent of the FOB (Free on board—price from the point of departure) price.

In the short run there were important gains for Peru. These revenues allowed the state to abolish barriers to capitalism such as the head tax, internal duties, and slavery, as well as pay off its debt. Some of the new wealth led to new sugar plantations on the north coast and drove up wages by 50 percent.

Unfortunately, the pot of gold also led to what is today known as the "Dutch Disease." A strengthened Peruvian currency led to massive imports, displacement of local artisans and manufacturers, and grandiose building programs. Aware that exports, which reached the herculean total of 50,000 tons in 1856, were far outstripping the cormorants' ability to eat and excrete, government officials sought to use the windfall (or perhaps "currentfall") to diversify and develop the economy for that not long-off day.

The government in Lima borrowed in Europe at a furious pace on the collateral of their guano deposits (one of history's most peculiar collaterals). Enormous railroad projects were undertaken. Historian Paul Gootenberg argues that these were far-sighted, if failed efforts, while others have accused them of being fraudulent and foolish. In either case, Peru's guano wealth led it to become Latin America's largest debtor and, in 1876, to declare what Gootenberg has called a "world-shattering default."

With easily mined guano deposits much depleted, Europeans turned to another source of nitrogen nitrates. Coincidentally, the greatest deposits were found in the area between Peru and Chile and what was then Bolivia. Although at first this appeared to be another windfall, in fact it proved to be another tragedy. Disputes over the nitrate lands led to the bloody War of the Pacific (1879–1883) between the three countries. Peru lost not only the war, but the southern part of the country and its nitrate fields.

Overmining of the guano islands, substitutes like nitrates, and eventually chemical fertilizers ended guano's golden age. Today, Peruvians have to work much harder at turning fish into gold; they catch and process fishmeal, not as a fertilizer as much as a dietary supplement for livestock. The cormorants, once the heroes of Peru's waste-to-wealth treasure chest, are unemployed.

The world economy, then, transformed waste into wealth. Unfortunately, to a considerable degree humans wasted the wealth.

4.7 Fur and Fashion in the Far East

When British traders first arrived at Canton, the main product from home that they hoped to sell was wool cloth. Since Canton is slightly farther South than Havana, generations of storytellers have made this a classic example of stupid marketing. But temperature was not the problem. (In fact some woolen goods were purchased and forwarded to the Mongolian frontier). Canton was the main international port for all of China, and from about 1650–1850, China was one of the world's largest markets for something even warmer than wool: furs.

China proper produced relatively little fur. An unusually high percentage of the land (especially in the relatively cold north) had been cleared for farms. Moreover, most of the remaining woodlands consisted of many small groves, rather than the few large blocks of consolidated forest preserved by aristocratic estates elsewhere. (Chinese elites, with a firmly civilian self-image, were more likely to bond by writing poetry together than by hunting and riding.) These many small groves were convenient for people who didn't have to haul their firewood very far. But they were too small to support many large furbearing animals.

Nonetheless, fur had long been known; it had been fashionable among the elite in the Tang dynasty (645–908), when it seems to have been associated with "exotic" peoples from Central Asia. (The ruling house itself was of mixed blood.) Its prestige faded during more self-consciously "Chinese" dynasties, but returned with a vengeance after 1650. (While fashions among the rich waxed and waned, poorer people mostly used jackets with cotton wadding, as they still do.)

At least three factors contributed to the new boom in furs. An unusually cold period (sometimes called The Little Ice Age) spanned several decades beginning around 1640. The new Qing dynasty (established in 1644), with its origins in Manchuria, brought with it Central and Northeast Asian fashions, in which wearing elaborate furs was an important sign of status. Meanwhile, the expansion of Russian power and settlement into Siberia created an important source of supply: fur exports (both to Europe and to China) were an important source of revenue for the czarist regime.

For about a century, Russian merchants, with tribal peoples as their hunters and trappers, dominated the market. Too much hunting began to reduce Siberian yields, however, new supplies came from the sea. The Russian merchants themselves drew more heavily on otters and sea beavers from Kamchatka, the Aleutians, and later Alaska. Because it was easier to move down along the coast than inland, the fur seekers (mostly indigenous Alaskan peoples, with Russians organizing the marketing) were catching otters as far south as San Francisco by the 1780s. By this time, British and American ships were also hunting in these waters. (The trade was particularly useful for the Americans, because they, like the British, bought huge amounts of tea in Canton—and unlike the British, they did not have a colony that produced large amounts of opium to sell there.)

The Spanish (and then Mexicans), who claimed California until 1848, were relatively minor players in the trade; they were never as successful as the Americans, British, or Alaskan natives at catching large amounts of furbearing animals. Instead, they tried to maintain their market share by banning others from the California coast, but their small navy was not up to the task. One of the few areas they could keep control of was Monterey Bay, but they were not very successful at exploiting it—with the result that seals and sea otters survived in large numbers there, while being severely depleted along most of the rest of the coast.

By about 1800, as even these supplies grew thin, others came on line. . Increasing exploration of the South Pacific gave Europeans and Americans access to a vast new source of furbearing seals. And (perhaps equally important) the settlement of and importation of livestock to New Zealand and other South Sea islands created provisioning stations for the fur hunters. And as a few U.S. citizens began to arrive overland to the Pacific Coast in the middle nineteenth century, they brought beaver and other land-based pelts to ship to China.

But by this time the trade was beginning to fade. Prolonged civil war depressed the China market in the 1850s, 1860s, and 1870s. More generally, as opium imports overtook tea exports, China had far less money to purchase foreign goods; and when opium imports finally started to recede in the late

1800s (owing to increased domestic production), it was machine-made cotton yarn and other manufactures that took over as China's major imports. By the end of the century, the declining prestige of an increasingly wobbly Qing court had lessened the power of their fashion example: elites who increasingly wished to be "modern" returned to cotton, silk, and linen. With global trade booming, there was no shortage of other ways to use ships and sailors; and as the North American frontier filled up, furbearing land animals became increasingly scarce. No longer desperate for goods with which to pry open China—and with enough demand at home for the furs they could find—Westerners stopped combing the globe for furs to send to China. For many seal and otter populations, the end came not a moment too soon.

4.8 Not Just Peanuts: One Crop's Career in Farm and Factory

The industrial revolution arrived in a Western Europe already short of many raw materials, with shrinking forests and often overworked soil; it was accompanied by unprecedented population growth. And since most nineteenth-century industrial goods still required large inputs of cotton, wood, or other natural products—only the twentieth-century chemical revolution would dispense with that—where were the necessary farm goods to come from?

The most famous answers—such as the rise of American cotton and wheat exports, and the development of rubber plantations—are the stuff of legends, but millions of humbler farm goods also had a brief day in the sun as coveted producer goods. The strangest case may be guano—vast deposits of bird excrement shipped from Latin America to Europe in the years between the discovery of soil depletion in Western Europe and the development of chemical fertilizers. When these new agro-industrial inputs already had a very different role in more locally oriented economies, strange transformations could occur. Consider the career of the peanut.

Like potatoes, corn, and tobacco, peanuts came to much of the Old World via the New. (They were known in Africa before Columbus, but seem not to have spread from there to Europe or Asia.) Spanish traders brought them to the Philippines, from whence intra-Asian networks took them to the mainland; and it was there that they attracted attention. A highly labor-intensive crop with a taste very different from basic grains, peanuts were never a staple anywhere—especially not in the sparsely populated New World. They remained the stuff of decorations, sauces, and snacks. But for poor people in densely populated areas they were nonetheless very important.

Peanuts would grow on the thinnest and sandiest of soils, and in fact gradually improved them and held them in place. This made them perfect for places where population pressure had led to earlier ecological mismanagement: when Chinese who cut down trees to make farms of the Yangzi Valley highlands found the soil eroding too fast, they found that switching to peanuts could help save their farms. Farmers in the post–Civil War American South, inheriting land exhausted from growing too much cotton, also made peanuts an important part of living with a legacy of ecological decay.

Moreover, every part of the plant was usable: the vines made excellent pig food and the shells a useful fuel, and the oil was good for both cooking and heating. And while peanuts required an enormous amount of extremely dull post-harvest work, such as cleaning (dirty peanuts easily get mildews that ruin the entire pile), this was work that even small children could do, thus adding one more contributor to the tight budgets of many poor families. The labor requirements were too burdensome for any family to put all its land into peanuts, but the enormous (and high-protein) yields per acre made peanuts an ideal homemade safety net for those taking a gamble in cash crops: many South Chinese and Indian peasants who were switching some of their land into lucrative but risky sugar in the nineteenth century switched the rest of it into peanuts, which became a home-grown food supply protected from the ups and downs of prices. (These same qualities made peanuts a favorite of reformers seeking to improve rural diets, from Georgia to Jiangsu: suggested recipe lists compiled by American 4–H clubs and Chinese Nationalist extension agents alike contain any number of ideas for sneaking more protein and vitamins into poor people via peanuts.)

Then, around 1900, everything changed. German and American chemists (including the famous George Washington Carver) discovered dozens of industrial uses for the peanut and its oil: as a lubricant, a paint ingredient, and a soap ingredient. (In parts of Europe, peanut oil replaced increasingly pricey olive oil in this process.) Demand boomed, and exports soared—first from China, then India, and then from West Africa. In Seattle, the main port for U.S. imports, special wharves were built in the 1920s just to accommodate peanut oil tankers. And with demand soaring, prices soared, too. Since peanuts were not a large part of the cost of any final industrial product, Western markets were not very price sensitive; needs kept growing faster than supplies, especially during and immediately after World War I.

But prosperity had its perils, too. Because much of the land on which peanuts had traditionally been grown would support nothing else, it was often land that none but the poor had bothered to claim: dry former riverbeds, sandy wastelands, and rocky hillsides. But now that these lands could generate *cash,* richer and more powerful people became interested in them, often "rediscovering" old deeds. In some cases, peasants had once paid a nominal fee to secure use of these lands from owners who were glad to get anything from land they couldn't or wouldn't farm themselves; now, all of a sudden, these rents could double or triple overnight. In parts of the North China peanut belt, local "sand land wars" raged throughout the 1920s, often ending with the eviction of the earlier peanut growers.

Even the winners in those battles found their triumph short lived. When peanut prices got high enough, large-scale production for the market expanded on lands more fertile than those traditionally set aside for peanuts in Asia. West African peanuts, in particular, soon claimed an ever-growing share of the world market. Thanks to higher productivity, they survived the 1930s slump in peanut prices that drove many Chinese and Indians out of the world market. Finally, a bubble created by industrial innovation fell victim to industrial innovation: a new round of chemical discoveries in the 1930s and 1940s created synthetic substitutes for industrial peanut products. Before long, peanuts were again marginal, except perhaps to North American children. But their rise and fall are more than a curiosity. They stand with many other now-forgotten booms created between the time when the industrial revolution placed massive new demands on the land, and the time when chemists rerouted much of that demand underground: to products of the mines, as transformed in laboratories.

4.9 As American as Sugar and Pineapples

How did sugar, a German grocer, gold in the Sacramento River, and a Republican protective tariff turn a Polynesian paradise into the fiftieth star on the American flag? The Hawaiian islands had enjoyed a prosperous anonymity, distant from the world's trade routes, before Captain Cook gave them the dull and inappropriate name of Sandwich Islands in 1778. The Englishman slowly brought the kingdom into the world economy. But there was little demand for their chief products of breadfruit and sandalwood, and the Hawaiians had few needs. The force for change would come from America, not Europe.

The gold discovered in California's Sacramento River brought hundreds of thousands of consumers to the West Coast and merchants to sell to them. One of the newcomers was a German immigrant who had arrived in South Carolina in 1846, Claus Spreckels. After working his way up in a Charleston grocery store to become its owner, ambition drove him a few years later to New York, where his new grocery store again prospered. Starry-eyed with the possibilities in the Golden State, Spreckels sailed to San Francisco in 1856 to mine the miners.

Spreckels was not the sort of man to let mere success stand in the way of real fortune. After a few profitable years in the mercantile business, he branched out into sugar refining. Headquartered on the West Coast, he naturally turned to Pacific producers of sugar rather than the conventional U.S. sources in the Caribbean and Louisiana.

So the offspring of Protestant missionaries in Hawaii—less otherworldly than their forebears—began to grow sugar to meet the new demand. Sugar changed the face of the islands. Foreigners, mostly Americans, began buying up the land for sugar plantations. The native population—around 300,000 when Cook first wandered to the kingdom—had fallen to 50,000 one hundred years later. Chinese laborers, imported as contract workers, soon outnumbered the native population.

This transformation gained speed after 1876, when the United States and Hawaii signed a reciprocal trade treaty that awarded Hawaiian sugar a privileged position in the U.S. market. Hawaiian sugar production ballooned almost twentyfold in the next two decades; virtually all of it went to the United States. Twenty-five years of sugar boom saw Americans come to own 80 percent of the sugar plantations and the number of native Hawaiians fall to 35,000. Hawaiians became strangers in their own home, as they neither owned the lands (Americans owned sugar production, Chinese rice, and Portuguese cattle) nor the companies that prospered in Hawaii's heady sugar economy; they did not even work in the sugar fields.

Spreckels was single-handedly responsible for much of the growth. On Maui, he developed one of the largest sugar plantations in the world, controlled most of the island's irrigation and docks, erected its electric lights and giant mills, and laid the island's railroad track. He joined with the kingdom's largest exporter and financed much of the Hawaiian crop. His Spreckels Oceanic Line then carried his sugar—and that of other planters—to California, where his refineries finished it. To secure his position he became the principal banker for King Kalakaua and one of the most politically important people in the kingdom.

The king was friendly toward Americans. In 1874 he had made a great hit in New York when he became the first reigning sovereign ever to visit the United States. However, Spreckels's political control and economic empire became endangered when he fell out with King Kalakaua. Legend has it that Spreckels and the king were playing a Hawaiian card game with two visiting admirals when Spreckels boasted that if this were poker, his hand (which held three kings and two smaller cards) would win. The British admiral—holding three aces—disagreed. But Spreckels insisted, saying he would win because he had *four* kings. "Where is the fourth king?" he was asked. Spreckels boldly replied "*I* am the fourth king."

King Kalakaua was so upset by the ex-grocer's arrogance that he bolted from the party and began plotting a way to reduce U.S. influence. His first step, in 1886, was to float a successful loan on London, a center of growing European interest in the islands.

The London loan worried Spreckels. More troubling still were the side effects of the American McKinley tariff of 1890. To increase trade with Latin America and Europe the tariff made sugar duty-free for everyone signing a trade treaty. The agreement effectively removed Hawaii's privileged position. Even worse, King Kalakaua was unwilling to accept America's draconian terms for a reciprocal treaty: President Harrison wanted in effect to establish a protectorate over the kingdom and claim Pearl Harbor. Without the trade treaty, painfully high duties would close the U.S. market to Maui sugar.

The only alternative was annexation. If Hawaii were to be annexed by the United States, the planters would not only find their sugar duty-free, but would have the windfall of a bounty, intended to help Louisiana's planters.

Ironically, most planters did not initially want annexation. They feared that American racism would prevent the immigration of Chinese workers in Hawaii just as it had in California. Refiners such as Spreckels feared that annexation would stimulate the creation of refineries on the islands that would break the monopoly of their West Coast refineries.

But when strong-willed nationalist Queen Liliuokalani ascended to the throne in 1891 the foreign planter minority overcame their reluctance toward annexation. Although a small group of foreigners owned 80 to 90 percent of the kingdom's wealth, native Hawaiians represented the overwhelming majority of the electorate. Planters feared that the queen would side with her indigenous subjects to reduce the power of the sugarcrats. Plotting with the U.S. consul Edwin Stevens, the annexationists arranged to have U.S. marines and sailors land just as a coup was set off. The queen was overthrown almost without bloodshed. The new government, headed by Sanford Dole, son of missionaries and cousin of the king of the pineapple, sought annexation to the United States.

Initially there was heated opposition to annexation. Royalists on Oahu threatened Spreckels's life. They posted a sign in bold red letters on the sugar king's Honolulu mansion: "Gold and Silver will not stop Lead." There was an anti-imperialist outcry in the United States as well that President Cleveland heeded when he refused to annex the islands on the grounds that the coup had been precipitated by a small minority.

However, four years later, in 1898, President William McKinley took Hawaii as a territory of the United States. The annexation of Hawaii was, as *The Nation* charged, "of sugar, for sugar, and by sugar."

4.10 Saved from Sugar Shock

Starting around 1500, sugar conquered the world—at a terrible cost. As Europe's sweet tooth grew, and cane replaced honey as the main way of satisfying it, tropical island after tropical island was deforested, covered with slave plantations, and committed so completely to export agriculture that they even imported their food. In Southeast Asian colonies, indebted or coerced peasants replaced slaves, but the results were not much better. Even today, most former sugar colonies are very poor and bear permanent ecological scars as well: Jamaica, Haiti, Cuba, northeastern Brazil, Java, the Philippines. But one of the early modern world's big sugar islands—Taiwan—wound up on a different path, which has led to a much happier present. One big reason was an unlikely benefactor—a combination merchant, pirate, and Chinese rebel named Zheng Chenggong, who conquered the island in 1662.

In the early 1600s, Taiwan was a sparsely populated island with a largely self-sufficient economy. Traders who stopped there were either getting supplies en route between China and Southeast Asia, or acquiring deerskins—a logical export for a place that was still overwhelmingly forest. But when the Dutch set up forts and trading posts there in the 1610s and 1620s, they began to think more in terms of what the conquered natives could produce for them; sugar, which fetched a high price in both Europe and Asia, was a logical choice. By the 1650s, the island was one of the world's largest sugar producers, even though most of the island was still forested, and much of what wasn't was producing rice.

Meanwhile, on the mainland, massive civil wars and an invasion by Manchus from the north brought down the Ming dynasty in 1644. But a number of officials swore never to serve the new "barbarian" Qing dynasty and grouped themselves around relatives of the last Ming emperor, who set up new "capitals" in South and Southeast China. Since the horse-riding Qing knew little about sailing, the Ming loyalists fared better on sea than on land—indeed, most of the financial support for the resistance came from the profits of overseas traders based along the South China Coast.

The most important of them was a combination merchant official named Zheng Zhilong, whose trading interests and personal fleet extended all the way to present-day Singapore. When Zheng Zhilong abruptly went over to the Qing in 1646, his sons remained with the Ming and took over his assets. By 1650 one son, Zheng Chenggong, had not only consolidated his father's vast holdings, but achieved a near monopoly over China's foreign trade, using the cover of civil war to subjugate his relatives (some of whom he murdered), his other Chinese rivals, and any foreigners, Asian or European, who were foolish enough to fight his navy rather than cut a deal with him.

Though most of his staggering wealth was located offshore, Chenggong's overriding obsession was always to bring back the Ming dynasty. Throughout the 1650s, he struck repeatedly at port cities on China's coast and up the Yangzi River as well. He captured several, but couldn't hold them—in large part, because he never held enough of the countryside to feed his mainland bases. Like the tiger and the shark, Zheng and the Qing were each supreme in their element and unable to subdue the other.

Desperate to gain lasting control of an area with a rice surplus, Zheng turned his eyes to Taiwan. In 1661 he invaded the island, with hundreds of ships and over 20,000 soldiers. The Dutch were far less numerous, and they had alienated most of the natives through their harsh policies. (In dispatches back home, the missionaries blamed greedy merchants and the merchants blamed intolerant missionaries; there was probably blame enough for both.) Within a few months, the island was Zheng's. (Twentieth-century Chinese nationalists later made Zheng's conquest into an "anti-imperialist" crusade against the Dutch, but there is no sign that he thought in those terms: for him the enemy was always the Qing.) Zheng himself became increasingly tyrannical and irrational as his dreams of reconquering the mainland faded; he died at age thirty-eight, soon after conquering Taiwan.

Nonetheless, Zheng's invasion had lasting implications. Once Taiwan had become an anti-Qing base, the Qing became determined to conquer it; when they finally did in 1683, it became part of the Chinese Empire for the first time. And though China had its own sweet tooth—indeed, per capita sugar consumption was probably higher there than in Europe until the early 1800s—the government had no desire to create the kind of sugar monocultures that Europeans created on so many islands that they ruled.

For European governments, sugar—a much coveted (and even mildly addictive) substance that could not be grown at home—was a perfect item on which to grant monopolies, levy heavy taxes, and pay for colonial and naval competition; for colonial authorities, a more exclusive concentration on sugar also meant more revenue; and for big planters, an island without much land left in food crops was an island on which runaway or rebellious slaves could not hold out very long.

But the Chinese regime—in part because of its experience with the Zhengs—had no desire to see major concentrations of wealth and power created on the edge of the empire; and being more concerned with internal stability than foreign threats anyway, they always made sure that sugar did *not* crowd out rice production on Taiwan, or destroy too much of the forests. (Preserving forests, the Qing reasoned, would enable the indigenous population to maintain enough of its old way of life to prevent rebellions.)

So Taiwan kept growing sugar, but sugar never took over the island. When the Qing weakened and the foreigners came again after 1860, sugar production on Taiwan boomed again; and when the Japanese took over in 1895, they did much to push sugar production, too. But even then, the island kept a base of rice production and diversified agriculture—Japan, short of rice itself by the twentieth century, could hardly afford to have its colonies become rice importers. Sugar mills (and roads and port facilities) came, but monoculture never did. That danger, in retrospect, had probably been greatest in the 1600s—and had been warded off, thanks to a wild-eyed trader turned would-be king maker.

4.11 How the Cows Ate the Cowboys

First there was Argentina's wide-open, fertile, treeless prairie known as the Pampa that stretched for hundreds of miles. Then came an expedition of Spanish conquistadors seeking precious metals. They found no wealth in the ground, but they left behind them some cattle that would bring Argentina future riches. With no natural predators and endless pasture, the number of bovines grew astoundingly. The Spanish population on the Pampa, however, rose slowly. Devoid of silver and gold, but rich in a hostile, intractable nomadic population, the Pampa held few charms for the Spanish. Until the nineteenth century, the Pampa remained very much a frontier, a huge area contested by the native indigenous peoples and the few Spaniards and ruled over by the swelling herds of cattle.

This land gave birth to the Argentine cowboy, the "gaucho." If ever a man was made for his work, it was the mixed-blood gaucho who roamed the Pampa—gypsy-like, trailed by his string of horses—herding cattle. Legs bowed by his almost permanent residence on horseback, his job literally shaped him; eating little other than beef, he consumed his work. Today the gaucho occupies the same romantic position in Argentine national mythology as does the cowboy in the United States: a symbol of individualism, freedom, masculinity, he became the quintessential Argentine.

In the nineteenth century, however, foreign visitors and the Argentine elite scorned him as idle, disorderly, "half horse, half man." He was both held in awe and disdained for his equestrian brilliance. One visitor noted, "In some respects they are the most efficient Cavalry in the world—dismount them and they are nothing, for they are scarcely able to walk."

The gaucho did almost everything from horseback—wash, fish, attend mass, draw water, beg. In fact, his boots left an open space in front for the toes so they could grip their stirrups better. These boots were relatively useless on the ground.

But until the last part of the nineteenth century, the Pampa needed horsemen, not peons. The cattle industry was essentially an organized hunting party. Semi-wild cattle, mostly left to fend for themselves, roamed the vast fenceless land holdings, some as large as 800,000 acres. Real estate in this sparsely settled frontier was largely a legal fiction. The rancher was much more a merchant than an agro-industrialist. His only contribution to the cattle industry was to provide the gaucho with a few cherished goods, such as tobacco, *mate* tea, alcohol, and sugar, in return for the hunted cattle carcasses and hides.

The gaucho owned his means of production and enjoyed his independence. The quality of the cattle in this system was unimportant; fresh meat would spoil aboard sailing ships long before it reached Europe, and cattle were so plentiful and people few in Argentina that there was essentially no home market. Only salted meat, prepared in salting houses (*xarquerias,* which, corrupted, produced the word "jerky") could be exported. But its quality was so poor that the major market were the slaves of Brazil and Cuba who had little choice over what they ate. This was a small market. In fact, most cattle carcasses were left to rot on the Pampa; the gaucho just cut out the tongue to eat and skinned the hide for export. Returns per cattle were of course low, but costs were virtually zero.

The gaucho began to slowly lose his way of life and freedom in the nineteenth century. Independence from Spain was a long, bloody, drawn-out affair that gave rise to many local warlords. Fighting became endemic. Now the gaucho's horsemanship, and his ability with the lasso, knife, and bolas became valuable military weapons. The Argentine cowboys, however, were truly self-interested. Not much concerned about questions of partisanship or patriotism, they had to be forcefully conscripted. Governors began issuing passports to confine their movement and pass vagrancy laws to force into the army those not employed on ranches. But it was Europe's hunger for beef that most doomed the gaucho lifestyle. Ironically, the growth of the cattle industry brought the decline of the cowboy.

Several forces combined to make Argentina one of the world's greatest meat exporters. Demand had grown in urbanizing Europe. The steamship made the Atlantic passage faster and more reliable and, with its larger carrying capacity, reduced freight rates.

Cattle on the hoof could be brought to Europe, but that was still a risky and expensive proposition. A major breakthrough was one of the miracle foods of the nineteenth century: Liebig's Meat Extract. Beef bouillon brought the taste of meat to tens of thousands of poor European households where it previously had been a rare visitor.

More revolutionary yet was the experimentation being done in Chicago with refrigerated railcars. Applied to ships, refrigeration permitted great amounts of dressed, chilled, or frozen beef to be transported across the Atlantic. Refrigerator ships, known as *frigoríficos,* proliferated in the last two decades of the nineteenth century and were perfected in the beginning of the twentieth.

But to take advantage of the new technology, Argentina had to improve the quality of its livestock. No longer admired were the creole cattle that were so well adapted to the wild Pampa. Ranchers began importing plumper, fatter European shorthorns. To ensure selective breeding, they erected fences across the plains.

The fences, with their palpable boundary limits, eventually put an end to the gaucho way of life. In a real sense, they created property. Ranchers who invested in improving their herds became much more concerned about branding their herds to prevent rustling (which gauchos considered simply hunting). Labor contracts were increasingly written to constrict the gaucho's freedom of movement. The draft and jail constantly hung over him.

The gauchos became an underclass on the plains where they once reigned, as being a migrant ranch hand became virtually a crime. Rued one observer in 1904: "The poor creole class that has lost all idea of the right to own land, sees it as unalterable patrimony of the grandees and vegetates with no other possibility than to be a soldier, a ranch peon or a rustler." And there was ever less need for ranch peons. A man with a herd dog in an enclosed pasture could do the work of four or five men on the open range. Some of the Pampa became populated by the cowboy's nemesis: the sheep. Most gauchos could find no more than part-time work.

The final insult came when the need for alfalfa pasture convinced ranchers to let out parts of their land on shares to farmers who would prepare the ground for feed. Believing "the gaucho on foot is fit only for the manure pile," ranchers attracted Italian and Spanish immigrants to till the pampa, marginalizing the gaucho even further. As the cattle industry prospered and fat domesticated herds filled the countryside, the gaucho passed into history. The need to feed beef cattle cost the gaucho his freedom and his existence. And that is how the cattle came to eat the cowboys.

4.12 The Tie That Bound

Chaos theory tells us that a butterfly beating its delicate wings in the Amazon can create a monsoon in India. Actions can have completely unexpected and distant consequences. So it was with the American wheat farmer, who, mechanizing his Midwestern farm with the most modern technology, unintentionally and unknowingly brought cruel archaic slavery to the Maya Indians in Mexico's tropics.

As the "Great West" around Chicago became tamed and tilled in the nineteenth century, settlers discovered that the flat, treeless expanses were perfect for grains. When rain was ample, the virgin lands offered astounding yields, more than anyone had ever heard of. Getting the bountiful harvests to urban consumers on the eastern seaboard or abroad remained a major problem until a web of railroads and canals linked the scattered farms to the Great Lakes, the Mississippi, and beyond.

This was capitalist farming almost from the outset. Land was surveyed and sold in segments of 160 acres or more by large land companies who extended credit to the new arrivals. The indebted farmers had to sell to market to service their debts. They were calculating and profit-seeking. It is no coincidence that the world's first commodity market and first futures market sprang up in Chicago. These capitalist-farmers realized that since the land was so fertile and relatively inexpensive, they could enjoy greater profits if they worked more land.

Their problem was labor. With land abundant and accessible, it was hard to convince the scarce rural population on the frontier to work for someone else, even for a reasonable wage. This bottleneck was overcome by machines. Cyrus McCormick brought his invention of the mechanical reaper to Chicago, where he opened a factory in 1847. His company improved the machine; sales mounted along with grain production.

Just reaping was not sufficient, however. Gathering the cut sheaves to bring to the thresher still required ample labor, especially since the wheat was so rapidly cut. Another inventor, John Appleby, solved this problem in 1878 when he invested a mechanical knotting device that led to the reaper-binder. This ingenious machine gathered up the cut grain, bound it together, loaded and carried it. Now two men with the machine could reap fourteen acres a day. Thus the yeoman Yankee family farmer used his investment in labor-saving devices to reduce production costs and provide low-cost food to the hungry populations of the eastern United States and Europe.

Completely unknown to the Midwestern grain agro-industrialist, his success at modern technological farming was impoverishing peasants thousands of miles away. The success of the reaper-binder depended upon a steady supply of low-cost binding twine. The place best able to supply it was Yucatán, Mexico.

A rather dry, infertile land, the Yucatán peninsula had fallen upon bad times in the seven hundred years since the collapse of the last Mayan Empire. A backwater of Mexico, the state was rich in only cactus and poor people. But since the cactus was henequen, whose fibers were well suited to binding twine, the local landed elite saw an opportunity.

In the decade after Appleby's invention, henequen exports swelled almost sixfold. But the raw material necessary for one of the world's most modern agricultural machines was produced in a very old-fashioned way. Men, women, and children used machetes to cut leaves off the henequen and then carted the heavy wheelbarrows to the simple rasper that separated the fiber from the pulp. Aside from rail spurs to carry off the heavy product, little technology was employed.

Tens of thousands of local Maya Indians were impressed into the back-breaking work through debt peonage or the threat of draft into the military. Others found their land seized by the planters; landless, they had to work on the plantations. Sometimes workers were sold from one plantation to another like slaves, and their children were obliged to pay off their parents' debts to perpetuate the slavery generation after generation. The bountiful harvests of wheat in North America brought hunger to the Maya, now stripped of their cornfields.

The most egregious case of enslavement involved the Yaqui Indians of the northern Mexican state of Sonora. Embroiled in a land dispute with Mexican farmers who sought to emulate Midwestern Americans, the Yaqui were hunted down by the Mexican army and marched in chains to the henequen fields of the Yucatán.

The henequen "divine caste" ruled, built grand palaces, and adorned their capital city of Mérida. They boasted that by supplying the twine that International Harvester craved (the successor to the McCormick company and the world's largest agricultural implement manufacturer), the divine elite brought progress to Yucatán. But what a difference a change of latitude made.

Although the Yucatán and the U.S. Midwest were bound together by the umbilical cord made of henequen, mother and child were virtual opposites. The mechanized, capitalist, family farm of the Midwest, with its labor-saving machines and wage workers, gave birth to the extensive Yucatecan plantation that relied on intense use of coerced labor with rudimentary tools. Wheat spread landownership among the newly arrived settlers; henequen appropriated the land from the Maya who had lived there since time immemorial. The labor that the reaper-binder saved in the Midwest was expended in the tropics. The consequences are often unpredictable and even contradictory when the butterfly of world trade begins to beat its wings.

4.13 The Good Earth?

In its first hundred years, the United States imported far more technology than it exported. Often, in fact, it stole know-how, especially from Britain. But by 1900, things had changed, and Americans began exporting "Yankee ingenuity" for prestige and profit.

Prospects were especially bright on the farm, where the United States could capitalize on the skills that had made it the world's agricultural leader. While Europeans often limited agricultural extension to their own empires—the British, for instance, stole rubber and tea plants so they could grow them where they had greater control—Americans dreamed of spreading better farming methods everywhere.

In particular, the missionaries of scientific agriculture turned to China—and especially to China's fledgling cotton industry. Sheltered from international competition during World War I, mechanized textile mills appeared in Shanghai, Tianjin, and Qingdao. At first, they all relied on foreign (mostly Indian and U.S.) cotton, for though China was one of the world's largest cotton producers, native cotton fibers were too short for machine spinning. Thus Chinese farmers who supplied raw cotton to hand-spinners stood to lose more and more of their own market as their compatriots turned to machine-spun thread.

The Chinese government intervened. Officials successfully tested U.S. breeds in North and Central China soils, where some U.S. varieties—Trice, Alcala, and Lone Star—grew better than native breeds, yielding 30 percent more cotton (by weight) per acre. And because modern mills could spin them, the U.S. breeds sold for 20 percent more per pound. Another unforeseen bonus: U.S. cotton flourished on the sandy wastes near the Yellow River, and on land where the only other profitable crop was opium.

Beyond supplying China itself, the crop had enormous export potential; it could be grown in China for about 20 percent less than in the United States itself. That caught the eye of Japanese mill owners in Osaka. In 1920, they approached the Industrial Bank of Japan, which was planning to finance a North China water-control project, to seek guarantees that the land reclaimed in the process would be planted with U.S. cotton.

Soon an army of American missionaries and agronomists, agents for Chinese and British-owned mills, and reform-minded Chinese officials were in the field, offering seed, advice, credit, and guaranteed markets. Japanese agents, whose ambitions worried Chinese officials (and the U.S. State Department—see reading 6.8, "Banking on Asia"), undertook a separate, parallel campaign, using American varieties that they had modified in their Korean colony. The colorful cast included Cornell agronomist John L. Buck, who married (and used as his translator) one Pearl Sydenstricker, the daughter of American missionaries; her experience yielded *The Good Earth* and other popular works that shaped American views of China for decades.

The American reformers knew they faced social as well as technical hurdles, but they were confident. Many had done agricultural extension work in the United States' own slice of the Third World—the Deep South—promoting these same cotton varieties. They felt sure that what had worked among poorly educated Americans—demonstration farms, fairs at which short plays about new farm techniques were performed, and a kind of early 4–H movement— would also work among poorly educated Chinese.

At times, their naïveté and cultural ambitions produced bizarre results. At the first Chinese agricultural fair, in Linyi, Shandong, the county's agricultural extension chief and an American missionary played themselves in a skit with the following plot: farmers, frustrated by the low price their native cotton is fetching, pray to a local god for help. The missionary lectures them on the vanity of "idolatrous worship," and sends them to the extension agent, who gives them seeds for the new cotton varieties. The new crop solves their problems and makes the old gods unnecessary. But Linyi was near places where Christian converts and other Chinese had killed one another in the Boxer Uprising just twenty years before; there were undoubtedly better ways to advertise the new cotton.

More material problems were a still greater impediment. The new crops sometimes interfered with well-established local customs in destabilizing ways. In western Shandong, the poor had a customary right to glean anything left in the ground after a certain date. But the new cotton grew more slowly than native varieties, and about 70 percent of its bolls were not yet open when, in the words of county agents, "tens and even hundreds of men and women" stood on their rights and rushed the fields, claiming most of the crop. In response, the local "cotton societies" that had been organized to distribute seed and information became armed vigilantes. Some county agents wound up leading a war against the poor, and even against old elites, who objected to the power that new seed, credit, and marketing arrangements gave outsiders over "their" peasants.

Where the crop did take hold, peasants of all classes reaped more lucrative harvests. But local spending for public security soared, too. Meanwhile, many farmers who used to hire their poorer neighbors to help with (and guard) the harvest were now unwilling to run the risk of miniature class wars; instead, their wives and young children began to do more field work. And increased dependence on outsiders had its hazards, too: one group of entrenched Japanese seed suppliers/cotton buyers even tried to pay for the crop in opium.

Despite such setbacks, the new crop did work. By statistical measures, Chinese peasants in some areas responded to the new crop as quickly as their counterparts in the American South—despite the added barriers posed by warlordism, shaky transportation, and other problems. But it was no panacea: as the costs of social conflict mounted, some Americans gained new respect for village elders who had banned a more efficient sickle on the grounds that its benefits were not worth the new struggles it would touch off between farmers, hired harvesters, and thieves.

Certainly Buck's hope that these efforts would ward off communism by showing that science could help the poor without class conflict did not come to pass. Ironically, in areas where gleaners had successfully disrupted the new cotton in the 1920s, it was left to the Communist regime of the 1950s to create an environment in which the rural poor stopped interfering with the new breeds. The idea of uplifting the world's poor through American botany, educational techniques, and involvement in world markets has a rich history: so do exaggerated hopes and ignorance of the varied ways in which world trade affects local societies.

4.14 One Potato, Two Potato

Sometimes the big story is buried in the fine print. When Spain conquered much of the Americas, the excitement in Europe was over silver and gold. As other Europeans followed, interest turned to exotic agricultural exports: tobacco, coffee, cocoa, sugar, all New World crops, or crops that could be grown there on an unprecedented scale. None was very good for you, but Europeans soon craved them all, and grew none of them at home. Huge plantations were cleared, slaves imported, companies chartered, royal monopolies created, fortunes made and lost.

But the New World crops that would keep the world's burgeoning population eating were humbler fare, which excited no such interest from big investors. One was maize, a corn variety that grew throughout the Americas; it spawned no new types of agribusiness for centuries, but it was so miraculously hardy and nutritious that even without big sponsors it was soon being planted by peasants around the world.

Humbler still was the potato, "discovered" by Spanish soldiers in the Peruvian Andes in the 1550s. Considered a second-class food even in its homeland, it had never made it north of Colombia and was rarely planted outside the marginal farmlands of mountain slopes. No London merchant ever formed a new company to trade potatoes; and the European masses gave it a far cooler welcome than its less nourishing, even poisonous, New World cousins. But crises created needs to which the potato was beautifully suited; today, potatoes are the second largest food crop in the world.

Potatoes were important in the Andes for four simple reasons. First, they would grow at extremely high altitudes, withstanding frosts that killed almost any other edible plant. Second, they yield a lot of calories per acre—more even than rice, and vastly more than wheat, oats, or other grains—and a wide variety of vitamins. Third, they required little labor, leaving highland people time to cut trees, mine ore, and gather the other mountain and forest products with which they paid the lowlanders for textiles, pottery, and fruit—and for not attacking them. Finally, they were easy to store— even without special buildings—and so a great protection against the constant specter of crop failure.

Spanish sailors carried potatoes to the Philippines, warding off scurvy in the process. In Asia, the same advantages that made potatoes popular in the Andes helped them find a niche wherever growing populations were pushing farther up the mountainsides. Potatoes and maize were particularly important in opening up the highlands along China's huge Yangzi River; thus, these New World crops were crucial in allowing eighteenth-century China to reach new levels of population, and in the nineteenth- and twentieth-century ecological nightmares that followed from hillside deforestation. But it was in Europe that potatoes finally conquered the towns and farms of lowland majorities.

The potato entered the Atlantic economy at its two extremes: as a luxury side dish for Europe's rich and as a staple for the enslaved Indians working the mines of Spanish Peru. At the high end, potatoes benefited from the belief that they were a potent aphrodisiac; and like most other vegetables and herbs in early modern Europe, they were grown in small quantities in the gardens of the rich. (A seventeenth-century recipe, though written by a rich Londoner, includes substitutes to use if potatoes were too expensive.) At the bottom of the scale, feeding miners on potatoes was an obvious move. Mining begat instant cities in places too mountainous to grow or import much else. But this use contributed to a strong popular belief that as a staple, potatoes were fit only for slaves; a belief that helped postpone for centuries the use of potatoes by the European masses.

As Europe's population boomed after 1600, an unprecedented food crisis developed, and a slowly growing chorus of botanists, reformers, and royal commissions became interested in the potato as a solution. But as late as 1770, a cargo of potatoes sent to Naples as famine relief was refused; in France, the belief that potatoes could cause leprosy lingered into the early 1800s. Where the crop made progress at all, it was usually in the wake of intense misery.

Such was the case in Ireland, the first place in Europe to live on potatoes. Potatoes arrived shortly before 1600, according to legend in the hold of a shipwrecked member of the Spanish Armada. Here no aristocratic reformers promoted the new miracle food, but the viciousness of Ireland's conquerors proved far more effective than benevolence could have been. Intent on subduing a series of uprisings, the British resorted to a scorched earth policy, burning storehouses, mills, corn, barley, and oat fields, and killing livestock to starve out recalcitrant areas. The rebels replied in kind. In such a setting, the potato's virtues stood out. They grew underground, in small wet plots surrounded by trenches and were thus hard to burn; they stored safely and compactly inside the farmer's cottage; they needed no mill processing; and families who had no plough left (much less a plough animal) could plant the crop with just a spade. In the seventeenth century, the fighting got worse; one account has it that 80 percent of the population died or fled during the rebellion of 1641–1652. By the end of the century, potatoes had become the dominant source of Irish food (and drink): an adult male consumed about seven pounds of them a day, and little else other than milk. Potatoes helped Ireland's population recover rapidly and then soar to new heights in the 1700s. Not only did the crop yield a staggering amount of food per acre, but one needed almost no capital to get started in potato farming—no storehouse or plough animal, and very few tools. A small plot of land was usually rented in return for free labor on some other piece of the owner's land. As a result, even very poor people could afford to marry and start having children earlier than their English or French counterparts. The combination of deep poverty, a booming population, and overwhelming reliance on one crop that never seemed to fail (until the catastrophe of the 1840s) made Ireland and the potato a subject of much discussion throughout Europe. But where some saw the salvation of a hungry continent, others saw a worsening nightmare.

The Enlightenment's new philosophers—economists—mostly anticipated disaster. While Smith, Malthus, and others disagreed on how much to blame the potato itself, they all agreed that population booms were dangerous. A crop that required so little in the way of a homestead was at best a mixed blessing, driving the socially acceptable "living wage" ever lower. Indeed, those who saw great opportunities in the potato during the 1700s were precisely those whose dreams depended on making it cheaper than ever to feed large numbers of poor people—the commanders of the continent's armies (whose costs were growing much faster than their tax receipts), and the owners of England's emerging factories (who were struggling to gain markets by producing more cheaply than artisans could).

In England, many manufacturers and reformers spoke glowingly of the potato's possibilities as a cheap, nutritious substitute for wheat-based bread. By the end of the 1700s, potatoes had moved out of the garden and become a field crop, especially in the rapidly industrializing north. Nonetheless, millions of ordinary people resisted its adoption: to many English workers, for instance, the Irish were low-priced rivals willing to live like beasts. Their favorite food proved the point: it was, after all, the same food the English had come to feed their pigs. For urban and especially agricultural workers, eating the same white bread as their "betters" was a prized status symbol; any attempt to substitute potatoes was fiercely resisted. What happened instead was a far cry from what at least the more nutritionally conscious reformers had imagined. As bread took up more and more of English workers' budgets during the harsh early years of industrialization, people did indeed eat more potatoes: as a substitute for the meat, cheese, and poultry they could no longer afford once they'd bought bread. Only the very poorest—those forced to eat the potato gruel of orphanages, relief stations, and workhouses—made potatoes their main starch. Thus, once English living standards began to rise again a generation or two later—and especially once protection against American grain ended—protein returned to poor people's diets, and potatoes remained forever a subsidiary starch in England.

War and famine created a larger and more lasting opening in Central and Eastern Europe, as they had in Ireland. The high yields and easy storage of potatoes made them the food of choice for armies, and of statesmen obsessed with military readiness. Frederick ("An army travels on its stomach") the Great of Prussia promoted the potato aggressively in what is now Eastern Germany and much of Poland. In the War of the Bavarian Succession (1778–1779; part of the Wars of the American Revolution), both sides were so dependent on the miracle tuber that people called it the Potato War; it ended when the potato crop of Bohemia was exhausted. The unprecedented strains of mass military mobilization during the twenty-five years of war that began with the French Revolution spread potato use across much of the rest of Europe; extensive government-sponsored plantings in Russia after an 1831–1832 famine completed the crop's sweep of the continent. Three hundred years after the Spanish "discovered" it, one of the New World's greatest gifts was now far more widely grown and eaten in Europe than it had ever been in its homeland; but it conquered the world's richest continent as the food of the poor, and despite its merits, each step of its advance had struck its new users as a defeat.

4.15 Trying to Get a Grip: Natural Rubber's Century of Ups and Downs

As we all know, motor vehicles made the twentieth century the century of oil—but as we sometimes forget, cars also made it the century of rubber. Rubber tires allowed cars to go over fifteen miles an hour without the ride being painfully jarring, thus helping them become popular; but the rubber business has taken people on a wild ride indeed.

The first rubber boom occurred in the late nineteenth-century Amazon rainforest, where *Hevea brasiliensis,* the most usable of various latex-producing plants, grew naturally. But big rubber consumers soon found importing from the Amazon unsatisfactory. It was hard to make rubber-tapping "efficient" in the wildly diverse rainforest—in many areas, they averaged fewer than one per acre, so tappers spent a huge amount of time going from tree to tree. This made it hard to raise productivity, and as demand soared, so did prices: even in nominal dollars, natural rubber cost roughly 10 times as much at its all-time peak in 1910 ($12.00 per kilo) as it does today.

The major consuming countries—all the industrial powers of the day— could not grow *Hevea* at home: it's a tropical plant, and they were all in the temperate zone. Britain quickly worked on transplanting rubber trees to its tropical colony in Malaya (now Malaysia), where they could not only have political control, but could clear indigenous rainforests and create plantations with nothing but rubber trees, neatly spaced as close as they could get. This eliminated the time "wasted" on walking from tree to tree in the Amazon and allowed workers to be kept constantly at work. The Dutch did the same in the Dutch East Indies (now Indonesia) with help from American investment. The workers—mostly imported Tamils from South India and Fujianese from South China—did not thrive. Among other things, clearing the forest canopy let more sunlight reach pools of water on the ground, creating ideal breeding conditions for malaria mosquitoes (previously rare in the area). Diseases, bad food and medical care, and often brutal discipline produced horrific death rates in the early decades—5 percent of workers each year on most estates, and close to 20 percent in the worst cases. (Health legislation and unionization later did much to improve this.) Nor did the land thrive: depleted by monoculture, it soon needed huge amounts of fertilizers. But the trees prospered, producing far better than they had in Brazil itself. Smallholders in both colonies soon followed the plantations' lead (though they never planted just rubber): these two colonies soon produced two-thirds of the world's natural rubber and continued to do so until recently. In fact, they did almost too well. Once rubber trees reached maturity, it cost very little to keep them producing for many years, so heavy planting soon generated gluts: prices had dropped to $2.00 per kilo by 1913. Producers have tried periodically to restrict supply ever since.

Other powers lacked this colonial option. The United States, which by the 1920s had 85 percent of the world's automobiles and bought 75 percent of its rubber, had one tropical colony—the Philippines—but its legislature refused to waive limits on landownership to facilitate giant rubber plantations. When the British and Dutch collaborated in a price-fixing scheme in the early 1920s, tire magnate Harvey Firestone turned to Liberia, the West African republic ruled by descendants of former American slaves. There he leased a million acres (almost the size of Delaware), built infrastructure, and refinanced the government's foreign debt. The government in turn assigned tribal chiefs in the interior quotas to recruit a certain number of laborers; their methods led to charges of slavery, affirmed by a League of Nations commission in 1930. Plenty of rubber was produced, but not nearly enough to sate American appetites. Meanwhile, Firestone's friend Henry Ford returned to Brazil, buying 2.5 million acres in 1927. But his "Fordlandia" plantation was a disaster. It turned out there was a reason why *Hevea* trees were rarely found close together in nature: this prevented a variety of pests from moving from one tree to the next. (These pests did not exist in Liberia or Southeast Asia, allowing successful plantations there.) Fordlandia turned into a feast for caterpillars and was abandoned in 1942. Rubber hunger had meanwhile induced other American entrepreneurs to try planting *Kok saghyz* a dandelion-like rubber producer that would grow outside the tropics, in Southern California; they gave up amidst low yield and Depression-era prices in 1931. (Rubber hit bottom at $.06 per kilo in 1932.) The USSR, also without tropics, even more concerned about self-sufficiency, and unconstrained by unprofitability, continued planting *Kok saghyz* in Central Asia for decades.

The rubber plant's natural limits also encouraged experiments with synthetic rubber. Germans took the early lead, rightly fearing that in the event of war, Britain's Royal Navy would cut them off from any tropical imports; Germans achieved partial success during World War I and improved the product further during the 1930s. (Despite a looming war, Germany's I.G. Farben shared this know-how with DuPont and Standard Oil of New Jersey; through the same deal, they later helped Farben manufacture improved airplane fuel.) But in addition to being more expensive, synthetic rubber was inferior, especially for tires that must bear a lot of weight. (Even today, when synthetic rubber has been improved further and makes up most of the average automobile tire, truck tires use mostly natural rubber.) This made it a poor choice for things like airplane tires or tank treads and left generals still craving natural rubber.

There was one more approach to a rubber shortage. Lacking both tropical colonies and top-notch chemical labs in the 1930s, Japan's leaders decided that their "security" amidst competing power blocs required seizing Indonesia and Malaya from their Dutch and British colonial masters—even though this was bound to mean war with the United States.

World War II proved to be the last time that war isolated major rubber producers and consumers from each other. For a time, it seemed that steadily improving oil-based synthetics would eventually squeeze out most natural rubber, but when oil prices jumped in the 1970s, natural rubber bounced back; it has had roughly one-third of the global market ever since. Today's industrial and military titans probably lose little sleep over *Hevea brasiliensis;* but ever-more of us have a lot riding on that quirky perennial.

– 5 –

The Economics of Violence

Commerce has often been seen as a civilizing passion, a *doux commerce* that obviates the need for violence. Rather than bloodying each other fighting for a fixed amount of resources, rivals could each specialize in producing wanted goods and trade them for coveted goods the other held. Specialization in production rather than destruction would increase surplus and reduce production costs. Peace would vastly lower the cost and danger of protecting property and facilitate exchanges. In the world of comparative advantage that classical economists Adam Smith and David Ricardo imagined, the race to acquire ever more material goods would lead to cooperation as well as competition. The market would channel aggressive individual militaristic urges to socially useful prosperity.

Some historians even argue that this vision came true—at least for a while. Once true capitalism emerged in the beginning of the nineteenth century, a Hundred Years' Peace reigned from 1815 to 1914. Struggle was confined to the marketplace rather than the battlefield.

This rosy picture of the healthy effects of the spread of market economy unfortunately hides the historic foundation of violence upon which it was built and the continuing use of force that persistently underlay it, particularly in the non-European world. "Primitive accumulation," that is, simply seizing property and coercing labor, has been a common activity for thousands of years. Tribute and booty funded the Babylonians, Assyrians, Egyptians, and Mayas. While some trade existed, coercion (explicit or implicit) was a much more important motor of accumulation than was voluntary exchange. Wealth was based much more on the size and power of armies and tax collectors than on productive technology and market operations. Economically rational market calculators were often impaled on the swords of Mongolian troops or Viking raiders. At other times, they concluded that force was indeed an effective cost-cutter and joined in the violence themselves.

The relationships between traders and those who gave them protection (including unwanted "protection") away from home has varied over time. In Venice, the government compelled all traders to travel in a government-organized convoy, organizing both protection and much of the actual trading through the state. The Portuguese and Spanish tried to export this model from the Mediterranean to the Atlantic, Pacific, and Indian Oceans, with mixed success. The Dutch and early English overseas traders took an opposite tack, with the state chartering private companies to handle both war-making and trading. So here, too, violence and commerce were in the same hands, though now they were private rather than public. As Frederic Lane put it, these firms "internalized protection costs" and could make them part of rational planning and calculation. On the other hand, the chartered companies had to pay those costs, which became increasingly ruinous for anyone but a government as the scale and price of warfare rose in the eighteenth and nineteenth centuries. Only then did Europeans come to think that there was a "normal" division of labor between merchants who traded but did not fight and a state that fought but did not trade—though it was not always clear whether that state was more a "night watchman," merely protecting property, or an armed robber "opening" new areas to new kinds of trade by force. And even then, the new division of labor was not permanent: faced with the high costs of creating and ruling colonies in the interior of Africa, for instance, various late-nineteenth-century European states once again chartered companies with monopoly rights in trade and the right to act as quasi governments. Even today, many companies—especially resource-based companies operating in remote areas—deploy large groups of private guards not easily distinguished from armies. Thus, while it has seemed at times that peaceful consensual trade and physical coercion were becoming more clearly separated, the separation has never been complete. (One finds the same range of policies at work in various parts of Asia, though in different proportions: from a few Venetian-style monopolies to large "free trade" areas, and even some concession areas where licensed violence and trade worked in ways much like those of the chartered companies.)

Moreover, economic violence is not just a base urge of the remote past, harnessed by the drive to "barter and truck." Although "Westerners" have a tendency to forget about them, the Ottoman Turks were one of the world's great empires for four centuries. At their height in the sixteenth century under Sultan Suleiman the Magnificent, the Ottomans stretched from the gates of Vienna and Regesberg, Germany, in the west to Azerbaijan in the east, north to southern Poland and south to Egypt. With one of the largest armies in the world, an admirable bureaucracy staffed in part by Christian slaves, and an indomitable will to spread the word of Allah, the Turks dominated Southeast European and Middle Eastern politics and brought relative stability to vast areas. The highways that connected China, India, and Persia with Europe were safe so commerce prospered. But the engine of accumulation was conquest; the principal expense, the army.

The Ottomans so milked the cash cow of commerce to finance their military and bureaucracy that European traders sought other routes to the riches of the East. Thus the Turks drove the Portuguese and Spanish south to circumnavigate Africa and west to unwittingly bump into a New World (see reading 2.2, "Better to be Lucky than Smart"). Africa had been in contact with Europe for millennia. The main links with sub-Saharan Africa were through the gold and slave trades, now dominated by the Ottoman, who controlled Africa's northern coast. So the Portuguese made an end-run and opened trading posts on the Ivory and Gold Coasts and established colonies on Africa's Atlantic islands such as São Tomé. But this trade in humans, which played a crucial role in early modern European growth (and even more, of course, in American growth), depended upon violence.

Once again, the relationships between violence and entrepreneurship varied, but they were always there. Most often, Africans did the original enslaving, but the Europeans played crucial supporting roles, from bidding up the price (and so encouraging more raiding) to providing firearms to favored groups of raiders. Moreover, the voluntary exchange of "property" between African and European slavers fundamentally changed the nature of the slave experience. Property though they were, most slaves within Africa had various sorts of rights—rights that often increased with time until they gradually joined the society that had captured them; and in many cases their children would be free regardless. But once they became transatlantic cargo, slaves could expect to be treated much more like pure chattel: a state that could only be maintained if one was willing to use vastly increased levels of violence. Although, as reading 5.1 illustrates, exchange and profit were key elements in the commerce, violence and state power were far more instrumental than entrepreneurship. The technology was one of power and destruction, not production.

Moreover, as long as slaves had mostly remained with the societies that first enslaved them, the need for supervision and the fear of rebellion had limited the number of slaves that it made sense to capture. Once two continents opened up as markets for these goods, this constraint collapsed. The slave trade experienced unprecedented activity and profitability in the seventeenth and eighteenth centuries. Europeans were unable to colonize Africa until the late nineteenth century. Hence, for slaves to be worth purchasing for Europeans they had to labor elsewhere. Unfortunately for the African chattel, Europe developed a sweet tooth at this time (see reading 3.6, "Sweet Revolutions"). American Indians would not work in sugar plantations. In the Caribbean they died off so quickly when infected by European diseases that virtually the entire pre-Columbian population (which could have been as high as 5 to 10 million people), died off within fifty years of Columbus's arrival. In Brazil, the native male population was unused to agricultural work (see reading 1.7). Despite brutal expeditions to enslave them, Indians simply refused to work long hours in tropical agriculture.

Poor whites were brought to some colonies as indentured servants, but always on the condition that they would be freed and given land after a certain term of service. Planters on small tropical sugar islands found this a burdensome condition to meet, and even the tobacco planters of Virginia, with a huge wilderness at their backs, disliked granting land to those who would soon plant their own tobacco and so glut the market. In the first couple of generations, the death rates of Europeans in the tropics (and the southern part of North America) were so high that few of the indentured lived long enough to be given land; but as these problems eased a bit, the costs of relying on poor white labor became too high for planters. It was cheaper, most planters figured, to pay a little more up front for a slave whom you could keep for his whole lifetime and never had to give land to. So African slaves sweating in the blazing sun enriched Europe; and, once again, the activities of peaceful traders and violent kidnappers were closely enmeshed. Still later, when Europeans turned against slavery, many tropical plantations still would not or could not pay competitive wages; instead indentures returned, this time usually involving Chinese or Indian laborers (see reading 5.9, "Looking for the Next Worst Thing").

Wealth came more directly (though fleetingly) to the Spanish by simply plundering the empires of the Aztecs, Inca, and other civilizations they encountered. Melting down golden sculptures and religious icons, the Spanish vastly increased Europe's supply of precious metals (much of which was then transshipped to Asia for spices, silks, and other goods). Then Peruvian Indians were forced to work in the great silver mine of Potosí (see reading 5.2). The *mita* labor tax that sent them into the deep shafts often was a death warrant. But the silver created inflation in Spain and great demand there for northern European goods. In fact, Spain sucked in imports so fast that it wound up with not much more silver than it started with, being forced to turn to copper for domestic coinage. The big winners from the looting of Mexico and Peru were the British, Belgians, Dutch, and Germans, who sold their wares to affluent Spaniards; and many of them probably didn't even realize that there was blood on the money they earned.

Some northern Europeans *did* understand the source of Spain's new wealth and decided to cut out the middlemen. Officially mercantile companies, British, Dutch, and French merchants were just as willing to plunder as trade. As reading 5.3 shows, privateers, claiming that they were acting as agents of national glory, tried to force trade upon Spanish and Portuguese colonials in Asia, Africa, and the Americas. Indeed, it was much easier to raise funds for overseas ventures if the investment prospectus mentioned plunder, glory, and national pride than if it kept to a discussion of commercial opportunities alone. And when the colonists or natives these adventurers encountered didn't want to trade, the pirates simply seized goods, raped women, and burned towns. This proved to be extremely profitable and, as a bonus, successful at reducing Spanish and Portuguese resources and naval superiority. The piracy of privateers and buccaneers so terrorized the residents of the Spanish Caribbean that they fled, leaving fertile areas such as Belize, Curacao, Haiti, Jamaica, and Trinidad to be seized as colonies by the British, Dutch, and French, and the Portuguese were driven out of the Red Sea and Indian Ocean. Honest merchants, engaged in the slave, Asian, or New World trades were virtually indistinguishable from pirates. Similarly, a national hero such as Sir Francis Drake, raiding the Spanish galleons with the authorizations of a letter of marque from Queen Elizabeth I, appeared very much a pirate to the Spanish. Reading 5.4, "The Tropical Dutch," shows how national geopolitics in Europe combined with greed for profit in the slave trade to convert the Calvinist Dutch into some of the world's greatest slave merchants. The British, too, overcame their scruples to enter into the luxury trade of piracy and slavery. As reading 5.5, "The Luxurious Life of Robinson Crusoe," reveals, even the famous island-bound, self-sufficient hero of hard work and self-sufficiency, Robinson Crusoe, actually was a slaver and an international trader.

Once the British and Dutch came to rule the seas and their merchants dominated world markets, pirates became a plague rather than the vanguard of a commercial invasion. As a result, the Royal Navy now hanged men they had formerly decorated. Reading 5.6, for instance, describes how the Royal Navy turned on the seaborne raiders of Sulu, even though British merchants had previously armed their expeditions, which helped provide goods that British merchants then sold in China.

Merchants and pirates had a close relationship, though the traders never referred to themselves as "pirates" when coercing trade at gunpoint. Violence was a great competitive advantage when it could be used to create monopoly conditions. As reading 5.7 demonstrates, the corporation first came into being in order to pay for corporate violence.

They also wanted to protect their markets from interlopers such as the buccaneers, whom they denounced. Reading 5.8, only partly in jest, suggests that the buccaneers of the eighteenth century were far better employers than their contemporary navy or modern-day corporate raiders. Despite the general perception that the service buccaneers provided was economically undesirable, in fact the cutthroats were rather democratic and concerned employers. Multiethnic, multinational sea rovers, they adhered to strict codes of conduct and morality. But there is no denying that they, just as their swashbuckling, bemedaled forebears, lived and prospered through violence. Although their service provided a more egalitarian redistribution of the wealth than did the slave trade, silver mining, or merchant raiding, they, too, relied

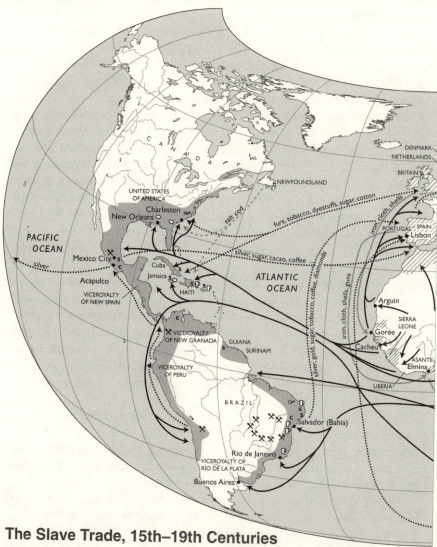

The Slave Trade, 15th–19th Centuries

Slavery has existed in many times, places, and forms, and the sale and transport of
slaves over long distances also has a long history. The two largest slave trades,
however, both traded in Africans. One, dominated by Muslims, took captives to North
Africa, the Middle East, and across the Indian Ocean, and lasted from the 800s to the
1800s. The other, perhaps even larger trade, took about 12 million Africans to
European colonies (and ex-colonies, such as the United States) between the 1500s and
late 1800s. These slaves provided much of the labor for major American cash crops
(sugar, cotton, tobacco, coffee, etc.), some of the labor for mines, and also played
other vital roles in the commercial and industrial development that made the Atlantic,
for a time, the center of a new kind of global economy.

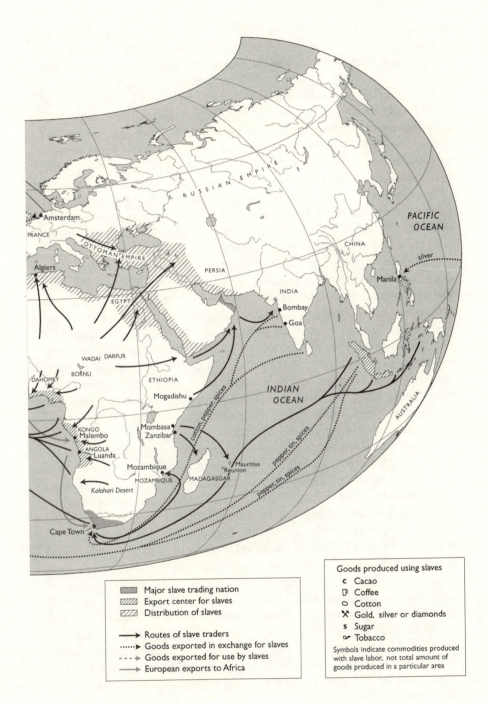

PACIFIC OCEAN

RUSSIAN EMPIRE

CHINA

silver

Manila

OTTOMAN EMPIRE

PERSIA

Amsterdam

FRANCE

Algiers

EGYPT

INDIA

Bombay

Goa

WADAI DARFUR

DAHOMEY

BORNU

ETHIOPIA

Mogadishu

INDIAN OCEAN

cotton, pepper, spices

AUSTRALIA

KONGO

Malembo

ANGOLA

Luanda

Mombasa

Zanzibar

Mozambique

MOZAMBIQUE

MADAGASGAR

Mauritius

Reunion

pepper, tin, spices

Kalahari Desert

pepper, tin, spices

Cape Town

Goods produced using slaves

c   Cacao
ᵱ Coffee
○ Cotton
✗ Gold, silver or diamonds
s   Sugar
☞ Tobacco

Symbols indicate commodities produced
with slave labor, not total amount of
goods produced in a particular area

⬛ Major slave trading nation
▨ Export center for slaves
▨ Distribution of slaves

→ Routes of slave traders
·····► Goods exported in exchange for slaves
- - -► Goods exported for use by slaves
→ European exports to Africa

on a technology of terror. Finally, an animal rights advocate might see an uncomfortable slippery slope connecting the various early modern trades that involved hunting humans and the same period's enormous increase in the efficient slaughter of whales, sea otters, beavers, and later, buffalo.

Many scholars have noted that great financiers (in both Europe and South Asia) financed early modern wars in part because they lacked enough other attractive outlets for reinvesting their profits. Local trade was usually too competitive to yield high profits; long-distance trade was not big enough (and was often closely intertwined with violence anyway, as we have seen); production, for the most part, required relatively little capital before the age of machines. In such an environment lending to cash-hungry, war-making princes (who could repay by squeezing the people harder, if necessary) was relatively safe and lucrative—and offered the crucial added benefits of heightened prestige and political access. Although there is much truth in this explanation of lending to governments, the rise of mechanized industry did not drain funds away from the financing of violence—even though fixed plant and equipment embodying the new technologies became a profitable way to invest unprecedented amounts of capital. Investments in war may have become a smaller percentage of the portfolios of capitalists, but the total volume of available capital grew so much that there was still plenty with which to finance an ever-growing amount of state violence. In fact, military budgets didn't just keep growing in the nineteenth and twentieth centuries—they have kept growing, for much of this period, at an increasing rate. This becomes quite clear when we look more closely at the supposed "century of peace" that followed the fall of Napoleon.

The industrial revolution that arguably began in the last part of the eighteenth century supposedly crowned capital and markets king. Warfare was now subsidiary to the business of making money by producing ever-more efficiently. The reign of haute finance is said to have created a century of peace. But this view is too Eurocentric. Yes, there were no major, prolonged wars in Europe between the Napoleonic wars and World War I. But this period was known to the rest of the world as the Age of Empire, which was anything but peaceful. Violence not only erupted as a tool of capital accumulation, it also served as a weapon for self-defense against the forces of world economy. Between roughly 1851 and 1870 some of the bloodiest wars ever known broke out on three continents, including the Civil War in the United States, the French invasion in Mexico, the Paraguayan War in South America, the Sepoy Mutiny in India, and the Taiping Rebellion in China. Modern weapons allowed age-old passions for killing to be expressed much more efficiently, and the increasing size of armies and expense of their weapons created huge opportunities for profit.

Violence reared its ugly head not only through slavery, piracy, and war. Sometimes destruction and death were directed at wealthy groups within the country. Nationalist and racist policies were trumpeted to win political power and seize the assets of ethnic groups. The group most commonly targeted in European history was the Jews. Reading 5.11 relates the story of a German trading family that first prospered on the tide of international trade and then was torn on the shoals of nationalist xenophobia.

Not only has violence been one of the main levers of accumulating wealth in the global economy, warfare has been a mother of invention. Many innovations such as the invention of synthetic nitrates, rubber, and textiles (nylon) were occasioned by war. New foods, such as beet sugar and cereal coffee (Sanka), and methods of canning also issued from combat-created conditions. And new mechanical techniques, such as Colt's assembly line, producing standardized replaceable parts, and new forms of transportation, such as submarines and airplanes, were driven as much by the urge to destroy as the love of creation.

No doubt the total economic costs of war have dwarfed any such benefits. Even if we just think about inventions, it seems likely that the destruction of so many minds, and the diversion of many others from constructive to destructive projects probably quashed more technical advances than war ever nurtured. And certainly destruction has decreased the world's total stock of wealth. But individual actors need not see or care about who loses from their gains, any more than slave traders and New World plantation owners had to think about what the millions of Africans they moved might have done in Africa. As historians, we can only look at what inventions *have* been made and at how wealth *has* in fact been accumulated and redistributed. When we tell those stories, we see that bloody hands and the invisible hand often worked in concert: in fact, they were often attached to the same body.

5.1 The Logic of an Immoral Trade

America was created by immigrants. We have all been taught that their hard work and ingenuity carved civilization out of the wilderness. Yet few people pause to consider from where the early immigrants came. In fact, before 1800 perhaps as many as three out of every four people who crossed the Atlantic were from Africa. Ten to fifteen million people were herded onto the cruel slave ships and transported across the Atlantic.

We are all at least vaguely familiar with the transoceanic slave trade. Yes, it was horrible, and yes, it was profitable. But one question is rarely considered: Why did Europeans take Africans all the way across the Atlantic to use in the Americas in the first place, rather than simply engage them in Africa itself?

After all, the trade had a very high "leakage." It has been estimated that for every one hundred Africans purchased as slaves in the interior of Africa, fewer than thirty would survive the Atlantic crossing and the first three years on the new continent. Moreover, a fifth of the sailors died in transit.

Surely, using slaves in African colonies would have been more efficient. They would have known the climate, crops, and technology. Slavery itself was a long-standing and widely used institution in Africa. Why then move them to another world?

The answer appears obvious: Europeans already had colonies in the New World and not in Africa. But that situation was as much a result of the slave trade as its cause. Why didn't Europeans colonize Africa first? After all, Europeans had a much longer acquaintance with Africa. The Saharan trade had provided most of Europe's gold for hundreds of years. And the first modern European colony on another continent was in Africa's Ceuta (next to modern-day Morocco), which the Portuguese conquered in 1415. Navigation of African waters was known earlier and better than the seas of the New World.

Certainly parts of Africa were appropriate for European exploitation. The first large-scale sugar plantations were built on African São Tomé. In the sixteenth and seventeenth centuries some 100,000 African slaves worked its fields and refineries, as its *fazendas* became the prototypes for Brazil's vast export complex (which eventually demanded some 40 percent of the Atlantic slave traffic).

Geography, history, and logic seemed to point to European use of slaves in Africa rather than the building of a new world in the American tropics. Yet that did not occur on any substantial scale until after 1880 when the slave trade was abolished. Why not?

In part, the answer lies in the large states and sophisticated warfare that Africans could use to defend themselves against imperialists. Long enjoying the horse, the wheel, and iron as well as obtaining firearms in trade, African soldiers were virtually on a technological par with Europeans. The cannon gave a slight edge to the northerners, but, as Joseph Conrad poignantly showed in *Heart of Darkness,* cannons could reach only a short way into the continent.

Still, this answer does not completely convince. The Aztecs and Incas, whom Europeans did conquer and colonize, had larger states and armies than their African contemporaries. Yet they fell much sooner to the Spanish and Portuguese sword and musket.

Could it be a question of values? Europeans could obtain what they wanted from Africans through trade because of their long-standing commercial intercourse. Amerindians, on the other hand, did not share enough values with Europeans to be interested in many exchanges.

This argument has some merit. Europeans gained the main goods they sought through trade in Africa. But they failed to open up the continent to trade. West African societies were not monetarized and did not embrace European goods until late in the nineteenth century. Africans didn't differ much from Amerindians in their indifference to most European goods.

So what is the answer? Why did over 10 million Africans cross the Atlantic? The main reason was disease. Amerindians had no experience with epidemic diseases; they had no immunities. When the Spanish brought smallpox and measles, the Indian armies and empires collapsed. In many places 90 percent of the population died within a few decades of the conquest. The Caribbean was almost entirely devoid of its indigenous inhabitants within half a century. Since there were no native epidemic diseases in the Americas, Spaniards survived much better. But surviving was not the same as prospering. Spaniards and later northern Europeans did not want to work with their hands. Africans came to take their places. Africans had long had contact with European disease because of the active trade between the two continents. Consequently, they were relatively immune to smallpox.

At the same time, disease protected Africa from European colonization. While Africans had developed some immunities to smallpox and measles, malaria, yellow fever, and other indigenous diseases were fatal to Europeans. Consequently, Europeans were loath to establish settlements on the African continent. They remained in small trading enclaves on the coast.

Silver and later sugar and tobacco paid for African slaves and in turn required the slave labor for production. A complementary triangular trade between Africa, North America, and South America arose. It became more profitable—and considerably safer and easier—to ship to the Americas African slaves often entrapped by other Africans than to create colonies in Africa itself. Disease and greed created an African diaspora.

5.2 As Rich as Potosí

Deep in the interior of South America, ten weeks from Lima by mule, stands the 16,000–foot-high Cerro Rico peak, which towers over a bleak, frigid, barren landscape. This was the end of the world, but it became the center of the world. It became a magnet for tens of thousands of people who founded the city of Potosí. The world of colonial South America became irreversibly changed, and the world economy transformed. This remote summit in this harsh land came to affect millions of people and the course of history, because it was a mountain of silver, the richest motherlode ever found.

The Incas had already worked Potosí with their flint picks. They used silver for their temples and jewelry. They were not anxious to share their secret with their Spanish conquerors, but by 1545 the Spanish were aware of the mountain.

At first the Spaniards employed Incan techniques and Indian labor. This was quite successful for about two decades, as long as they could mine the four unbelievably rich veins that lay close to the surface. But the voracious Spanish appetite soon exhausted the easily exploitable veins. Potosí's boom threatened to be very brief.

Spanish technology came to the rescue. Production was revolutionized in the early 1570s under the tutelage of Viceroy Toledo. The discovery of the rich mercury mine at Huancavelica, Peru, in 1565 made feasible the patio method of extracting silver from ore by applying mercury.

But first the ore, with its declining silver content, had to be crushed. Rich merchants and government officials turned miners invested millions of pesos in creating a maze of waterworks. To ensure water all year around in this dry land, four large reservoirs were built. Thirty dams and tunnels and canals brought the water to the crushing plants to provide hydraulic power.

Equally important, the viceroy solved the labor shortage. Labor was a major problem because Potosí was so far removed from population centers and because Peruvian and Bolivian Indians were not anxious to work for wages. They preferred their subsistence, barter economies. Toledo instituted a labor corvée system inherited from the Incas known as the *mita*. Indian villages were obliged by Spanish authorities to supply a certain number of men for the mines.

State coercion had to be used early on because Indians feared the dangerous mine work. The men worked six or seven days a week deep in the sweltering, dusty tunnels. They sometimes had to carry out fifty-pound loads of ore, climbing up ladders as much as two hundred fifty meters long and then face the frigid air at the mine's mouth. To avoid the labor draft, some villages paid off government officials. If they failed in their efforts and had to provide laborers, funeral services were held in the village before the men's departure. Funereal music was appropriate. A priest newly arrived in Potosí gasped at seeing miners trudge by: "I don't want to see this portrait of hell."

Indians unable to avoid the mita trekked to Potosí and remained there a year. As many as fourteen to sixteen thousand Indians were used at a time. Whole families often accompanied married men in order to provide the men's food. By 1650 there were some 40,000 Indians living on the outskirts of Potosí. This was only one-fourth of the city's population, however.

The barren, remote mountain gave birth to the largest city in the Americas, indeed, one of the largest cities in the world. By 1600 there may have been as many as 160,000 people living in Potosí, making it as large as Amsterdam, London, or Seville. Said one amazed observer in the 1570s: "New people arrive hour by hour, attracted by the smell of silver."

But no more than about 15 percent of Potosí's vast population came to work the mines. The rest came to mine the miners. There were hundreds of carpenters, hat makers, tailors, weavers, cooks. Government treasury officials who ran the mint kept a stern eye on activities. Numerous sumptuous churches sprang up as Dominicans, Franciscans, and Jesuits competed to save souls. This was not another sprawling, dusty frontier boomtown. Built on an orderly Spanish grid pattern, Potosí's stone buildings in the town center lined at least thirty regular blocks.

But it certainly had its share of saloons, gambling dens, and, by one count, 120 prostitutes. With some 30,000 transients, violence and gang warfare were common. An exasperated judge complained in 1585 that Potosí was a den of thieves with "the most perverse sort of people the world has created."

All of these people had come to this distant place because for over a century it was the economic heart of South America and one of the most dynamic places in the Spanish world. With the most silver, Potosí also had the highest prices on earth. This made it a magnet for merchants, because the city's inhospitable surroundings demanded that all food and goods be imported.

The poorly paid Indian population could not afford much. But they purchased lots of potatoes, corn beer (*chicha*), and coca leaves. So much chicha was drunk on festival days that "small rivulets of urine" ran through Potosí's streets. Coca under the Incas had been restricted to the aristocracy. But under the Spanish it became more "democratic" as thousands of workers chewed it to deaden hunger and energize themselves. It came from Cuzco, 600 miles away. Pack trains of 500 llamas regularly entered Potosí to bring these goods. The mining center required a total of 100,000 llamas to attend to its transportation needs. (One can imagine the fragrance.)

The Hispanicized population had far greater wants, turning Potosí into the center of a complex international trade network. Wine came from Chile and Argentina, as did mules, cattle, and wheat; cloth arrived from Ecuador. Brazil provided African slaves. Potosí's millionaires also craved French hats and silks; Flemish tapestries, mirrors, and lace; German swords; and Venetian glass. These arrived not only on the legal Spanish fleets via Seville and Panama but also through smugglers who circumvented the mercantilist routes. *Peruleros,* Lima merchants who bought directly in Spain and avoided the expensive fleets and royal taxes, joined French, Dutch, and Portuguese traders who landed goods in Argentina's Río de la Plata and then carted them overland. At least a quarter of Potosí's silver exited through these illegal routes.

Potosí also reached across the Pacific. Peruvian merchants sent silver to Acapulco, Mexico, partly in trade for Mexican cacao and cochineal, but mainly for Asian goods. From Acapulco the Manila Galleons shipped Cerro Rico's treasure to the Spanish-owned Philippines, which was an emporium for Chinese porcelain and silks, Indian and Persian carpets, perfume from Malacca, cloves from Java, cinnamon from Ceylon, and pepper from India. Anything available in Seville, London, or Amsterdam could also be bought in Potosí—at a much higher price. But when one owns a silver mountain, price, distance, and difficulties shrink in importance. Potosí brought the world to it. Potosí's wealth was legendary. "To be as rich as Potosí" was the ultimate dream.

Then the silver gave out. After more than a century of prosperity, declining quality of ore and increased problems with production forced mines to close down. By 1800 the thriving metropolis, once the equal of any of Europe's leading cities, had become little more than a ghost town. And the world, which had once strained to serve its greatest delicacies and luxuries to the distant miners, forgot about Potosí. But its legacy had rearranged the map of the world and had fueled the world economy. The silver of Potosí and Mexico excited the avarice of the British, Dutch, and French, who set out to wrest away and imitate the Iberian colonial empires.

5.3 The Freebooting Founders of England's Free Seas

Between 1550 and 1630, England took the first major steps toward becoming what would be the world's greatest commercial empire. Colonies were founded all along the coast of North America and in the Caribbean. The famous East India Company—often considered the world's first multinational—was created, and quickly set up numerous trading posts. Other companies were formed to trade with Africa, the Levant (our "Middle East"), Russia, and elsewhere. In all, roughly 13 million pounds was invested in joint stock companies that sought profit overseas. But the largest chunk of that money—more than a third—went into one kind of venture: government-licensed and -regulated piracy, mostly targeted at Spain and its possessions.

Privateering wasn't just the biggest part of England's investment in expansion, it was the most profitable. One historian has estimated that from 1585 to 1603, British pirates returned profits to their investors that averaged 60 percent of the cost of outfitting their ships. (By comparison, investors in the East India Company realized dividends that rarely exceeded 20 percent, and the Virginia Company never made any money at all.) And piracy provided much of the pizazz that lured investors skeptical of commerce into financing overseas expansion.

Although merchants would invest in anything that looked profitable, much of England's aristocracy and gentry still disdained commerce and invested very little in enterprises that expected to do nothing but trade. Brochures for them emphasized the opportunity for even passive investors to reap glory as well as profit by helping English privateers weaken Spain and pave the way for colonies that would open up the field for converting heathens and other noncommercial pursuits. (One brochure for a Newfoundland project went so far as to emphasize the excellent sporting opportunities the project would open up, giving potential investors a detailed description of a critter most had never seen: the moose.)

The glory (including a knighthood) heaped on the most successful pirates, such as Francis Drake, became the stuff of popular ballads, broadsheets, and even sermons, doing much of the work of prospectus writers for them. And while nonmerchant investors usually didn't put up much money (about half as much, on average, as merchants), their participation was crucial, making what might otherwise have been an exclusively land-oriented aristocracy into powerful supporters of a navy. And in the end, piracy—both British and Dutch—probably had more to do with the eclipse of the Spanish and Portuguese empires than whatever commercial superiority the Northern Protestant powers might have enjoyed.

Why was piracy so important? Because of the nature of early modern European trade. With one important exception—the growing Baltic grain trade—virtually all of Europe's seaborne commerce was in luxury goods: spices, gold and silver, furs and high-quality textiles, and later, slaves and sugar. These cargoes made especially rich prizes, so a pirate needed to hit only one target to return to port with a big profit. And because shipping costs were a small percentage of the final costs of these products, there was no great incentive to minimize these costs: better to increase security by having a larger crew and a lot of gunports than to risk disaster by cutting costs that didn't matter much anyway.

The resulting pattern fed on itself: because every merchant ship was armed for defense, any one of them *could* turn to piracy to supplement inadequate earnings if the opportunity arose. For centuries, all that changed was the players, not the game.

First Genoans and Venetians vied for primacy; then the Spanish and Portuguese carried the biggest prizes; then the Dutch and British began to beat them at their own game. (By contrast, Chinese, Indian, and Arab merchant ships more often carried a mixed cargo, including lots of bulky staples, and kept few weapons on board because piracy was an episodic, rather than constant, feature of the Indian Ocean and South China Sea. Consequently, for all their skills in commerce and navigation, these traders were ill-prepared for the kind of armed trading the Europeans brought to their waters.)

But bit by bit, a new kind of trade emerged in Europe, and with it a new kind of shipping. As Holland's cities began to live off of grain from Eastern Europe in the 1500s, suddenly there were lots of seaborne cargoes too cheap and bulky to be attractive prizes for pirates. Thus captains plying this route could afford to worry much less about protection; and with the relatively narrow profit margins on grain, timber, and other Baltic trade goods, these captains couldn't afford *not* to trim costs.

Soon the Dutch were building a new kind of ship, the *fluitschip*. Fluitschips were slow and no more seaworthy than other European vessels, but they required barely half the crew for the same size ship, and with little worry about having to fight, Dutch captains in the Baltic could take full advantage of the lower wage bills these ships allowed. With a large fleet of these ships, the Dutch were soon in a position to move into other European waters and undercut their rivals. They soon dominated almost all of Europe's nonluxury ocean shipping, including the routes that brought Egyptian and other grain to several of Southern Europe's major cities. And Dutch control of the provisions trade became a wedge they could exploit to become the dominant trading community in most of Europe's ports. (In wartime, when any ship was a target, the Dutch convoyed their fluitschips with warships built for that precise purpose—the logical complement to the new specialized merchant ships.)

Undercut on intra-European routes and plundered on intercontinental ones, Southern Europe's seapowers collapsed, leaving the Dutch and their British imitators to fight for naval and commercial supremacy.

Eventually, the British won; and, wishing to make the seas safe for cost-minimizing merchant ships (and a growing long-distance trade in bulk goods such as New World farm products), maintained a standing navy pledged to rooting out piracy—now mostly an activity of non-Europeans pushed to the margins of international shipping—all over the globe. In the new order, any armed trader would be suspect and harassed by a navy that proudly proclaimed its descent from Francis Drake and Martin Frobisher. But in fact, the British navy was really enforcing a world more like that of premodern Asia, and its illustrious forebears had been far more like those it now condemned as criminals.

Without pirates, neither of the two kinds of English sailor into which that role eventually split would have come to rule the waves.

5.4 The Tropical Dutch: How the Burghers Became Slavers
by Julia Topik

In 1596 the townspeople of Middleburg in the Netherlands protested when one hundred and thirty African slaves were brought to the port for sale. The Calvinist Dutch morally objected to the institution and freed the slaves; yet within forty years the Dutch had replaced the Portuguese as the world's leading slave traders. How did this happen?

Certainly when investors from the Dutch provinces founded the West Indies Company (WIC) in 1621 their intention was not to acquire human cargo or to establish colonies. As a joint stock company, the WIC's goal was profit for its stockholders. But as a monopoly company with a government subsidy, the WIC was also powerfully driven by geopolitics. The stock prospectus circulated in the Netherlands proclaimed that the WIC would wrest trade away from the Catholic Spanish.

Clearly, the campaign against the Spanish was more than a simple commercial rivalry. The stark religious divide between the Calvinists and the Catholics was exacerbated by the fact that the Spanish Habsburgs had ruled over and fought in parts of the Lowlands for most of the sixteenth century and continued to control the Spanish Netherlands (today Belgium). So the WIC was fighting not only for wealth and religion, but also for revenge against their former masters.

The Dutch, by opposing the Spanish, also found themselves in a battle with the Portuguese. The Portuguese were the dominant slave traders and sugar producers in the sixteenth century. They owned trading stations along the West African coast, as well as sugar plantations in Brazil. In 1580 the Portuguese and Spanish crown united and would stay together until 1640. This gave the Portuguese the *asiento* trade, which was a spectacularly lucrative contract with the Spanish government, making the Portuguese the sole legal slave purveyors to all Spanish-held possessions.

The Dutch saw the wealth and prestige that came from trade in the New World and wanted a piece. So they opened the door to Spanish markets, first through piracy, then outright conquest. This allowed the Dutch to reap the benefits of a new colony while inflicting damage on Spain at the same time. The WIC decided on Brazil because it was vulnerable due to Spain's overstretched European obligations, and because they anticipated that Brazilian natives and African slaves would revolt in favor of the Dutch. They also hoped that profits from Brazil's prosperous sugar trade would pay off the debts the WIC would incur in the colonization effort.

Failing to hold Bahia in 1624, the Dutch tried Brazil once again in 1630 after Piet Heyn's privateers captured the Mexican silver fleet off of Cuba in 1628. This piracy financed the conquest of the Brazilian province of Pernambuco, which had large sugar profits but little defense.

The Dutch excursion to Brazil brought them to overcome their religious scruples and acknowledge the benefits of entering the slave trade. As the Dutch found themselves in control of Pernambuco, they also found themselves in debt and in a complicated situation. Many of the sugar plantations were abandoned, because more than half of the Brazilian owners had fled with their slaves and capital. Production fell sharply, which Dutch farmers were not able to or willing to replace. As a report lamented in 1637: "It is not possible do anything in Brazil without slaves." To resume sugar production, the Dutch required slaves, but Portugal controlled the supply. The solution was again military. Dutch forces conquered the leading African slave ports of El Mina, Luanda, and Benguela in the Congo area initially to provide workers for Pernambuco's sugar industry.

The WIC was left with a 15 million-guilder debt and was making a 115 percent profit in commerce prior to their engagement in the slave trade. The Portuguese were making an estimated 900 percent from slaves, which must have looked extremely tasteful. The Dutch saw that they could use slave labor to boost sugar production, but they also saw that they could make enormous profits by just engaging in the slave trade. The added incentive of depriving their Iberian rivals of trade whetted their appetite for human cargo still further.

In 1654 the Portuguese regained control of Pernambuco and their African slave ports. But the Dutch had been transformed by the experience. The stern Calvinists were seduced by the slave trade. They opened other sources on the African coast and began to ship human chattel to the French and British Caribbean colonies, where they introduced sugar technology and undercut Brazil's domination of the world sugar market. This Calvinist country ignored moral objections in order to make a profit and as a result helped spread the institution of slavery throughout the Caribbean.

5.5 The Luxurious Life of Robinson Crusoe

Robinson Crusoe would not seem to be someone enamored of luxury. On the contrary, Crusoe is usually taken as a symbol of hard work, frugality, and austerity. The book, published already in 1719, is seen as a inspiration for Max Weber's Protestant ethic, an explanation of the relationship between worship, saving, and investing, not a tribute to leisure or conspicuous consumption.

But the book and Daniel Defoe's message have been often misconstrued as something quite contrary to Defoe's intention. Instead of a celebration of self-sufficiency, the story is actually a tribute to world trade, especially in luxury goods and a celebration of slavery.

It is true that early on in the novel (arguably the first novel ever written in the English language), Robinson's father gives him a speech *against* luxury.

Crusoe spends the rest of the novel regretting that instead of listening to his father and joining England's middle class, he takes to the sea to trade.

Robinson Crusoe, is indeed in part a celebration of hard work. He never submits to pleasure or leisure activities while on the island. He has the mentality of an accountant (which for a while Defoe was), keeping close track of his warehoused stores, of the passing days and years. He husbands the liquor he brings ashore from the wrecked ship for special moments rather than downing it in one drunken spree. He spends his free time studying the Bible, not exploring the island. In fact, he waits eighteen years before he walks to the end of the island!

Not only does he disdain idleness and celebrate labor, Robinson as a good middle-class Englishman, rejects luxury. He does not bring ashore any fine clothes from the ship; instead he crafts a crude goatskin wardrobe, which he only wears at all because he is afraid of sunburn. On the island, cut off from others, Robinson concludes that things are valuable only according to their usefulness. He prefers a carpenter's chest of tools, with which he can make things, to money, which he disdains as "stupid stuff" because there is nothing to purchase.

Self-sufficiency, frugality, and moderation don't seem to be values that would fuel world trade. But, in fact, Robinson Crusoe, as well as his inventor, Daniel Defoe, were very much involved in international trade, a trade often based on luxury goods.

Defoe was an entrepreneur before he was a writer. He bought French civet cats to use in the production of perfume, insured British men-o'-war in struggles with the French, invested in a project to salvage sunken treasure, wrote propaganda in favor of the Guiana colonization project, took shares in the infamous South Sea bubble, and participated in the African slave trade. He believed that England's success would depend on international trade, not on self-sufficiency.

This view in fact underpins *Robinson Crusoe.* Although Robinson is isolated on his island in the Caribbean and he arrives with few mechanical skills, almost everything he has that sustains him comes from the foundered ship that he was crewing to Africa. Guns, powder, food, tools, everything is imported. Without these goods, Crusoe sees the island as "barren," useless, rather than a utopian tropical paradise.

Why were these goods on board the ship in the first place? Robinson had disregarded his father's advice to take the middle station and enter either trade or the law, instead entering into the African slave trade, one of the most profitable of enterprises. He does very well on his first trip, exchanging "toys and trifles" for slaves, investing much of the profit. On his return for a second sales trip to Africa, he is captured by Moroccan pirates and spends four years himself as a slave. But his fortunes change again as he escapes with a fellow slave by stealing a boat. He sells the boat and his fellow slave to a Portuguese slave trader, who rescues them on the Atlantic and brings them to Brazil. There he invests his capital in land and begins growing tobacco and sugar, the principle American luxury crops of the era. When he is later marooned on the island it is because he has set out on another trip to Africa in order to buy slaves more cheaply than then available in Brazil.

So to this point, Robinson's life has been occupied either in trade or in purchasing others to labor for him. He trades in the main luxury goods of his time: slaves, tobacco, and sugar. During his twenty-eight years on the island, he is self-sufficient; he survives and becomes modestly comfortable. But he does not accumulate wealth. He never searches for any resources that would be good export commodities, indeed he is blind to anything that he didn't already know previously. Consequently, when he is rescued, the only wealth he has are the coins he salvages from the wreck, money intended for commerce, not the products of his own labor.

He later begins a colony by importing people onto "his" island. But that is paid for by the profits from his Brazilian sugar plantation and the returns from the invested profits of his first slaving trip, not from wealth from the desert island. After being reunited with the world economy and its luxuries, Robinson returns to a life of "rambling" around the world and further adventures, not to self-sufficient hard work. Robinson Crusoe and Daniel Defoe were so entrenched in a world of luxury trades, that even this paean to sober Protestant values could not avoid the enticement and wealth of luxuries—and slavery.

5.6 No Islands in the Storm: Or, How the Sino-British Tea Trade Deluged the Worlds of Pacific Islanders

The tea for opium trade may not be one of the nicer stories in the history of world trade, but it's one of the best known. As the British got hooked on Chinese tea in the eighteenth and nineteenth centuries, they needed things they could sell in China—but the Chinese didn't want any European goods. For a long time, the British simply shipped silver coins East, but eventually political pressures back home to stop the silver drain grew irresistible.

Casting about for an alternative, the British hit on opium, which they could produce in large quantities in their new Indian colony. Eventually, the drug caught on, solving the English East India Company's problems, but creating massive addiction in China. When the Chinese tried to stop the trade in the

1840s, a fateful conflict resulted, forcing China to open itself to free trade, missionaries, and other more subtle Western influences.

In reality, though, it was not so simple. The British did find some other items they could market in China that had powerful, and mostly negative, effects on the places that produced those goods.

It's true that the European goods that the East India Company wanted to sell in China didn't go over too well—British woolens, for instance, were not widely welcomed in subtropical Canton, where English ships docked. But the English traders were no fools, and long before opium, they had found other things that the Chinese customarily bought from other parts of Asia: shark's fins and birds' nests (both very expensive delicacies), pearls, special woods (especially sandalwood), and more ordinary goods such as Indian cotton (which was spun, woven, and then often reexported by people near Canton) and Vietnamese sugar. But each had its own complications.

The market for cotton was fairly large, but not easy to expand farther, since China produced most of the raw cotton it needed; the same was true for sugar. Sandalwood, on the other hand, was something the Chinese seemed to have an infinite appetite for, so the problem was getting enough supply. The wood grew on many Pacific islands, but not in huge quantities. In an era that knew little of planned, sustainable forestry, European ships would find an island (including some as far off as Hawaii), buy as much of the standing timber as they could, and then move on when all the conveniently located trees had been cut. Island after island was introduced to long-distance trade in this way, had a brief commercial boom, and then was abandoned, often after severe ecological damage had been done. Indeed, some of these islands would probably have been completely devastated by chieftains desperate to keep the flow of foreign goods coming (which heightened their prestige) had the rise of the opium trade not provided an alternate good for the China market. Meanwhile, the search for resins from other tropical trees, and for sharks' fins, birds' nests, and pearls, produced even stranger results.

The problem was that none of these goods could be cultivated; they could only be gathered in from the seas, jungles, and other forbidding settings in which nature produced them. Most of those settings were on or near the jungle-covered islands that today make up the southern Philippines and eastern Indonesia. In each case the work was dangerous, unpleasant, and—especially in the case of pearl-diving—highly skilled. Since these islands and their neighbors were sparsely populated, making laborers scarce enough to have some bargaining power, there was simply no way to get enough free workers to do this work at a rate that the British were willing to pay.

Into the breach stepped the Sultanate of Sulu, a kingdom set on several islands claimed by Spain, but in reality independent. Always looking for allies—and revenue—to continue his ongoing war with the Spanish, the sultan coveted British guns, money, and various foreign goods (such as cloth and brass items) that made good presents for his main followers. Decades of on-and-off warfare with the Spanish had helped the sultanate hone two of its specialties—seafaring and slave-raiding—to the point of fine arts.

As Muslims, the Sulu could not theoretically enslave other Muslims. But Filipino Christians and followers of the area's many local religions were fair game, and slave owning had long been an important sign of status and a source of wealth in Sulu society. As the British provided vastly better connections to the Chinese market for tropical ocean and jungle products and provided guns that made the sultanate's forces stronger, Sulu slave-raiding reached new heights in the early nineteenth century.

In order to keep slaves from wandering off when they went out to gather jungle products, various incentives were used—including a share of the profits, the opportunity to become the master of other slaves, and eventually, the right to freedom. Huge pyramids of masters, slaves, and slaves of slaves grew up; raiding for slaves switched from being an intermittent threat to a constant and severe problem. Many weaker kingdoms simply collapsed or became dependencies of Sulu. The Spanish responded by stepping up their campaign to conquer the sultanate. For many years the Spanish got the worst of most battles, but in the end, they did eventually conquer the islands in the 1870s.

If the British—a much stronger power than Spain—supported what the sultanate was doing, one might wonder how the Spanish ever won. That question leads to a final peculiar twist in the story: the British essentially supported the crushing of the Sulu kingdom that sold them these coveted goods. Britain's Parliament outlawed the slave trade in 1807, and the Royal Navy was supposed to help enforce the ban worldwide. Thus, even though demand from British merchants was behind the boom in Sulu slave-raiding, it made the sultanate an outlaw kingdom in the eyes of the British state.

Had the East India Company retained its government-licensed monopoly on British trade with China, and had the Company not come up with opium to pay for its tea purchases, perhaps the navy could have been induced to look the other way. But the monopoly was abolished in 1834, and long before that, opium had made pearls, birds' nests, and the like much less important. Meanwhile, Sulu ship captains, having developed a specialty in naval violence, were not above developing a sideline in piracy, one that became increasingly important to them as their trade to China became more marginal, but which certainly won them no friends in Manila, Singapore, or London.

By mid-century they were pariahs, while their erstwhile silent partners—

having now moved on to drug dealing—were using the world's largest and most powerful navy to chase them down in the name of civilization.

5.7 The Violent Birth of Corporations

Why did seventeenth-century Europeans create the world's first corporations? Looking back from 2005, the answer seems obvious: the corporation seems like such a logical way to do business, especially on a big scale, that the wonder is that they weren't invented sooner. But the real answers turn out to be more complicated, and only loosely related to the advantages of the corporate form today.

The first real corporations—the Dutch and English East India Companies, West India Companies, and so on—were hardly the first big business partnerships, but they were new in several ways. They were anonymous—the partners did not all have to know each other. They separated ownership from control: elected directors made decisions while most investors had only the choice of accepting those decisions or selling their shares. They were permanent: if one or more partners did want out, there was no need to renegotiate the whole arrangement. Finally, they were legal entities separate from any one owner, and they had unlimited life. The big trading partnerships of the sixteenth century and earlier were created with a planned date of dissolution—sometimes at the end of one voyage, sometimes after a set number of years—at which point *all* the firm's holdings would be liquidated and divided among the partners. The new firms, like modern corporations, did not self-liquidate: they *built up* their capital over the years rather than distributing it back to its separate owners.

Clever innovations, to be sure—but how many people at the time needed them? Very few. Over the next 200 years, almost no corporations were created for either manufacturing or intra-European trade. The capital needs of virtually all production at this time were small enough that people could raise the funds they needed without taking the risks of dealing with strangers. Even the new mass-production factories of the industrial revolution—Wedgwood china, Schneider (Le Creusot) iron, and virtually all the English cotton mills—were family firms, as were the coal-mining companies that fueled the new economy (turnpike and canal-building were partial exceptions). Not until the post-1830 railway boom was there finally an industry that required so much capital, and so long a wait before the profits started to roll in, that the corporate form was really essential.

Where lots of patient capital was needed, even in the 1600s, was for economic activities that ranged beyond Europe. A round-trip voyage to East

Asia could take three years to complete, and if a partnership wished to spread its risks over several voyages, the partners would have to wait still longer for the final payout. But even this did not require that the corporation have *permanent* life: the English Muscovy Company, which traded with Russia, for instance, did not have this feature. Moreover, there was considerable resistance to the idea among investors: with share markets not yet fully developed, they didn't know if they'd ever get their principal back unless the company had to dissolve at a certain date. Partly as a result, the Dutch East India Company was originally chartered with a long but finite life—it was to be liquidated in twenty-one years—and with compulsory high dividends. And Asian merchants who handled trade over distances almost as long—and who often continued to outcompete the Europeans on routes between the Middle East, India, Southeast Asia, Japan, and China all the way through the eighteenth century—apparently had no need of the corporate form.

So what made the turn to permanent life necessary? In a word, violence. The East India Companies were not just licensed to trade, but to make war on the Portuguese, who had created fortified colonies and used their navy to claim a monopoly on trade from Asia; the West India Companies faced similar Spanish and Portuguese claims (and much stronger colonies) in the Americas. To compete, the Northern Europeans reasoned, they would need to play the same game: seizing and fortifying territory and arming ships to patrol the waters. But this meant enormous costs for fixed capital in forts and ships, and for working capital, such as provisions. (Asian traders largely refused to play this game, concentrating on the vast stretches of the ocean and coast where the Europeans could not enforce their monopolies. As a result, they had far lower overhead, and could consistently undersell the Europeans wherever force could not create monopolies, which meant almost everywhere besides a few strategic straits.) In the New World, distances were shorter, but other problems were more demanding. Unlike fortified European bases in Asia, which could buy supplies and hire laborers from highly commercialized neighboring societies, New World bases needed to be much more self-sufficient, and so had to be real colonies with productive agriculture—something that took much longer to create.

Because they needed so much capital to fend each other off, Europe's overseas ventures could not possibly be organized without bringing in many unrelated partners. And because they needed so much fixed capital, only a very large trading volume would generate enough profit to make these ventures worthwhile. And a very large trading volume, in turn, meant that very large amounts of working capital had to be tied up in inventories held overseas, awaiting the right moment to exchange them for goods that would sell back in Europe. Indeed, the founder of the Dutch East India Company's empire in Asia, Jan Pieterszon Coen, waged an almost constant battle with Amsterdam for more capital. The European directors kept suggesting that, having achieved naval superiority, he could monopolize the spice trade back to Europe without much more capital by raiding; he replied that he could indeed do so, but that raiding discouraged trade, and so would never yield a large enough volume to cover costs, even if he did achieve monopoly. To make the forts pay off, whole new lines of trade needed to be developed and others greatly expanded—and that meant more capital and more patience. After years of conflict, and many revolts by shareholders who wanted the company to wind down rather than grow, Coen and his successors won: the company was rechartered rather than liquidated after twenty-one years, the directors got the flexibility to lower dividends when they needed to build up capital, and Dutch investors learned to operate like shareholders today.

The idea of companies that took care of their own protection costs did not last, of course. As the costs of war-making soared in the eighteenth century, both the English and Dutch companies staggered under the burden; when they tried to make back these costs on goods they monopolized they found themselves very unpopular, and often undercut by smugglers. (The English East India Company's problems with tea sales in America are only the most famous example.) By the 1830s, all these companies had collapsed, and their colonies had been taken over by governments—just as a new era of capital-intensive industry was about to create more productive uses for the corporate form that they had pioneered.

5.8 Buccaneers as Corporate Raiders

Pirates have gotten a bad name. They are seen as savage, predatory dictators, as parasites and wastrels, "monsters in human form." They were men outside the law and outside accepted morality. Financiers, on the other hand, are often viewed as creative, intelligent men who direct resources to the most deserving enterprises to increase productivity. The pirate is a threat and a defiance to the capitalist system of profit and property, while the financier is its guardian angel, ensuring its successful operation. Yet in many cases the differences between the two are not so large. The corporate raider, like the pirate, often makes nothing from something, tearing apart carefully assembled structures and leaving their victims marooned and desperate. Like pirates, corporate raiders use other people's money to profit themselves.

But this comparison of the pirate and the modern corporate raider does an injustice—to the pirate. Detailed studies in the last few years show that in fact the financier could learn something from the pirates of the sixteenth, seventeenth, and eighteenth centuries, not just about raiding, but about personnel relations. Ironically, pirates tended to follow closely a moral economy. Outside the reach of the state's law, they had to craft laws for themselves, laws that they obeyed across seas and continents.

Piracy of some sort has existed for thousands of years and over most of the world. Who was a pirate was usually defined by the power with the greatest navy. As a famous pirate is said to have told Alexander the Great: "You who seize entire kingdoms are celebrated as a great emperor. I, who merely take ships, am but a lowly pirate."

The pirate business picked up in the sixteenth century when shipbuilding and navigational technology created a boom in international overseas trade. It became especially noteworthy in the Caribbean after the Spanish discovered silver and gold in the Americas. The first pirates in the Americas, men such as John Hawkins and Francis Drake, attempted to encroach upon the Spanish Lake to sell contraband. When rebuffed, they entered into piracy. During times of war between England or Holland and Spain the privateers were issued "letters of marque," which made them volunteers in their country's navy. For these sixteenth-century raiders, then, piracy was simply an extension of trade and warfare. The ships were outfitted by merchants much as in any commercial venture, and the stockholders received a large share of the booty. Certainly, pirates employed predatory trade practices.

But the early merchant pirates gave way in the mid-seventeenth century to buccaneers who were not black princes of commerce or part-time irregulars in her majesty's navy. They were multinational, multiethnic democratic bands of sea rovers. Originally they consisted of castaways, runaway slaves, escaped criminals, and religious and political refugees who scrounged an existence on a remote part of the island of Hispaniola. Though the buccaneers were peaceful and innocuous, the Spanish governor could not abide these men beyond his command; so he sent troops to hunt them down. The buccaneers retreated to the small island of Tortuga, created the "Brethren of the Coast," and declared war on all Spaniards. Together with privateers, they proved so devastating that not only did they force the Spanish into an expensive system of escorted transatlantic fleets and coastal forts, but they seized many silver-laden galleons and even sacked some of the major Spanish port cities such as Cartagena and Porto Bello. The Spanish Caribbean was largely abandoned, and even along the continental coast, cities were built at least fifty miles inland to avoid the threat of pirates.

How did the buccaneers become so numerous and fierce? They were joined by many British, French, and Dutch privateers who became self-employed mercenaries of sorts when wars ended and their activities were no longer condoned by imperial powers. Although their actions were the same as when they were privateers, they trespassed the line that separated patriotism and glory from piracy and infamy. But that was not the only difference.

Buccaneers operated as partnerships in which each crew member had a stake. Before setting out, the crew drew up articles of conduct. The leader was agreed upon by the crew according to his naval and martial ability and his capacity to command respect and discipline. No one ever became captain of a pirate ship because of influential parents, college connections, or strings pulled by absentee investors. Unlike in the royal navy, the corsair captain was no despot. Noted one observer: "They only permit him to be captain on the condition that they may be captain over him." Rules were enforced by a council of the crew. Although drinking, gambling, whoring, and pederasty were permitted on most ships, some antisocial behavior was severely punished: hiding some of the loot was punishable by marooning on a desert island or death.

Buccaneer ventures were essentially partnerships. They were all paid on commission: "No prey, no pay" was their motto. Once a prize was taken, the booty was distributed among the buccaneers, who voted on the amount of individual shares. Generally the captain received two shares, some of the staff such as the surgeon received one and a half, and all others received one share. Since their ship was owned jointly by the crew (usually it had been seized from someone else), none of the proceeds were paid to investors back in Europe as with the early pirates. The buccaneers applied their own labor theory of value. Buccaneers also had their own disability and life insurance. Monetary awards were doled out for the loss of body parts, and widows were sometimes given the share of their departed pirate husbands.

Buccaneers tended to treat the crew and passengers of captured ships well if they did not resist capture. They would be left with food and ship or else brought to a safe port. The pirates would, however, "distribute justice" to the captain of the conquered ship if he had mistreated his crew, which was frequently the case. Often the captive crew preferred the democratic life of the pirate and joined their captors. As explained by pirate captain Bartholomew Roberts, who had seized four hundred ships, "In an honest service there is thin commons, low wages, and hard labor; in this, plenty and satiety, pleasure and ease, liberty and power and who would not balance creditor on this side, when all the hazard that is run for it, at worst, is only a sour look or two at choking?"

Therein lies another difference between the pirate and the corporate raider. The latter, who disdains and dismisses his own crew, sinks captured ships and abandons their crews and passengers, and seizes wealth with a fountain pen rather than a sword. He therefore has no fear of choking and retreats, pockets full, to his own Caribbean island with the law on his side. Ah, for the days of pirate justice.

5.9 Looking for the Next Worst Thing: Emancipation, Indentures, and Colonial Plantations After Slavery

Nineteenth century Western societies were unmatched in their faith that free markets and human freedom generally went together. And there were few prouder achievements of that liberal faith than the abolition of slavery: in the British Empire in 1833–1834, the United States in 1865–1866, and elsewhere at various points in the nineteenth century. Although many people wanted abolition at any cost, others went along in part because they were sure that relying on free labor would not only prove more moral, but more profitable. But when things did not turn out so neatly, abolition—and labor policies more generally—took some strange turns.

Colonial sugar plantations posed the biggest problems. As emancipation neared in the British Caribbean, Lord Elgin confidently predicted that wages would make ex-slaves work even harder, and would convince slaveholders worldwide to abandon the whip. But he probably had no idea how hard many slaves actually worked. (Consider that on some U.S. plantations, slaves ate more than 5,000 calories a day—more than you use climbing Everest—without getting fat.) Given a choice, they preferred anything else—subsistence farming on unclaimed hillsides, renting better land to grow crops for local markets, or leaving agriculture altogether. (Men who were newly emancipated, and thus had become "real" household heads, were often particularly eager to keep "their" women out of the fields.) Desperate to keep labor costs down, some colonial legislatures mandated "apprenticeships" on plantations for the newly freed—though nobody had to teach them how to cut cane. For decades to come, colonial authorities repeatedly argued that Africans and Afro-Caribbeans were an exception to the universal rational self-interest that they believed would make all other people work hard and budget adequately if the alternative was hunger; consequently, ex-slaves still "needed" forced labor until they were ready for a market-driven world. Once in place, this idea was also applied to Africans in new colonies who had never been slaves: it rationalized forced labor in mines in Natal, on Senegalese roads, and elsewhere. In fact, though many Africans—among others—chose not to focus exclusively on maximizing their earnings, many others were unavailable for plantation work precisely because they were busy producing for local markets. (Early twentieth century British colonies in southern Africa were all too aware of this—and banned black small farmers from growing market crops to protect the profits of white settlers.)

But such measures still did not suffice—so old and new tropical colonies imported indentured servants. More than 2 million such people, mostly from India and China, were transported to plantations in the Caribbean, Indian Ocean, Hawaii, and East Africa. Even more went to Southeast Asia, though under conditions so varied that it is hard to tell how many count as "indentured." Like the indentured whites who had come to early colonial North America, the newly indentured had their passage paid in return for a set term of labor (usually five years); unlike those whites, the bonus awaiting them at the end was not usually a piece of land, but a ticket home, which many declined.

From the beginning, some people called this a new slavery—which it both was and wasn't. Workers had finite obligations, were paid wages, and had signed contracts (though what they knew when they signed is hard to tell). Since they remained legal persons, rather than private property, some governments regulated their treatment in ways that mattered. Ships and passengers headed for the British Empire got at least a minimal health inspection, and death rates on those voyages were one-third those on the essentially unregulated route from China to Cuba. Some colonies insisted that a third of those imported be women—which allowed the indentured to create something much more like other immigrant communities. Most importantly, where laws were enforced, masters were much less likely to extend indentures or dock wages illegally. (Wages eventually reached almost the level of those of farmworkers in the poorer parts of Europe—well above those in India or China.) But the law was still mostly the bosses' tool—absenteeism, for instance, could lead to prison, making it hard to call this "free labor."

But still plantation owners could not recreate what they had under slavery. In the British Caribbean, they regularly complained that indentured Indians did barely half as much per day as enslaved Africans had. Even allowing for some nostalgia, this suggests just how much work slavery had squeezed out of people and how impossible it was to duplicate that, once coercion was even somewhat limited. By 1920, both China and India had banned the "coolie trade," and indenture disappeared as a legal way of recruiting labor (though it survives underground even today). While it lasted, it made big profits for some; and some of those indentured bettered their lives as well. It certainly changed the ethnic mix of many parts of Africa, the Americas, and other places. But in another sense it was bound to fail—an embarrassing reminder that merely calling slavery "backward" didn't dissolve the reliance of some very modern enterprises—and their customers, bankers, and others—on forced labor.

5.10 Bloody Ivory Tower
by Julia Topik

Billiards seems an innocuous pastime, a diversion little connected to the currents of world history. But the balls that rolled on the tables of nineteenth-century sportsmen were made of ivory, which had a long history. The tusk of the elephant, first used for decorative purposes more than 20,000 years ago by Stone-Age men, later inspired Egyptians, Minoans, and Greeks to carve figurines, jewelry, and gods. The Bible's King Solomon had an ivory throne. Churches and temples in the Middle Ages were decorated with ivory images.

Then the industrial revolution found new uses for the ancient precious material: billiard balls, piano keys, knife handles, and chess pieces. The volume and value of the trade swelled. By the turn of the twentieth century, more than 1,000 tons of ivory was imported yearly into London, Antwerp, Hamburg, and New York. The gentlemen coolly stroking balls across elegant felt, while the piano gently played in the background, were not aware of part of the story. Ivory's lavish, fine-grained texture and opaque shell was doused in the blood of hundreds of thousands of elephants and millions of Africans. Ivory created colonies.

Colonies were on the mind of King Leopold II, the monarch of Belgium, a rather small country that was devoid of colonies in a mercantilist era. Leopold knew that if he would ever hope to control a territory he would have to look toward Africa, the only continent that had been left almost completely unsettled by the European powers. Eighty percent of the entire land area of Africa was still under indigenous rulers, making the continent "ripe for conquest." He used a series of shrewd diplomatic maneuvers to gain control of his Congo region. As Adam Hochschild remarked in a recent study: "If he was to seize anything in Africa, he could do so only if he convinced everyone that his interest was purely altruistic." In a stupendously ironic and tragic moment in history, he found his allies in the European abolitionist movement! He would reinvigorate the slave trade in Africa after the international traffic in humans had all but died out, exactly the opposite of what the abolitionists sought.

Leopold began to show his interest in Africa at first by voicing his concern over the illegal slave trade that continued to thrive despite the treaties and the proclamations of many powerful European governments. Leopold claimed to help protect Africans by sending his military to rid the area of slave traders and to modernize the Congo. He created the International African Association to open routes into the interior to create hospitals, scientific, and pacification bases. The association purportedly was to establish peace among the chiefs and procure them just and impartial arbitration in order to abolish the slave trade. Leopold convinced the world that his intentions were purely philanthropic.

But philanthropy does not pay and is a weak foundation for a colony. Leopold's eyes strayed toward the abundant source of ivory in the region: the herds of elephants protected by the tropical forests. However, Leopold had to first control the area before he could start to exploit it.

Leopold started using African mercenaries in 1879 to control the Kongo, Pygmies, Kunda, and other peoples who could not comprehend the idea that someone could own the land that they had inhabited for thousands of years. In 1888, Leopold organized his mercenaries into the Force Publique, which was divided into small garrisons that were usually composed of several dozen black soldiers under one or two white officers. The king gave bonuses to white agents according to the number of men they impressed into the Force Publique and the number of laborers they captured. The white agents usually delivered their "ready and willing" workers in chains.

Leopold ran his territory mostly through military power. He carved out small areas and gave willing Europeans complete control over their inhabitants. The king left white men alone in charge of areas for months at a time; there was little or no punishment meted out to soldiers who mistreated the Kongo.

The natives were brutalized. White men sailing down the Congo River would shoot Lunda or Mongo for sport. They justified their cruelty with their belief that the indigenous people were simply animals, inferior and devoid of human emotion. The common practice in the Congo was to punish the captive peoples with whippings, chaining them to the ground and giving them thirty lashes in a row, sometimes more. Sometimes ears and limbs would be cut off.

With the native Kongo and Lunda cowed, Leopold began to treat both vacant and nonvacant land—as well as everything on them—as his property. His soldiers left piles of dead elephants, and Africans were forced to carry tusks on their backs. The self-proclaimed abolitionist depended on slavery, while cruelly naming it the Congo Free State. Ivory and produce filled the holds of ships sent to Belgium, but returning ships were practically empty when they arrived in the Congo, because the workers in Africa were not being paid. In search of billiard balls and piano keys, the Belgians were stripping the Congo of its resources. This was theft, not development.

Leopold conquered the Congo region behind a badge of justice. He cried out for civil rights and for the abolition of the atrocity called slavery. Yet he ran the territory with a whip. The blood spilled along the banks of the Congo, of the five to eight million Africans and the hundreds of thousands of elephants who were killed, went unseen by his royal eyes. And ever more billiard balls rolled in the elegant parlors of New York, London, and Antwerp.

5.11 Never Again: The Saga of the Rosenfelders

Before corporations, partnerships were the premier form of business organization. Blood ties, rather than impersonal stocks, bound together enterprises that traversed the continents. Often ethnic groups viewed as "outsiders" by the majority population formed closed communities that specialized in specific trades. Their outsider status allowed them to move between different national groups, but also made them vulnerable to nationalist and racist attacks.

Take, for example, the Jewish trading house of Samuel Rosenfelder und Sohn that was centered in the fur capital of Europe: Leipzig. The company was founded by Samuel Rosenfelder, who was born in the 1820s in Nordlingen, Germany. Beginning as a small-time peddler, he woke up each morning before 3:00 A.M. to travel out to the surrounding farms to deal with farmers before they left for their fields. He bought their surplus cattle hides or whatever other skins they offered and then sold them to factories. Since the farmers mostly raised animals and grew food for their own subsistence, each stop garnered few skins—if any at all. Samuel eked out a living. He continued, to the end of his days, to be extremely thrifty. He took third-class trains, lived in a small apartment, and rather than rent an office, did his business in the street.

In the middle of the century, Samuel took a gamble and moved to the fur capital of Europe, Leipzig. There he peeked into the world of the international fur trade. In the days before synthetic materials and efficient heating, when mink coats and beaver hats were still in fashion, there was a large market for the most varied types of furs and skins. Many of the more exotic animals were still trapped, though there was a movement toward raising animals for their furs. The natural distribution of furbearing animals meant that each country specialized in different furs, encouraging international trade.

Samuel first met the traders from other lands at the great Leipzig trade fair that brought together men from all over Europe. Personal connections he made there permitted him credit in other markets. So he sent a representative abroad—his son Max—who would become heir to the Leipzig company. His other son, Adolf, moved to Paris and established his own fur company, which continued to have trading relations with the German firm. (As we shall see, family ties were as much a centrifugal force as a magnet.) The great fair at

Russia's Novgorod offered fox, martin, weasels, and sable for luxurious coats. In Ismir, Turkey, Samuel bought thousands of cat skins (reputed to cure rheumatism) and dog skins for gloves. Rabbit skins came from Italy, Spain, Australia, and Argentina.

Initially, Rosenfelder was simply a middleman between producer and manufacturer. Since the fur and skin businesses were so subject to the fortunes of fashion, climate, and disease, he made most of his profit from hoarding and waiting for price rises rather than establishing an efficient high-volume, low-mark-up business. Sometimes this was quite successful. In the 1920s the company made a fortune by buying up monkey skins in Africa, which suddenly came into demand.

Gradually, his firm began cleaning furs and sorting and tanning skins as well, employing a dozen people in these jobs. But the company continued to be principally a middle-sized trading house. By the early twentieth century the core of the company was Max and his three sons, Felix, Gustav, and Eugene. At an early age they took up the job of visiting trade fairs throughout Europe. But there was a falling out. The three sons created their own firm, though customers must have been confused because they gave it the same Rosenfelder name as the original. Gustav maintained his ties to Rosenfelder und Sohn, but from a distance. He traveled to Argentina in the 1920s where he invested in rabbit and paca (a large South American rodent), then moved to Danbury, Connecticut, then the largest hat producer in the country. (A large sign outside of town boasted "Danbury Crowns All.") There he set up his own company. He branched out from the furs to the hair business, establishing the Federal Fur Company. He sold leftover animal hairs, which were spun together with wool for expensive clothes. Gustav Rogger, a relative by marriage, opened a branch in London in 1931, turned it over to his son Walter, and returned to Leipzig.

The company had sometimes prospered when crises struck Europe. During World War I, for instance, Rosenfelder made out handsomely, selling Russian lamb and sheepskins to the German Wehrmacht. But the war also divided the family. Brother Adolf in France, who had married into the French aristocracy and hidden his Semitic background, fought for the French, while Max supported the German army. The two brothers would not speak for years after the war.

This was a minor problem compared with the crisis the company faced when the Nazis came to power in Germany. Aware of the threat that the Nazis presented to Jews, Felix left for the United States (Eugene had already died) and charged their relative Gustav Rogger with getting the company's assets out of Germany. This was no small feat since Jews were prohibited from taking money from Germany. Rogger was to send the best furs to Gustav

Rosenfelder in the United States priced below value so the profits would accrue in the United States. Unfortunately, Rogger was not aware of the scheme, and intent on making a profit as any born trader would, he sent low-quality furs to the United States so he could show a greater return in Germany. Unfortunately, Rogger was sent to a concentration camp before he could liquidate assets.

Fortunately, the U.S. connection saved him. In an act of tremendous courage, company employee Joe Ackerman (himself Jewish) rented a large black car, prominently displayed an American flag in front, and brashly drove to the concentration camp insisting on speaking with the commandant. His brass and self-assurance won him an audience. There his money freed Rogger, who eventually left for the United States. Rosenfelder und Sohn was no longer a German company. Family members fled to England, Israel, Sweden, Peru, Argentina, and the United States. The dispersion that business began was accelerated by racist politics.

Gustav Rosenfelder maintained his company for a few years after World War II, selling hair for felt to the Stetson hat company. But synthetics began to replace natural skins, and furs and hats faded from fashion. By the late 1940s the company ended, selling out to competitors. There was one last effort to resurrect the family's stake in the fur business. In 1947 two nephews of Gustav, Kurt and Fred Tschopik, bought into the Spencer Rabbit Company in Los Angeles. The firm slaughtered rabbits, selling dried skins and meat. But by 1953 they, too, withdrew from the skin business, the first becoming a realtor and the second a university professor. Today, the descendants of Samuel Rosenfelder are spread over the globe; none maintains the business that occupied four generations over three continents. Rosenfelder und Sohn was swept apart by the tides of the international market and world history. The family and ethnic ties that for so long were valuable assets led to the demise of the family business and to the death of some family members. But we remember.

– 6 –

Making Modern Markets

For a true world economy to come into being, with vast amounts of commodities, capital, and technologies traveling around the globe, laws and practices had to become more predictable and universal. Standardization and impersonal relations were the key conceptual changes. The great transformation of subsistence production and exchange of use values to a market-driven notion of commodities and profits required a host of important changes. For people to find the world market "natural" and be driven to sell and profit in it required new international institutions and a conceptual revolution. It involved concepts that have become so embedded in our everyday lives that we cannot conceive of their not existing or of their being socially invented: time as a commodity, gold as money and the measure of all things, consistent and translatable standards and measurements, sacrosanct property rights, limited liability corporations, product packaging, corporate trademarks. Most of these would have been strange to people only two hundred years ago. Each one involves ideological concepts, social conventions, political struggles, and historical processes.

Although, as we have seen, ample long-distance trade existed in the absence of money, it is still true that for world traders money makes the world go round. Of course, for most of history there was no general agreement on what constituted money. Indeed, early exchanges were much like that of the Brazilian Oueteca: direct barter of one good for another. Money, a symbol of value that was important more for what it could purchase than for its own intrinsic use value, was slow to develop. For people of the Northwest of the United States it was shells; for the Aztecs it was cacao beans. In parts of Russia tea tablets served, while in many places salt was currency. In undermonetarized societies such as El Salvador, supposedly even soap and rotten eggs served as money (though one can't imagine accumulating much wealth in rotten eggs). But how did one convert shells into cacao beans?

Over time, as the problem of converting the monetary systems of diverse peoples intensified, two precious metals, silver and gold, came to dominate as symbols of value. Although there was much disagreement over whether their value was intrinsic, as commodities much sought after for their appearance and use (this Marx called commodity fetishism), or their representation of value, international traders increasingly came to recognize them. There was early international agreement from China and India to Africa, Europe, and the Americas that silver and gold were valuable.

The fixing of value of currency was simplified because, as readings 6.1 and 6.2 discuss, the Mexican peso was the world's predominant coin for some two centuries. The great bonanzas of Mexico and Peru monetarized world commerce in a way that had never before taken place. The silver flowed from the Americas to Europe, Asia, and Africa. In the nineteenth century a problem arose, however, with enormous gold discoveries first in California (see reading 4.4, "California Gold and the World"), then in Australia, South Africa, and Alaska. It took more than half a century to agree upon the relative value of silver to gold and fix it in currencies. Only after World War II would the gold standard be abandoned.

The invention of money and the establishment of currency equivalencies were only two steps on the way to integrating the world economy. Agreements on other weights, measures, and instruments of trade were also necessary. The metric revolution of the nineteenth century, discussed in reading 6.3, was necessary to create universal, unchanging measures. Myriad local measures, which had defined local custom and sovereignty, succumbed to the homogenizing power of international trade and state power. The trader in Amsterdam or New York now knew how much guano he was getting in Peru without having to guess about the measures being used. This was a key step on the road to commodification, the production of goods for sale and the ability to translate one good into a certain amount of another good by quantifying their attributes. It also undercut the local merchant who had been expert in local weights and measures.

The process of commodification was further illustrated (reading 6.4) by the creation of an international grain market around 1900. Railroad storage elevators literally homogenized the wheat of numerous farmers in the United States or Argentina, as they were all thrown together. The shipping revolution caused an integration of Asian rice markets that had previously been quite distinct. In times of drought in rice-growing areas, Indians who normally purchased rice would switch to the cheaper wheat. Now, for the first time, the international price of rice affected the price of wheat, creating an integrated international grain market. One could actually think about and measure how much rice one needed to purchase a certain amount of wheat. Consequently, the size of the wheat harvest in Saskatchewan, Canada, was felt in the rice paddies of Sichuan, China.

The transportation revolution of the nineteenth century not only affected the price and interchangeability of goods, it affected time itself. Although telling time was thousands of years old, it was fixed by the local position of the sun. A plethora of different time zones presented no problem as long as people and goods moved slowly and time was not yet money. But the fact that the United States had some 300 different time zones and 80 different railroad times in 1870 (reading 6.5) became a major problem for the railroads. Railroad companies, deciding that it was bad business and extremely dangerous to have two trains at the same place on the tracks at the same time, joined together to establish national time zones in 1883. International railroads in Europe and the advent of the telegraph in the second half of the nineteenth century demanded that time zones be agreed upon internationally.

Time became not only standardized, but commodified in the nineteenth century with the advent of commodity futures. Commodification of grains, described in reading 6.4, referred to existing grain. But soon farmers wanting to borrow on the future and traders, seeking to hedge against rapid price changes as well as speculate on the future, sold claims on future crops. Now traders in major markets all over the globe were not only purchasing goods thousands of miles away, they were purchasing goods that did not yet exist.

Buying pieces of paper that granted the right to future crops did not seem so strange to traders, in part because they had already institutionalized the notion of corporate stocks. Reading 5.7, "The Violent Birth of Corporations," discussed the fundamental departure of the impersonal joint stock company from the partnerships that had prevailed previously. Investors could buy into a company, indeed, take it over or sell its stock without meeting any other of the stockholders. The company was greater than its owners and could outlive them. The personal reputation and word of the stock owner were not even in question. One's obligations were equal only to the amount of stock one owned.

Ironically, such an impersonal institution as stock shares were promoted by one of the first institutions for bourgeois sociability. The coffeehouse (reading 3.4) in seventeenth-century London was one of the first men's clubs, one of the first sites for organizing political parties, and became the first stock market, mercantile exchange, and insurance company. The business of the coffeehouse became business.

Not only did corporations develop their own juridical identities and lives to be traded on the stock markets, but so did bonds. Lending was a longstanding institution, of course. We read of it in the Bible. But loans had usually been made by merchants or banking houses to individual borrowers or rulers. The nineteenth century saw the birth of bonds, shares of debt (rather than shares of assets as were stocks) that were to be repaid with interest. Unlike previous debts, bonds could be bought and sold by parties not involved in the original transaction. Governments favored this kind of borrowing, which spread the liability and control among a multitude of lenders. Sometimes the bonds had exciting social lives. Such was the case of the little blue bonds issued by Emperor Maximilian of Mexico in the 1860s, discussed in reading

6.6. Rather than simply being resolved by the market mechanisms of supply and demand, five decades of international diplomacy involving a half dozen countries were necessary to put the blue bonds to rest.

Bonds had long been the jurisdiction of international banking houses, family-centered partnerships. But, as the saga of the *petits bleus* demonstrates, joint stock company banks began to encroach on the market at the end of the nineteenth century. U.S. banks, which had been overshadowed in international finance by European competitors, began to enter the contest. The settling of the petits bleus had given American capitalists an opening into Mexico, which became a laboratory for American corporations, often headed by financiers (see reading 6.7). Success south of the border encouraged banks such as City Bank to look over the Pacific at China during World War I where the American International Corporation secured important construction contracts. Unfortunately, as reading 6.8 shows, Japanese and British bankers who had a head start used their financial and diplomatic power to thwart this precocious U.S. foray.

While impersonal representations of value such as bonds can develop social lives as do banks and other corporations, very personal things such as the product of one's labor are often alienated, removed from the control and identity of the producer. The development of the world economy and the rise of industrial technology has turned on its head the customary notion that one knows best what is closest to home. Packaging technology combined with advertising (reading 6.10) led to the more distant, even foreign, becoming more familiar and more trusted than the local. Advances in canning and government inspections meant that industrial goods were thought of as more sanitary than their homemade competitors. Advertisers told us about the faraway, and much about ourselves, particularly that sweat was a sign of underdevelopment rather than a sign of wholesome labor (see reading 6.12, "Learning to Feel Unclean"). Packaging, as "Packaging" discusses, went from protecting goods to being a publicity agent for marketing them. The exotic is made familiar and desirable.

But what was new about advertising was a new form of value: the trademark. As reading 6.11 discusses, intellectual property in trademarks was a nineteenth-century invention. The notion that a company could buy, sell, and own a name, and that consumers would continue the same loyalty to the name even if the company were owned by completely different people of a different religion, nationality, and expertise, would have been absurd in the past. One trusted the person in charge, the content of the package, not the name on the box. But trust in the impersonal, huge corporation and increasing government regulation gave rise to this conceptual revolution.

Part of the reason for trust in trademarks is the implicit assumption that if a company is large enough to advertise it must be good enough to have a valuable product. This is an extension of the Social Darwinist notion of "survival of the fittest." Those companies or products that succeed are those that are the best. However, in industry the triumph of one standard, be it the gauge of railroad track, the sort of video system, or the computer system, has not been dictated so much by the choice that in any objective sense is the best. The railroad gauge that was chosen for railroad worldwide (see reading 6.14) was too narrow to support large, fast trains. But it was the first gauge. Its success meant others had to adapt their tracks and their locomotives to the narrower gauge. The same was true for the typewriter keyboard (reading 6.15). Often it is a case of survival of the first and the company with the largest market power.

Just as historically the world economy has not always rewarded the best, neither has it been true that necessity is the mother of invention. Reading 6.15 demonstrates that frequently a very long time transpires between the apparent necessity, say the tin can, and the invention, the can opener. Other less optimal solutions are found. Or a good solution, such as the dishwasher, is invented and few people want to use it. Necessity is not obvious. Invention depends on not just the need and the idea, but the willingness of consumers to apply the idea. Sometimes, as with the vast array of soaps, deodorants, mouthwashes and the like that have become common in the last 150 years, the new necessity succeeds so well that we can't imagine that the people didn't always feel the need. But in fact advertisers, scientists, missionaries ("cleanliness is next to godliness"), governments, and educators did change our notions of personal hygiene. And behind that lay an even deeper change: a change in whom we relied on for information about ourselves. Ads told people that they had bad breath, body odor, and other ills that might not make them sick, but would cause them to lose jobs, husbands, and so on; and that their friends and loved ones could not be counted on to tell them these unpleasant truths. Fortunately advertisers and impartial, anonymous experts would inform them of their real needs.

More recently, postwar campaigns for Coca-Cola promoted another shift in reference groups, convincing millions of European youth that the people they wanted to imitate were not their immediate peers, but healthy, Coke-drinking Americans, especially GIs. When parents complained that if their children drank Coke rather than beer or wine they would be diluting their Belgian or French heritage, Coke pled no contest—and reaped the youth market with a strategy repeated endlessly since then. Today, millions who will never visit New York, Paris, or Tokyo nonetheless "need" the goods that would make them fit in there—or in some version of "there" that they imagine with the help of mass media.

Finally, it is worth remembering that the expansion of world trade and the process of commodification rests on an anthropocentric view of the world. As goods became commodities, humans increasingly came to believe that the world existed to satisfy human needs and wants. All efforts were bent toward turning nature into "natural resources" or "factors of production" and making these useful and profitable for people. As a result, wondrous worlds, such as Brazil's Atlantic Forest (reading 4.1), were cut down to leave barren, denuded hills. Other historically remote places such as Andorra, tucked away in the Pyrenees Mountains, became important players in the world economy, even without an air- or seaport because the Internet erased the barriers geography had erected. Clearly, the world economy that trade created is a complex social phenomenon that did not always maximize benefits or conform to the edicts of neoclassical economics or even follow what many would call common sense.

6.1 Silver Lining

In 1905 Mexico switched from the silver standard to the gold standard. This apparently unremarkable event represented, in fact, the funeral of one of the world's oldest, most esteemed, and storied currencies, the Spanish silver peso.

The world 500 years ago had little species currency. Most exchanges were barters. Into that older world came the wealth of the New World. The gold and, later, silver that crossed the Atlantic on Spanish galleons vastly increased the medium of exchange and stimulated European commerce. They also helped spark a price revolution in Europe that facilitated the accumulation of wealth in the Northern European countries and launched the industrial revolution.

After the Spanish melted down Incan and Aztec golden images, masks, and jewelry, and after alluvial deposits of gold panned out, silver replaced gold. In the sixteenth century, Peruvian silver—extracted from the Potosí mountain of silver—dominated global exchange.

By the seventeenth century, however, Mexico's peso became the world's currency, capturing the world's imagination as it attempted to slake the thirst for silver. The peso lured thousands of Caribbean pirates and helped finance some of the largest armies Europe had ever mounted. To protect the peso's passage to Europe, the Spanish built the world's largest navy and the most extensive system of fortresses anywhere.

And, while the peso bound the Americas to Europe, it strengthened European links to Asia as well. Europeans, with their foul cuisine and coarse clothes, were desperate for Asian spices and silks. But Europeans owned little that Asian peoples valued. Except silver. Silver provided the means to pay for the Oriental trade, for it was highly prized in the East. Indeed, the Mexican peso, coveted for its purity of silver and consistent weight, was circulated widely in China, India, and the Philippines, often serving as the local currency. Although there were several devaluations of the peso's silver content in the eighteenth century, it remained throughout most of the world the dominant currency, playing much the same role that the dollar does today.

Nothing lasts. The peso's decline came in the nineteenth century when other nations followed the yellow brick road to the gold standard. The British were first: In 1821 the pound sterling (based on sterling silver) went to gold. As the British became the world's dominant commercial power and London the world's financial center, the gold pound slowly became the preeminent currency.

The adoption of the gold standard—and the demise of silver—was made easier by great gold rushes in California and Australia in the 1840s and 1850s. The abundance of specie sparked an unprecedented boom in world trade between 1848 and 1873. Later in the century, finds in South Africa, Alaska, and the Yukon—as well as the adoption of the cyanide process that made the recovery of gold from low-grade ores viable—augmented the gold supply. By the beginning of the twentieth century more gold was being produced each year than had been mined in the entire period between 1493 and 1600.

Not everyone was pleased. Several nations worked to forge an international bimetallist agreement. Napoleon III wanted the agreement based on the French franc, hoping to seize through diplomacy the supremacy the pound won through commerce. The United States sought to defend its own silver miners who began producing enormous amounts from the Comstock Lode in Nevada and the Rocky Mountain strikes after the 1870s. The United States hoped that a stable silver coin would enable it to wrest away some of the Asian trade.

But the British were unwilling to don Dorothy's silver slippers. (Samuel Goldwyn painted them ruby red for Technicolor appeal). London's financial district remained firmly goldbug; no international bimetallist agreement was reached.

Eventually the mountain came to Mohammed. With the growth of international banking and commerce, it became clear that a single, stable monetary standard was necessary. The Germans were the first to capitulate, taking French gold in reparations after the German victory in the Franco-Prussian War in 1871; Germany was soon on the gold standard. The United States and other European powers quickly followed suit.

The result was a dramatic drop in demand for silver and for the peso at precisely the time Mexico and the United States were employing more sophisticated techniques to exploit rich new veins. Silver prices dropped by one-half between 1873 and 1900.

The fluctuations in the value of the peso relative to gold caused grave concern among silver's remaining Asian users. Asia's retreat from the peso came when European powers began minting their own gold coins for Oriental commerce. With the accelerated trade and lowered transportation costs between Europe and Asia caused by the opening of the Suez Canal in 1869, Europe was able to pay with goods what it had previously paid with silver. While in 1873 almost half the people in the world still considered the peso legal tender, by 1900 only the Mexicans and the Chinese still recognized it.

The paradox of a backward, dependent country producing one of the world's premier currencies was solved in 1905. Mexican monetary reform that year was part of a larger effort by the United States to convince Mexico and China to join the newly won U.S. colonies of Cuba, Hawaii, Panama, Puerto Rico, and the Philippines in a currency based on the dollar. In return for accepting the gold dollar as the basis of value for the peso, Mexico would receive U.S. aid in propping up the international commodity price of silver. Mexico agreed. The silver peso died a quiet death.

6.2 Currency over Country?

Most of the European Community has agreed to a common currency, the Euro, which had its debut in 1999. By 2003, pesos, francs, and marks had become things of the past. This sort of a union is unprecedented. In the past only imperial states were able to impose their currencies; major sovereign nations have rarely agreed to submit to another's currency. Even if they do, they tend to rename the currency—for example, in Panama where the dollar is legal tender, they have renamed it the balboa. Of course, the unification of European currencies is not yet complete—and it might never be, particularly if history is any guide.

The growth of the world economy and international trade, as well as the intensification of markets, has created ever greater monetarization and homogenization. Before the nineteenth century, most parts of the world usually bartered. To the extent that there were any media of exchange, they often used natural products, such as sea shells, cocoa beans, jaguar skins, or man-made products with some utility, such as blankets or soap. Even Europe was slow to develop full monetarization. Money was simply not a part of most people's lives.

The growth of the world economy, transportation, and communication in the nineteenth century brought money into far wider use. For the first time, nations considered currency integration. The Enlightenment's expansion of scientific thought led to demands for universal standards. This was the era of the creation of the meter and the gram, of international law and time zones, and other conventions such as postal service and treatment of war participants. The nineteenth century also saw the first efforts at creating a pan-European currency. Napoleon III, anxious to reclaim the glory of his uncle, tried to tie other European money to the franc (a new currency created only under the French Revolution). Napoleon III argued that the reform would make monetary systems rational and facilitate exchanges. The British refused to change the value of the pound sterling to be an even multiple of the franc and the dollar, however. They recognized that behind the appearance of scientific rationality lay the true French goal of substituting Paris for London as the international center of finance. The French turned to their southern neighbors instead and created the Latin League in which all propped up each other's currencies.

All century long there were efforts to stabilize the value of silver relative to gold and fix the relationship between the largest national currencies. This also failed largely due to English intransigence.

The last major effort at a hemispheric currency in the nineteenth century was the Pan American Conference of 1889, which proclaimed the need for an American silver dollar based on the U.S. dollar and the Mexican peso. The silver issue, heatedly debated in the United States at the time, had strong advocates in both parties. Indeed, the year of the monetary conference Republicans passed the Sherman Silver-Purchase Act, which required that the U.S. government purchase essentially the entire U.S. production of silver and coin it. Virtually every Latin American country at the time was on silver or, as with Argentina and Brazil, on inconvertible paper currency hypothetically based on gold. A continental coin was certainly possible.

Republicans hoped a silver coin would allow New York to replace London as the financial center of the Americas. All Latin American delegates enthusiastically endorsed the idea of a common coin, as did one of the U.S. delegates, and the conference passed it.

The next year a Pan American Conference took place in Washington, DC, to work out the details. Some countries such as Argentina and Uruguay, which borrowed and sold overwhelmingly in Britain, were reluctant to abandon gold.

But the scheme's death throes began when the Democrat goldbug Grover Cleveland was elected U.S. president. When confronted by a run on U.S. currency and a shortage of gold in the 1893 depression, he canceled the Sherman Act, avowing that cheap silver currency was the cause of the financial disruption. He turned to London to borrow gold, essentially jettisoning any chance of turning New York into the pan-American financial center. The international price of silver collapsed during the depression, sealing the doom of a continental silver coin. The United States did coin silver export dollars for trade with its colony in the Philippines and the Orient, but refused to participate in a pan-American coin. Only time will tell if nations have progressed sufficiently past internecine jealousies and the temptation to blame currencies for economic crises in order to allow Europe to maintain and expand what neither Europe nor the Americas could bring off in the nineteenth century.

6.3 Weighing the World: The Metric Revolution

When a French traveler visiting the Soviet Union shortly after World War I lavished praise on the universal applications and benefits of the meter, his Russian hosts laughed in disbelief at the foreigner's stupidity: "As if the centimeter could measure our Russian roads!" This would be as much folly as making Russian vodka out of French grain.

We don't understand the Russians' reaction. Today we think of weights and measurements—if we think of them at all—as something natural and neutral. They are simply categories used to facilitate trade and calculations with no inherent values or ideology of their own. Yet our notion of weights and measures would have been extremely alien and troubling not only to those dumbfounded Russians but to most people throughout time. Measurements are the result of historic processes, social struggles, and conceptual revolutions.

Most measures have been anthropomorphic. People measured with their arms (the fathom), their hands (span), their feet (feet), and their elbows (the el). They also measured according to their strength, sight, or hearing. Nomads in the Sahara Desert, to whom the distance to the next oasis was a matter of life or death, used categories such as a stick's throw, a bowshot, the distance one could see from level ground, and how far one could see from a camel's back. Latvians used the distance one could hear a bull bellow.

Agricultural peoples measured their land by its usefulness, not abstract dimensions. In France the *argent* was the area that one man with two oxen could plow in a day. This of course would vary according to terrain, rocks, and trees. Many other measures similarly were scaled to the amount of human labor needed to prepare land for harvest. In precapitalist societies with no functioning land market, this was the relevant calculation.

Productivity figured in places ranging from Brazil and Colombia to France and Italy to Japan. A unit of land was often determined by the amount of seed it produced. Thus the same unit might cover very different dimensions of territory and indeed might vary from year to year. For subsistence farmers, the size of the harvest was a much more important statistic than the dimensions of land worked.

These measures, even sometimes when they had the same name, varied tremendously in size. One department of France had nine different sizes of *argent;* the largest was five times the size of the smallest.

The use of very many different weights and measures resulted in good part from small, compartmentalized economies with little intercourse and strong senses of tradition. Local measures were the product of local feuds and struggles, were understood locally, and helped people define who they were and who was the "other." Change was considered subversive; new measures were seen as means of cheating producers or consumers who were not familiar with them. Populations were barely numerate and did not even all use the same numerical system. In the early modern world systems based on twenty (the number of toes and fingers) were more common than systems based on ten. Anything more than simple division was mysterious. Thus translating from one measure to another was extremely difficult and suspect.

The plethora of measuring systems was not simply a result of folk wisdom (or ignorance), however. For thousands of years weights and measures were seen as attributes of justice and sovereignty. Authority meant the power to define the scales. When the definer of measures was also the tax collector and lender, abuse often followed. In prerevolutionary China there were two *dou* that differed by over a third. Officials often used the larger to collect peasant dues and the smaller when lending grain. Under feudalism each lord set his own standards and his court judged them. This complexity was compounded in places such as Silesia, where in addition to the multitude of small seignorial potentates, there were church and municipal authorities, each with their own weights and measures.

The definition of measures sometimes varied intentionally to hide price differences. Great changes in price were unsettling for precapitalist peoples to whom difference might mean the difference between life and death. Often they responded not by going to a different seller, but by revolting. To avoid this, merchants often varied the measures. In pre-metric Europe an apothecary's pound was minuscule, the spice merchant used a larger pound, and the butcher a larger one yet. In the Piedmont of Italy in 1826 merchants agreed on using the *libra*. However, for sugar, coffee, and groceries it weighed 12 Milanese ounces, for candles 14 ounces, good quality meat and cheese used 32 ounces. Bread, the most important and politically charged food in early modern Europe, was sold by the loaf. The price remained the same, but like today's candy bars, the size of the loaf varied substantially, depending on the price of grain. As the Polish historian Witold Kula insightfully observed: "It is reasonable to look upon the whole process, within limits, as a safety-valve or a buffer against social reaction to market developments."

The first three major efforts to unify measures were by-products of attempts by the Greeks, Romans, and Charlemagne to spread and solidify their empires. The need to expand tax collection drove these attempts. But since they did not reflect or create any revolution in local perceptions, they largely failed.

Success only came at the end of the eighteenth century when French revolutionaries created and spread the metric system. Based on impersonal and unvarying astronomical calculations (the meter is one ten-millionth of the distance along a meridian from the equator to the pole) rather than local anthropomorphic usages, the meter required a revolution in thought: acceptance of the notion that all people are equal before the law, that is, that the lawgiver or measurer not be arbitrary; and development of the process of commodification. As goods became produced for a distant market they lost the distinctiveness bestowed by the individual producer or consumer, becoming mass products with common attributes that could be measured.

As goods became commodities and their attributes were abstracted in measurable quantities, they became fungible, commensurate. This protected peasants from arbitrary local officials or merchants but destroyed the business of many international traders. Only the traders had been able to understand the plethora of local weights and measures and had been able to translate between them. Once their skills were no longer needed, their pivotal position was taken over by large-scale importers in the biggest consuming markets. Measures ceased symbolizing local history and traditions, struggles and victories, and became the mundane boxes and scales we think so little about today.

6.4 Growing Global: International Grain Markets

What forces create a world market for a commodity?

Transporting it more efficiently might help, enough so that, say, iron from Minnesota could compete in Europe with the stuff from Sweden. Or governments could have a change of heart and reverse protectionist policies that inflate its price. But would-be global commodity barons may discover that another kind of barrier is harder to eliminate: indifferent or hostile consumer tastes—tastes that make people think, for instance, that Indian rice and Chinese rice are entirely different commodities.

Of course, "grain" has a cold, biological definition as well—a set of starchy crops that share certain nutritional characteristics. And contemporary Americans might not blink if asked to substitute corn for wheat in their diets. But try telling that to eighteenth-century Neapolitans, who in 1770 rioted against attempts to feed them potatoes—a "slave food" in their eyes—even during a famine.

Looking back, creating a global market for the world's most basic commodity group—grain—involved convincing millions of people that foods often basic to their cultural identities were interchangeable with the "weird" stuff eaten by foreigners—a task that proved to be particularly challenging. For as long as such strident feelings were widespread, there could be no commonality among the prices of different grains, and thus, no world market in "grain."

For a world market in "grain" to come into being, then, certain events had to take place: first, the emergence of unified markets in wheat—the great staple of the Atlantic world—and rice, the main grain of the Pacific and Indian Ocean worlds; second, people from all three regions had to alternate their consumption from rice to wheat and vice versa, depending on price. None of these conditions existed in 1840, yet all of them existed by 1900.

The emergence of an Atlantic wheat market is the simplest and best-known story: Mid-nineteenth-century industrializing Europe was experiencing soaring demand for wheat, demand that fueled the settlement of the American Great Plains. Barges plying the newly constructed Erie Canal passed the grain to trains, which then unloaded in New York City; and advances in ocean shipping cut the cost of taking wheat across the Atlantic by two-thirds in thirty years.

But even the creation of "wheat" was tricky—and in part accidental. When grain moved by boat from the Midwest to Manhattan, it made the journey in the same sacks in which it left the farm. It reached New York Harbor still identified as farmer Jones's or Smith's wheat, and still belonged to that farmer; the middlemen up to this point were commissions agents. New York traders would sample the wheat, appraise it, and only then would they buy it from the farmer. Jones and Smith might get very different prices, depending on quality of their wheat; no set price for "wheat" as such existed.

Railroads changed all that. Because it was very expensive to keep a train sitting under a full head of steam while it was being loaded or unloaded, the process needed to be completed quickly. Thus, before long, shippers had made the switch from hauling individual sacks to using grain elevators that opened and released a torrent of grain into a boxcar. But this meant that Jones's and Smith's wheat were hopelessly intermixed in the elevator. Thus, grain had to be sold by the time it reached the railhead, and one farm's output became interchangeable with that of another.

While wheat continued to be graded, it was now divided into just a few classes, within which one load was assumed to be exactly the same as another. "Wheat" was born; and because now a ton of this year's "number 2 spring wheat" was also interchangeable with a ton of next year's, wheat futures trading, options, and the Chicago Board of Trade were born.

The story of rice is more complex. Because it stores and ships better than wheat, it had been traded across long distances for centuries: the rice trade along the 1,000–plus miles of China's Yangtze River, for instance, dwarfed the famous trade in grain from Eastern to Western Europe. But the rice tide flowed within rigid cultural boundaries, because people had strong preferences for the particular kind of rice they were used to. Most rice exports, in fact, were built around those preferences and followed human migrations. India's Kaveri Delta sent rice to the tea plantations of Sri Lanka, many of whose workers were also from the delta; labor contractors who supplied Chinese workers for the tobacco plantations of Sumatra also imported the kind of rice those workers were used to.

So, although the mid-nineteenth century saw a huge boom in international rice trading—fueled by the growth of cash crop plantations in Southeast Asia and the creation of "rice bowls" for these plantation workers in the recently drained Mekong (Vietnam), Irawaddy (Burma), and Chaophrya (Thailand) river deltas—no one rice market existed.

But as more and more rice was used as a source of industrial starches—mostly in continental Europe—a consumer emerged who would "eat" rice based on price alone. Now, when a bad harvest in South China raised prices in Vietnam (which produced a similar variety of rice), European purchasers would abandon Saigon and buy more Burmese rice, raising its price. Cantonese still might not touch the rice that Sinhalese preferred, but now, price swings affected what consumers paid, regardless of where the commodity was originally cultivated. And before long, rice futures traded in Singapore much as wheat futures did in Chicago.

To achieve a truly global grain market, that vital connection between rice and wheat had to be made—and that link was forged in India. Though we tend to forget it today, nineteenth-century India was one of the world's major grain exporters. This reflected both a genuine surplus and British colonial policies that promoted exports at the expense of peasant and working-class consumption. Indeed, India exported both rice and wheat and consumed both. Millions of Indians were accustomed to a cuisine that used both grains—and were too poor not to base their purchasing decisions on price. Thus, when world rice prices rose in the late nineteenth century, Indian exporters responded. And since India's internal rice prices rose, too, consumers shifted to wheat. That meant less Indian wheat made its way to London—and farmers in Kansas faced that much less competition.

For the first time, a worldwide market existed in the most basic of commodities, and for the first time—like it or not—the impact of harvests in Saskatchewan was felt in Sichuan, no matter what the local population grew, or ate.

6.5 How Time Got That Way

You have no doubt sometimes sat in a fancy restaurant and looked at the clocks on the wall and noted that it was midnight in New York, five o'clock in London, six o'clock in Paris, and the next day in Tokyo. This seems so normal, so logical that we accept it as a part of nature, like the sunset or dawn.

But standard time is far from part of nature. Even today parts of the world do not subscribe to it. All of China is on Beijing time. So when the radio announces dawn and calisthenics in the early morning light in Beijing, people in the west, say in Urumqi, are waking in the pitch black.

Until the last quarter of the nineteenth century, there were neither standard time zones nor time imperialism of the capital in most parts of the world. Rather, time was local. Clocks were set to the sun by inexact measurement. Since travel was on foot or horseback, distances were small and travel infrequent. There were no regional radio or television broadcasts. It did not really matter that time was off by fifteen minutes in a neighboring town. The railroad changed all that.

With the railroad, travel and freight shipments became faster and integration over larger spaces became important. As rail companies grew in the 1840s and 1850s they suffered from the multitude of time zones. How could one coordinate timetables, ensure that trains were on the sidings at the proper time, provision them if every town was on its own time? The problem was clear but the solution difficult. Each town felt its time was the proper one, for it was based on the sun at noon in that town. That is, each town was in a sense the center of the universe for the determination of the hour. How could most towns submit to someone else's hour? This was a grave question of civic pride.

The answer was that instead of attempting to convince local leaders to agree on specified times, the railroads struck up agreements between themselves. Business, rather than science or politics, initially set the clocks to the same time. Towns on the same rail line adjusted to the time of their railroad. But in hub cities this created more confusion than clarity. For instance, at Brazil's busiest train depot in São Paulo, three clocks were set to three different times: one clock for the trains arriving from Rio de Janeiro, one for those from the interior of the state, and a third for those from the port of Santos. In the United States the chaos could be even greater. The Buffalo station had three clocks on different times and Pittsburgh had six!

England, the first in building railroads, was also the first to create standard railroad time in 1842, basing it on Greenwich time. The United States, with its vast distances was slower. There were still some 300 different local time zones in 1870 and 80 different railroad times. As the country's westward expansion stimulated more long-distance traffic, routes crossed more time zones. The merger movements of the 1870s and 1880s created ever larger networks, which made coordination imperative—and possible. November 18, 1883, was called the "day of two noons," because at noon the clocks in the eastern part of each zone were set back to finally create a national standard railway time. The government moved more slowly. It took six years for the country to be divided into four time zones, and only in 1918 was standard time legally recognized.

But this does not explain how Paris or Tokyo came to agree to similar arrangements. Clearly the railroad did not extend over such vast areas. Political arrangements would have to be made, and they floundered for decades on the shoals of nationalism. The size of the world was known, longitudes were generally accepted. So dividing the world into twenty-four time zones was an easy task. The ticklish part came in deciding where the acceptable correct time should be housed. In a sense the disagreement was over what point should be the standard for the rest of the world. The French, who had made many efforts in the nineteenth century to standardize weights and measures—the meter and the kilo were their most notable successes—naturally wanted Paris to be the center of the world. The British, at the time the most powerful nation in the world—wanted England, specifically Greenwich. Throughout the nineteenth and twentieth centuries a number of international meetings were held to sort this out. But several countries, chiefly France and Brazil, refused to join until just before World War I.

This led to some serious problems in those countries. In Brazil, a study done around World War I discovered that every state capital had a different time, even though they should almost all have been within the same time zone. The differences were often minute. Niteroi, the capital of Rio de Janeiro state, differed from Rio de Janeiro city, ten miles across Guanabara Bay, by only one minute. In other cases, the differences were greater. A candidate for federal deputy led a crowd of supporters into the remote district in the interior where he was candidate only to discover the polls closed because the district was three hours ahead of the national capital. This also had serious repercussions in business as the national economy became increasingly tied to the world economy.

Of course we know that these problems were eventually hammered out. The ease with which this was done in the nineteenth century was a testimony not only to rationalism, but also to imperialism. The European powers were able to convince Asian and African leaders to accept standard time, even though their relatively minimal integration into international commerce and transport did not necessitate it, because so many of the leaders were themselves colonial governors. Between 1870 and 1914 one-quarter of the globe fell to European and North American powers. These powers saw an advantage in standard time and imposed it upon the rest of the world. It took a long time for these decisions made in fancy European drawing rooms to filter down to the people in villages in central Africa or the highlands of the Andes. But slowly, as the world economy reached into isolated corners of the world, they were brought into standard time. We all know that time is money. We are less aware that time is a historical invention of businessmen.

6.6 The Ghost of Maximilian

The future appeared as bright as the blue skies over Veracruz as French soldiers helped unload Emperor Maximilian von Habsburg's ornate gilded coach that was supposed to carry him to a triumphal welcome in Mexico City. European royalty at the helm of state would surely end the fratricide that had rent and impoverished this once wealthy American colony and restore its former prosperity. Napoleon III, Maximilian's sponsor and protector, hoped to restore the glory of the House of Bonaparte with this foothold in the Americas. To finance this imperialist adventure, the Habsburg emperor tripled Mexico's already onerous foreign debt by issuing in 1864 and 1865 bonds worth 534 million francs. Known as the *petits bleus* (little blues), the bonds represented the first large-scale French investment in independent Latin America. They were supposed to be only the first step in ever closer Franco-Latin American economic relations. Instead, the petits bleus provoked forty years of bad feelings and bad business.

When Maximilian's dream of conquest ended before a firing squadron on a lonely hill in Querétaro, the bonds' story should also have ended. The government of the victor, Beníto Juárez, refused to repay bonds that were used to finance a war *against* him that had claimed perhaps one hundred thousand Mexican lives. However, thirteen years passed before France quit her claims for repayment and resumed normal relations.

But the saga had not yet ended. A consortium of French speculators purchased a majority of the radically discounted outstanding bonds. They mounted a vigorous press campaign in Paris and purchased the alliance of some deputies in Parliament to prevent official quotations of Mexican bonds on the Paris stock market.

The Mexican government responded by offering French companies privileged concessions in Mexico for ports and railroads with tax reductions, the purchase of French weapons and capital goods, and duty reductions on other Mexican imports from France, if Mexican access to the Parisian stock market was opened. These favors, worth substantially more than was supposedly owed on the little blue bonds, were offered to some of the richest and most powerful corporate leaders in France.

There is no way that this campaign by a handful of speculators should have succeeded in keeping Mexican issues off of the Parisian Bourse. France's most influential financial houses such as the Rothschilds and Paribas had substantial interests in Mexico and sought more. Major manufacturers and arms producers wanted access to the market that the goodwill of the Mexican government promised. The Panama Canal scandal of the early 1890s and the Dreyfus Affair at the end of the decade had enraged sentiment against speculators and Jews. (Apparently the holders of the petits bleus were Jewish.) Moreover, French hatred of Germans was high. Without official quotations on the Paris Bourse, Mexican bonds were being negotiated in Germany and then sold in the French secondary market. The ultimate capital was French, but the commissions were mostly earned by Germans.

Yet the French government turned down appeals by Mexico in 1898 and again in 1901. Either repay the petits bleus or no official quotation. As a result, major Mexican loans were floated by German banks rather than French.

The surprising willingness of the French government to abandon its haute bourgeoisie in favor of stock speculators was probably related to politics more than economics. The weak French government was being battered from Socialists on the left and monarchists and Bonapartists on the right. To win political favor by appealing to French chauvinism, they embarked on a policy of imperialism in Africa. Support for colonizing northern Africa would be jeopardized by failure to support the bondholders from another imperial era—Napoleon III's—in another continent—America. Hence the symbolic importance of Maximilian's bonds for early twentieth-century French colonialism caused the French state to sacrifice the interests of major French manufacturers and exporters.

Only in 1904 was the issue finally put to rest. The Paris stock market was officially open to Mexican issues because the petits bleus were paid off—by American house of Speyer, using German and French capital. Maximilian's ghost was finally exorcised from international financial markets to be replaced by Yankees and a new form of imperialism.

6.7 How the United States Joined the Big Leagues

Today it seems natural to think of the United States as a major player in international capital markets. Until the 1980s the United States was the world's largest capital exporter. But the United States only began exporting capital on a large scale in the twentieth century. In the nineteenth century, and even as late as 1914, the United States ran by far the world's largest trade deficit—partly because the country was the world's largest recipient of foreign investment.

Historians have typically regarded World War I as the turning point—the watershed moment when American financing of the Allied war effort converted the United States for the first time into a creditor nation. But even before the war, Yankee capitalists had begun asserting their position abroad.

The first concerted foreign effort was in Mexico. Indeed, Mexico became something of a laboratory for new forms of industrial combinations and international agreements. Mexico had long been important to the United States, of course. Her silver mines had captured the imagination of Americans since the Mexican peso was legal species in America until 1857.

But despite the fact that the United States gained half of Mexico's territory through the Texas and Mexican-American wars of the 1830s and 1840s, investment was slow to migrate south. British capital far outweighed American gold as late as 1900. Aside from a few large railroad lines, fairly small, individual direct investments predominated.

All this changed radically after the Great Depression of the 1890s, when some of America's most prominent moguls, men who rarely invested abroad, began investing in Mexico. American banks that had restricted credit during the depression now eagerly looked for borrowers, and found them in the men restructuring the U.S. economy. The best known result of abundant liquidity was the Great Merger Movement. Financiers such as J.P. Morgan took advantage of the concurrence of available capital and companies still wobbly from the depression to create the largest corporations the United States had ever known. The merger that created the $1.4 billion United States Steel still ranks, relative to the size of the economy, as one of the largest ever.

The same financiers and stock raiders reshaping American corporations looked to Mexico. J.P. Morgan, Jacob Schiff of Kuhn, Loeb and Co., James Speyer, William Rockefeller, E.H. Harriman, and the Guggenheim family took advantage of close—often familial—ties to British and German capital markets and control over the burgeoning U.S. capital markets to raise finance over industry. Their Mexican projects were intimate parts of international plans they began laying. E.H. Harriman was planning a rail and ship network that would link the United States to South America and Asia. He attempted to gain control of most of Mexico's railroads with this in mind. William Rockefeller, who cooperated with Harriman on several projects, sought to include Mexico in his petroleum and copper empire by controlling transportation and production in the mineral-rich northern part of Mexico. He took over Mexico's largest copper mine and bought options on vast oil fields. The Guggenheims' ASARCO, which soon came to refine most of the world's silver and was a major producer of lead and copper as well, dominated Mexican mineral refining.

Because of the south-of-the-border ambitions of these plutocrats, American investments grew fourfold in the fifteen years before World War I, far outstripping the foreign investments of all other foreign countries combined. By 1914, $1 billion of U.S. capital was invested in Mexico—half of all American foreign investment worldwide. But Mexico was important not only because of the flow of direct investments and the creation of incipient multinational corporations there. The participation of American financiers in Mexico also transformed the role of the United States in international capital markets. For the first time, Wall Street bankers were applying European funds abroad and voting their proxies. The houses of Speyer and Kuhn, Loeb and Co. used continental and American funds to buy a controlling interest in Mexico's major railroads. Speyer then founded in Mexico one of the first American-dominated banks abroad. The two merchant banking houses joined with other major financiers in 1904 to lend $40 million to the Mexican government, one of the first foreign loans ever denominated in dollars. Quickly subscribed in Europe, it was the first American bond issue ever floated in Paris. One newspaper noted that the loan "marks an epoch in international finance." Four years later, Speyer's consortium issued $500 million in bonds for the Mexican National Railways, the largest bond issue in U.S. history until the 1920s.

The massive infusion of American-controlled capital brought with it U.S. economic hegemony. It was the first area of major importance that the United States was able to wrest away from the great powers. England, Germany, and France all had substantial investments in Mexico. But by 1910 they had to recognize that, in the words of the German minister, the Americans had come to "exercise a veritable protectorate." Yankees dominated such key sectors as mining and railroads, and came to own fully one-fifth of Mexico's territory. American advisers shaped Mexican monetary, banking, and railroad reforms. Even culturally Mexico was becoming Americanized, as beer began to replace tequila and baseball and boxing competed with bullfighting.

Within a few years of 1900, the Germans and the French acknowledged that they had to accept a subordinate position in Mexico, under the shadow of American economic and political might. British investors placed great sums in Mexico through American financiers, as New York slowly began challenging London as an international financial center. Europeans had long been worried about the potential of the fledgling North American republic and its threat to their influence. In Mexico after the turn of the century, this potential first was realized. The German minister warned: "The American Danger is not a specter but a reality."

6.8 Banking on Asia

Years of political and military conflict have ended with one power bloc's victory; the losers, governed by former dissidents, are on the brink of economic collapse. Impoverished countries elsewhere worry that rebuilding Europe, and funding the chief victor's deficits, will make it harder than ever for them to get capital. And in one country that still has huge amounts of capital to export—a country that stayed on the sidelines for most of the military struggle—a high economic official immediately circulates a plan to turn his nation's overwhelming financial power into political influence and to take markets away from its former allies.

This is not the plot of an early 1990s paranoid best-seller about Japanese ambitions. The struggle was World War I; the debt-plagued victor, Great Britain; the secret document a December 1918 memo from a U.S. Commerce Department official. And as Washington set out to harness American financial power to reshape the world, officials were in for a shock. The American banks they were counting on had become "international" in more ways than one. Having created new ways of working with their counterparts in London, Paris, and elsewhere to finance the war, keep trade moving, and keep financially shaky governments (especially China's) afloat, most of Wall Street had little interest in promoting a particularly "American" agenda. Wall Street's unwillingness to rock the boat was a source of stability and a particularly great relief for cash-short empire-builders in London and Tokyo; it was a disappointment to others, such as Chinese liberals, who had hoped for a "peace dividend," including infusions of both American cash and supposed American ideals.

Even before peace arrived, London and Washington clashed over virtually every aspect of the postwar financial order, including how to finance Germany's indemnity and how to reschedule U.S. loans to the other allies. But nobody expected the United States to become the dominant lender in Europe itself; what officials in Washington dreamed of was the influence that a dominant financial role would give the United States in Asia and Latin America. Some American bankers, such as Frank Vanderlip (CEO of National City Bank, today's Citicorp), shared this goal and sought a business-government partnership to pursue it; some Americans with strong interests in exports, such as the shipping and timber magnate Robert Dollar, were also enthusiastic. (For Dollar, who grew rich selling Oregon lumber in Asia, the vision was literally carved in stone: his corporate headquarters featured bas-reliefs of "the world's three great harbors"—New York, San Francisco, and Shanghai.) But as they soon discovered, most of Wall Street was not.

The pilot vehicle for America's new financial diplomacy was a financial consortium formed in 1916 and appropriately named the American International Corporation, exclusively dedicated to investing in less developed countries. The idea for AIC was jointly hatched by Vanderlip and the U.S. ambassador to China, Paul Reinsch, while its board included the names synonymous with American economic might: Rockefeller, DuPont, Morgan, and others. Its first efforts were directed at China and were as much political as economic. The scarcity of European loans—and European political influence—after 1914 had created a vacuum into which the Japanese had moved expeditiously. Before long, Chinese politicians, looking for a counterweight, began soliciting U.S. involvement in numerous projects, including a few that had previously been off-limits to all foreigners. By late 1916, AIC had signed agreements for a series of flood-control projects in Shandong (where Japan had seized control of a former German sphere of influence), Jiangsu (a somewhat less formal British sphere), and elsewhere, which would use American contractors only; plans were under way for a U.S.-built and -financed railroad in Manchuria (where a standoff between Russian and Japanese interests had turned into Japanese dominance); and there were discussions of reorganizing all of China's railways with U.S. loans, engineers, and rolling stock. The terms on the flood-control projects were so favorable to AIC that Reinsch was moved to wonder whether they were "too severe for China." European diplomats and businessmen feared that American loans would soon secure control of everything from China's iron deposits to its politics.

But by 1920 all of these projects had collapsed; no work beyond surveying was ever done on any of them. And in the process, the diplomats and financiers behind AIC discovered that they had sharply divergent ideas about how "dollar diplomacy" should work.

The trouble began when Japan lodged a diplomatic protest against the Shandong project, claiming a right of first refusal on all such ventures as successors to Germany's privileges in the area. Stand firm, the State Department told AIC; Japan's protest was purely formal. Besides, Japan itself wanted American loans for development at home (particularly for building electric power and other utilities) and wanted American investment in its Chinese projects as long as management remained Japanese (a development strategy that some Japanese cabinet members nicknamed Japanese brains and American money); thus, it was unlikely to press the point. But the interdependence that state saw as a source of American muscle looked different to many of the bankers involved in AIC: since Japan was a much bigger market for them than China, they were unwilling to offend their Japanese counterparts. Instead, AIC promptly offered 41 percent of the project's financing to the Industrial Bank of Japan, a similar share of the contracting, and a share of the loan's political prerogatives (supervisory rights over Chinese water control officials, and the right to stop remittance of certain local revenues to the national government if loan payments fell behind). For Washington—and Beijing—this partnership worsened the political situation they had hoped it would ease. Though many of the Chinese signatories were so desperate to improve flood control that they continued to support the project, both Washington and Beijing cooled, and the project soon collapsed amid recriminations; so did the dikes that it had been supposed to repair.

The same sort of failure, on a grander scale, soon engulfed AIC's participation in loans to the Chinese central government. Loans to China had long been handled by an international consortium led by Britain's Hong Kong and Shanghai Bank; the United States had sometimes participated and sometimes preferred to play a lone hand. At the end of World War I, the United States returned to the consortium, assuming that as the largest contributor of capital, it would play the leading role in shaping the loans' conditions. But the managing agent for AIC's participation—J.P. Morgan partner Thomas Lamont—had other ideas. The House of Morgan's huge stake in Great Britain (they were by far the largest holders of British war bonds, for instance), their close cooperative relations with numerous other European banks, and their high hopes for expanded activities in Japan made them unsympathetic to Washington's plans to replace the various powers' spheres of influence with one China open to free trade, American investment, and Wilsonian liberalism; their idea of financial internationalism was one in which cross-cutting trade and investment gave all the major powers an interest in *respecting* each other's special privileges in different corners of the Third World. (Lamont worked out just such a deal for China with Charles Addis of the Hong Kong and Shanghai Bank; they then presented it to their governments as a fait accompli.) Such a collegial imperialism was perhaps a formula to make another World War I less likely, but hardly one for a new economic order. Had they looked south to Mexico, which had provided the dry run for America's rise to financial dominance, the ambitious—and sometimes starry-eyed—diplomats might have seen it coming; once they were bankers to the world, Wall Street's elite became part of a world of bankers—a club whose rules could override borders, governments, and national sentiments.

6.9 Fresher Is Not Better

At Halloween, children are warned about the perils of accepting fruit or foods prepared by neighbors; wrapped or packaged candies are much safer. We have heard this so often that it seems common sense. Yet for anyone living any time before the last century, and even many people still today, the notion would be absurd that a food is safer when prepared in a factory by an anonymous faraway stranger who might well be of a different nationality, race, and religion, than when given out by a neighbor. How is it that we have come to put so much faith in the faraway producer?

For the vast majority of human existence most people ate only what they themselves killed or harvested. When they obtained food from someone else, it was done in face-to-face barter in which one still knew personally the food producer. Foods that came from a longer distance were unusual. They were purchased mostly as raw materials, such as rice and wheat, so one knew the ingredients and processed them with one's own hands. The few food makers, such as bakers, were overseen by guilds to ensure quality. In the age before refrigeration, the nearer the fresher and the fresher the better.

The nineteenth century, with its population boom, transportation revolution, and explosion of international trade, undermined traditional values of freshness. The massive production of food staples such as grains and the shipping of meat allowed an international specialization of labor. Lower prices somewhat ameliorated consumer suspicion of faraway producers, though there were considerable battles over imported food. Home farmers used tariffs to protect agricultural goods and meat producers appealed to concerns over hoof-and-mouth disease to limit international flows.

Technology was partly responsible for the growth of a complex long-distance trade in food. Salting and drying of foods had long been known, but salted food such as beef jerky, while edible, was considered so unpalatable that it was fit only for slaves and cowboys. The nineteenth century saw the art of canning transform food into industrial raw materials suitable for long-distance shipping. The first foods canned by the French inventor Nicholas Appert beginning in 1810 were so overcooked that few sought them. Not surprisingly, soldiers (of similar social standing to cowboys and slaves) were the first consumers of canned goods as they would be later guinea pigs for food concentrates. The U.S. Civil War coupled with improvements in vacuum cooking and the use of tin cans gave birth to important late-nineteenth-century canners such as the H.J. Heinz Company, Campbell's Soup, the Franco-American Company, and Borden.

Refrigeration also played a large role in bringing far-off foods into the kitchen. Ice, of course, had been used for millennia, but before steamers and the railroad it melted too fast for preservation over distance. Commercial refrigerators were widespread in industrialized countries by 1890, but weighing five tons, their usefulness for transporting was limited. Frigidaire and Kelvinator sold the first refrigerators for home use in the United States during World War I, and by 1940 half the households in the country owned mechanical refrigerators. The relationship of freshness, nearness, and recent production changed.

But technology alone did not bring distant foods into our mouths. Even after preservative technology improved, disease and adulteration threatened foods produced by others. The unfettered market was also a dirty market. Factories were more often viewed as slimy, filthy pits as described in Upton Sinclair's *The Jungle* than as shiny, spotless, sanitary laboratories as they sometimes are today. State and then the federal government came to the rescue. Modeled on British laws of the 1880s, U.S. government agencies began policing the production, transportation, and marketing of foodstuffs. The Pure Food and Drug Act of 1906 gave the U.S. Department of Agriculture's seal of approval to industrialized foods. Since U.S. consumers had faith in the scientific authority and honesty of food inspectors, they were willing to buy more and more processed foods.

Urbanization and supermarkets accelerated this trend. People no longer had sufficient land to grow their own food as they moved to the cities. But after the 1950s they had large supermarkets that carried the products of the large canning companies. The local grocer, who prided himself on knowing his customers personally and putting his reputation behind his products, many of which were in bins, not cans, lost ground to the large, impersonal, but cheap supermarkets, easily accessible by car to the country's burgeoning suburban population. Supermarkets made possible a concentration of processed foods by a relatively small group of companies that spent fortunes establishing and trading on brand names. These brands became familiar through advertising.

In the end, the world of two hundred years ago was turned on its head. The far-off became familiar through advertising, while the nearby became unknown. The factory-made, cellophane-wrapped became sanitary, while the handmade became suspect. The seal of government inspectors became more trustworthy than the proximity and reputation of neighbors. And so our children throw away the Halloween cookies and unwrap the candies.

6.10 Packaging

You have been told that you shouldn't judge a book by its cover. It is the contents that counts, not the container. Indeed, containers and wrappings have negative connotations. To "package" a political candidate is to present him or her in an appealing, but dishonest light. The box is often seen as misrepresentative, hiding or distorting the contents and creating an avalanche of waste. Certainly packages fill our dumps.

But packages have played a central role in the creation of long-distance trade and in mass commodity markets. Not just innocuous by-products, packages work integrally in the production process of many goods, serve as haulers in transportation, preserve goods, and pitch products as sales-men. They are closely tied to the rise of brand names, supermarkets, and convenience products.

Although the use of packages has grown enormously in the last one hun-dred years, they have existed in some form for millennia. Nature provides packages to protect life in the form of seeds and fruit. The egg, the orange, the coconut, and the banana all have natural wrappers. Their objective, how-ever, is usually not to attract consumers but rather drive them away until the seeds have reached maturity. Insects and animals are prevented from eating the contents of the plant. But, once the seeds are mature, the cover is sup-posed to encourage consumers to disperse the seeds to improve the species' chance of survival or, in the case of the egg, the package is supposed to be sufficiently brittle for the mature chick to break through.

The first man-made containers were organic, handmade, and custom made for the particular purpose of the moment. Animal skins and woven fibers served to carry and transport goods long before they were market-oriented commodities. Pottery was useful not only for storage, but also for produc-tion. We have evidence of five thousand-year-old wine jars and beer contain-ers found in western Iran that were crucial to the fermenting process. Containers were laborious to make. Requiring substantial effort, they were handicraft achievements that were recycled over and over again. They were some of the most important possessions individuals owned. Craftsmen marked them with their own personal insignia to stamp on their individual creations, and anthropologists and archeologists identify whole cultural groups by the pots they designed.

The nature and role of packages changed with the industrial revolution in the nineteenth century as new materials became popular for packaging. Ma-chines came to make mass production of containers possible, but they also made large-scale production necessary, because the rapidly growing pile of production had to be preserved, stored, and shipped.

In the early nineteenth century, the growth of packaging was more for luxury goods than for necessities. Beautiful, often handblown bottles showed off perfumes, patent medicines, and wines. But the cost of making a large number of bottles and transporting them precluded even a local market for, say, water; the thought of sending Italian Peligrino or French Perrier around the world would have been madness.

Several inventions and innovations in the nineteenth century caused a pack-aging revolution: the ability to mechanically produce mass goods, the rail-road and steamship, which allowed rapid transport of large batches of goods, urbanization, which created a greater commodity-consuming public, and, certainly not least important, the introduction of new techniques and machines to produce glass bottles, tin cans, paper bags, and cardboard boxes. The twentieth century would see the plastic revolution release a flood of different shapes and sizes of containers.

Containers did more than just allow storage and transport of goods. They allowed the packer, who also often was the distributor, to wrestle away the definition of the products' purpose, appeal, and size of serving. Since consumers were buying from strangers and could not see, touch, or smell the goods imprisoned in the bags, cans, and boxes, the predictable quality and healthfulness of packaged goods became extremely important. Brand names were used to make familiar and reliable the strange and remote producer and canner. A result was that an ever larger share of the final sales price went to the processor, packer, transporter, and distributor, and an ever smaller part to the farmer and rancher.

This trend accelerated in the twentieth century with the rise of the supermarket. Consumers purchased foods that were increasingly preprepared and branded, from Quaker Oats and Campbell Soup down to TV dinners and frozen pizza. More and more of the work was done in the factory rather than in the kitchen. Packers had to protect the preprepared food.

Packages became much more than just containers or advocates for a brand's property rights; they became salesmen. With beautiful boxes, bright wrappers, and shapely bottles, they were the engines of "self-serve" stores. Instead of going through a clerk, the consumer wandered the aisles being seduced by ad campaigns. The producers and packers could directly touch the consumer. Tony the Tiger and a Hunt's Ketchup bottle, which have a permanent place on the kitchen table, became more friends of the family and more familiar than the distant and temporary grocery clerk. Packages embraced and elided internal contradictions: a breakfast cereal being related to a friendly tiger.

We can see this in the concept "shelf life," which was designed to refer to the lively advertisements animating packages, not to living things inside of the boxes. Indeed, consumers want to be sure both that the contents once were alive (organic foods being preferred over inorganic foods) and that nothing is left alive inside the can or box.

We revel in our consumer autonomy. Freedom, at least to most Americans, means the freedom to buy what they wish. But what they wish is very much shaped by the package in which the product comes. Packages may well be wasteful from the social point of view of the landfill, but they are central to the creation of the modern world economy. They are a key to modern mass-consumer society. They might not be beautiful, but they certainly are important. Maybe sometimes you should judge a book by its cover.

6.11 Trademarks: What's in a Name?

A love-struck Juliet, distraught that Romeo's name was Montague, mused: "What's in a name? That which we call a rose would by any other name smell just as sweet. So Romeo would, were he not Romeo called, retain that dear perfection which he ow[n]es without that title." Lovers for five hundred years have agreed with Juliet that the essence is more important than the name. But a copyright lawyer would give very different advice. The name itself, not the essence, is legal property that should be defended. Indeed, the name has become sometimes more important than the object that it signifies. Clearly, something very important has changed in the last five centuries, and it is not just our sense of romance. That something is the rise of corporations and trademarks. Business historian Mira Wilkins has even argued that the emergence of trademarks and corporations are intimately linked.

In the olden days, which means any time until well into the nineteenth century, there were no brand names. Seamstresses might be known for beautiful dresses, a cook for fine recipes, a farmer for a tasty type of tomato or breed of cattle. But only locally would the name of the producer be associated with the product. Once porcelain left China, it was just "china." Syrian reversible woven material was known as "damask" and leather from Córdoba, "cordovan." Agricultural goods, to the extent that they were differentiated by name, also referred to the location of origin: Mocha for coffee that passed through Yemen's port of Mocha and Valencia for oranges from Spain's Valencia. Semimanufactured goods such as wines followed the same pattern: sweet wines from the region of Oporto, Portugal, were ports; from Jerez, Spain, came sherries, and Champagne, France, gave its name to a bubbly beverage. The designations referred to the region of origin, not the company or person producing it and certainly not to any quality associated with it, such as "zest," or "jolt." And these were exceptional. Most products lost their birthplace in their denomination once they left their home area.

The distinctive quality of the good—its sweetness, delicacy, strength—inhered in the product itself. Few of the goods were packaged, and none were advertised. Their fame was spread by word of mouth and merchants seeking new markets.

There were no trademarks or legal protection for the consumer. Under the domain of caveat emptor, "let the buyer beware," the personal reputation of the seller and the consumer's ability to detect quality were the only guarantees. Sales were limited, and the relationship between the buyer and seller was personal.

This began to change as larger companies manufactured goods intended for a mass market and set up marketing and advertising networks. The nineteenth century's industrialization saw the emergence of companies that could produce large numbers of fairly identical goods. The actual producer was an anonymous worker; it was the company that purveyed its name. The purchasers were spread over ever-greater distances as economies in the carrying trade made it profitable to sell nonluxury goods over wide areas. And the same company built factories in a number of locations, so the product was not associated with a particular place.

Of course, this meant that there was no personal relationship between producer and consumer. The good was known by the name of the company, not the producer. The mass market that brought small profits from each transaction also meant that ever-more companies sought repeat trade, satisfied customers who would continue to purchase their wares. This required not only a good product and price, but standardized quality. (For that reason John D. Rockefeller chose "Standard" Oil and many other early conglomerates used "standard" or "general.")

As packaging and tinning spread in the nineteenth century, people increasingly bought products essentially sight unseen. They had to trust the information on the package and particularly the name of the company to ascertain the contents. For consumers to trust in the quality of the good, the name of the company had to be protected from copy-cats and adulterers. The impersonal commercial relationship demanded trust in a producer who was at once anonymous (no one knew who specifically had produced the good) and also had a brand name to designate the company that became very familiar. In other words, the rise of the corporation meant that the name of the actual producer became far less important, while the name of the company became paramount.

Unfortunately for the first large manufacturers, some of the pioneers in brand names were not entirely reputable. Patent medicines, which sold sometimes lethal concoctions under fanciful names in captivating bottles, were selling a hope of cure as much as a product. The spectacle of the medicine show was one of the first forms of advertising campaigns. Some of these medicines generated considerable profits. But the companies themselves were usually fly-by-night concerns, which simply set up elsewhere under a different name if their product was denounced.

Large companies with great investments in capital goods did not have the luxury of disowning their name. They had to protect it. As is usually the case, these champions of free enterprise had to turn to the state to defend them from their competitors. The first states protected trademarks in the 1840s, and the first federal legislation was passed in 1870 under the constitutional authority to legislate on copyrights and patents. But the Supreme Court overruled the law on the grounds that trademarks are unlike copyrights and patents: "The ordinary trademark has no necessary relation to invention or discovery. . . . At common law, the exclusive right to it grows out of its use, and not its mere adoption. It does not depend on 'novelty, invention, discovery or any work of the brain.' It is simply founded on priority of appropriation."

Thus trademarks were not based on invention, but on custom, on the accepted use of the company's mark for specific products. As a result, although trademarks have been registered in the Patent Office in the United States and in similar offices in foreign countries, it is in the courts where battles over trademarks have been mostly fought.

The federal government, using different authority, passed legislation protecting trademarks in international trade in 1880 and in internal trade in 1905. The protection was not seen as a spur to invention, as is a patent, but rather as a defense of a property right, an intangible asset.

The massification and then globalization of commerce gave rise to potentially enormous profits if a product gained wide acceptance. Corporations had two tasks. First, they had to stimulate demand for their good. That involved enormous advertising expenses. Increasingly, advertising was not about educating the public about the product's uses and ingredients, but rather product differentiation and associating goods with feelings or ideas often intrinsically very remote from the product: the Pepsi Generation, the Marlboro Man, a hint of Springtime, the Budweiser frogs. Brand loyalty brought with it a premium on price, as anyone knows who has shopped in a supermarket and compared brand products with generic ones.

Corporations' second task was to avoid allowing their product to become so popular that the trade name became a generic name. This happened to Bayer, which lost their control of aspirin. Kleenex, Xerox, and Coca-Cola have fought back vigorously against the popular uses of their names as generic titles. (Coca-Cola won the Coke war, but lost the cola war.)

The "goodwill" of corporate brand names has often been their main asset. It doesn't matter to consumers that Colonel Sanders has long had nothing to do with Kentucky Fried Chicken or that Baskin Robbins changed hands. The products are perceived as remaining the same. Trademarks make franchises possible and aid the concentration of business in conglomerates. Companies can enter areas in which they have no expertise simply by buying popular brands.

Trademarks are useful because they have a history; consumers have familiarity with them. But rather than being old friends, the brands are impersonal assets that serve the demands of capital. It turns out that although a rose by any other name might smell just as sweet, indeed, under another name, a rose might even conjure up more arresting images, it would be a less valuable corporate asset. What is a name? "It is nor hand, nor foot, nor arm, nor face." But it *is* corporate profit.

6.12 Learning to Feel Unclean: A Global Marketing Tale

To most of us, the need for soap seems obvious, but one hundred years ago it didn't. All around the world, hygiene products have been among the most heavily and creatively advertised goods of the last century, giving us the first product wrappers that could be returned for prizes, the first promises to give a percentage of sales to charities, and radio and TV "soap operas." Why? Because many people didn't see the need for lots of soap.

People have always cleaned themselves—but often without much soap. Nineteenth-century chemistry made soap cheap for Europeans and Americans, while the emerging germ theory of disease argued for using it: without effective antibiotics (still decades away), scrubbing more seemed the best defense. But not everybody was convinced, so other appeals, more social than biological, were mobilized.

An 1887 British magazine's ad for Pear's soap is illustrative. A case of soap has washed up on a beach and broken open; an almost naked black woman holds one bar (and a spear). "The Birth of Civilization" says the title, and the bottom of the ad elaborates: "The consumption of soap is a measure of the wealth, civilization, health and purity of the people." Many Pear's ads were set in a fanciful "Africa," though Pear's sold virtually nothing there until much later. Their target was nonelite British consumers, who were being shown how to align themselves with their betters (and their triumphant empire), while separating themselves from "savages." In some American ads, supposedly dirty immigrants replaced the Africans, but the message was similar: civilized people used appropriate soaps for skin, hair, dishes, clothes, and so on.

The manufacture of demand for soap is most visible at a distance: in colonial Africa itself, for instance. Twentieth-century marketers were preceded by missionaries emphasizing that cleanliness was next to godliness, and by colonial schools that emphasized Western-style hygiene. Although many were sure they were bringing the first alternative to native "filth," their predecessors had known better: pre-1870 Europeans visiting Southern Africa did not see the natives as dirty and note that they used various reasonably effective indigenous methods, using local oils, fats, and clays. Only after colonialism was more advanced (and many natives forced to abandon migratory lifestyles) did the "dirty African" became a problem to be cleaned up with new commodities. Women, especially, were told they were responsible for the success of "their" men, who would never get good jobs or otherwise advance, unless their clothes, bodies, hair, teeth, breath, and wives met European standards. The ads also said that if women didn't use the appropriate products, nobody would ever tell their husbands directly that this was why they were being passed over and passed by: a worrisome message in societies where old status markers were disappearing and new ones still confusing. Gradually, the strategy worked—by the 1970s, people in most of Africa not only bought brand-name soaps in quantity, but did so as a matter of course.

The problem was not unique to cross-cultural marketing. Consider a forgotten "crisis" close to home: the fear of a soap glut in the United States after World War I. Overseas markets won during the war were threatened, and so was the home market: manufacturers feared that switches from dirt to pavement, horses to cars, coal to gas stoves, and oil lamps to electric lights would mean less need for soap. Instead of just pushing their individual brands, they mounted a concerted effort "to convince Americans they were still dirty."

One result was the industry-backed Cleanliness Institute. Along with some peculiar crusades (including one against handshaking), it launched successful efforts to increase soap use, especially among the young. Schools were encouraged to require frequent hand-washing: some created washroom monitors, who issued tickets that students had to show in order to enter the lunchroom. Women were supposedly natural targets. "Surer than the appearance of the robin or the tender crocus leaves as the first sign of spring is woman's urge to clean house from attic to cellar," said one Cleanliness Institute release; another said that scrubbing the refrigerator was excellent exercise and represented "kneeling before the altar of beauty and health." New scourges were created and traditional remedies forgotten: bad breath became "halitosis," and Listerine (originally for sanitizing wounds) replaced breath-cleaning customs like eating parsley (probably the reason it still appears on restaurant plates). Almost unknown in 1920, mouthwash was ubiquitous by the mid-1930s; the use of toothpaste, deodorant, and so on also spread. And Americans also heard in dandruff, mouthwash, and deodorant ads that without the right cleansers, they'd lose the job, the date, the spouse . . . and nobody would ever tell them why. In some ads a child too young to know better tells her kindly but lonely aunt that she smells bad. But since one can't count on such a niece appearing when needed, the larger message of the ads was that one should instead trust the experts—like those at the Cleanliness Institute—about how to be sure one was sufficiently clean. And since the "experts" spoke to everyone at once through ads, the best policy was to buy and use the same cleansers as everyone else.

The soap habit we have all acquired is a small thing, and probably a good one. But the larger principle—learning to rely on strangers in ads to tell us what is acceptable, rather than expecting to learn from real-life peers—has had enormous social, economic, and psychological consequences. The messages about how we look at, talk to, judge, and compete with one another might be less blunt when they don't come from colonial powers—but they matter, nonetheless, selling much more than soap.

6.13 Things Go Better with Red, White, and Blue: How Coca-Cola Conquered Europe

Few brand names say "U.S.A." as clearly—and successfully—as Coca-Cola. But when it first went to Europe, things didn't go better with (or for) Coke. It took a war, diplomatic intervention, and some clever marketing to turn things around and set a pattern that has transformed global commerce and culture in the last sixty years.

When it was first sold in the United States in the 1880s, Coke was supposed to have health benefits: part of its appeal was that it was nonalcoholic, and, thus, a suitable temperance beverage. But when the company tried expanding into Europe during the 1920s, it found that its product was suspect on health grounds. It was, after all, loaded with sugar and caffeine, specially targeted at the youth market, and contained a mysterious ingredient that the company refused to reveal. Regulators and medical associations were suspicious, and the counterargument that Coke was an alternative to alcohol cut much less ice in Europe than in the United States.

What being an alternative to alcohol did do didn't help Coke: it added protectionist pressures from vintners and brewers to doctors' arguments. (At least in France, the vintners made the rather logical argument that since U.S. customs regulated wine and liquor exports, Coke should be subject to French beverage regulations, which it resisted.) And it did something more, which was vague, but important: it touched a nerve among nationalists, who, recalling that "you are what you eat," worried about whether young people who substituted Coke for wine or beer would not become less French or German in the process. The product had made only limited progress in Europe by 1939 (though somewhat more in Latin America); but when things resumed in 1945, the situation was vastly altered.

On the one hand, the Cold War meant that any aggressive American firm faced new suspicions, especially from parts of the political left. Some Communist parties and newspapers claimed Coke was a poison, that its salespeople were part of a spy network, and that its bottling plants could be transformed into atomic bomb factories. French rumors included a less apocalyptic but equally insulting danger—that Coke planned to advertise on the facade of Notre Dame Cathedral. Since most postwar governments regulated foreign investment (as well as food and beverage content), the addition of a new partner to the anti-Coke coalition mattered. Coke was briefly banned in Denmark, slowed by health-related lawsuits in Belgium and Switzerland, and had a very hard time getting past French regulators without revealing its secret ingredient.

On the other hand, American power was vastly greater in the postwar world, and Washington pushed hard for the folks from Atlanta. (The fact that Communists were active in the opposition, naturally, increased American determination.) European governments were threatened in various subtle and unsubtle ways about the effects of banning Coke; the French foreign ministry came to fear that its Marshall Plan aid might be in jeopardy. Hoping that this was ultimately a small issue—though fearing that it was instead part of a fearsome tide of Americanization—European governments dropped their opposition.

As with many other companies, being strongly associated with the United States became a great boon for Coke. Indeed, the war itself had done much to tighten this association. Coke had spent vast amounts of money making their soda available at low prices to GIs—even to the point of moving in quickly with bottling plants as parts of Western Europe were liberated. And with Coke's signature bottle, the people being liberated didn't need to look closely—or know English—to see what their liberators were drinking.

Though the company presumably had patriotism and perhaps public relations at home in mind when it spent so much to get Coke to the troops, doing so also helped open up the European market. Not only did it associate Coke with a very positive U.S. contribution to Europe, but it must have helped undermine the health fears as well: if the army that drove Hitler out of Western Europe (and was, in fact, probably the best-fed and healthiest army in history) drank Coke in such quantities, how bad could it be for you?

Whether this association had come about deliberately or accidentally, the company soon played it for all it was worth. Although companies that had tried to sell food overseas in the past often tried to hide the product's foreign origin behind a local brand (both to allay fears that it wasn't fresh and those based on "you are what you eat"), Coke trumpeted its association with "the American way of life" and American triumphalism. For the Helsinki Olympics, the company even refurbished a D-Day landing craft and sailed it into the harbor—filled, not with troops, but with 720,000 bottles of Coke and various promotional materials. The Yanks were coming again.

Though in-your-face Americanism alienated some people, Coke's campaign for Europe was a big success. And for better or worse, it ushered in a new kind of marketing. Those who worried that people drinking Coke rather than beer would be a little less German were not entirely wrong: what was emerging was an international consumer culture (especially for youth) in which people increasingly looked abroad—especially to the United States—to find the peers whose consumption habits determined what was "cool." And for millions of them, Coke was it.

6.14 Survival of the First

In business, competition has not always led to survival of the fittest. Rather, it has often simply caused survival of the first; precedence won over capability. And after being victorious in one market, the early products have often gone on to capture the global market.

Take, for example, one the greatest technological leaps of the modern age: the railroad. The locomotives that first began to pull train cars in Great Britain in 1825 traveled on a number of different gauges of track, since each railway was free to lay down whichever gauge it chose. Transferring from one line to another was a costly headache. Subsequently, railroads in other nations also employed an array of track widths. Over time, this chaos ceased; one gauge triumphed. But the survivor was not the one that was technically best suited to moving freight and passengers.

The first railroad used a narrow gauge of four feet eight-and-one-half inches. This spacing was not chosen on the basis of any technical criteria of excellence. Rather, precedence dictated it. The horse-drawn coal cars of the nearby coal mines had long used the four-foot, eight-inch width. It has even been suggested that the coal cars' gauge was itself a vestige of the width of Roman chariots that had left their mark in Britain almost two millennia before. That standard was passed from ancient times to the industrial age because of custom. The first steam-powered railway, the Stockton and Darlington, was mainly used to carry coal from the mines to ports. And its concession stipulated that the track had to be available to the coal mines' horse-drawn carts. Thus the narrow gauge continued from horsepower to steam power. When George Stephenson designed the first railway primarily intended to carry merchandise and passengers, he copied the existing gauge.

But other railroads chose wider tracks that could more easily sustain the much larger and higher freight cars of the steam railway and would allow the construction of larger locomotives. From any technical standpoint, Stephenson's narrow gauge was not optimal. Yet it ultimately prevailed for two principal reasons.

First, all railroad lines soon came to recognize that standardized tracks allowed easy integration of wider networks. Since Great Britain was so small and its rail system so dense, this problem was confronted very early on. The precedent of the Stephenson gauge encouraged other lines that wanted to link up with it to adopt the same track size. The advantage of the first continued to grow as its network did. Competition continued, nonetheless. The Great Western Railroad, using a broader track, proved the advantage of the wider gauge in time trials. Nonetheless, the British government concluded that, although a wider gauge was superior for carrying passengers, the advantage did not outweigh the benefits of an integrated system. Since the narrower track had a far greater constituency, the government decreed that new lines should adopt the narrow gauge.

The second reason for the triumph of the coal car width was that over time technology was adapted to the narrow track, rather than the track being changed to conform to technology. Locomotives and cars were enlarged with numerous refinements in suspension, axles, and wheels that allowed them to move swiftly and carry ever-greater burdens on the narrower track.

In the United States, the problem was a little different than in Britain. Because of the vastness of the country and the proliferation of regional rail networks, numerous lines intentionally used unusual gauges to create a monopoly for themselves within their district. This continued until after the Civil War. Then the Westward expansion of the population and the railway system created greater demand for long-distance trade. As the demand and profitability of through-freight grew, so did the impetus to standardize track. By the last decade of the nineteenth century, virtually all rail in the United States was of the English gauge.

Indeed by the end of the nineteenth century, the English standard had become virtually a world standard. Europe gradually adopted the British gauge, though in some cases such as at the French-Spanish border, different gauges were seen as a means of national defense. Elsewhere standardization was easier. Britain's technical head start and its great investments abroad in the budding railways of its far-flung colonies and the rest of the Third World allowed it to stamp its imprimatur across the continents. From horse-drawn carts to steam- and then diesel-driven locomotives to today's high-speed trains, the gauge has remained mostly unaltered. The standard is used not because it is optimal, but because it is custom. Therefore some of the most sophisticated vehicles of the nuclear age still run on the four-foot, eight-inch tracks of the Romans and the coal carts of England.

6.15 It Ain't Necessarily So

Necessity is the mother of invention. Of course she is. We have been told this so often and from such an early age that this aphorism is accepted as natural and self-evident. Yet what does it actually mean? Who decides when something is necessary, and what sort of invention does it mother? Historically this has been a complicated and not altogether satisfactory relationship.

Take, for example, the lowly can. It was introduced first in England in 1810 to nourish His Majesty's navy so they could kill the enemy. Canned rations were a great advance from the meager and bug-ridden diet sailors had historically known. Of course, every solution carried with it its own problem. In this case, the obvious first hurdle to overcome was opening the can. Here, surely, we have a necessity. Yet the invention of a practical can opener had to wait for half a century!

Not that all those cans piled up for fifty years before anyone could open them. At first sailors used knives, bayonets, or hammers and chisels. They worked, if not terribly well. Nobody concerned themselves for decades with improving the situation. This was partly because the first cans were large, heavy, thick-walled iron canisters. As a tool of war, they needed to survive trying conditions and serve sailors in bulk. Their customers generally carried knives. Moreover, they were men who could wield and thrust a knife or hammer a chisel.

Two things needed to change to create the necessity of a more convenient can opener. First, the art of metallurgy improved, allowing the construction of lighter-weight tin and steel cans. Second, packing techniques improved so that a whole host of foods could now be safely canned without fear of botulism or spoilage. Hence more and more housewives were interested in purchasing canned goods. But they usually did not have a bayonet or hammer and chisel handy, nor were they anxious to apply them. Only in 1870 did an American inventor, William W. Lyman, finally patent the device that would revolutionize the food marketing industry: the can opener.

Sometimes the solution preceded the necessity. In the 1880s Josephine Cochrane of Illinois was upset that her servants frequently broke her treasured china when washing it. She therefore invented a dishwasher. A large wheel with metal compartments was placed in a larger copper boiler, which squirted up water over the dishes. It worked well.

But housewives refused to buy the new invention. There were technical problems, to be sure. Many homes lacked sufficient hot water to run the machine, and water was often too hard to allow the soap to suds and clean the dishes. But there was an important cultural barrier that was probably more important in delaying the "necessity" of a dishwasher: women did not object to washing dishes by hand. Before the large incorporation of females into the workforce, women were mostly not doing double duty on the job and in the home. Moreover, washing dishes was considered a relaxing and social activity at the end of the day that often brought the family together in a common chore. Only in the 1950s, when women entered the labor market and had the wherewithal to purchase dishwashers, did Mrs. Cochrane's invention become a necessity.

Sometimes necessity led to a quick, but poor, solution that outlived its usefulness because of precedence, as in the case of the typewriter keyboard. The first typewriter was invented in 1829 by William Burt. But the machine was slow. It was a clumsy circular contraption that used the principle of the piano key. It went no faster than the fastest penmen, who set the handwriting speed record in 1853 at thirty words a minute. This became a serious problem when the electric telegraph began transmitting messages faster than anyone could write them down. Christopher Sholes created a machine they called the "type-writer" in 1872 that allowed considerably faster typing. There was only one drawback. The keys continually jammed when typed fast. The first stenographer who tested the machines destroyed one prototype after another, testing the patience of the inventor. No matter how hard he tried to solve this, no matter how he tinkered with the apparatus, Sholes could not keep the keys from locking together. So he finally hit upon the logical remedy: if he could not speed up the machine, he would slow down the typist. After much experimentation, he hit upon the keyboard as we know it today. The keys were placed in such illogical and difficult positions that the typist was forced to slow down and the machine did not jam. Even after later improvements were made to retract the keys so that the jamming problem ceased, the keyboard remained essentially the same. The electric typewriter and now the computer all adopted an intentionally inconvenient and cumbersome keyboard because of custom. Rather than adapt the keyboard to the typist, millions of typists have had to spend hour upon hour searching for the "b," the "e," or the "i."

Alas, necessity is not always a good mother. She is sometimes barren, sometimes fickle, sometimes precocious. The problem, the solution, the inventor, and the customer are all symbiotic interacting agents that can lead in many different directions—or nowhere at all.

6.16 Where Is Andorra?

How did a tiny principality, tucked away on the roof of the world and seemingly ignored by the tides of history, skip from the medieval to the postmodern, from the feudal to the international, without ever passing through the modern and the national? How did this medieval Shangra-la with no seaports, no airports, and no railroads, connected to the outside world only by a thin tissue of narrow roads, become a center for international trade and business?

Andorra is ancient. Humans inhabited the 180 square miles perched atop the Pyrenees between Spain and France five to eight thousand years ago. War indirectly brought statehood to the Basque people of the land. One of the last areas the Islamic Moors occupied during their conquest of the Iberian Peninsula, it became one of the first they evacuated. Charlemagne anointed it one of the numerous march states that served as buffers between the Islamic and the Christian worlds. Its fierce, independent shepherds and warriors blocked passage, rather than facilitating it. As a result, history seemed to pass by Andorra. It became the sole surviving march state.

As late as 1900, a visitor noted that "Andorra has kept its medieval usages and institutions almost unchanged." Its 5,600 inhabitants continued to live from agriculture and livestock herding. The visitor remarked that "the local industries are of the most primitive kind, merely domestic as in the middle ages." Lacking capital, coal, and communications, the isolated principality lived an almost insular life in the middle of the European continent. Aside from one municipal road, the other communication "arteries" were bridle paths on which mules brought Andorra's few imports.

Andorra lacked most of the attributes commonly associated with sovereignty. It had no budget until 1954, no ordinary taxes except for customs duties, no currency—French francs and Spanish pesetas were and are the legal tender. And this former warrior state has no real army. A popular folk song of the 1960s used Andorra to make an antiwar statement since here was a country without an army. Aside from a half dozen professional soldiers, the army was composed of a volunteer militia. Every member was treated as an officer. That has posed no problems because they have not fought a war for seven hundred years. With only 2 percent of Andora's miniscule territory arable (surprisingly, they grow tobacco on the slopes of the Pyrenees) and few natural resources, neighboring France and Spain have been content to allow the Andorrans a large degree of self-rule and a national language, Catalan, borrowed from its neighbors to the south.

But it is a strange sovereignty, because there are two co-princes, neither of them Andorrans. Since 1278 rule has been divided between the count of Foix in France—eventually passed on to the king of France and now the president—and the bishop of Seu d'Urgell in Spain. The Andorrans pay a token yearly tax to the co-princes, acknowledging their suzerainty. The co-princes still have final say over Andorra's international treaties.

Andorrans have only recently begun to extend their rights of citizenship. Women received the franchise only in 1970. The country's constitution was not ratified until 1993, finally legalizing political parties and labor unions. By that point Andorra had already joined the outside world.

Its population has swelled from 5,800 in 1954 to 70,549 in 2005, only a quarter of whom are legal citizens, and property values have skyrocketed. Perhaps more to the point, some 12 million tourists a year wind their way up the narrow, treacherous roads. The police force has been expanded thirtyfold so that the policemen can direct the traffic of the clogged roads of Andorra la Vella and other towns. What does this geographically challenged land, with few natural resources, have to offer the hoards of visitors?

Long a route for small-scale smuggling between France and Spain, Andorra became a free port and a major smuggling center. Although it produced little, its fragile sovereignty allowed the principality to charge low or no taxes on goods. Tourism followed in the wake. While applying its own traditions, such as medieval communal property and applying customary Catalan law, Andorra nonetheless required the acquiescence of its neighbors, so the tax-free goods could leave their mountain fastness. After all, its roads are maintained by the French and the Spanish. French and Spanish policemen search for contraband—especially cigarettes—in cars that have come from Andorra.

International recognition became even more important as Andorra sought to become a center of international banking and finance by allowing tax holidays. Taxes on consumer goods replaced customs duties and obviated the need for an income tax. The three-quarters of the residents who have no voting rights come more for the tax shelter than for the clean air.

It was necessary to draft a constitution so the principality could join the international community, particularly the European Union, which was seeking to make taxes uniform. Andorra revealed the new importance of internationalism by finally opening its first diplomatic mission abroad in 1993. Rather than posting it in another country, the mission was to the United Nations! Two years later, in 1995, it established diplomatic relations with the United States, although the U.S. representative to Andorra is stationed in Barcelona, Spain.

Andorra has leaped from a feudal enclave to an international free port, without ever really going through the process of nation building. This transformation is reflected in a simple fact. In the libraries of the University of California there are but 169 books dedicated to Andorra. On the World Wide Web, however, there are more than 41.5 million Web sites and more than eight million pages in English on the Web relating to Andorra! The vast majority of the sites relate to commerce, finance, and tourism.

This hybrid mix of ancient and postmodern, of local and international, has served the people of Andorra well. Everyone over the age of sixteen is literate, per capita annual income is $18,000, and life expectancy, one of the highest in the world, is over 86.6 for women and 80.6 for men, with infant mortality an extremely low eight per thousand.

Andorra has no airport, railroad, or seaport, but it has the Internet. And that has made tax laws more important than geography. Remote Andorra is now in the center of the world.

– 7 –

World Trade, Industrialization, and Deindustrialization

Eighty years ago, the historian T.H. Ashton was already calling the industrial revolution a "thrice squeezed orange"—a subject that had little juice left. He nonetheless wrote another book about it, and touched off new debates. Today we still have little consensus on exactly how industrialization—the movement of most of the workforce out of agriculture, fishing, and forestry, into jobs where they used increasingly powerful mechanical devices to transform objects—occurred, or what role trade played in that transformation. The effects of trade between already industrialized areas and those that are still primarily agrarian are even more controversial—in particular, under what circumstances did such trade make it easier or harder for the "less developed" trading partner to industrialize itself? Since today, virtually all prosperous economies are industrial (or postindustrial), this question is one version of a still more basic one: Does participation in international trade really benefit all parties, or do inequalities of wealth and power cause some participants to lose out? The historical complexities of this question stem in part from the fact that very few countries have ever done in practice what elementary economic theory tells them is obviously good for them: namely, institute free trade with all other countries, regardless of relative levels of development. So somebody—maybe everybody—must be confused.

World Trade and Early Industrialization

People have made things for millennia, so when does "industrialization" begin? Workshops that employed huge numbers of workers go back centuries, mostly in a variety of royal and imperial factories making weapons, uniforms, and certain luxury goods. And although most processes were powered by human and animal muscle (the very word "manufactured" once meant "made by hand"), waterpower, coal, and other mechanical and chemical power sources were not unknown: the salt works in China's Sichuan Province even burned natural gas close to two thousand years ago. But if one looks for the first place where large numbers of workers worked very intensely and in a coordinated way (not each working separately side-by-side under one roof), with the timing of tasks determined by the physical needs of a fuel-intensive

215

production process yielding a standardized product, the prototype for modern factories might be found in an unusual place—the sugar mills of Latin America, where cane (which rots quickly if not processed) was crushed, boiled, and made ready for its transatlantic journey (see reading 7.1, "Sweet Industry"). And in that case, not only did factories originate outside Europe; the first laborers to adjust to factory life were not wage earners but slaves, and not Europeans but Africans.

More conventional versions of the industrialization story begin with English textiles, and here trade looms large. The first cotton textiles produced in England were imitations of Indian fabrics. For a long time, Indian cloth remained the gold standard, especially in the strategically critical African markets where cloth was exchanged for slaves. England's early mills found much of their market overseas. The opening of these markets was linked to empire in at least two senses. First, in an era in which most countries protected their home and colonial markets from foreign competition, the strength of the British navy was crucial in prying open markets around the world (particularly the Americas), in reducing the shipping costs to distant markets (in part by reducing piracy), and, in some cases, in preventing interlopers from competing with English goods in British colonies. Second, British dominance of India (especially Bengal, the leading textile-exporting region, and Britain's first area of dominance on the subcontinent) proved quite important. It was Indian goods that first gave Britain a toehold in the textile markets of the Ottoman Empire, Persia, Southeast Asia, and various parts of Africa, dealing a significant blow to at least some part of the local textile industry in each of these places. Mechanization eventually gave British producers a huge advantage in their struggle to replace those Indian textiles with their own; but the transition occurred sooner that it might have, thanks to various East India Company policies. Though the Company was only trying to make sure that Indian weavers sold exclusively to them and at very low prices, their plans instead drove many Bengalis who had woven for export to give up that work entirely (see reading 7.4, "Killing the Golden Goose"). Later in the century, when British textiles had lost their competitive advantage in much of the world, India provided a huge, protected market that was essential to keeping Lancashire alive.

Finally, trade was central to British industrialization because the principal fiber of the textile revolution, cotton, was always an import that Britain could not grow at home. The mechanization of wool and flax spinning and weaving developed more slowly than with cotton; but more important, Britain could never have supplied itself with enough flax or wool to expand textile production as it did. Flax was both extremely labor-intensive and quite hard on the soil, so that in Western Europe it was largely a garden crop, grown on a very small scale where dense populations provided both labor and fertilizer. Despite numerous attempts over two centuries by Parliament to subsidize flax-growing throughout the British Isles and the North American colonies, the results were quite modest. And as for wool—well, raising enough sheep to replace just the cotton Britain imported in 1830 (still rather early in the industrial era) would have required more or less the entire arable and pasture land of the United Kingdom (see reading 7.2, "Fiber of Fortune").

To be sure, the early industrial age involved much more than textiles. But in almost all accounts cotton remains a critical leading sector of industrialization—and so foreign trade remains a critical, though sometimes underappreciated, part of the story. When we turn to other sectors, we again often find that foreign supplies of primary products were crucial.

At an even more basic level, we must remember that the industrialization of a society—as opposed to one particular sector—is almost certain to depend on vast imports of other goods. Unless the rapid growth of the nonfarming population is matched by equally rapid growth in agricultural productivity, workers will not be able to eat without an increase in food imports, much less will they be able to purchase the vastly expanded range of consumer items (all of which contain some raw material) that provide much of the motivation for accepting the alien environment, often harsh discipline, and peculiar new habits of industrial life. Thus—as we discuss in more detail in chapter 4, our section on commodities—industrialization almost always goes with a sharp increase in trade. Shortages of various goods now needed in much larger quantities created bottlenecks that caused merchants to scour the globe for exotic substitutes. The soaring demand for copper wire that came with electrification is just one example (see reading 7.7, "Lighting the Night and Darkening the Day"). And in the twentieth century, industrialization all over the world came to be powered (quite literally) by a global trade in oil, which has radically transformed both producing and consuming societies (readings 7.11 and 7.12).

Dependence on any one import, or even any one class of imports, may well be temporary. For instance, Europe, which imported unprecedented amounts of food between 1830 and 1950, has more or less regained self-sufficiency since World War II. Nonetheless, imports were often quite indispensable for long periods. This leads to a different kind of question: If industrialized (and generally powerful) nations need some other countries to remain specialized in agriculture, forestry, and raw materials exports, have they taken steps to prevent these countries from industrializing? If so, have those steps been effective? Or, on the contrary, have relations with already industrialized countries accelerated industrialization elsewhere, at least for those countries that did not face particularly serious *internal* obstacles?

World Trade and the Spread of Industrialism:
Two Sets of Issues

The role of world trade in diffusing industry to other countries is even more complex, because there are so many different cases to consider. But the questions can at least be grouped under two separate general headings.

One concerns how trade affects the development of economic conditions for industrialization. Does the export of primary products to industrial countries that can pay top dollar for them help other countries accumulate the capital needed to industrialize? Does the availability of industrial imports discourage industrialization, since it means factory-builders could not even be sure of their own home market? Does it impoverish artisans who might have been more likely to invest in early industrialization than were the landlords who benefited from a boom in agricultural exports?

A second set of issues concerns the spread of industrial technologies themselves. At first, it seems that the net effects of global trade on the diffusion of technology must be positive. Having somebody in the world who knows how to do a certain thing does not reduce the chance that somebody else will invent it, too; so when one adds to that unchanged probability the chance that people will learn about the technique from elsewhere, the chances that they will obtain it somehow must increase. But it isn't quite that simple, at least once enforceable patents make it illegal for people to use processes others invented first, even if they would have gotten it themselves soon. More concretely—and in most periods more importantly—it is crucial to see how global trade has influenced the *distribution* of the best technological processes across the map at various times: through spreading knowledge and stimulating competition, but also through deliberate polices by certain firms or countries that seek to create or preserve a monopoly on some best practice. How such efforts work—and what effects they have—has changed enormously, in large part because of changes in the nature of the technologies people seek to control. We shall return to these questions in the last part of this chapter.

Trade, the Global Division of Labor, and
Prospects for Industrialization

In most contexts, it is not hard to imagine that terms negotiated between two self-interested parties with vastly different amounts of wealth and power might well work to the disadvantage of the weaker party, leaving it even farther behind. But since the days of Smith and Ricardo, economics has told us that such worries are misplaced in the area of international trade: free trade will benefit both parties by forcing them to specialize in the activities that are most profitable for them, while maximizing the total amount of wealth created. This might well mean, for some countries, a prolonged period of specializing in primary products, but this would only occur if it was beneficial to them—it would in no way lock them into continuing such a specialization once circumstances made it more advantageous to them to industrialize. Ricardo's famous example drew on the trade in wine and wool between England and Portugal, showing how much better off both were than if they tried to produce some of both commodities themselves. On the blackboard, the argument works even when one country is more efficient than the other at everything—the laggard still gains from specializing in the thing(s) where it is least far behind and importing the others, compared with what it could achieve through self-sufficiency. In the abstract, it is hard to make a case for protectionism.

But reality is not always so clear-cut. Indeed, Ricardo's own example could make one wonder—how well did Portugal do during its centuries of free trade with England? Are we sure it would have done worse otherwise? The matter gets more complex when we realize that there are virtually no examples of successful industrialization with "pure" free trade (or for that matter with pure self-sufficiency). Even in the supposed heyday of free trade, the United States and Germany achieved their impressive late-nineteenth- and early-twentieth-century growth behind high tariff walls; many other countries also had some kind of protection.

Even Britain's record is mixed. For most of the nineteenth century, Britain championed free trade, but its own textile industry was sheltered from cheap Indian imports in the seventeenth and eighteenth centuries by tariffs of roughly 100 percent; only after it had become the world's most efficient producer did it dismantle those walls. And even at the height of free trade in the late nineteenth century, Britain's Indian empire remained an important exception, with markets for various industrial goods essentially closed to non-Britishers. This guaranteed market became more, not less, important, as British industry began to lose its competitive footing against the United States and Germany (see reading 3.7, "How Opium Made the World Go 'Round';" reading 7.8, "No Mill Is an Island;" and reading 2.9, "Guaranteed Profits and Half-Fulfilled Hopes").

Oddly enough, one of the best cases of agricultural and raw materials exports fueling industrial growth comes where we might not expect it—in Japan (see reading 7.9, "Feeding Silkworms, Spitting out Growth"). Though hardly a resource-rich country, Japan did export large amounts of silver in the late nineteenth century, and even more silk. Taking advantage of a silkworm blight in Europe, and of homegrown technical innovations that enabled them to coordinate rice-growing and silkworm rearing better than before (basically by heating silkworm sheds to trick the worms into producing earlier in the year, when the rice paddies were not so busy), Japanese farmers seized a huge worldwide market share and provided much of the country's foreign exchange; meanwhile the high rents they paid became both the capital that landlords invested in spinning mills and the taxes that the state invested in its pilot projects, mostly in heavy industry. Thus, while more recent experience has made us think of Japanese (and Korean and Taiwanese) agriculture as economically inefficient vestiges subsidized by payments from powerful industrial economies, just the opposite was true earlier in the century. To whatever extent we wish to speak of a pre-1945 "Japanese miracle," that miracle looks very different from the post-1945 pattern often taken to be typical of East Asia. (It was also different from postwar patterns, in that the heavy industrial sectors of the pre-1945 Japanese economy, which had the closest ties with the government, were the least successful in economic terms—though they did help create an impressive military machine. It was the less coddled light industrial sectors that succeeded.)

In many other cases, even larger surges in agricultural exports have failed to lay a basis for industrialization. The Philippine case discussed in "Sweet Success" (reading 7.6) may be extreme, but it is hardly unique in kind. In this case, the goal of British consul Nicholas Loney was to *destroy* the handicraft textile industry in the Philippines, so as to open a market for British goods; the development of sugar plantations was essentially an afterthought, which he pursued at first largely in order to provide a return cargo for boats bringing in cloth. Workers on the sugar plantations that developed were paid dismally, while a small landholding elite preferred European to domestic goods. The one relatively large group whose incomes did rise—longshoremen—tended to be single men who spent heavily on entertainment and services, in sharp contrast to the female weavers, whose earnings, much higher before Loney's arrival, tended to support household consumption. Under these circumstances, it is hardly surprising that a boom in export earnings did nothing to promote industrialization and may even have retarded it. It is not only the effects of trade on total national income that matter, but the effects on distribution as well. While there are no hard and fast rules, export booms that use lots of labor and/or resources whose ownership is widely dispersed (e.g., Japanese silk, which is arguably a light industrial product rather than a "natural resource," or Scandinavian timber) seem to do better at creating the conditions for long-term development than booms in resources owned by just a few people.

The effects of primary product exports on government may matter even more, but they are not easily predictable. Enormous oil revenues made it much less necessary for various regimes to extract fiscal sustenance from taxes on the mass of their citizens, while making relations with foreign companies and a particular subset of workers crucial. The results could vary from populist politics and subsidization of industrialization efforts (as in Mexico, see reading 7.11) to a system with many welfare benefits, but no political rights, an easily demobilized set of "guest workers," the import of huge amounts of foreign manufactures, and very limited industrialization at home (as in Saudi Arabia, see reading 7.12). A gusher of mineral royalties may also make exporting states feel they have more interests in common with their industrialized customers overseas than with their own people, especially if the foreigners also provide military security for the regime. But they may also feel that producing a vital industrial input enables them to stand up to foreigners with whom they do not perceive shared interests. Confusingly enough, most cases involve some of both tendencies.

Technology

Although joining the international economy may not increase the financial resources or incentives available for industrialization, it is bound to increase knowledge of technological alternatives. But learning about other ways of doing things doesn't always lead to implementing them. Sometimes the new technique may not be more advantageous—expensive labor-saving machinery, for instance, may be counterproductive in an economy with very cheap labor. The plight—and health—of workers is ignored, especially if they are not organized in unions. The miners of Baja California, bringing to the surface copper, which supplied the wiring for the electrical revolution that lit the night and powered the machines in the United States and other industrialized countries at the end of the nineteenth century, used candlelight and human muscle, as Dennis Kortheuer shows in reading 7.7, "Lighting the Night and Darkening the Day." In other cases, the new technology might have been economically efficient, but judged deleterious in some other way. But even a technique that people could see would be advantageous was not always adopted. Transfers of early industrial technologies were often hindered by the cultural and organizational differences between workplaces; transfers of more advanced technologies were more often complicated by legal and financial hurdles.

Early industrial technology often involved artisanal knowledge that was embodied in people as much as it was embedded in pieces of equipment. Under the circumstances, the cost of building the necessary "machinery" (if that is even the right word for many of these items) was usually not a great barrier to imitation; patent protection, even if it existed on paper, was rarely very effective (especially across borders). A knowledgeable artisan going to a new place could often recreate the equipment from scratch. And though Britain, in particular, tried banning the emigration of "mechanics," this was impracticable in the long run. Enough of them went to wherever the rewards were good—continental Europe, the Americas, and some parts of Asia—to frustrate such legislation.

On the other hand, reproducing the necessary equipment did not always complete the process of technology transfer. The historian John Harris provides a wonderful set of examples of failed technological transfer even between two countries that were, in the great scheme of things, relatively similar: England and France. Eighteenth- and early-nineteenth-century Frenchmen made scrupulously accurate copies of the furnaces in which the English were making iron, glass, and many other basic materials using coal—but for several decades almost all of these new facilities failed. To make any of these materials properly, as it turned out, required all sorts of knowledge that was almost impossible to put on paper: exactly how to tell by looking and listening that a piece had been in the fire long enough, at what angle to hold it, how slowly to turn it, and what sort of noises indicated that something was wrong. Indeed, these small but essential nuances were so completely different from those that a French artisan used to working with wood-burning furnaces would know that it was hard for accomplished English craftsmen to even know which of the practices they took for granted needed to be explained to others. Only when whole teams of English workers came over after 1830 were these processes really transferred. If so much miscommunication could occur across the short hop of the English Channel, is it any wonder that technological transfer across larger geographic and cultural gaps often failed? Technology may often have traveled poorly in this period, but probably not because of deliberate attempts by "advanced" countries to monopolize it; the nature of the process itself was often barrier enough.

This particular form of "natural stickiness" of technology and technological leadership became much less important as industrialization proceeded. New machines and processes were increasingly designed by people who shared a common engineering language, and who did not emerge from a craft tradition. Such machines required less and less artisanal knowledge to operate; indeed some of them were designed specifically to enable people with no prior knowledge to replace more expensive and independent craft operatives. Much of the new equipment required plenty of skill to operate, yet it was skill that was invented anew, recorded in books, and impossible to keep secret. But if these barriers to technology transfer were eroding, new ones were taking their place.

First of all, as technology was increasingly embodied in big, expensive machines, the costs of acquiring it became more burdensome for the country playing catch-up; and increasingly, technology depended on various kinds of networks that could be extremely expensive. (Computers and modems may be relatively cheap, but reliable electricity and static-free phone lines are not.)

It became much easier to define, and therefore patent, inventions that consisted of equipment, not skills; much more worthwhile to acquire a patent, as both the cost of the item in question and its potential market rose (as late as the eighteenth century, many inventors did not bother to patent their creations, even in England), and much easier to enforce a patent as information became easier to store and send and intellectual property laws converged (sometimes through changing attitudes, sometimes through pressure by richer countries). As technological change became something that was consciously planned and invested in (the R & D budget was itself a late-nineteenth-century innovation), it became an object of policy for governments and firms all over the globe; this involved both promoting further innovation and taking steps to control diffusion and catch-up that had not been fully paid for.

For many years in much of the world, colonialism complicated the picture still further. The British presence led to unusually rapid railway-building in India (see reading 2.9,"Guaranteed Profits and Half-Fulfilled Hopes") and to the first mechanized textile mills in Asia, but neither created the sort of linkages that would have promoted further growth. Indian railways used all British equipment, British engineers, and even mostly British coal. Consequently, new industries were not stimulated, nor many new skills transferred. Bombay's textile mills, like their slightly younger counterparts in Osaka and Shanghai, boomed during World War I, when shortages of shipping provided protection from European goods (see reading 7.8, "No Mill Is an Island"). But those same shipping shortages meant that mills running at full tilt could not import enough spare parts, much less the machinery to build new capacity. In China and especially Japan, where steel mills and arsenals had been built and maintained for national security reasons, these uncompetitive enterprises now suddenly paid off: the machinists, mechanics, and engineers they had nurtured took advantage of this opportunity to make spinning and weaving machinery, and a local capital goods sector was born. Colonial India lacked similar resources, so a precious opportunity was lost. Because the era in which much of the world began to trade with industrialized economies coincided with the period in which many of these same countries were subordinated politically, we can never fully sort out how much increased trade might have stimulated industrialization had that trade not come wrapped in imperialism.

Sometimes, however, even measures *designed* to thwart industrial development didn't do so, at least in the long run. In colonial New England, the

The World Economy in the Late 19th and Early 20th Centuries

A combination of technological and political changes in the 19th century connected economies around the globe more tightly than ever before, while also creating unprecedented differences in wealth and political power between "have" and "have-not" economies. Europeans and their descendants, who had ruled about 35% of the world's territory in 1800, ruled about 85% of it in 1900, and most of the world's most prosperous trade routes ran through Western European ports. But some other nodes of mechanized industry and international finance were also developing; by the late 20th century, far more trade would cross the Pacific than the Atlantic each year.

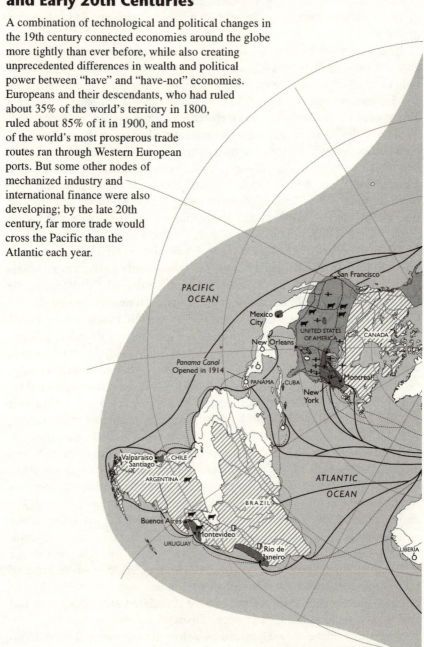

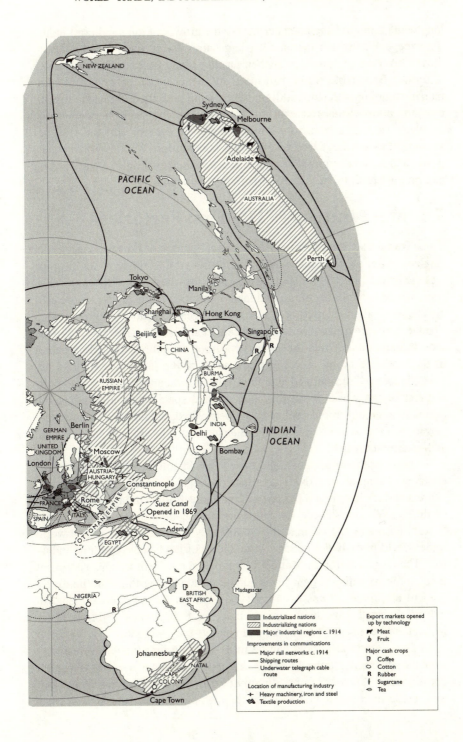

NEW ZEALAND

Sydney
Melbourne

Adelaide

PACIFIC
OCEAN

AUSTRALIA

Perth

Tokyo

Manila

Shanghai   Hong Kong

Beijing   Singapore

CHINA   R   R

BURMA

RUSSIAN
EMPIRE   INDIAN
                                          OCEAN
INDIA

Berlin
GERMAN   Delhi
EMPIRE
UNITED   Bombay
KINGDOM
London   Moscow
          AUSTRIA-
FRANCE   HUNGARY
Rome   Constantinople
ITALY
SPAIN   OTTOMAN EMPIRE
                         Suez Canal
                         Opened in 1869
               EGYPT   Aden

NIGERIA   Madagascar
           R   BRITISH
                              EAST AFRICA

Johannesburg
                NATAL
         CAPE
         COLONY
Cape Town

Industrialized nations   Export markets opened
                                              up by technology
Industrializing nations
                                                  Meat
Major industrial regions c. 1914
                                                  Fruit
Improvements in communications
                                              Major cash crops
——— Major rail networks c. 1914
                                              ₽   Coffee
——— Shipping routes
                                              ○   Cotton
······· Underwater telegraph cable
        route   R   Rubber

Location of manufacturing industry   ↓   Sugarcane

 +   Heavy machinery, iron and steel   ⬦   Tea

 ⧲   Textile production

long winters might have been perfect for the growth of the handicraft industry, except that British mercantilist legislation discouraged it. As a result, those who couldn't make it from their farming alone either moved on (mostly to upstate New York, which had more and better land), or went into commerce, shipping, and shipbuilding, which were permitted. After the revolution, the connections made in those trades and the skills learned in the shipyards served early factory-builders well, and the lack of handicraft development meant they faced no low-wage competition. With plenty of water-power and stolen designs to complete the picture, New England was soon up and running as the first factory center in the Americas.

7.1 Sweet Industry: The First Factories

When we think of the first factories, we usually think of Europe, particularly England. After all, factories were the definition of the "modern" and Europe was the leader in modernization. We assume that they were first built in Europe, where capital, machines, and labor combined to create ever-more efficient and productive methods. European ingenuity and entrepreneurship together with previously accumulated capital and budding markets led to the industrialization that was the secret of Europe's centuries-long domination of the world economy. According to this story, the globe was divided between industrial Europe, and later the United States, and the agrarian exporting rest of the world. With this international specialization of labor, the agricultural countries only belatedly industrialized. In fact, there is good reason to turn this version on its head: the first factories arose in the colonial, export-oriented world.

To be sure, the importance of the New World colonies for the rise of industry was long recognized. Karl Marx observed a century and a half ago: "Direct slavery is as much the pivot of our industrialism today as machinery, credit etc. Without slavery, no cotton; without cotton, no modern industry. Slavery has given the value to the colonies, the colonies have created world trade; world trade is the necessary condition of large-scale machine industry." The Cuban historian Manuel Moreno Fraginals echoed this sentiment much more recently: "Sugar received and gave a strong thrust in the development of capital: it was essentially a big motor that accelerated English industrial growth." In these versions, however, the colonies lead to industry *in England* because of the capital and markets they provided.

In fact, a good argument can be made that the first industrial factories were the sugar mills of the Americas. It is not surprising that one of *Webster's* definitions of "factory" refers directly to the colonies: "a place where factors reside to transact business for their employers, as, the British merchants have factories in the colonies." But the colonies also had factories in the more standard definition: "an establishment for the manufacture of goods, including the necessary buildings and machinery." Usually we think of the manufacture of goods as involving the production of a finished product from raw materials through the use of machinery on a large scale and a division of labor.

The last part is crucial. Although sizable workshops had existed since ancient times, bringing together scores of cobblers, tailors, or weapons makers who used tools to transform raw materials into finished products, they did not have specialized labor. Each cobbler made the entire shoe; there was no integration of effort. One worker's product was not dependent upon the work of his neighbor.

The emergence of factories is usually credited to the presence of wage laborers who were able to master the more sophisticated techniques demanded by industrialization. For Karl Marx, industrialization and capitalism came hand in hand. But the fact is that arguably the first factories were the sugar mills of the Atlantic islands such as São Tomé and then the Caribbean. They not only did *not* issue from a natural process of domestic capital accumulation with their product intended for the domestic market, but they also did not use much wage labor, nor did they make great demands of expert laborers. On the contrary, sugar was refined by large slave forces for export to Europe.

Already in the seventeenth century, sugar plantations involved perhaps two hundred slaves and freemen, with a mill, boiling house, curing house, distillery for rum, and storehouse. This involved not only some of the most sophisticated technology of the era, and a large workforce, but also investment of several thousand pounds.

True, nine-tenths of the workforce were field hands engaged in brute labor. But the 10 percent in the crushing, boiling, and distilling plants were very much specialized labor. More importantly, the scale, complexity, and social organization of the sugar mills made them the first factories. Time was a ruthless master in the sugar production process. Once harvested, cane had to be rushed to the mill to prevent loss of sugar content. In the mills, especially the larger ones, close care of temperature was necessary. The boilers' fires had to be constantly stoked; the liquid sugar had to be moved from kettle to kettle without permitting unwanted crystallization, while running off the sediment at the right time. Then the sugar had to be quickly brought to the curing house where the molasses was run off. Sugarcane produced various qualities of sugar, as well as molasses and rum. The closer the attention to production, the better the final product and the greater the returns.

We think of labor-saving machinery when we think of factories. Indeed, technological advances from the sixteenth century on meant that the sugar mill was able to process much more sugar with far less mill labor. But the great cost of the mill and its voracious appetite meant that large armies of slaves were put to work twenty hours a day feeding the sweet monster. Technological improvement created the demand for greater and more disciplined labor. This was no leisurely tropical enterprise. A Barbadian colonist reported in 1700 on the sugar mill: "In short, 'tis to live in a perpetual Noise and Hurry . . . the Servants [read: slaves] night and day stand in great Boyling Houses, where there are Six or Seven large Coppers or Furnaces kept perpetually Boyling . . . one part is constantly at the mill, night and day, during the whole Season of making Sugar."

This led to sugar mills becoming the first factories ruled by the discipline of industrial time. The specialized work gangs had to coordinate their efforts: cane had to be quickly cut when mature; carters had to carry it to the mill; the hungry crushers were constantly fed cane; the leftover cane, the bagasse, was carried to the boiling room to stoke the fire. The time exigencies of the production process meant that slaves had to work together as so many parts of a well-oiled machine. Efficiency and slavery, labor saving and labor intensification were combined.

The vast amount of sugar that this method produced caused the price of sugar to drop vertiginously, turning the one-time luxury spice and medicine into a mass food and eventually into a food additive. In the early stages of England's industrialization, from 1650 to 1750, per capita sugar consumption rose, while that of bread, meat, and dairy products stagnated. Sugar fueled not just the industrial revolution, but the European industrial workforce.

Sugar, which we think of as a leisure and pleasure product, an import from the balmy Caribbean lands of mañana, was actually the first industrial product and a cruel master to the hundreds of thousands of slaves who labored to turn out sweet delights. Marx observed that "the veiled slavery of the wage-workers of Europe needed, for its pedestal, slavery pure and simple in the New World." He could have added that the factories of the Caribbean were holding a mirror in which Europe could see its industrial future.

7.2 Fiber of Fortune: How Cotton Became the Fabric of the Industrial Age

"He who says the Industrial Revolution says cotton," according to one standard text, and cotton textiles were among the first products produced in recognizably modern factories. But as the story proceeds, we usually focus on the machinery, not the fiber; it seems coincidental that the birth of the factory coincided with a switch in Europe's principal fiber crop. In fact, it was anything but. Had cotton (long the fiber crop of choice in most of Asia) not replaced flax and wool as Europe's leading cloth source, it is hard to imagine the industrial revolution taking the same course. And had Europeans had to grow the crop themselves, rather than rely on New World plantations, the increased demands on their land, water, and labor supplies could easily have short-circuited the process.

Cotton was known in India more than 2,000 years ago (as was a machine quite close to the modern cotton gin); it spread slowly to the east, north, and west. It was easier to twist into yarn than hemp and much more comfortable to wear. By roughly 1300, it had spread from west Africa to Japan. It was not cultivated in Europe, but it was known there as well; during a medieval wool shortage, Venetian merchants brought the new fiber from Aleppo (in modern-day Syria), where it was combined with wool to make an ersatz cloth called fustian. But these imports were limited. For the next 400 years, cotton largely bypassed Europe while conquering Africa and Asia.

In China, cotton cloth gradually became the fabric of choice for almost everybody; peasants wore the coarser grades, and even the very rich wore some cottons in rotation with their silks. The range of quality—and price—was enormous: an eighteenth-century document records that some of the cotton cloth used in temple rituals cost 200 times as much per yard as the grade used by most ordinary people. In India, there were not only cottons of all qualities, but a wide variety of cotton-silk blends, which became the standard of excellence throughout the Old World. Buyers as far away as West Africa and Southeast Asia would draw patterns that merchants would then take back to India, where a particular village with whom that merchant had connections (usually indirect ones) would create fabrics to order for the next trading season. In the 1600s and 1700s, the Europeans got in on the act, too, purchasing so many cheap, high-quality Indian cottons that they provoked riots among English woolens workers and various acts of protective legislation by Parliament.

But unlike with silk—where the Europeans made endless efforts to learn to produce the yarn at home—cotton plants were never imported to Europe on any significant scale. This may have been just as well for Europe, because self-sufficiency in cotton fiber came at considerable ecological cost for various parts of Asia. In China's Lower Yangzi region (near present-day Shanghai), huge amounts of soybean cake fertilizer had to be imported (mostly from Manchuria) to replenish the overworked soil; by the peak of the trade in the late eighteenth century the quantity of soybeans used for this purpose could have fed about 3 million people per year.

In Japan, it was the sea that provided the needed ecological relief for cotton-growing land. Japanese fisheries expanded enormously in the eighteenth and early nineteenth centuries, mostly in the direction of Sakhalin

Island (leading to various tense encounters with eastward-moving Russians), but most of the catch was not eaten; instead, it, too, was used mostly as fertilizer, and mostly for land growing cotton. (Paddy rice, the biggest food crop in both China and Japan, produces very high per-acre yields with a minimum of fertilizer.)

And cotton is a thirsty crop, too. By the early nineteenth century, North China peasants growing cotton were finding that they needed to re-dig most of their wells because of a sinking water table—a problem that has reached crisis dimensions in that region today.

Europeans, meanwhile, were still using much more flax and wool than cotton, even in the mid-eighteenth century; through much of the seventeenth and eighteenth centuries, Parliament kept passing subsidies to encourage more flax production (with very limited success) rather than trying to secure greater supplies of raw cotton. But two related events—industrialization and population growth—made continuing with those fibers more or less impossible. First of all, eighteenth-century inventions made it possible to spin cotton into yarn and weave the yarn into cloth, mechanically, achieving astonishing results: a roughly one hundredfold gain in yarn spun per hour over a few decades. Figuring out how to machine-spin oily, rubbery flax took considerably longer, though the problem was eventually solved.

Europeans did quickly figure out how to spin and weave wool mechanically—though not quite as well or as quickly as with cotton—but wool presented different problems. First of all, it was not what was wanted in many strategic markets—especially in the tropics, where cloth was exchanged for slaves in Africa and used to clothe them in the Americas. Worse yet, wool production faced serious ecological limits. Sheep-raising requires far more land per pound of fiber obtained than raising fiber crops, and as population grew, there simply wasn't enough land available for this relatively low-return-per-acre use. In fact, replacing just the cotton imported by Britain in 1830 with wool would have required over 23 million acres: more than the entire farm and pasture land of Britain! And the problem would only have gotten worse over time, since Britain's cotton imports rose by twenty times from 1815 to 1900.

The solution, of course, was cotton from the New World, especially the American South. Imported slaves did the labor, while rural Europe disgorged workers to become factory operatives. Though cotton was very tough on the soil, the land supply in the New World seemed virtually limitless. England's new textile mills hummed along, heralding a new economic era, while those who produced their own cotton close to home wrestled with environmental decay, land and water shortages, and the need to *increase* their agricultural labor forces to keep local looms and spindles going.

7.3 Combing the World for Cotton

The world's largest industrial power—and most of the others—depend on an essential, imported, raw material. One region supplies most of it; and that region is politically unstable. Before things blow up, the world's leading power begins planning to develop alternate sources.

The United States and Middle Eastern oil? No. The description above is of Britain in the 1850s, contemplating the possibility that Civil War in the United States could wreak havoc on its cotton supplies. In some ways this was an easier task than replacing oil; after all, cotton can be planted in new areas, whereas oil can only be extracted where it happened to form millions of years ago. But despite many years of lead time and concerted efforts, Britain had limited success in staving off a "cotton famine." The reasons tell us much about how the nineteenth century world differed from our own.

Britain had begun by 1850 to make considerable efforts to increase its cotton supply. Yet in spite of these efforts, "the supply of raw material . . . prov[ed] obstinately inelastic."

The major focus of British efforts was India. The colonial government was pursuing a "cotton-oriented policy of annexation and railway construction," during the 1850s, targeting promising cotton lands for conquest and investing huge sums in transportation, but had little to show for it for the first decade. A big jump in cotton exports did occur in 1861—much of it at the expense of domestic consumption and shipments to China rather than by expanding output—but Indian shipments were still less than half of U.S. shipments to Britain in 1861. Moreover, exports rose only 8.6 percent further after this, even though this was when the Union blockade became effective and cotton prices soared.

The other relative success—with far less outside effort—came in Egypt. This was possible because the Egyptian government itself had been committed to expanding cotton output since the days of the early nineteenth-century reformer Mohammed Ali: and once the mills he had ordered built proved uncompetitive, the cotton crop was available for export. Exports began in 1821, passed 27 million pounds in 1824, and almost 50 million pounds by the 1850s. Yet despite years of landlord pressure on cultivators, backed by a state inspired by Lancashire's success, these were limited achievements. Even the 1850s level of cotton output was about that of the United States in 1803—just a decade after Eli Whitney's cotton gin. In fact, up until the 1860s, Egyptian cotton growing did not spread far beyond the lands of Mohammad Ali's descendants and their relatives. Even at its peak during the American Civil War, Egyptian cotton exports reached only 200 million pounds (about 12 percent of U.S. exports in 1860) and cost much more than U.S. supplies had.

What's more, even that level of Egyptian production was probably not sustainable, much less capable of further expansion.

During the U.S. Civil War, about 40 percent of the Nile Delta was growing cotton in any given season; given the rotations being used, it appears that cotton was grown in every Delta field at some point between 1863 and 1865. With only a limited amount of well-watered land in Egypt, this probably represented an absolute maximum of possible cultivation without the kind of irrigation made possible by twentieth-century megaprojects. Even on this land, costs of cultivation quickly rose to levels that were profitable only at the absolute peak of prices in 1864; and at those prices (in fact, even at the lower ones of 1862), raw cotton was actually more expensive than coarse yarn.

Britain's less-focused efforts to stimulate exports from other promising-sounding sources—Brazil, West Africa, Queensland, and Burma—produced almost nothing, even though prices soared. Thus, even though U.S. cotton shipments were cut off for only three years (the blockade became effective in mid-1862, and the war was over in 1865), British cotton consumption fell 55 percent between 1861 and 1862. The price of cotton relative to wool more than tripled from 1860 to 1864. Mill employment fell by roughly half in 1862, and total hours worked by close to 80 percent. Numerous firms went bankrupt.

With such powerful efforts, why such meager results? In part because the United States cast a long shadow: since its production would not be off the world market for ever, it made little sense to switch to cotton in areas where that would require large fixed investments (in irrigation for instance) that were otherwise not needed. In part because many peasants were quite reasonably skeptical of greater reliance on the market: with the transportation and marketing institutions available in some places, people could not always be sure that the cash they might get for cotton would turn into a secure supply of grain. Meanwhile the aggressive tactics of British promoters sometimes backfired. Much of the land targeted for new cotton-growing in India was forest, and people often protested its sudden elimination. The rapid extension of the rail network that was also tied to trying to obtain more cotton was a significant factor in the Sepoy Mutiny of 1857: the biggest threat to British power in the subcontinent before the twentieth century.

Finally, for all its seeming modernity, nineteenth-century industry still belonged to a natural world. British wealth and might could try to make more cotton grow; British science could not yet make artificial fibers. Nor could they quickly produce seeds that would grow cotton in new places, or that would replace the short-staple cotton grown in much of the world with the longer fibers needed by mechanical spinners. For the time being, industry had simply grown faster than the science it needed.

New hybrid seeds and cheap power to pump water long distances eventually solved these problems; but they arrived only in the twentieth century, transforming cotton planting in much of China and India and making cotton growing possible in California and Arizona. (Had it been possible to extend cotton cultivation—and thus slavery—into the American Southwest back in the 1850s, the lead-up to the Civil War might have been very different to begin with.) When those new cotton varieties were developed, they were descendants of seeds from the Egyptian cotton boom: a long-delayed off-shoot of an episode that seemed to have ended in failure.

7.4 Killing the Golden Goose

When Vasco da Gama arrived in Calicut, India, in 1498, he found as inter-preters some north African Muslims who had been in the city a while and knew the ropes. Legend has it that they took him aside to tell him his gifts for the port officials had been laughable—next time, they said, better bring gold. And how, da Gama asked, should he acquire gold? Go to the kingdom of Kilwa, on the East African coast, they said—and be sure to bring textiles made in Gujarat, the Northwest Indian weaving center.

Before long, of course, the Europeans found in Latin America piles of precious metals beyond anything in Kilwa. But when the Dutch arrived in the Moluccas (Indonesia) a century after da Gama's voyage, they found their New World loot was not acceptable as payment for the spices they sought. Instead, the local nobles and merchants wanted to be paid in textiles from Coromandel, in Eastern India; before long the Dutch East India Company found it necessary to have a trading post in Coromandel in order to carry on its Southeast Asian procurement. And over the 200 years following that (all the way down to 1800), a variety of European powers found that Indian tex-tiles were the preferred way to pay for African slaves. These cloths made up more than 50 percent of the goods exchanged by French traders for slaves in the two years (1775 and 1788) for which we have complete records; one Frenchman noted ruefully that while Francophone planters in the Caribbean could be forced to take French goods for their sugar, African traders refused, insisting on top-quality products. The British experience in Africa was simi-lar until very late in the century, when their artisans finally learned to make passable imitations of Bengal and Coromandel fabrics. (The American-cen-tered accounts in high school books usually tell us that the trade was a tri-angle of "molasses to rum to slaves," but destructive Euro-American goods actually had much less appeal to African chiefs than fine fabrics, furniture, and so forth: alcohol was about 4 percent of the goods that the English ex-changed for slaves, and guns about 5 percent.)

In much of the world, then, Indian textiles were more liquid than money. They were also probably the first industrial product to have a worldwide market. Fine Indian fabrics reached more than just Southeast Asia and Africa: in the 1700s they drove most of the Ottoman silk industry to the wall, conquered Persia, and won a big chunk of the European market; indeed, they might have wiped out the English weaving industry if the Spitalfield weavers riots of 1697 had not been followed by strict quotas and high tariffs against all grades of Indian textiles. (Daniel Defoe, the novelist whose *Robinson Crusoe* is often regarded as a manifesto of free trade and the rising English merchant class, here lent his talents to the protectionists, publishing a pamphlet against imported cloth.) Probably the only court in the eighteenth-century world not graced by Indian cloth was that of the Chinese emperor. Meanwhile, the cheaper grades of Indian cloth traveled equally well, clothing laborers from Southeast Asia to North America, including many of the slaves who had been sold for fancier Indian cloths. (As with fine fabrics, the European market for coarse cottons was also on the verge of being conquered when mercantilist princes and parliaments intervened to limit India's market share.) All told, India probably produced over 25 percent of the world's cloth; and since its own population (at most 15 percent of the world in 1800) was poor and lived mostly in hot climates, a good two-thirds of that was available for export.

What accounted for this fabulous success? In part, it was careful attention to customers' changing wants: even in the 1400s, it appears, Indian merchants often returned from Southeast Asia with drawings of new patterns that their trading partners wanted copied for next year's fabrics. In part, it was superior access to a huge crop of high-quality cotton; except in China, no comparable source existed until the post-Independence American cotton boom. But above all, it was highly skilled labor—much of it available at extremely low wages.

Indian wages in general were probably lower than those in China, Japan, or Western Europe; and in Bengal, where huge rice surpluses kept food cheap, nominal wages were especially low. (Indeed, both Indian and other merchants redirected many of their orders for coarse cloth from Gujarat on India's West Coast to Bengal as the gap in food prices between the two regions grew in the late seventeenth and eighteenth centuries.) But within the general category of weavers were different levels of craftsmen, who presented very distinct problems to cost-conscious merchants.

While many weavers of coarse cloth were part-time weavers and part-time farmers, weavers of the finer cloths tended to be full-timers who lived in and around a few big cities (especially Dacca, today the capital of Bangladesh). Virtually all weavers received advances from merchants; these not only paid for needed raw materials, but paid the weavers' living expenses until the cloth was finished and accepted. The merchants, of course, always tried to use these advances as leverage over the weavers; in time, they did succeed in reducing many skilled workers to perpetual indebtedness, and so broke their power to bargain. But for the more highly skilled weavers, the strong demand for their work enabled them to accept advances with impunity. If necessary, they could usually find a new buyer for their cloth so they could repay an advance from a particularly unreasonable merchant; or, better yet, they could find a new patron who would protect them when they reneged on their original contract without repaying the advance. Coarse cloth weavers had much less assurance that they could market their goods to a new buyer at the last minute; but if the harvest season looked busy enough, they might just abandon their cloth and go back to agriculture full time, supplementing work on their own farm with peak-season wage labor. Even politically connected Indian merchants could not always keep control of their weavers under these circumstances; and the correspondence of eighteenth-century European merchants is full of complaints about lost advances.

What finally brought an end to the reign of Indian textiles? In the long run, England's industrial revolution, begun by firms largely dedicated to imitating Indian cottons for sale in African and American markets. But even before that, Englishmen in India, trying to hold back the challenge from Lancashire, had begun to kill the goose that laid the golden egg. When the English East India Company conquered Bengal in the 1750s, it immediately set out to eliminate all other buyers of cotton textiles for export and finally bring the weavers under thorough control. Various discriminatory measures hobbled other merchants: a new law made it a criminal offense to work for anybody else while someone had an outstanding advance from the EIC (even if he finished his work for both buyers). The EIC agents were empowered to post guards at the homes of weavers under contract to them. The EIC admitted that it paid anywhere from 15 to 40 percent less than other buyers, but expected these measures to help it get all the cloth it needed anyway; a Company official told Parliament in 1766 that now that it ruled Bengal, the EIC expected to double its cloth exports within a few years.

Instead, though, weavers took the only recourse they had against what was now effectively a state monopsony; they left their looms entirely, migrating or becoming agricultural laborers. Within a generation, the specialized weaving communities around Dacca had disappeared, and the city itself shrank to a fraction of its former size. Countless looms in peasant homes that had once produced for export now only made cloth for fellow villagers. The EIC's goals were no different in kind from those that had always motivated the merchants in this trade; but by pursuing them with a new ruthlessness and consistency, they had done the seemingly impossible, destroying their era's premier industry in order to save it.

7.5 A Triangular Trade in Ideas: Early Modern Europe, China, and Japan

In the centuries before international trade in cheap everyday goods took off, much of what was traded—silk, precious metals, and so on—directly affected just a few people. The biggest benefit of these trades probably came from the accompanying exchange of knowledge. Artisans copied foreign products. Ship's doctors studied local herbs, and ships themselves had added on useful features observed elsewhere in the harbor.

Few examples of this interchange were as important—and as poorly understood—as the exchanges among China, Japan, and Western Europe between the first European arrival in the 1500s and the first Opium War of 1839. The conventional story is of two one-way streets. First knowledge flowed from Asia to an eager Europe; then, once Europe pulled ahead, the flow reversed, with a worried Japan copying the West and a proud China refusing to learn. But the real story is more complicated.

Europe did learn the most in the early years, and much less toward the end. But even in 1800, China had some things to teach. For instance, the breakthrough of the Scottish engineer John McAdam (from whom we get "macadamized" roads)—that a thin layer of broken stone, free to expand and contract with temperature changes, was better than the thick, rigid slabs used in Roman roads—was old hat in China, and observations of this probably influenced McAdam.

China's alleged obliviousness to Western advances is also much exaggerated. First, it turns out that Europeans brought less knowledge than one might think. Catholic missionaries, for instance, brought advances in astronomy (and with them, Euclidean geometry) but withheld the heretical insights of Galileo, Kepler, and Newton. Consequently, some of their calculations did not add up. Thus, when the Chinese learned of them, it did less to whet their appetite for Western knowledge than to make them suspicious of their visitors. Chinese science still benefited—in part because the prod of foreign mathematics led to a rediscovery of forgotten Chinese work in this area—but much less than it might have.

In technology the response—often from ordinary people—was more enthusiastic. Western gadgets—from cuckoo clocks to windup toys to telescopes—became fashionable along the South China coast, and local craftsmen learned to make them: by the 1700s, the better copies made in Chinese cities were indistinguishable from the originals. This required enormous skill in areas like gear-making and precision boring, which one might have expected to be transferred to other kinds of production. That it wasn't—at least not much—remains a puzzle, which might be partly explained by a pattern of extreme specialization, subcontracting, and mutual separation between different urban crafts.

The Japanese case might be the most complex of all. In the 1500s, Japanese craftsmen were learning eagerly from foreign sources. They quickly learned, for instance, to reproduce foreign weapons, which were used extensively in the civil wars of the 1500s. Once peace returned, the guns were destroyed, and the Westerners restricted to a limited presence at a single port (Nagasaki). Yet through that port, a group of Japanese intellectuals kept close watch on both new developments in Western medicine and technology (known in Japan as "Dutch studies") and on innovations from China. Not until very late were the Europeans perceived as being on a fundamentally different and faster track, in part because technology everywhere was still thought of as mostly a matter of discrete innovations made by producers in a field; the idea that new techniques represent "applied science" is largely a nineteenth-century notion.

In fact, many Western innovations reached the Japanese through Chinese translations or copies, and, even as late as 1870 (by which time we usually think Japan had left China in the technological dust), many innovations in basic economic activities (especially farming and food processing) continued to come from China. Japan did not "take off" simply by being a "pupil" of the West's best practices.

Where Japan did quickly outpace China was in finding new uses for foreign technology. Thermometers, for instance, first became known through Nagasaki as medical instruments, but within just a few years they were also being used out in rural silkworm sheds, where temperature control was crucial for the improved quality control—the kind of internal transfer of knowledge that seems to have been slower in China. Through efforts like this, Japan did indeed gain the most in the nineteenth-century flow of knowledge. But from beginning to end, the flow was triangular, not a set of one-way streets.

7.6 Sweet Success

It was not a promising beginning for a world trader. Nicholas Loney arrived in Iloilo, a provincial capital in the central Philippines, on July 31, 1856. His carriage didn't arrive from Manila until the following February; annual monsoons made the roads impassable and the seas too dangerous. And the place where he hoped to build a wharf was a swamp full of crocodiles.

Nor was it a happy ending. Thirteen years later, Loney died, shaking and feverish, of malaria. One hundred carriages and, an observer noted, "lots of buffalo carts" carried him to his grave. By then the transformation of the area by world trade was well under way. A native textile industry that had once employed half of the area's women was dying, undercut by the Manchester mills for which Loney was an agent. To provide a return cargo for ships bringing cloth, Loney started something that would become much bigger than the textile trade: the export of sugar from nearby Negros Occidental. It is for this side interest, which made Negros planters rich and still dominates Philippine trade, that Loney is remembered. But in Iloilo City, it's a bittersweet memory.

Loney arrived as the first British consul in Iloilo, just months after the Spanish suspended laws routing all foreign trade through Manila. He was also the agent of several British textile firms and a partner in his own trading company. In those days, even the mighty British Empire had a small civil service, and a businessman actually willing to live in such a remote place was welcome to wear two hats at once. Loney wore several. For a while the only resident "Anglo-Saxon," Loney also served American firms, did research for a book the governor of Hong Kong was writing, and even took on a task for a British anthropologist—procuring three skulls from a local graveyard.

The place he explored and eventually transformed was a puzzling mixture of extremes. On the one hand, Loney was often moved to compare Iloilo to the Garden of Eden and to describe its inhabitants as unspoiled "savages"; he seems to have preferred them to the Spanish officials and priests. On the other, there was much to remind him of England a century or so before. Almost every home contained a loom, some as many as six. Thousands of women worked them, producing cloth "of an admirable beauty which is impossible to imitate in Europe because the cost of production would be prohibitive." *Mestizo* merchants—the offspring of male Chinese traders and local women—supplied cotton, silk, and hemp-spun yarn, and paid the women months in advance, turning them into "virtual slaves." Their output went first to Manila and then under sail for the rest of Southeast Asia, China, and even Europe and the Americas.

In fact, the native cloth was so good that Loney despaired of ever winning the upper-class market. He reasoned, however, that cheap British textiles could appeal to the "laboring population"—if he could do something about shipping costs. But that meant bringing oceangoing steamships directly to Iloilo, replacing the island-hopping, shore-hugging sailcraft that had carried the area's trade for centuries. That meant finding something for big freighters to take away, too.

Loney, an amateur naturalist (he caught the malaria that killed him while exploring a local volcano), found that something. He realized that nearby, sparsely populated Negros was perfect for sugar; some was already grown for local use. At Loney's urging, British and American firms lent him money to develop sugar estates and to build a waterfront at Iloilo, making it the area's break and bulk port. The British-built steamships he promoted took the guesswork out of shipping schedules—which had never been a big problem for cloth merchants, but would have played havoc with easily perishable sugar. Loney's own firm and others for which he was an agent bought the sugar and marketed it in Australia, Europe, and the United States.

They also brought in British and American cloth, which soon dominated even Iloilo's home market, destroying a formidable regional competitor. Families that had once depended on women's weaving and a little farming fled the depressed weaving villages—only to discover a new debt bondage in Negros, where plantation owners (often former cloth merchants) regularly used bribes, title fraud, and deceptive credit arrangements to turn these pioneering farmers into landless laborers; after that, foremen with whips disciplined the truculent. In fact, Loney encouraged reform of the region's credit laws—to modernize Iloilo's economy, he said. But the new law wound up making debt harder to escape—thereby reinforcing near-feudal labor relations. Negros boomed, with sugar exports surpassing 10 million tons by 1932. The province still generates much of the Philippines' foreign exchange, and sugar remains the basis of most of the country's richest and most powerful families.

For Iloilo, even the boom years had a double edge. The weaving industry had paid its workers poorly, but it had kept families together. Women generated enough cash to pay taxes, which allowed men to concentrate on food production. Loney's waterfront gave the city a different feel. It was a rough-and-tumble place where groups of muscular young men would gather at five in the morning to seek work; wages were paid daily, and lunch was "served" by dumping rice and vegetables into the men's hats. The town became nationally famous for its working-class culture: workers patronized the bars, restaurants, vaudeville theaters, and brothels, because they had no hope of saving for a family. When waterfront unions became strong in the 1920s and 1930s, shippers started skipping Iloilo and loading directly at the plantations. Loney's plans had destroyed first weaving, then the port. Yet a monument to him stands at Iloilo, near the once-swampy waterfront that bears his name. As a man for whom trade was a civilizing mission, he would have been proud.

7.7 Lighting the Night and Darkening the Day
by Dennis Kortheuer

When Thomas Edison threw the switch on the nation's first electric power plant in 1882, he turned the night into day for fortunate consumers of the

New York generator. But, unknown to him, he also sent Mexican farmers from their sunny fields into the darkness of copper mines.

Although the world was passing out of a dark age even before electricity, with candles, oil lamps, and gas lanterns, much of life had still been lived to the rhythms of the spinning Earth. But now with electricity, work and play could continue ceaselessly. Factories could run around the clock, and restaurants and dance halls could stay open all night long. City streets, where the shadows of night had masked sins that proper people dared not even imagine, would be flooded with the redemption of white cleansing light, returning the streets to proper gentlemen and ladies. These promenading citizens couldn't imagine that they owed some of their new-won pleasures to Mexican *campesinos*, who, instead of tilling their fields as had their ancestors, dug round the clock in the sweltering desert of Baja California, extracting the red metal that made wiring, and hence the transmission of electricity, possible.

Locals had known there was copper around Santa Rosalía on the east coast of Baja California since at least 1868, but not much had come of it. Here was a desolate, virtually uninhabited wasteland. This changed in 1885 when the French Rothschilds of the wealthy banking family joined with the bank of Mirabaud-Paccard-Puerrari to found the Compagnie du Boleo. Capitalized at 12 million francs, the company began building a smelting plant, a dock and harbor, a railroad, and offices for the company and for the Mexican customs office.

The El Boleo mine was clearly an enclave. Building materials, food, and equipment were imported. Forty administrators came from France. But the foreign capital and know-how were not sufficient to extract the copper. Mexican miners had to be attracted to this desolate area. Hundreds of workers, many of them Yaqui Indians, came across the Sea of Cortez from Sonora. What had been a desert dotted with scattered small shafts became within a few short years a town of thousands and one of the world's most important copper mines. The local population grew more than twentyfold in less than a decade.

Most of them came to El Boleo and Santa Rosalía, as the town soon became known, with little or no mining skills. They were farmers or ranchers, who had found that whatever work they did on the land was not enough to support themselves and their families. They heard of the mine from friends or from *engancheros* (labor contractors) hired by the company to recruit workers. Many claimed they were not told that they had to pay for their own boat ticket from Sonora. They felt little better than indentured servants for the first months of employment. Others had a worse experience: the job promised them at Santa Rosalía did not exist; they were left to wander the streets, no way home and no other work to be had in the company town.

But most found work. The big smelting oven had to be fired twenty-four hours a day, seven days a week, or the cooling and heating would cause costly damages. This meant that the mines themselves had to also operate round the clock. Miners worked twelve-hour shifts at temperatures above 100 degrees. They wore nothing more than loincloths, sandals, and leather hats, upon which they placed the tallow candles used to light their way. (Ironically, electric lighting would not come to the mine until decades later, the comfort of the consumer obviously being more important than the comfort of the producer.) Mine work was largely unaided by mechanization, even though they were enabling the electric revolution. The elite of the mine crew, the men who worked the picks, usually worked in pairs, one man holding the pick, the other hammering it with a ten-pound sledge. Between strikes the pickman would rotate the steel bar, so that as it dug into the rock it would break out chunks, which could then be carried up and out of the shafts, where others waited to sort and load it into railcars, which carried it to the smelter where it was further sorted and melted in the huge ovens of the smelter. Fathers would often team with sons, the senior teaching his junior the craft, and the junior taking longer shifts at the hammer as dad aged. The rest of the family lived in urbanized "barrios" outside the mines, because the area was too barren for agriculture.

It is unlikely that Thomas Edison thought of the miners of Santa Rosalía when he pulled the switch in New York. But he certainly affected them. Electricity, which would turn the night into day and power labor-saving machinery created a tremendous demand for copper. The labor saved in New York was expended in Baja, California, where Santa Rosalía became a thriving community, a successful industry (the largest copper mine in Mexico for a while), and an internationally known harbor. The community included thousands of people who had, since time immemorial, worked the land as farmers in the glare of the sun and now sweated in the cavernous dark of the mine. The ladies and gentlemen strolling under the streetlamps of New York had nothing in common with those miners—except the thread of copper that tied them together in a world that got smaller with ever-flowing watt of electricity.

7.8 No Mill Is an Island

Take a quick guess. Which city had the first mechanized textile mill in Asia: Osaka, Shanghai, or Bombay? The answer is Bombay, roughly twenty years before Osaka; and by 1914, India had the world's fourth largest cotton textile industry. And where was almost 85 percent of continental Asia's railroad track in 1910? In British India, with the third largest rail network in the world. So when World War I provided a brief respite from Western competition in Asia's markets, and new export opportunities as well, a savvy observer might have figured Bombay was ideally placed to benefit. So why did Osaka achieve major industrial breakthroughs, Shanghai important and lasting gains, and Bombay only a bubble of growth that disappeared once peace returned?

In all three cities, World War I brought a surge in industrial profits; but beyond that Bombay and its Far Eastern counterparts diverged. In Osaka and Shanghai, the capacity of modern mills soared, both during the war and for a couple of years afterward, with enough domestic growth to more than take up the drop in imports. In Bombay, the total number of spindles barely changed during the war, and India's consumption of machine-made cloth dropped over 20 percent.

Perhaps even more important, some Chinese and many Japanese firms took advantage of demand for more textile machinery amid a shortage of imports to start producing this equipment at home; and at least some of these firms survived to become the core of new capital-goods producers. Nothing comparable happened in India. And while the whole world went through a postwar recession, Osaka and Shanghai simply grew more slowly than in 1914–1918; Bombay mills sank back to prewar output levels, and to a market share well below what they had had in 1913.

Why the difference? Some Britishers blamed a lack of entrepreneurial spirit, but that makes little sense. The Bombay mills were, after all, run by the same people who had successfully chased British yarn out of the low end of the market over the previous few decades—not only in India but in East Asia. And India certainly had no shortage of cotton or of willing laborers.

In large part, Bombay's paradox had a simple root—it was part of a colony, not an independent state. For one thing, British-imposed tariff policies had long encouraged Bombay mills to concentrate on production of coarser yarns, aiming at markets elsewhere in Asia, while leaving the more lucrative end of the home market to Manchester; this meant that mills faced tricky adjustments if they were to engage in wartime import-substitution. But Shanghai and Osaka mills managed precisely this transition. The ways in which colonial status hobbled Bombay most become clear if we look at the downside of what at first seem like advantages: in particular, at how India got its precocious rail network and at the absence of precocious and uncompetitive heavy industries like those built for the militaries of China and Japan.

On the one hand, British rule had helped the country get a huge rail grid well before the volume of commercial freight would have made it profitable to build one, in part because the British wanted to be able to move their troops around quickly. (In China, which remained independent but suffered many foreign interventions, the same concern worked the other way: rail construction was often resisted by Chinese who saw in it a way that foreigners could make a few troops go a long way.)

But the same colonial relationship allowed Britain to insist that all the railroad equipment, engineers, and steel be imported from Britain: indeed, providing this outlet for British capital goods (and investors) had been another central reason for pushing rail construction. But since everything was imported, this massive construction did little to nurture Indian ironworks or machine shops that might have later filled Bombay's orders for modern spinning or weaving equipment.

Second, as a colony, India never built government-subsidized arsenals, or allied facilities like coal mines and steel mills, as part of a program of defense-oriented industrialization; both Japan and China did. A quick accounting might suggest that this was to India's advantage: the arsenals were expensive, and even Japan's iron and steel industries were not internationally competitive until after World War II. (China's still aren't.) But these seeming white elephants paid huge dividends for China and Japan in 1914–1918. While a shortage of Western-made capital goods was proving to be a big bottleneck in Bombay, machinists, mechanics, and others originally trained in China and Japan's arsenals were turning their attention to the needs of Shanghai and Osaka's textile mills, match factories, and other light industries; and while domestic steel for these machines may have been pricey, at least it existed. (Meanwhile, Japan's military industries also paid for themselves another way, extracting valuable land and cash indemnities from the country's neighbors—until this led to disaster in the 1940s.) And while foreign competition was gone, even fairly high-cost production yielded profits that could be invested in better techniques to try and hold market share after the war: Shanghai industrial *investment* actually peaked in 1918–1923, while competition was intensifying. Bombay mills, which had added more workers but not more plant during the war, simply cut their work force (and its wages) when imported yarn and cloth returned. These were perfectly rational decisions for each individual mill owner to make, but collectively they signaled a huge opportunity lost for industrial leadership—one that, thus far, has not come again.

7.9 Feeding Silkworms, Spitting out Growth

Mention Japanese agriculture today, and the first phrases that spring to mind are *not* "competitive," "export-oriented," or "subsidizing industrial growth." Since we all know that today it is Japan's phenomenal industrial success that makes its economy strong, we often tend to read that story farther back in time than we should. But from Japan's opening to the West in the 1850s until World War II, it was agriculture that supplied most of Japan's exports, fed its burgeoning cities cheaply, and paid the taxes that made it possible to build infrastructure. And in sharp contrast to their noncompetitive descendants, Japan's late-nineteenth- and early-twentieth-century farmers got mostly grief for their contributions to building modern Japan.

Until World War I, manufactured goods accounted for only about one-fourth of Japanese exports; silver and timber made up some of the rest, but farm goods were dominant. Above all, Japan's first sixty years of modern imports (including the textile machinery that finally created a competitive industrial export in the 1920s) were paid for with silk; this fiber alone made up 40 percent of Japanese exports year after year until 1900, and was still over 30 percent on the eve of World War II. Meanwhile, though the population doubled, rice imports never went above 20 percent of consumption. All of this was achieved while the number of farmers stayed about the same. How did it happen?

Though some new inputs played a role—chiefly chemical fertilizers after the 1920s—the key to the story was hard work and more humble technical innovations. New labor-intensive methods of transplanting rice seedlings increased yields; an increased diligence about gathering and burning rice husks immediately after the harvest (when older generations of farmers would have taken a few days off for a festival) made it harder for pests to breed. These and other innovations made it possible to double per-acre rice yields between 1870 and 1940. But above all, what happened was that cash-hungry farmers—hard-pressed by high taxes, rising rents (about 58 percent of an average harvest in 1878, and up to 68 percent by 1917), and other burdens—found a way to produce both silk and rice on the same farm.

Silkworm raising and paddy rice growing share a virtue that makes them perfect for crowded Japan—they yield a lot of output per acre. However, they also share an offsetting problem: they demand extraordinary amounts of labor, much of it packed into a few intense periods. When the fields are flooded in the spring, rice seedlings must all be planted at perfect intervals within a few days; even families with a small plot find they need to work as long as they possibly can.

Silkworms are, if possible, even more exhausting at peak season. As the silkworms near maturity, they need to be fed eight times a day (they eventually eat 30,000 times their weight), and their trays must be cleaned at least three times. Worse yet, silkworms require fresh-cut mulberry leaves at each feeding, so that keeping even a small group fed at peak season means having somebody at work twenty-four hours a day. And nature being what it is, silkworms naturally hatch and spin their silk between April and June—exactly the same times that rice needs to be planted. Thus, while Japanese farms had long produced both rice and silk, few farm families could do both—most Japanese silk came from families up in the hills, who grew crops other than rice.

This began to change slowly in the early nineteenth century. The secret, somebody discovered, was that by keeping the silkworm shed at a controlled temperature, one could make the silkworms hatch (and eat) faster. The result was an even more hectic few weeks, and plenty of risk: temperature control was no mean trick in a world of wood fires and no thermometers, and getting the temperature wrong could mean ruining the silk crop (which most people borrowed to raise) entirely. But if it worked, one at least shortened the overlap between rice season and silkworm season; with luck, one could prevent the women of the family (who fed the worms and worked in the fields only on the absolute peak days) from having to be in two places at the same time. Bit by bit, more rice-growing households began to try doing both things. Then, after 1870, came the real breakthrough: a new silkworm variety, which, with proper care and the aid of some chemicals, could be tricked into hatching between July and September. It wasn't cheap, it wasn't easy, but it worked. Silk production rose almost tenfold between 1880 and 1930, while the average number of days that a farmer worked during the year went up about 45 percent.

And what did farmers get for working harder and working smarter? Not a whole lot. In real terms, rice prices peaked in 1880; by 1930, they were down almost one-third. True, farmers were selling twice as much rice, but they were also spending a lot more (especially after 1900) for fertilizer, pesticides, and so forth. While consumers benefited greatly from increased production, most farmers saw no growth in their net income from rice-growing, and a decline in the per-hour returns to their labor. For a long time, silk was a compensating bright spot, but it, too, had its limits. When American demand for silk stockings nosedived during the depression, Japanese silk exports did, too; a little bit later, the invention of rayon delivered the coup de grâce. By most measures, rural Japanese on the eve of World War II were no better off than their forebears seventy-five years earlier. The payoff came to later generations: those who found jobs in the new factories, those who sold their farms for burgeoning suburbs, and those few who, still on the land, are now propped up by the modern sector their ancestors gave so much to build.

7.10 From Rocks—and Restrictions—to Riches: How Disadvantages Helped New England Industrialize Early

When Europeans "discovered" North America, those who hoped to get rich quick went to the South, or to New York or Philadelphia; New England was for those more interested in godliness than high living. Of course, some resource-poor areas get rich through industry, but here New England faced man-made barriers: English colonial policy was designed to make the colonies suppliers of raw materials and importers of manufactures. So how did New England become the first area outside England itself to master new technologies in areas ranging from mechanized cotton-spinning to brass production? In part because its natural and man-made disadvantages combined to keep it out of some of the blind alleys of pre-factory manufacturing.

At first glance, New England seemed able to keep some self-reliant frontier folk alive—but not much more. The growing season was short, the soil rocky, and the hills and forests to the West forbidding; coal and iron were scarce, too. By combining indigenous farming methods with their own, the immigrants learned to produce enough for a healthy subsistence. Indeed, the crops were good enough, and the area sufficiently free of both the contagious diseases of the Old World and the mosquito-borne plagues that raged in the Southern colonies that by the late 1600s New Englanders may have had the highest life expectancies in the world. (The only other likely contenders were in Japan.) And New Englanders also multiplied impressively: from 33,000 in 1660, the population had soared to about 700,000 in 1780.

But rapid multiplication could also mean a spartan standard of living. Indeed, after the first waves of Puritan zealots, few people were attracted to New England, no matter how long one could live there: over 90 percent of the population in 1790 were direct descendants of people who had come by 1660. (The mid-Atlantic colonies drew more immigrants, and the South, of course, imported huge numbers of involuntary immigrants.) At a very early date, New Englanders had realized that their farms would yield only a small surplus above their own needs, which made it hard to buy much of anything else. In 1646, the General Court of Massachusetts was already urging local people to produce more of their own clothing, shoes, boots, glass, and ironwares, because the colony simply couldn't sell enough to pay for English imports. (The South sold tobacco and later cotton, while the mid-Atlantic colonies, with larger harvests, fed the plantations of the West Indies.)

Had this program succeeded, New England might soon have had the same sort of "proto-industrial" landscape that was spreading across much of Western Europe (and for that matter, much of Asia): villages in which many families had too little land to survive on, but supplemented their income by spinning, weaving, making roof tiles, and other activities *for the market*—often under the direction of a merchant who loaned them the necessary tools and raw materials—and buying some of their food. Indeed, the long New England winters might have been perfect for these activities.

But two crucial factors undermined this strategy. First, the existence of empty land to the West (especially in what became upstate New York) provided an alternative, though not a very popular one. Second, Parliament forbade most commercial manufactures in the colonies: and since needed raw materials (from cotton to iron) would have had to be imported, this prohibition was surprisingly easy to enforce. New England farmers did whittle, weave, and so forth to make goods for their own use and keep expenses down, but rural manufactures to sell never took off. And that meant trouble for, say, a group of brothers left a farm that had supported their parents well enough, but would not yield enough to let them all raise families.

The answer to this squeeze lay in the forests and the sea. Shipbuilding was one industry that England was glad to see spread through the colonies, since England itself was far too deforested by the 1600s to meet its own needs. New England was well supplied both with trees and with rivers, which moved logs and powered sawmills. And the builders of ships also became important users of ships. First New Englanders took over much of the cod fishing that had drawn Europeans to their coasts in the first place. (Being easy to preserve, cod was an increasingly important protein source back in Europe, where pressure on the land was forcing meat prices ever higher.) Once a base of necessary ships and skills developed, New Englanders moved increasingly into whaling and merchant shipping.

Most likely, New Englanders did not prefer these occupations to weaving or other crafts that would have let them stay closer to their families and friends; but once forced on them, the choice proved a blessing in disguise. When Independence voided British colonial legislation, New Englanders were free to turn to manufacturing, and had a clean slate to write on. The area's first textile mills, created by infringing English patents, were built within a few years of the revolution; and unlike early textile mills elsewhere, they faced neither economic competition nor political opposition from low-tech, low-wage weavers and spinners scattered through the countryside. Boston, Providence, and New Haven soon commanded the industrial markets of their hinterlands and the region's cities grew without being swamped by rural migrants whose livelihoods had been destroyed by the new factories. Preexisting overseas contacts helped secure raw materials and markets; the profits of trade provided start-up capital; and carpenters who had learned in shipyards proved adept at copying early factory equipment. Within a very short time, New England was competitive with Britain in a number of manufactures. New York, with less waterpower, lagged behind, and the South far behind. As it turned out, the "handicaps" of rough natural conditions and restrictive legislation had interacted to leave New England perfectly positioned to copy much of the early industrial revolution.

7.11 American Oil

Petroleum became the world's most valuable internationally traded good in the twentieth century, which is why it has been christened the century of oil. Petroleum's uses had evolved from patent medicines, lighting and heating, building material, and lubricants in the nineteenth century, to mainly fuel for internal combustion engines and raw material for plastics and fertilizers in the twentieth. Today, we think of the Middle East when we think of oil. But for most of its first century, as a commodity, it was largely an American story. American not only because of the vast production and consumption of petroleum in the United States, but also because Mexico and Venezuela were early world oil production leaders. The oil stories of the three countries were closely intertwined.

The story, as usually told, was directed by heroic entrepreneurs, such as the American John D. Rockefeller of Standard Oil and the Dutch Henri Deterding of Royal Dutch Shell, who with other leaders of the multinational Seven Sisters, dominated world oil production its first half century. The common view is that the world was their theater, where they directed with minimal government support or interference. Places such as Mexico and Venezuela were simply sites of oil reserves, not actors in the drama. But in fact, national governments and oil workers took starring roles. Decisions and profits in the industry did not flow out of simple calculations of demand and supply, profit and loss. As oil came to substitute for coal as the blood of the industrial revolution, it was not only "black gold" but a symbol of the modern. National sovereignty, pride, development, and defense, as well as the class struggle, competed with the profit motive in powering the growth of the oil industry and the world economy.

Forms of petroleum had been known and used in the Middle East, particularly Iraq, since 3000 B.C. But its modern history began in the United States in 1859 when Edwin L. Drake struck it rich in Titusville, Pennsylvania. The industry soon spread to Ohio where John D. Rockefeller began Standard Oil after the Civil War. Initially supplying the needs of the burgeoning and urbanizing U.S. population, by the 1870s and 1880s the majority of kerosene was exported, becoming the fourth largest U.S. export. Pennsylvania's dominance would be challenged by Los Angeles fields by the early 1890s. Then in 1900 came East Texas's Spindletop gusher.

Mexico was brought into the oil age as an importer of kerosene from a Standard Oil subsidiary and, to a lesser extent, from Texas companies such as Gulf and Texaco. Royal Dutch Shell, a Dutch-British enterprise also fought to sell into the fast growing Mexican market. The government of Porfirio Díaz, (1876–1911) had sought to attract foreign capital by subsidizing Mexico's rapidly growing railroad network, protecting foreign investment, coercing domestic workers, and privatizing subsoil rights, which had been a government monopoly since the Spanish colonial regime. He sought to maintain national sovereignty during the Age of Empire by diversifying dependence. Mexico became one of the most hotly contested areas in the world for European and U.S. capital (see 6.7, "How the United States Joined the Big Leagues"). Oil became a major theater in the international contests when a California oilman, Edward Doheny, found crude in Tampico, Mexico. Other wildcatters and the major companies quickly began explorations. The Mexican government began to worry. To slacken the ever-tightening commercial bonds between Mexico and the United States, forged by the connecting railroads and avoid the sort of industrial and financial trusts that were monopolizing the U.S. economy, the Díaz regime gave lavish concessions to the British construction company headed by Weetman Pearson. Pearson in turn sold a major share to Royal Dutch Shell. Soon many other U.S. companies were bringing in oil wells and refining the black fuel for the swelling Mexican market. Before long, production outstripped domestic consumption. Mexico became the world's second leading petroleum producer by 1921 at about the same time that the U.S. Geological Survey mistakenly claimed that American reserves were running out. More attention than ever focused on Mexico.

The vertiginous ascent to becoming a major world player was startling, because oil was gushing while Mexico was swept by one of the bloodiest revolutions of the twentieth century. As a spectacularly lucrative enclave, petroleum companies could afford to post guards, buy off government officials, and bribe revolutionaries. Just looking at Mexican oil export figures, one would have no idea how troubled the country was.

But the oil companies, by now almost all foreign-owned, could not remain safe from the revolutionary tide. There is much debate about the causes and aims of the Mexican Revolution. However, it is clear that at least some combatants were fighting for nationalism and social justice. The 1917 Constitution promulgated them in Article 27, which returned purview over mineral rights to the national government. This led alarmed oil men in the United States to demand an invasion of Mexico to overturn the new constitution. The saber rattling brought about compromise under which existing concessions would remain in force but new ones would not be signed. Since the foreign oil companies still had many unexploited concessions, and climbing oil prices made their existing fields spectacularly profitable, warfare was avoided.

But Mexican nationalism was not quieted. The higher pay, better quarters, and coveted management positions that Americans and Dutchmen received, as well as foreigners' racism, learned from experience with race relations in Texas, Oklahoma, and California, made the oil fields a breeding ground for radicalism, just as they were at the same time in Russia's rich Baku fields, whose workers Stalin helped organize. The growing nationalism of the Mexican postrevolutionary state, prodded in part by U.S. invasions, first of the port of Vera Cruz in 1914 and then General Pershing's fruitless expedition into Mexico in search of revolutionary hero Pancho Villa in 1916, led to legislation that favored Mexican workers over foreigners. The tide of corporatist Catholic thought that was sweeping over southern Europe persuaded Mexican leaders that the state should organize and co-opt labor and turn it into a foundation of the regime, rather than treat it as a threat. Government-sponsored unions strengthened the position of Mexican workers who came to occupy the most important positions in the industry. Taxes on the multinationals also rose.

The foreign oil companies became fearful of labor strife and state radicalism in the wake of the Soviet nationalization of the vast Russian deposits. This and a decline in production as the most prolific deposits in Mexico became tapped out increasingly turned Standard's and Shell's attention toward Venezuela in the 1920s. Reluctance to compromise on both sides finally led Mexico's president, Lázaro Cárdenas, to nationalize the Mexican oil industry in 1938 and create a state petroleum company: Pemex, run by Mexicans. Timing was crucial in allowing Mexicans to assert their sovereignty in the face of the threat of their northern neighbor. The oil-starved Nazi German market provided a welcomed alternative to the United States for Mexican exports as the Seven Sisters tried unsuccessfully to boycott Mexico.

Mexico's exports continued to decline in the 1930s and 1940s. The usual explanation, especially popular with Standard Oil's management, was that Mexicans could not run the industry without American or European technicians. In fact, the decline in exports in part reflected the success of the Mexican government's import substitution industrialization policy. After an initial decline, production levels surpassed those of the boom years. But the oil was sold at below international market rates to subsidize industries within Mexico. Pemex later became one of the world's largest oil companies, especially after the Tabasco and Campeche fields were struck in the 1970s. At the beginning of the twenty-first century Mexico was the fifth largest oil producer in the world and Pemex the second largest petroleum company. The Mexican government received one-third of its revenue from Pemex oil profits.

Venezuela proved to be a temporary relief from Mexican nationalism for the energy multinationals. It was attractive initially because its longtime strongman, General Vicente Gómez, whom Mexico's nationalist educator and writer José Vasconcelos called the "Porfirio Díaz of Venezuela" offered generous concessions to the foreign companies. By 1928 Standard, Shell and Gulf caused Venezuela to surpass Mexico and become the world's leading exporter. By 1948 they provided almost half of the world's internationally traded oil, selling mostly to the United States and western Europe.

The oil companies transferred to Venezuela the policies they had developed in Mexico. As one observer noted, there were country clubs for the American employees and tropical shacks for the others. General Gómez was pleased with the oil income, which allowed him to buy off potential political rivals. However he died in 1935. His successors maintained cordial relations with the multinationals, but could not ignore the swelling wave of nationalism. Cárdenas's nationalization of Mexican oil created a worldwide sensation. Some of the same epithets thrown about in the Mexican fields were now heard directed at foreigners in Venezuelan camps, because not only managers and engineers had decamped from Mexico to Venezuela, but so had workers and labor organizers. The calls for greater tax revenues from the petroleum companies and better treatment for their workers could no longer be ignored, as Argentina, Bolivia, Brazil, and Cuba also nationalized their oil industries. Even the conservative military leaders were attracted by concerns of national sovereignty and the possibility of greater government revenue. Though siding with the United States in the Cold War, they exacted an increasingly higher price for their friendship. State control over the industry gradually grew. Finally, in 1976 the national oil monopoly was created, Petróleos de Venezuela S.A. (PDVSA).

The Venezuelans went beyond the Mexican example that had inspired them. In addition to a state monopoly, they negotiated with their Middle Eastern competitors to regulate the international oil market. In 1960 they organized OPEC, the Organization of Exporting Countries. By 1973 these countries had a strong hold on the world's most lucrative trade, which they retained past the end of the twentieth century. By the year 2000, six of the world's ten largest oil companies were state-owned. Pemex and PVDSA were the second and third largest and the pillars of government finances in Mexico and Venezuela. Government leaders, rather than "heroic entrepreneurs" are now in command of the global oil industry. But they have not always acted as public servants concerned foremost with the national welfare. Reigning in these companies to act in the "public good," rather than as "a state within a state," led to tensions in Mexico and dramatic strikes and conflict in Venezuela under President Hugo Chávez at the beginning of the new millennium.

As an epilogue, rich oil deposits eventually led not only to export economies. Brazil and Mexico have become two of the world's largest economies and major automobile producers. U.S., European, and Japanese automakers have mounted massive factories that produced more than a million cars a year, making Brazil one of the world's ten largest producers and Mexico the fourteenth. Brazilians elected Ignacio Lula da Silva, a social democrat of the Workers Party (PT), who rose from an autoworker and labor organizer to the presidency in 2002. However, he found his opportunities for great reform curtailed by the threats of international bankers, many of whom worked closely with the major private oil companies, which remain powerful in the world economy.

American oil has been dynamic, and it has led in directions never envisioned by the U.S. and European investors at the beginning of the twentieth century. Its shifts and turns make predictions for the future difficult. But its central place in world trade is secure, at least for the coming decades.

7.12 Running on Oil, Building on Sand

What coal, railroads, and steamships were to the nineteenth century, oil, automobiles, and airplanes have been to the twentieth: sinews of power and symbols of progress (and fear). Actually, worldwide oil use did not surpass coal use until after 1965, and coal still makes up most of the global energy reserves. But well before it became the world's main fuel, oil had been used to make something that coal had never made: countries.

Perhaps the most important of these oil states—who ever speaks of "coal states?"—is Saudi Arabia. And its story is full of surprises.

Looking at the Arabian peninsula 200 years ago—or earlier—it was pretty clear where you'd expect any future unifier to come from. A strip along the western edge of the peninsula (bordering the Red Sea), called Hijaz, includes the largest populations, including the Muslim holy cities of Mecca and Medina. A second choice might be the western edge of the peninsula, called Hasa, which included prosperous Indian Ocean merchants. The extremely dry and poor center of the peninsula, including Dir'iyyah, home of the Al Sa'ud clan, would have much longer odds.

Indeed, while the Ottoman Empire claimed this territory, in practice they made little effort to rule it, because it was unlikely to ever yield them much revenue. They did pay attention when Sa'ud ibn 'Abd al-'Aziz allied with a puritanical Islamic sect from the area, the Wahhabi, and led a group of Bedouin soldiers into Mecca in 1803, banning all "innovations" that they felt threatened original Islam (but represented normal religious practice to millions) and challenging the Ottoman role as protectors of the holy places. But troops from much more populous and wealthy Egypt had no trouble driving these forces out, and went on to sack the Sa'ud's hometown. A second Sa'ud-Wahhabi attempt at expansion—this time to the east—ended again in defeat and exile in 1891. Meanwhile, long-term trends around the world—especially booming population and more intensive land use—certainly favored farmers and urban-dwellers over nomads. The Sa'ud's moment might seem to have passed, without ever really having come.

The British, who soon arrived cash in hand, subsidizing local rulers around the edge of the Ottoman domains, seem to have thought so—they looked first to Qatar, Kuwait, Bahrain, and other coastal states, largely ignoring the interior until World War I (the era of "Lawrence of Arabia"). But Ibn Sa'ud (1880–1953), who had returned home from Kuwaiti exile in 1902, proved both militarily and politically skilled—making the most of a small British stipend and the political chaos surrounding Ottoman collapse, he reconquered by 1925 what his ancestors had briefly held more than a century earlier, including Mecca. By promising not to threaten more important British interests in Iraq and Jordan, he obtained British recognition of his kingdom the next year; other major powers followed.

But Sa'udi control was in some ways as fragile as in 1803. They eschewed nationalism, ruling as monarchs in the name of Wahhabi Islam—and their religious enforcers proved quite unpopular, even provoking a rebellion among Ibn Sa'ud's Bedouin troops. (Britain's Royal Air Force helped crush the rebellion—airplanes ending the mobility advantage of mounted warriors in the desert, who surrendered to the British in 1930 rather than to Ibn Sa'ud.) Meanwhile, the British had withdrawn Ibn Sa'ud's allowance, leaving him only one significant source of revenue—taxes on pilgrims to Mecca (and accompanying merchants). When annual pilgrimages dropped by 80 percent during the Depression, the new state neared bankruptcy, and still had no administrative bureaucracy to speak of—its money went largely to the royal clan and for gifts to important followers. Unable to continue those gifts, it faced collapse.

Then oil came to the rescue. While coal still ran most factories, locomotives, and seagoing freighters, oil was the fuel of cars, airplanes, and big, fast, naval vessels—and thus a military necessity. When fields in California began to decline (ca. 1920), the U.S. Geological Survey proclaimed an imminent shortage. Exploration boomed, and both Standard Oil of California and the Anglo-Persian Oil Company sought permission to try Saudi Arabia. The Americans offered more cash up front; Ibn Sa'ud took it in 1933. Commercial production began in 1938; and during World War II, the kingdom came under American protection. By 1945 state revenues had risen 900 percent, thanks almost entirely to oil. From then on, the money kept flowing, and the United States—by 1945, the world's preeminent power—continued to guarantee security. (The United States itself used little Middle Eastern oil until the 1970s, but its Western European allies used a lot.)

A durable state had been created, based almost entirely on revenues from foreigners (first British subsidies, then pilgrims, then oil companies), foreign recognition and military support, and—in the crucial oil fields and elsewhere—foreign workers. Even today, Saudi Arabia levies no income taxes on its own nationals—many of whom receive government payments—and more than half the labor force is foreign.

The situation abounded in surprises—at least if one expects national states to be built by mobilizing the local population. In the early 1950s, the U.S.-owned Arabian American Oil Company (ARAMCO) had more than five times as many employees as the Saudi government—and in addition to handling the oil, it built much of the country's infrastructure. The foreign employees lived in an "American camp" said to resemble Bakersfield, California, and had little contact with most of the population. In theory, this allowed the Americans to live as they pleased without coming into conflict with a society governed by strict Wahabbi principles. (In practice, the barriers were often leaky. ARAMCO, for instance, ran its own TV station so that Americans could watch their favorite shows without exposing Saudis to them. Inevitably, locals figured out how to tap into the signal. More seriously, the huge difference in conditions between the "American camp" and an adjacent "Saudi camp" aroused great resentment.) And since the Saudi population provided neither the state's essential revenues, nor its essential workforce, nor its essential security forces, the rulers faced little pressure to grant them political rights. No representation without taxation, one might say.

The roller coaster of world oil prices since 1971 first exaggerated these conditions, then began to change them. Saudi GDP quintupled between 1971 and 1974 as oil prices soared, and ambitious development plans, many first hatched in the 1960s, became reality. Population soared, educational and other benefits multiplied, and imports (many of them hard to reconcile with Wahhabi austerity) rolled in; the kingdom became a political force to be reckoned with, and a more engaged populace began to make new demands. The oil industry itself was nationalized. Then oil prices crashed in the 1980s, and 1970s social benefit levels plus high-living royals led to chronic budget problems. Add powerful cultural tensions, nearby wars, and increasing discomfort with the American presence, and Saudi Arabia may face a rocky road toward becoming "normal"—toward basing itself on revenue and soldiers from its general population. But so far, the foreigners and the hydrocarbon they love still remain—along with the potential for more surprises.

Epilogue:
The World Economy in the
Twenty-First Century

There is widespread agreement that we live in an era of "globalization," but very little agreement about what that word means. Although we do not propose to definitively solve that question here, we believe that viewing the current intensification of transregional connections in the context of earlier globalizations can at least make clear some of the things that "globalization" has not been, as well as some insights into what it is. Living in a world of immediate gratification, instant communication, ephemeral fads, overnight pop heroes, and advertising that trumpets that image is everything, students of today's world (especially those who are well off themselves) can be swept away by short-term apparent trends and controversies. This volume is based on the assumption that even in our postmodern times, there is a place for understanding the slowly evolving underlying structures of social and economic change and the cycles of conjunctures as well as the more exciting and busy world of events. We have attempted to assemble analyses of worldwide episodes over the last five hundred years to give us a better sense of where we are and how we got here.

So, what is "globalization" *not?* It is not a process in which economics always writes the story by subordinating political and cultural concerns. Just as we have seen that missionaries, warriors, scientists, and others who were not primarily interested in material acquisitions often drove the intensification of global interconnections in the past, so Amnesty International, the Red Cross, Red Crescent, Falun Gong, and al Qaeda all represent relatively new networks of transregional (if not quite global) reach that have little to do with the profit motive. Nonetheless, they clearly are instrumental in strengthening or inhibiting interregional relations. Profit-seeking corporations certainly do not always succeed in overriding the influence of less market-oriented organizations when the two clash: the international movement to boycott apartheid-era South Africa, for instance, imposed real costs on some of the world's mightiest multinationals and led to the abolition of that heinous practice; and the continued paucity of foreign investment in various zones from Russia to Central Africa that would seem promising on purely material grounds (e.g., the abundance of natural resources and/or educated but low-cost labor) make clear that, for better or worse, local institutions do influence the degree to which global networks penetrate.

Second, as the above examples indicate, globalization is not about either the inexorable expansion of the state and public sphere as was formerly expected, nor the withering away of the state, which is a more popular expectation today. Indeed, as one professor has quipped, it may be that the only place the state is really withering away is in the minds of some political scientists. Central banks may not be able to set interest rates as they wish, but the period in which they could do that was actually a rather brief one—and occurred only in some countries, anyway. Even states that were already strong half a century ago have many new and expanded capabilities, such as enforcing intellectual property rights in new areas like the Internet and genetics. Surveillance technologies that already exist or are on the near horizon raise the possibility of much greater control over society and the market. Polling gives leaders today a much better notion of what their citizens think and how to convince them of new ideas or causes than Roosevelt, Churchill, or Stalin had. (Whether they use those tools as skillfully is another matter.) And if we consider some states that were weak (or nonexistent) a generation or two ago, the growth in their power to affect their citizens' lives is often quite striking. Compulsory primary and often secondary education has come to most, though not all, of the children in countries decolonized since World War II; a large share of the world's remaining nomads have been forced to settle down, respect borders and private property in land, and in some cases, accept displacement by dams and other government-sponsored projects in remote areas. Moreover, increased engagement with the world economy has both strengthened and weakened states, even in recent times. Consider on the one hand various oil states that often lacked the means to tax their people— and thus to affect them in other ways—until petroleum revenues made it possible to build a state from the top down; Saudi Arabia, where the state had only a very rough idea of what its population was in 1970, is just one of several cases in point. But on the other hand, consider the many countries that, having accepted "structural adjustment" policies as the price of access to international credit, were forced to dismantle their welfare states: they have often seen popular loyalties shift away from the nation and toward ethno-religious movements (including offshoots of Islamic fundamentalist groups in the Middle East, Hindu nationalist groups in India, and Protestant Evangelicals in the Americas) that provide some of the basic health care, education, and other services people no longer receive from the state. Elsewhere, as in Colombia and El Salvador and even in parts of the urban United States, drug cartels and street gangs have assumed welfare and policing functions. Even in these instances, however, the state is needed to protect property and enforce general public order. Indeed, with the safety net of the welfare state seriously fraying, the state's role as gendarme has been reemphasized.

Third, it is important to realize that "globalization" is not one-way "Westernization," much less "Americanization." Economically, it is well-known that the most rapid growth of the last thirty years has been in East and Southeast Asia; what is less widely known is that this is as much a matter of growing intra-Asian trade as of Asian trade with the West. Indeed, intra-Asian trade has been growing faster than world trade as a whole for almost the entire period since the 1870s. Culturally, it is certainly true people recognize Mickey Mouse almost everywhere, but much of the growth of transnational popular culture is regional: South Korean and Taiwanese pop culture in China, the exchange of *telenovelas* among various Latin American and southern European countries, the widespread popularity of Indian cinema in Asia. And as the success of everything from curry to sushi to *manga* comics suggests, the West receives cultural influences as well as originating them.

In all these ways, the dynamic of contemporary "globalization" seems more continuous with what we have described for earlier decades and centuries than is sometimes acknowledged, and more uncertain in its outcomes. For instance, the drug trade that we point to as an important, though generally unacknowledged sector of the early modern world economy remains one of the largest sectors of international commerce today. Piracy, both on the Internet and on the high seas, as well as bandits on land are still widespread, as are forms of slavery and coerced labor. Yet the cumulative effects of 500–plus years of "globalization" have certainly made the world a very different place than it was in 1492. And many of the transformations are *because* of the growth and penetration of the world economy. What are the principal differences?

First, there are clearly far more people on the face of the earth. The Earth's population crossed the one billion mark only around 1800. A hundred and twenty years passed before it reached two billion. In the next seventy years humans' count exceeded six billion! In most parts of the world, life expectancy has almost doubled in a hundred years, so people occupy space for much longer. At each stage, world trade has played a role in population expansion: bringing maize and potatoes to African and Eurasian farmers, and guano and other fertilizers to later generations of cultivators; creating vast wheat and rice export zones in the nineteenth century, and spreading green revolution technologies and new medical techniques in the twentieth century.

At the same time per capita consumption has exploded, so that the environmental impact of each person has expanded. Humans, seeking to maximize their individual and collective incomes, have come to dominate the earth's plants and animals to a degree simply unimaginable for a Ming bureaucrat, Spanish explorer, Dahomey chief, or Aztec warrior 500 years earlier. Roughly half of all energy used by humans since the first emergence of hominids has been used since 1900. Of all the energy from the sun that winds up being used by living things each year, probably close to 40 percent is ultimately appropriated by humans. The world is known down to the square yard, as satellite eyes in space calculate GPS locations while bathyscaphs explore the bottoms of the ocean (yet insurgents in the backcountry of Pakistan and Afghanistan or the Amazon are still almost impossible to track down). It has been reckoned that there is no place on earth free from human-made noise.

As humans swarm over the face of the Earth, the border between nature and property is being erased. Humans claim, harness, clone, and patent evermore living matter, while at the same time domesticating or exterminating creatures and plants. Hunting for genomes and synthetic goods, people seek to control and replace nature rather than just expand its production and enjoy its fruits as in the past. Some genetically modified seeds are so commodified that they have built-in obsolescence so that they cannot be harvested and reused by farmers without them making a new purchase from the multinational seed marketer. We find that many solutions, such as introducing exotic insects (the African bee) for more honey production, exotic fish, such as the walking catfish to clean out waterways, and exotic plants, such as kudzu (introduced as animal feed), cause their own almost insurmountable problems. Increasingly the world is, rather than a garden or a field, a massive marketplace. Property rights, which are after all human constructs and inventions rather than inherent in nature, are being invented and extended constantly. In addition to ownership of existing plants, livestock, and areas of the surface of the world, property has become much more inventive. Large futures markets bet on anticipated production; professional athletic teams trade in the right to sign athletes to contracts that remove their liberty to choose other employers. Companies trade in pollution quotas, allowing them to dirty one area in which they manufacture because a cleaner producer elsewhere sold its virtue as a permit to pollute. Youths purchase fictional cyberspace identities and tools for use in online computer games. Web site names are bought and sold. Cultural and intellectual property rights have become a major new battlefield.

In one of the strangest cases of commoditization run wild, the Pacific island nation of Nauru gradually sold first its territory, and when that ran out, its privileges as a sovereign state. First its land made its inhabitants comparatively prosperous for years by selling phosphate mining concessions, piling up assets abroad that allowed payments to its citizens. These payments became increasingly important as the island itself largely disappeared, thanks to this same mining—today, 90 percent of the island is a wasteland, so that the country essentially became a set of financial assets held in New York, London, and Melbourne, and citizenship a share in those assets. When those assets dwindled due to mismanagement, the country took a further leap into abstraction, seeking to recoup by commoditizing its national existence: it allowed foreigners to set up "Nauru" banks without even visiting the island and became a center of money laundering and tax evasion (for the Russian mafia, among other groups). It also allegedly offered, for a fee, to set up an "embassy" in China that would provide cover for various operations by American intelligence services.

The same momentum that makes some people argue that today's world economy is uniquely free of constraints—be they those ones imposed by states, by cultural limits on acquisitiveness, or by unconquered nature—makes others wonder whether our economy is headed for an ugly collision with one or more of these constraints. Although such arguments are almost infinitely varied, they can be roughly sorted into three categories. Some deal with inequality, predicting that if unchecked it might lead to a crisis of under-consumption and/or growing political opposition. Others deal with culture, pointing to the possibilities for countermovements spawned by objections to the homogenizing tendencies of commodity culture. And yet others deal with nature, pointing either to finite supplies of key resources or to the possibility that massive pollution will make the earth far less hospitable to human activities than it is today. Without offering prophesies, let us look at each of these briefly to see how different the contemporary world economy is from what we have seen before.

The growth of inequality over the long term is unmistakable. As late as 1750, the Yangzi Delta, China's wealthiest region, probably had a per capita income roughly equal to that of England, the richest country in Europe. In 1800, it has been estimated, the ratio of the per capita income of the richest countries to the poorest ones was still only 2 or 3 to 1. By 1900, however, that ratio was 12 or 15 to 1; by 2002, 50 or 60 to 1. And of course, countries are not homogenous either. If we look at individuals, it has been estimated that in 1988 the richest 5 percent of people had incomes fifty-seven times those of the poorest 5 percent; just a few years later, in 1993, that ratio had soared to 114 to 1. Even in the United States, which prides itself on a democratic middle-class culture, at the beginning of the new millennium the net worth of one individual, Microsoft founder Bill Gates, was estimated to be greater than the combined net worth of the United States' 100 million least affluent residents. And the Waltons of Walmart fame are richer than Gates. The concentration of wealth has been institutionalized as a handful of massive corporations not only dominate the most profitable areas of the world economy such as, oil, energy, electronics, aviation, and automobiles, but also have moved into the service sector beyond banking and insurance to craft enormous international store chains such as Walmart which alone imports one-third of the United States' consumer durables exported from China. A handful of companies control the press, radio and television media, publishing, and telecommunications. Never have so few people controlled so many so intimately.

Yet the crisis of capitalism that Karl Marx forecast one hundred and fifty years ago has not happened in the form that he expected. The Great Depression of the 1930s and the petrodollar shock of the 1970s as well as the bursting 1980s financial bubble and the stalling of Japan's apparent stratospheric takeoff in the 1990s threatened the world economy. But the underconsumption scenario did not happen: this has been in part because of the invention of new financial tools such as the credit card and the automatic teller machine (ATM), which have facilitated increased consumption and debt among the more affluent, in part because collective action by the poor has enabled at least some of them to increase their access to the world's wealth, in part because, while the poorest countries continue to lose ground, large consuming "middle classes" have now developed within a number of largely poor societies (India, China, Brazil, Mexico, etc.) and because the Chinese government has invested its trade surplus in U.S. bonds rather than share it with Chinese workers and consumers.

Because of worries over underconsumption, consumption is now given more emphasis than production. We are now told that it is consumption, not production or savings, that drives the U.S. and the global economy. The old nightmare of a world awash in profits needing to be reinvested, which would then beget a glut of high-powered machines producing far too many products for people to buy does not seem to be on the horizon, partially because it has proved possible to invest products in "machines" (such as televisions) and labor (such as advertisers) that produce ever-more ardent consumers. In other words, the modern world economy has revealed an ability to produce not just ever-more goods, but also contrarily, ever-more insatiable appetites by emphasizing what people *lack* in order to create dissatisfaction. To satisfy their swelling desire capitalists, merchants, and state administrators have invented methods for easy borrowing. In some cases, such borrowing allowed for less affluent people to make investments that ultimately narrowed wealth gaps, as subsidized home loans in the United States of the 1950s and 1960s did, and as student loans probably continue to do; in others, cheap credit just expands indebtedness and inequality.

Pointing to the ever-larger role of consumption and advertising in people's lives, critics have predicted an eventual cultural reckoning. Some point to resistance from groups strongly attached to noncommercial values (e.g., religion, the environment) threatened by various kinds of commodification. Other people object to highly sexualized advertising, or to the way marketers encourage youths to imitate their peers elsewhere in the world rather than model themselves on the adults of their own society. Retailers are accused of cultural desecration as in the case of Walmart de Mexico which is building a superstore in the shadows of the revered two thousand-year-old pyramids of Teotihuacan. Some essayists have noted that the emphasis on leisure activities undermines the work ethic and leads to societies of passive, obese spectators. Ecological groups stress humans' debt to other living creatures and the ecosystem. They remind us that it is not only our own nest that we are dirtying. They argue that the most precious goods are collective and perhaps should be outside the market: clean air, clean water, uncontaminated seas, unspoiled soils. Others, by contrast, fear that consumerism may succeed all too well: that by creating people who really are as narrowly focused on their own self-interest as the "rational actor" of Economics 101, the world economy will undermine the extraeconomic institutions (e.g., family and nation) and loyalties to them that make a functioning society possible. Even neoliberals who profess great allegiance to the efficiency and liberating forces of the market where self-interest reigns supreme, often also emphasize patriotism, community activism, and religious morality as necessary for continued collective social life. After all, the market requires cooperation as well as competition.

Certainly cultural conflicts are common today; but they are not new, as this volume has shown. And both marketers and consumers themselves continue to use markets to increase the perceived value of mass-produced products by deploying them in ways that resonate with the particular cultures they live in, rather than by rejecting those cultures. Christian rock downloaded to an iPod, "affinity" Visa cards that generate income for one's alma mater or favorite cause, and rural Chinese inserting new consumer goods into an elaborate version of old gift-giving rituals (reaffirming their place in their community in the process) are all examples of this tendency. While the global economy homogenizes in some ways, people continue to find ways to make distinctions and assert difference. Indeed, many of the most successful corporations are successful in part because they respond to these differences. Thus we find MacDonald's franchises in places with many Muslims that feature Ramadan cookies and stay open late during that period, others that have no beef items (in India), and others (in various countries) that, having become hangouts for young people in societies with few other such places, encourage customers to linger, so that they are no longer "fast food places."

The other broadly cultural concern—that as we all become ever-more focused consumers, we will lose the capacity to assume other vitally important social roles—poses more subtle problems. It does seem to be true that the marketplace model is invading other realms and changing the content of terms such as "citizen." It is striking, for instance, how often governments at all levels in the United States now speak of satisfying their "consumers." Half a world away, a Chinese media campaign encouraged retail workers to conduct themselves in the spirit of Lei Feng—a Cultural Revolution-era hero who indeed said he lived to "serve the people," but meant by that something far more transformative than giving them prompt, cheerful help with their purchases. How much these trends have to do with what seems to be a declining willingness in many countries to pay for collective goods through taxes is hard to say; and how far that trend is likely to go is even less clear. These "cultural contradictions of capitalism," to use Daniel Bell's phrase, are real enough, and are bound to produce continued contestation. But it is not clear that they are about to derail high-speed globalization. And the more radical prediction of Marx and Engels—that rebellion would result as the commoditization of almost everything destroyed other ways of investing things with meaning, leaving "no other bond between man and man than naked self interest," and so leaving the exploitation of workers unveiled—does not appear to be on the horizon.

And yet the march to a global market with capital flowing freely over borders, as the European Union spreads over ever-more of Europe and the United States attempts to bring in its American neighbors into a "free trade" zone, looks less inexorable than it might have just a few years ago. First there is the impact of dramatic, unforeseen events. More than the towers of the World Trade Center were destroyed on September 11, 2001. The dream of a new "century of peace" (as Karl Polyani referred to the hundred years between the defeat of Napoleon and the outbreak of world war I) was shattered. Suddenly the countertrends in the world economy, less spectacular than the September 11 bombings, but perhaps more important structurally and likely to limit some of the momentum toward globalization, were etched in sharp relief.

The United States, which has been the most important political actor pushing for a regime in which capital and products (though not people) can move unencumbered, currently runs the largest trade and government budget deficits of any country in history; although it is not certain that this will dim American enthusiasm for global neoliberalism, the possibility is certainly a real one. Vigilantes patrolling the southern border with tacit acquiescence of the government, is one dramatic example of a countermovement in the United States. Europe is at least equally ambivalent about globalization, even as it creates a superregion above the nation. As we write this, France has just voted against a new constitution for the European Union. It is not surprising that most "no" voters explain their motivation as opposition to unfettered transnational capitalism; what is striking is that a large percentage of "yes" voters also said that they were voting against global capital, arguing that only a stronger Europe could defend a humane social contract in today's world economy.

Part of what propels resentment in the richer countries is that it is no longer just manufacturing jobs that are moving overseas; information technology has now made it possible to outsource many services as well. The estimated 3.6 trillion dollars of services sold across national borders still pales next to the 14.9 trillion dollars in merchandise traded, but it is growing rapidly and means that skilled middle classes no longer have a guaranteed safe haven in the service sector. Hostility toward the ever-more frequent outsourcing of both services and production often mixes with chauvinist distrust of immigrants, to stir nationalist sentiments opposed to internationalism. Meanwhile, new efforts by poorer nations to protect their interests have also complicated matters, whether one characterizes these efforts as "pro" or "anti" globalization. The recent Cancun round of global trade talks of the World Trade Organization collapsed when a group of mostly poor countries (led by India, China, Brazil, and South Africa) turned the tables on the leaders of the world's richest economies (who most often preach the virtues of free trade), shining an embarrassing light on the heavy agricultural subsidies and barriers to trade in farm products in the wealthy countries that make it very difficult for poorer countries to compete. (The EU subsidizes every cow to the tune of more than $900, and developed countries' subsidies to their own farmers are more than six times what they spend on development aid.) At the local level, peasants and ethnic minorities have revolted against the perceived consequences of globalization. Bolivian Aymara and Quechua, Chilean Mapuche, and Mexican Maya, among many others native peoples, have protested the commodification of their homelands and foreign investment. Opposition is also often articulated in nationalist rhetoric, reviving and intensifying old rivalries such as those between China and Japan, France and Algeria, Korea and Japan, Russia and former members of the USSR and a more generalized anti-Americanism, especially in the Middle East.

Resistance to globalization has also appeared in the area where one would expect the dominance of the few most powerful actors to be most in evidence: the unprecedented concentration of the forces of destruction in the hands of a few countries have been undermined by international arms dealers profiting from the sales of sophisticated weapons, as well as simple improvised devices and suicide bombers. directed against the spread of market society. Nor have racial/ethnic and gender division faded away as Marx expected.

It is also important to remember that, despite the stunningly rapid circulation of humans and of information, a very large proportion of the world is only partially plugged in to these circuits. Though the often heard claim that half the world has never made a telephone call is almost certainly exaggerated, a figure of a third or a quarter is still quite plausible. Not that those people are untouched by global connections—indeed, they could be among those most affected when global commodity prices or currency exchange rates change, because they tend to be people who live close to the margin. But it remains the interplay between what is locally rooted and what is not that shapes our world—as it has for at least five centuries.

That interplay makes attributing changes to any one process very difficult. Despite rising inequality and global population growth, economic growth during the last twenty-five years has reduced the number of people in poverty (at least according to World Bank measurements) by about 350 million people. Closer examination, however, shows that virtually the entire net decline is accounted for by the reduction in poverty in China. So what does that tell us? To be sure, China has opened up to the world economy dramatically during this period. Its share of global merchandise exports more than doubled from 2.8 percent in 1994 to 6 percent in 2003. This has had much to do with that decline in poverty: not only because exports have generated jobs and incomes, but because imports have kept a lid on price increases for primary products that would otherwise have become increasingly scarce. But at the same time, China has followed a number of policies—from currency controls to Keynesian stimulus through government spending, state investment, and various forms of continuing state ownership (both local and national)—that hardly suggest simply leaving things to the market. Moreover, the state has intervened very aggressively (in all meanings of that word) to limit population growth and control internal migration. Whatever one thinks of the costs and benefits of those policies, they have presumably had something to do with the rapid capital accumulation of recent years; they hardly suggest a withering state. (Nor, if we accept the arguments of some scholars that a prerevolutionary history of family planning by extended families in China helped make these policies more acceptable, can we ignore the specificity of local culture.) Moreover, while the relatively closed Maoist years saw much less per capita economic growth, they did see huge leaps in life expectancy, literacy, and other basic goods—enough to account for close to half the improvement in *worldwide* life expectancy since 1945—making it far trickier to say exactly when the "Chinese miracle" occurred, or what the contribution might have been of human capital built during a decidedly antiglobal period to the increasing prosperity experienced during a globalizing era.

It is not only among humans, of course, that we find winners and losers from the growth of world trade. Other species have been massively affected. Many have disappeared, or become much less common (though some of these are now being preserved, thanks to other kinds of global networks). Others, such as cows and chickens, have become far more common, but live so differently from their ancestors on the less industrial farms of a century ago—not to mention their much more distant wild ancestors—that they hardly seem to be the same creatures at all. The decline of biological diversity over the last one hundred years has been large enough to be notable, even on the scale of a billion years—to cite just one example: more than half of all the loss in diversity of terrestrial vertebrates in the history of the biosphere has occurred since 1880. Usually this has been a result of the intensification of land use and consequent loss of habitat, less frequently due to increased hunting; both of those trends, of course, are linked to growing human populations, rising living standards, and expanding markets.

Our own environmental future—and the environmental sustainability of the growing world economy—are particularly unpredictable. The issues include both questions about the health of the planet in general if our activities continue unabated—for example, the effects of global warming—and questions about finite supplies of the resources we use in those activities. Concerns about energy supplies—intensified by mounting, though still contested, evidence that the annual production of oil is near its peak—take pride of place here, because industrial civilization rests to a great extent on turning coal and petroleum by-products into just about everything: fertilizer (which substitutes for land), plastics (which substitute for all sorts of metals, fibers, and so on) and, of course, motive power. Here we are clearly skating closer to the edge than humans ever have before—but that does not enable us to see what lies ahead with any certainty. On the one hand, technological changes could still come along that will lessen the predicted impacts of continued growth in global production and consumption. On the other hand, change could suddenly become much more rapid, because many scientists warn us that what seem like slow but steady changes in nature can suddenly accelerate, if certain still unknown thresholds are crossed.

One area where strains are already being felt is in the supply of freshwater. Here change has been especially rapid in recent decades: more than half of all the net decrease in Earth's supply of freshwater over the past 12,000 years has occurred just since 1955. Serious shortages already exist in many areas; a huge range of economic processes rely on water, and standard of living improvements for millions are hard to imagine without higher water use. Substitutes for water in many of its functions are hard to find; and at least at this point, a large-scale international trade in freshwater to bring supplies to particularly hard-pressed areas is impracticable. Under the circumstances, a common recommendation has been to encourage conservation and efficient delivery of water by privatizing it and raising prices. Placed in a longer perspective, this solution would simply add water to the list of "natural" goods—wood, land, minerals—that have become commodities over the past few centuries. And, as often happened with those earlier commodifications, efforts to place water on the market have provoked furious and often successful protests, in Bolivia, South Africa, Uruguay, India, and elsewhere. The impetus for this opposition, it seems, arises not just from people's self-interested *calculation* that this would remove one more thread from their already precarious safety nets. In many cases there is also *indignation* arising from ideas that water is somehow so basic, so connected with life itself and with people's sense of relationship to the earth, that it feels wrong to let it become simply another traded good.

Thus, we must take into account *moral economy*—what people perceive to be just, and the cultural orientations that influence the value they assign to goods and labor—as well as *market economy* to understand our world. In some cases, cultural difference drives exchange by giving the same thing different uses and value in different places, making arbitrage profitable; in other cases, it fuels opposition to exchange. But cultures—we emphasize the plural—continue to matter, in often surprising ways.

Meanwhile nature, which once seemed on the verge of being completely subordinated to human wants and skills—in short to culture, acting through markets—has also reappeared on stage. Or perhaps more accurately, we have rediscovered that "nature" was on stage all along: modern civilizations that found substitutes for almost everything through the massive application of energy are now realizing that by generating all that energy we have been changing the planet in ways that might fundamentally threaten both natural and human-built habitats. Both nature and culture continue to place limits on the world economy, even as they continue to be transformed by it. We know that the future will be different, but we cannot be sure how. We will have to wait to see what the future has in store for the world that trade created. Or perhaps we have a larger role than that of couch potato spectators. As the world was being shaken by the first industrial revolution in the nineteenth century, a German philosopher presciently said: "The philosophers have only interpreted the world in various ways. The point, however, is to change it."

Abbreviated Bibliography

Adas, Michael. *Prophets of Rebellion. Millennarian Protest Movements Against the European Colonial Order.* Chapel Hill: University of North Carolina Press, 1979.
———. *Machines as the Measures of Men. Science, Technology and Ideologies of Western Dominance.* Ithaca: Cornell University Press, 1989.

Al-Rasheed, Madawi. *A History of Saudi Arabia.* Cambridge, UK: Cambridge University Press, 2002.

Andrews, Kenneth. *Trade, Plunder, and Settlement: Maritime Enterprise and the Genesis of the British Empire, 1480–1630.* Cambridge, UK: Cambridge University Press, 1984.

Anscombe, Frederic F. *The Ottoman Gulf: The Creation of Kuwait, Saudi Arabia, and Qatar.* New York: Columbia University Press, 1997.

Appadurai, Arjun. *The Social Life of Things. Commodities in Cultural Perspective.* New York: Cambridge University Press, 1986.

Arrighi, Giovanni. *The Long Twentieth Century: Money, Power and the Origins of Our Times.* London: Verso, 1994.

Aveling, Harry, ed. *The Development of Indonesian Society.* New York: St. Martin's Press, 1980.

Baer, Julius B., and Olin Glenn Saxon. *Commodity Exchanges and Futures Trading.* New York: Harper, 1949.

Bairoch, Paul. *The Economic Development of the Third World Since 1900.* Trans. Cynthia Postan. Berkeley: University of California Press, 1977.

Bakewell, Peter John. *Miners of the Red Mountain. Indian Labor at Potosi, 1545–1650.* Albuquerque: University of New Mexico Press, 1984.

Barlow, Colin. *The Natural Rubber Industry: Its Development, Technology, and Economy in Malaysia.* Kuala Lampur: Oxford University Press, 1978.

Barlow Colin, Jayasuriya, Sisira, and Tan, C. Suan. *The World Rubber Industry.* London: Routledge, 1994.

Bayly, C.A. *Imperial Meridian: The British Empire and the World, 1780–1840.* London: Longman, 1989.

Bennett, Alan Weinberg, and Bonnie K. Bealer. *The World of Caffeine.* London: Routledge, 2001.

Blackburn, Robin. *The Making of New World Slavery.* New York: Verso, 1997.

Blussé, Leonard. *Strange Company: Chinese Settlers, Mestizo Women, and the Dutch in VOC Batavia.* Dordrecht, Holland: Foris, 1986.

Boxer, Charles R. *The Dutch Seaborne Empire, 1600–1800.* London: Hutchinson, 1965.

Braudel, Fernand. *The Structures of Everyday Life.* New York: Harper and Row, 1981.
———. *The Wheels of Commerce.* New York: Harper and Row, 1982.
———. *The Perspective of the World.* New York: Harper and Row, 1984.

Burke, Timothy. *Lifebuoy Men, Lux Women: Commodification, Consumption and Cleanliness in Modern Zimbabwe.* Durham: Duke University Press, 1996.

Chandler, Alfred D., Jr. *The Visible Hand: The Managerial Revolution in American Business.* Cambridge: Belknap Press of Harvard University Press, 1977.

Chaudhuri, K.N. *Trade and Civilization in the Indian Ocean.* New York: Cambridge University Press, 1985.

———. *Asia Before Europe.* New York: Cambridge University Press, 1990.

Clarence-Smith, Willian G., and Steven Topik, eds. *The Global Coffee Economy in Africa, Asia and Latin America.* New York: Cambridge University Press, 2003.

Cochran, Sherman G. *Encountering Chinese Networks: Western, Japanese, and Chinese Corporations in China, 1880–1937.* Berkeley: University of California Press, 2000.

Cooper, Frederick, Holt, Thomas C., and Scott, Rebecca J. *Beyond Slavery: Explorations of Race, Labor, and Citizenship in Postemancipation Societies.* Chapel Hill: University of North Carolina Press, 2000.

Cortes Conde, Roberto. *The First Stages of Modernization in Spanish America.* Trans. Toby Talbot. New York: Harper and Row, 1974.

Cronon, William. *Nature's Metropolis: Chicago and the Great West.* New York: W.W. Norton, 1991.

Crosby, Alfred W., Jr. *The Columbian Exchange: Biological and Cultural Consequences of 1492.* Westport, CT: Greenwood, 1972.

———. *Ecological Imperialism: The Biological Expansion of Europe, 900–1900.* New York: Cambridge University Press, 1986.

Curtin, Philip D. *The Atlantic Slave Trade: A Census.* Madison: University of Wisconsin Press, 1969.

———. *Cross-Cultural Trade in World History.* New York: Cambridge University Press, 1984.

Dayer, Roberta. *Bankers and Diplomats in China 1917–1925: The Anglo-American Relationship.* Totowa, NJ: F. Cass, 1981.

Dean, Warren. *With Broadax and Firebrand: The Destruction of the Brazilian Atlantic Forest.* Berkeley: University of California Press, 1995.

Deerr, Noel. *The History of Sugar.* 2 vols. London: Chapman and Hall, 1949–50.

Dillon, Richard. *Captain John Sutter.* Santa Cruz, CA: Western Tanager, 1967.

Earle, Peter. *The World of Defoe.* New York: Atheneum, 1977.

Elvin, Mark. *Pattern of the Chinese Past.* London: Eyre Methuen, 1973.

Farnie, Douglas A. *The English Cotton Industry and the World Market, 1815–1896.* Oxford: Clarendon Press, 1979.

Farnie, Douglas A. and Jeremy, David J., eds. *The Fibre that Changed the World: the Cotton Industry in International Perspective, 1600–1990s.* Oxford: Oxford University Press, 2004.

Flynn, Dennis O., and Arturo Giraldez. *Metals and Monies in an Emerging Global Economy.* Brookfield, VT: Variorum, 1997.

Frank, Andre Gunder. *Capitalism and Underdevelopment in Latin America.* New York: Monthly Review Press, 1967.

Gallagher, John, and Ronald Robinson. "The Imperialism of Free Trade." *Economic History Review,* 2d series, 6, no. 1 (1953): 1–15.

Gardella, Robert. *Harvesting Mountains.* Berkeley: University of California Press, 1994.

Gerschenkron, Alexander. *Economic Backwardness in Historical Perspective.* Cambridge: Belknap Press of Harvard University Press, 1962.

Gootenberg, Paul. *Between Silver and Guano: Commercial Policy and the State in Post-Independence Peru.* Princeton: Princeton University Press, 1989.

Gudeman, Stephen. *Economics as Culture. Models and Metaphors of Livelihood.* Boston: Routledge and Kegan Paul, 1986.

Habib, Irfan, and Tapan Raychaudhuri. *Cambridge Economic History of India.* Cambridge, UK: Cambridge University Press, 1984.

Hamashita, Takeshi. "The Tribute System and Modern Asia." *Memoirs of the Research Department of the Tōyō Bunko* no. 46. Tokyo, 1988.

Hattox, Ralph. *Coffee and Coffeehouses: The Origins of a Social Beverage in the Medieval Near East.* Seattle: University of Washington Press, 1985.

Hayami, Yujiro. *The Agricultural Development of Japan: A Century's Perspective.* Tokyo: University of Tokyo Press, 1991.

Hine, Thomas. *The Total Package. The Evolution and Secret Meanings of Boxes, Bottles, Cans, and Tubes.* Boston: Little, Brown, 1995.

Hirschman, Albert. *The Passions and the Interests: Political Arguments for Capitalism Before Its Triumph.* Princeton: Princeton University Press, 1977.

———. *Essays in Trespassing. Economics to Politics and Beyond.* New York: Cambridge University Press, 1981.

Hobsbawm, Eric. *The Age of Capital.* New York: Scribner's, 1975.

———. *The Age of Empire, 1875–1914.* New York: Pantheon Books, 1987.

———. *Age of Extremes. The Short Twentieth Century, 1914–1991.* London: Abacus, 1994.

Hobson, John A. *Imperialism: A Study.* London: Allen and Unwin, 1938 [1902].

Hochschild, Adam. *King Leopold's Ghost.* Boston: Houghton and Mifflin, 1998.

Holliday, J.S. *Rush for Riches. Gold Fever and the Making of California.* Berkeley: University of California Press, 1999.

Hossain, Hameeda. *The Company Weavers of Bengal.* Delhi: Oxford University Press, 1988.

Israel, Jonathan. *Dutch Primacy in World Trade, 1585–1740.* Oxford: Oxford University Press, 1989.

Kenwood, A.G., and A.L. Lougheed. *The Growth of the International Economy, 1820–1960.* London: Allen and Unwin, 1971.

Kling, Blair. *Partner in Empire: Dwarkanath Tagore and the Age of Enterprise in Eastern India.* Berkeley: University of California Press, 1976.

Kortheuer, Dennis. *Santa Rosalía and Compagnie du Boléo: the making of a town and company in the Porfirian frontier, 1885–1900.* Ph. D. dissertation, University of California, Irvine, 2001.

Kuisel, Richard. *Seducing the French: The Dilemma of Americanization.* Berkeley: University of California Press, 1993.

Kula, Withold. *Measures and Men.* Trans. R. Szreter. Princeton: Princeton University Press, 1986.

Latham, A.J.H. *The International Economy and the Undeveloped World.* Totowa, NJ: Rowman and Littlefield, 1978.

Latham, A.J.H., and Larry Neal. "The International Market in Rice and Wheat, 1868–1914." *Economic History Review* 36 (1983): 260–80.

Lery, Jean. *History of a Voyage to the Land of Brazil, Otherwise Called America.* Trans. Janet Whatley. Berkeley: University of California Press, 1990.

Lewis, W. Arthur. *Growth and Fluctuations, 1870–1914.* Boston: Allen and Unwin, 1978.

Lu, Hanchao. *Beyond the Neon Lights: Everyday Shanghai in the Early Twentieth Century.* Berkeley: University of California Press, 1999.

Marchand, Roland. *Advertising the American Dream: Making Way for Modernity, 1920–1940.* Berkeley: University of California Press, 1985.

Marshall, P.J. *Bengal: The British Bridgehead.* Cambridge, UK: Cambridge University Press, 1987.

Marshall, P.J., and Glyndwr Williams. *The Great Map of Mankind: British Perceptions of the World in the Age of Enlightenment.* London: Dent, 1982.

McAlpin, Michelle. *Subject to Famine: Food Crises and Economic Change in Western India 1860–1920.* Princeton: Princeton University Press, 1983.

McCoy, Alfred. "A Queen Dies Slowly: The Rise and Decline of Iloilo City." In *Philippine Social History: Global Trade and Local Transformation,* ed. Alfred W. McCoy and Eduard de Jesus, pp. 297–358. Manila: Ateneo de Manila University Press, 1982.

McCreery, David. *Rural Guatemala, 1760–1940.* Stanford: Stanford University Press, 1994.

McNeill, William. *The Pursuit of Power. Technology, Armed Force and Society Since A.D. 1000.* Chicago: University of Chicago, 1982.

———. *Plagues and Peoples.* Garden City, NJ: Anchor Books, 1976.

Marx, Karl. *Capital.* New York: International Publishers, 1996.

Miller, Joseph C. *Way of Death. Merchant Capitalism and the Angolan Slave Trade, 1730–1830.* Madison: University of Wisconsin Press, 1988.

Mintz, Sidney. *Sweetness and Power: The Place of Sugar in Modern History.* New York: Penguin, 1985.

Mitra, D.B. *The Cotton Weavers of Bengal.* Calcutta: S.P. Ghosh, 1978.

Morris-Suzuki, Tessa. *The Technological Transformation of Japan: From the Seventeenth to the Twenty-First Century.* Cambridge: Cambridge University Press.

Ng, Chin-Keong. *Trade and Society: The Amoy Network on the China Coast, 1683–1735.* Singapore: Singapore University Press, 1983.

Northrup, David. *Indentured Labor in the Age of Imperialism, 1834–1922.* Cambridge, UK: Cambridge University Press, 1995.

Ortiz, Fernando. *Cuban Counterpoint. Tobacco and Sugar.* Durham: Duke University Press, 1995.

Panati, Charles. *Extraordinary Origins of Everyday Things.* New York: Harper and Row, 1987.

Parker, William. *Europe, America, and the Wider World.* 2 vols. New York: Cambridge University Press, 1984–91.

Perlin, Frank. *Invisible City.* Brookfield, VT: Variorum 1993.

———. *Unbroken Landscape.* Brookfield, VT: Variorum, 1994.

Platt, D.C.M. *Business Imperialism.* Oxford: Oxford University Press, 1977.

Polanyi, Karl. *The Great Transformation: The Political and Economic Origins of Our Times.* Boston: Beacon Press, 1957.

———. *The Livelihood of Man,* ed. Harry W. Pearson. New York: Academic Press, 1977.

Pomeranz, Kenneth. *The Making of a Hinterland: State, Society and Economy in Inland North China, 1853–1937.* Berkeley: University of California Press, 1993.

———. *The Great Divergence: China, Europe, and the Making of The Modern World Economy.* Princeton: Princeton University Press, forthcoming.

Rabb, Theodore. *Enterprise and Empire: Merchant and Gentry Investment in the Expansion of England, 1575–1630.* Cambridge: Harvard University Press, 1967.

Reid, Anthony. *Southeast Asia in the Age of Commerce.* 2 vols. New Haven: Yale University Press, 1988–93.

Richards, John F. *The Unending Frontier: An Environmental History of the Early Modern World.* Berkeley: University of California Press, 2003.

Sahlins, Marshall. *Stone Age Economics.* New York: Aldine, 1972.
————. *Culture and Practical Reason.* Chicago: University of Chicago Press, 1976.
Sauer, Carl. *Agricultural Origins and Dispersals.* New York: American Geographical Society, 1952.
Schivelbusch, Wolfgang. *Tastes of Paradise: A Social History of Spices, Stimulants, and Intoxicants.* Trans. D. Jacobson. New York: Vintage, 1993.
Schwartz, Stuart. *Sugar Plantations in the Formation of Brazilian Society: Bahia, 1550–1835.* Cambridge, UK: Cambridge University Press, 1985.
Shepherd, James, and Gary Walton. *Shipping, Maritime Trade, and the Economic Development of Colonial North America.* New York: Cambridge University Press, 1972.
Slatta, Richard. *Gauchos and the Vanishing Frontier.* Lincoln: University of Nebraska Press, 1983.
Smith, David, Solinger, Dorothy, and Topik, Steven, eds. *State and Sovereignty in the Global Economy.* London: Routledge, 1999.
Steensgaard, Neils. "The Dutch East India Company as an Institutional Innovation." In *Dutch Capitalism and World Capitalism,* ed. Maurice Aymard, pp. 235–58. Cambridge, UK: Cambridge University Press, 1982.
Stein, Stanley. *Vassouras: A Brazilian Coffee County.* Cambridge: Harvard University Press, 1956.
Stross, Randall. *The Stubborn Earth: American Agriculturalists on Chinese Soil, 1898–1937.* Berkeley: University of California Press, 1986.
Subrahmanyam, Sanjay. *The Political Economy of Commerce: South India, 1500–1650.* Cambridge, UK: Cambridge University Press, 1990.
————. *The Portuguese Empire in Asia, 1500–1700.* New York: Longman, 1993.
Taussig, Michael T. *The Devil and Commodity Fetishism in South America.* Chapel Hill: University of North Carolina Press, 1980.
Thompson, E.P. *Customs in Common. Studies in Traditional Popular Culture.* New York: New Press, 1993.
Tilly, Charles. "Food Supply and Public Order in Modern Europe." In *The Formation of National States in Western Europe,* ed. Charles Tilly, pp. 380–455. Princeton: Princeton University Press, 1975.
Topik, Steven. *Trade and Gunboats: The United States and Brazil in the Age of Empire.* Stanford: Stanford University Press, 1996.
Topik, Steven, and Allen Wells. *The Second Conquest of Latin America.* Austin: University of Texas Press, 1998.
Tracy, James D., ed. *The Rise of Merchant Empires: Long Distance Trade in the Early Modern World, 1350–1750.* New York: Cambridge University Press, 1990.
————. *The Political Economy of Merchant Empire.* New York: Cambridge University Press, 1991.
Trouillot, Michel-Rolph. "Motion in the System: Coffee, Color and Slavery in Eighteenth-Century Saint-Domingue." *Review* 5, no. 3 (Winter 1982): 331–88.
Ukers, W.H. *All About Coffee.* New York: Teas and Coffee Trade Journal, 1935.
Vinikis, Vincent. *Soft Soap, Hard Sell: American Hygiene in an Age of Advertisement.* Ames: Iowa State University Press, 1992.
Vlastos, Stephen. *Peasant Protests and Uprisings in Tokugawa Japan.* Berkeley: University of California Press, 1986.
Von Glahn, Richard. *Fountain of Fortune: Money and Monetary Policy in China, 1000–1700.* Berkeley: University of California Press, 1996.

Wallerstein, Immanuel. *The Modern World System.* 2 vols. New York: Academic Press, 1974–80.

Wells, Allen. *Yucatan's Gilded Age.* Albuquerque: University of New Mexico Press, 1985.

Williams, Eric. *Slavery and Capitalism.* New York: Capricorn Books, 1966.

Wills, John E. *Mountain of Fame.* Princeton: Princeton University Press, 1994.

———. "Maritime Asia, 1500–1800: The Interactive Emergence of European Dominance." *American Historical Review* 98, no. 1 (February 1993): 83–105.

Yergin, Daniel. *The Prize: The Epic Quest for Oil, Money, and Power.* New York: Free Press, 1992.

Index

Kenneth Pomeranz is Chancellor's Professor of History at the University of California, Irvine, where he has taught since receiving his Ph.D. from Yale University in 1988. He is the author of *The Making of the Hinterland: State, Society, and Economy in Rural North China, 1853–1937* (1993), which won the John King Fairbank Prize of the American Historical Association as the best book in modern East Asian history, and *The Great Divergence: China, Europe, and the Making of the Modern World Economy* (2000), which also won the Fairbank Prize and was co-winner of the World History Association's best book prize. He is also co-editor of the forthcoming *History of World Trade Since 1450*, and founding director of the University of California's multi-campus research group in world history.

Steven Topik received his Ph.D. from the University of Texas, Austin, in 1978 and is professor of history at the University of California, Irvine. He is the author of *The Political Economy of the Brazilian State, 1889–1930* (1987), *Trade and Gunboats: The United States and Brazil in the Age of Empire* (1996), and co-author of *The Second Conquest of Latin America: Coffee, Henequen, and Oil During the Export Boom, 1850–1930* (1998). He co-edited *States and Sovereignty in the Global Economy* (1999), *The Global Coffee Economy in Africa, Asia, and Latin America, 1500–1989* (2003), and *Latin America and World History: Commodities, Societies, and Economies* (forthcoming).